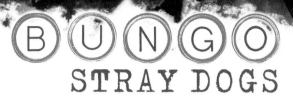

BUNGO STRAY DOGS

Story by KAFKA ASAGIRI
Art by SANGO HARUKAWA

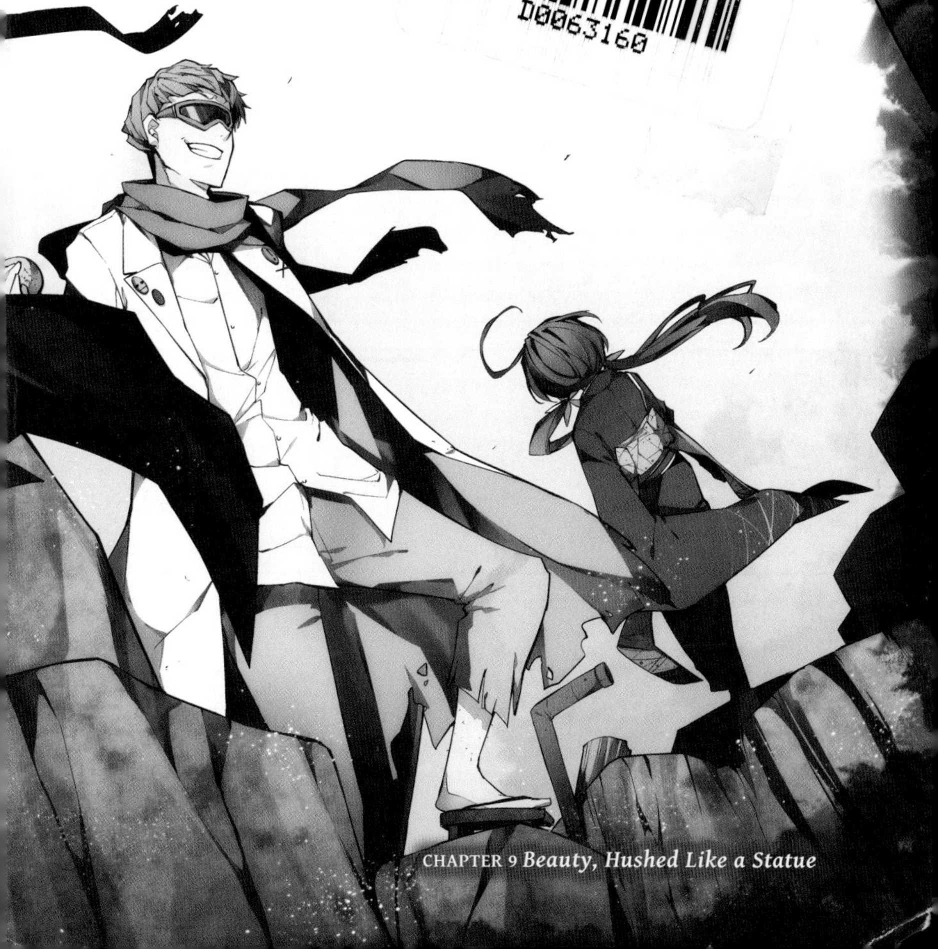

CHAPTER 9 *Beauty, Hushed Like a Statue*

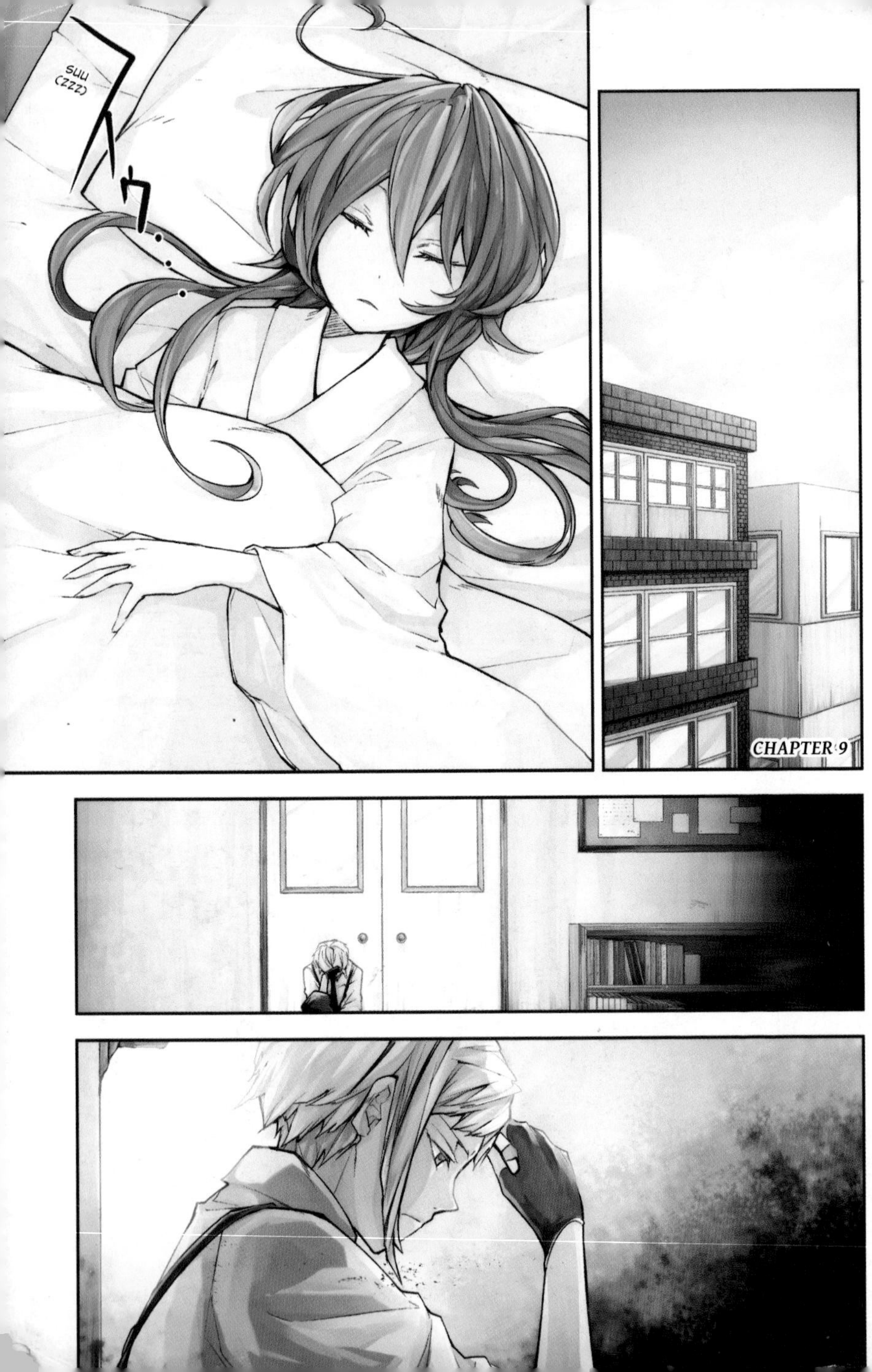
CHAPTER 9
スゥ…
suu
(zzz)

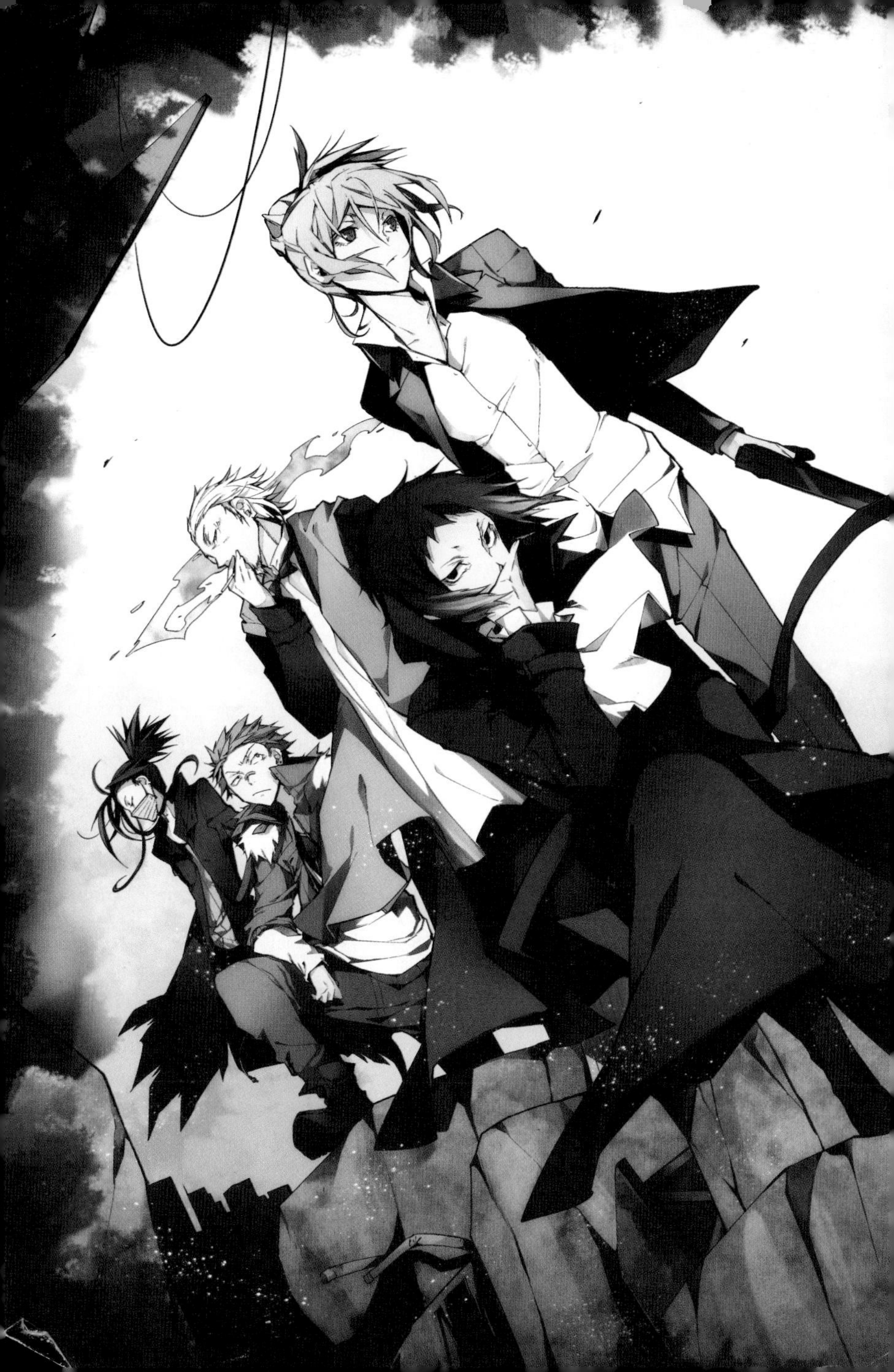

TABLE of CONTENTS

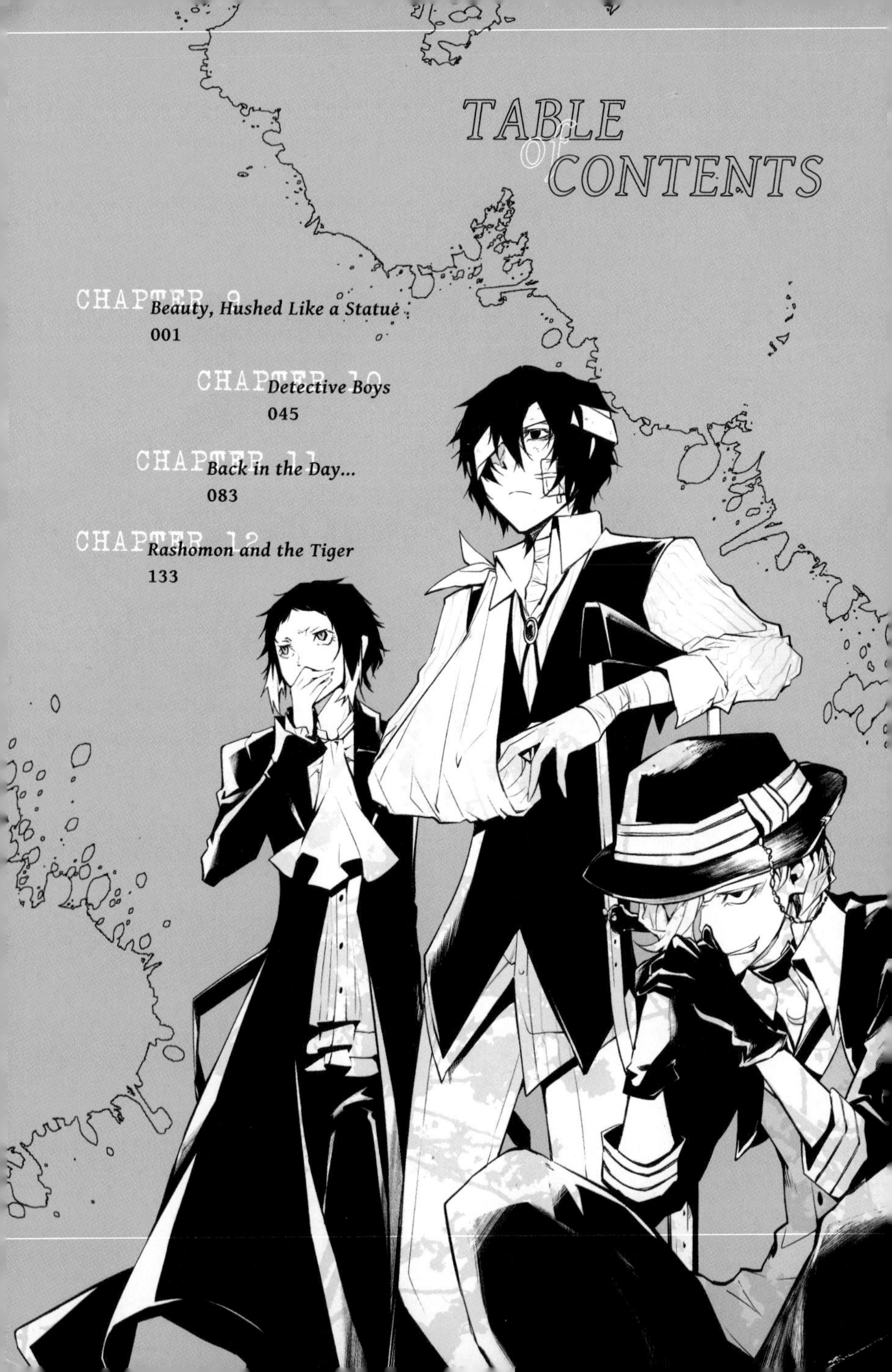

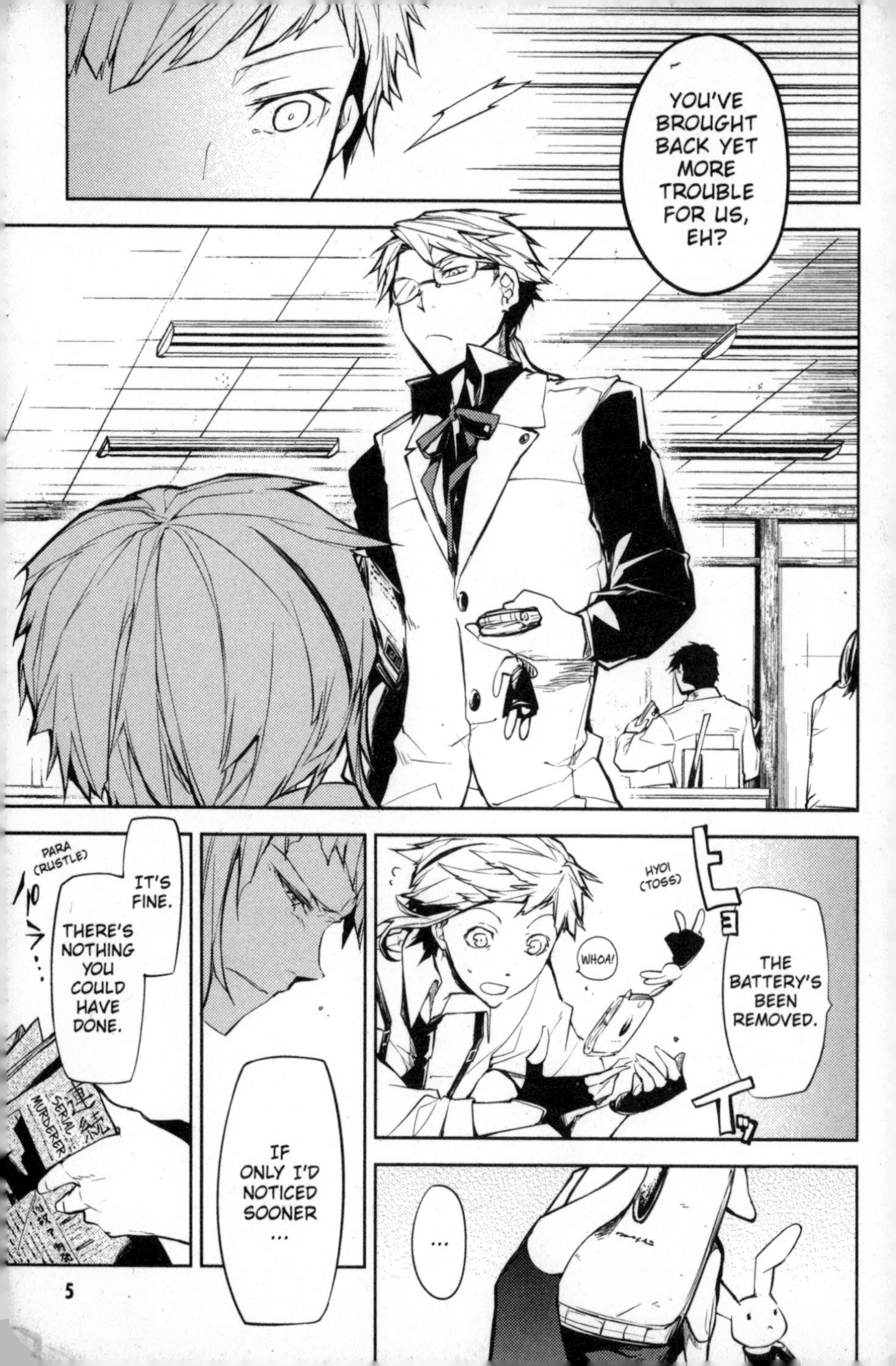
YOU'VE BROUGHT BACK YET MORE TROUBLE FOR US, EH?
HYOI (TOSS)
WHOA!
THE BATTERY'S BEEN REMOVED.
...
IF ONLY I'D NOTICED SOONER ...
IT'S FINE.
THERE'S NOTHING YOU COULD HAVE DONE.
PARA (RUSTLE)
SERIAL MURDERER

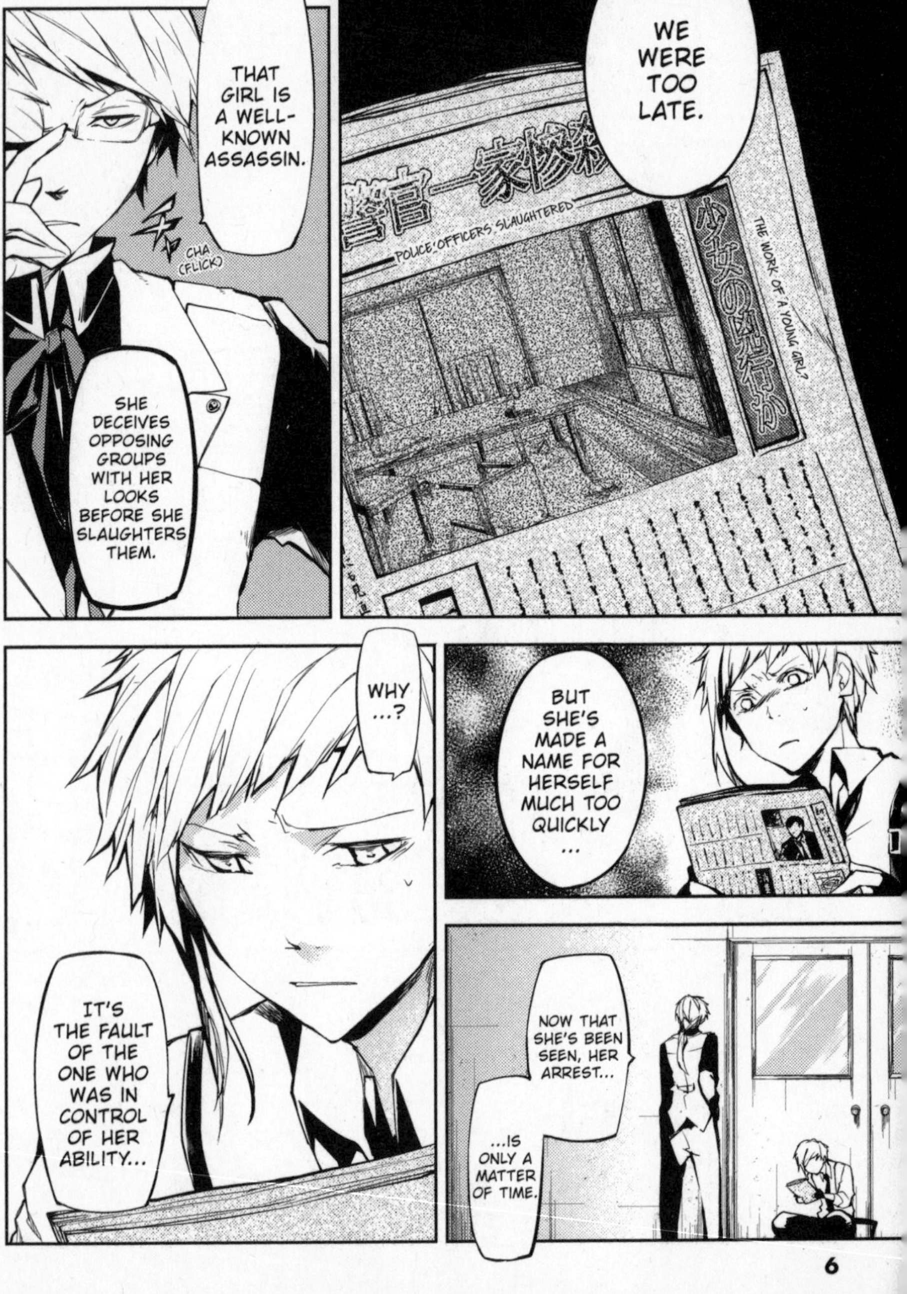
WE WERE TOO LATE.
警官一家惨
POLICE OFFICERS SLAUGHTERED
少女の凶行か
THE WORK OF A YOUNG GIRL?
THAT GIRL IS A WELL-KNOWN ASSASSIN.
CHA (FLICK)
SHE DECEIVES OPPOSING GROUPS WITH HER LOOKS BEFORE SHE SLAUGHTERS THEM.
BUT SHE'S MADE A NAME FOR HERSELF MUCH TOO QUICKLY ...
NOW THAT SHE'S BEEN SEEN, HER ARREST...
...IS ONLY A MATTER OF TIME.
WHY ...?
IT'S THE FAULT OF THE ONE WHO WAS IN CONTROL OF HER ABILITY...

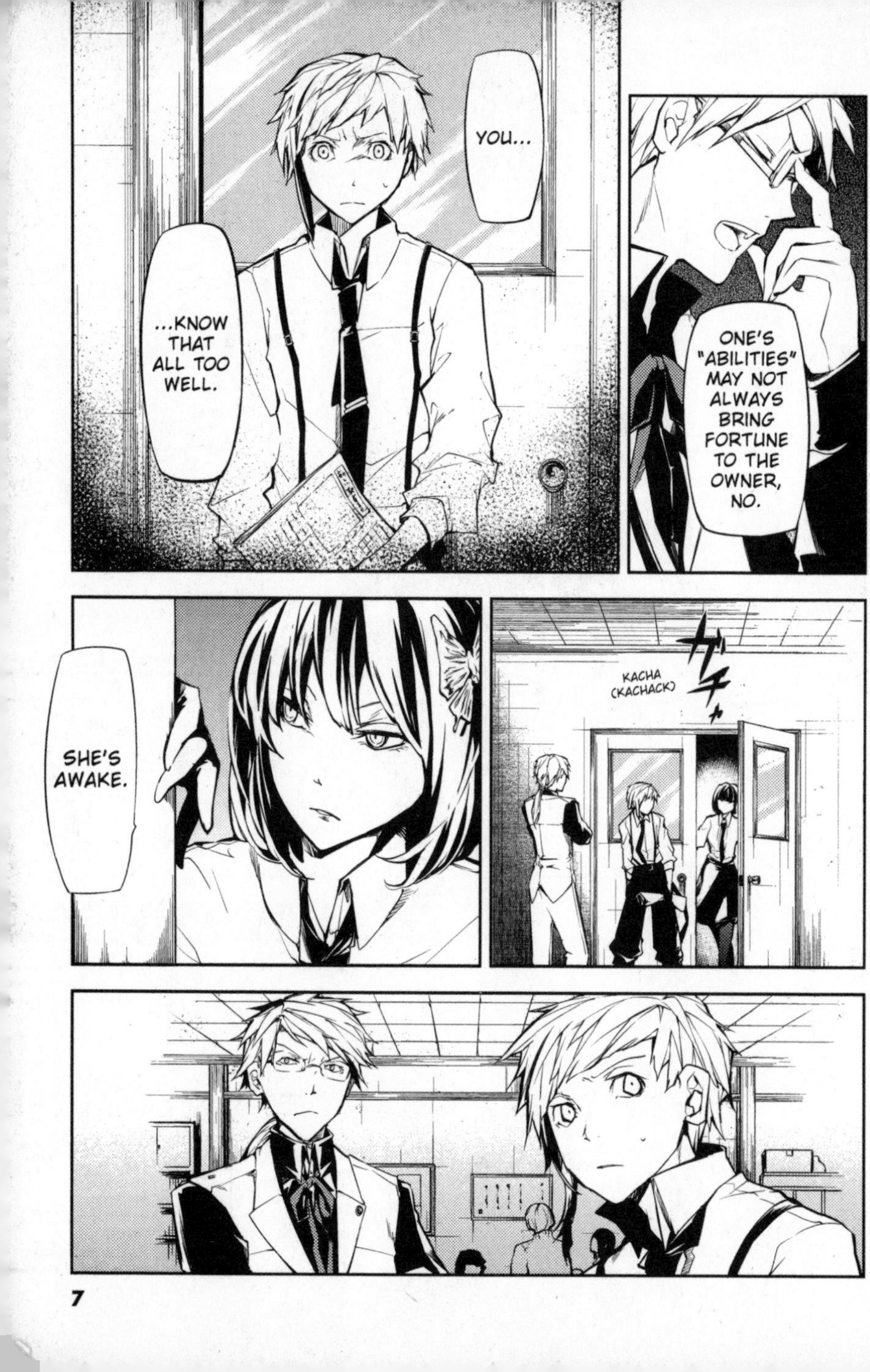
ONE'S "ABILITIES" MAY NOT ALWAYS BRING FORTUNE TO THE OWNER, NO.
YOU...
...KNOW THAT ALL TOO WELL.
KACHA (KACHACK)
SHE'S AWAKE.

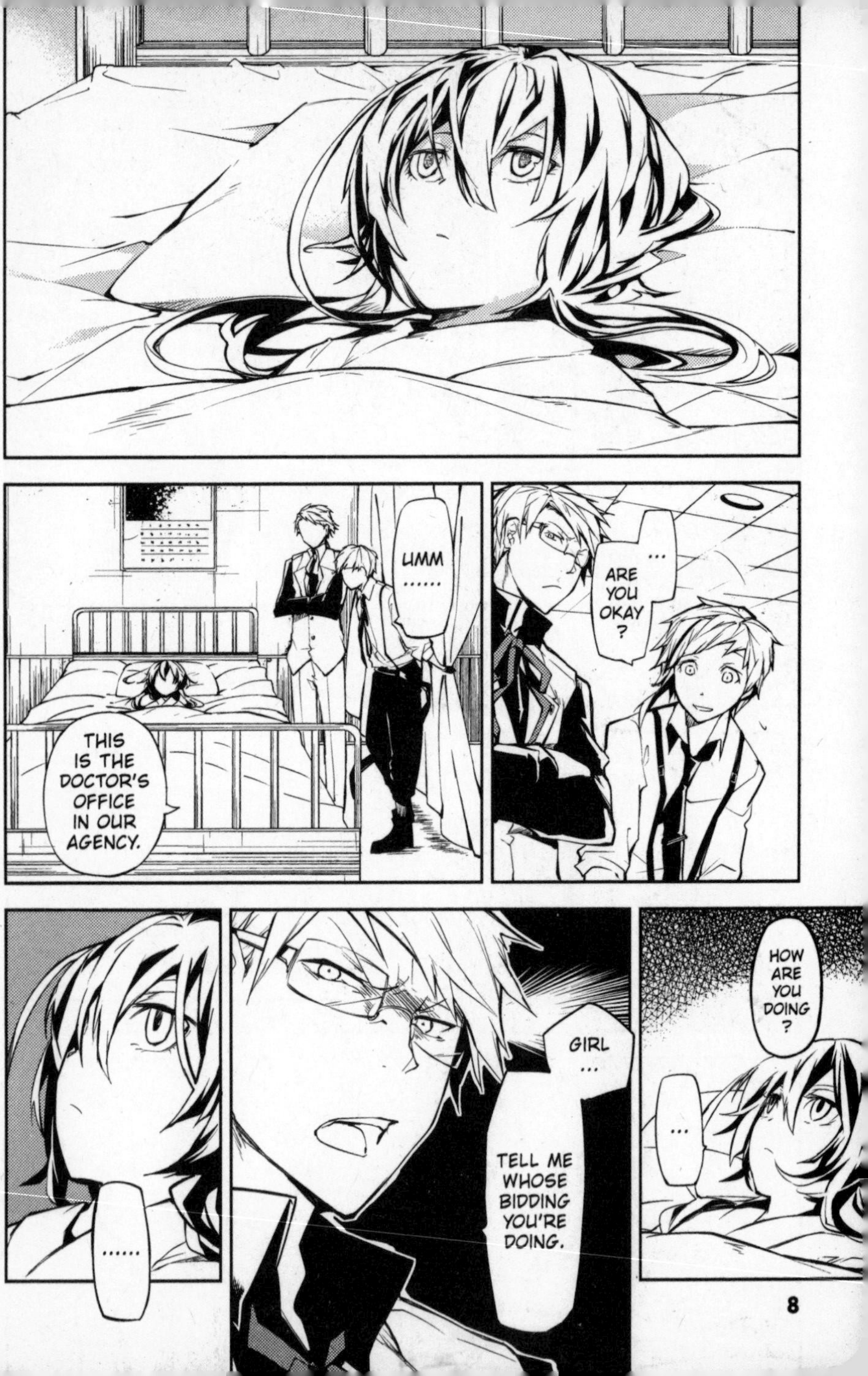
... ARE YOU OKAY ?
UMM ......
THIS IS THE DOCTOR'S OFFICE IN OUR AGENCY.
HOW ARE YOU DOING ?
...
GIRL ...
TELL ME WHOSE BIDDING YOU'RE DOING.
......

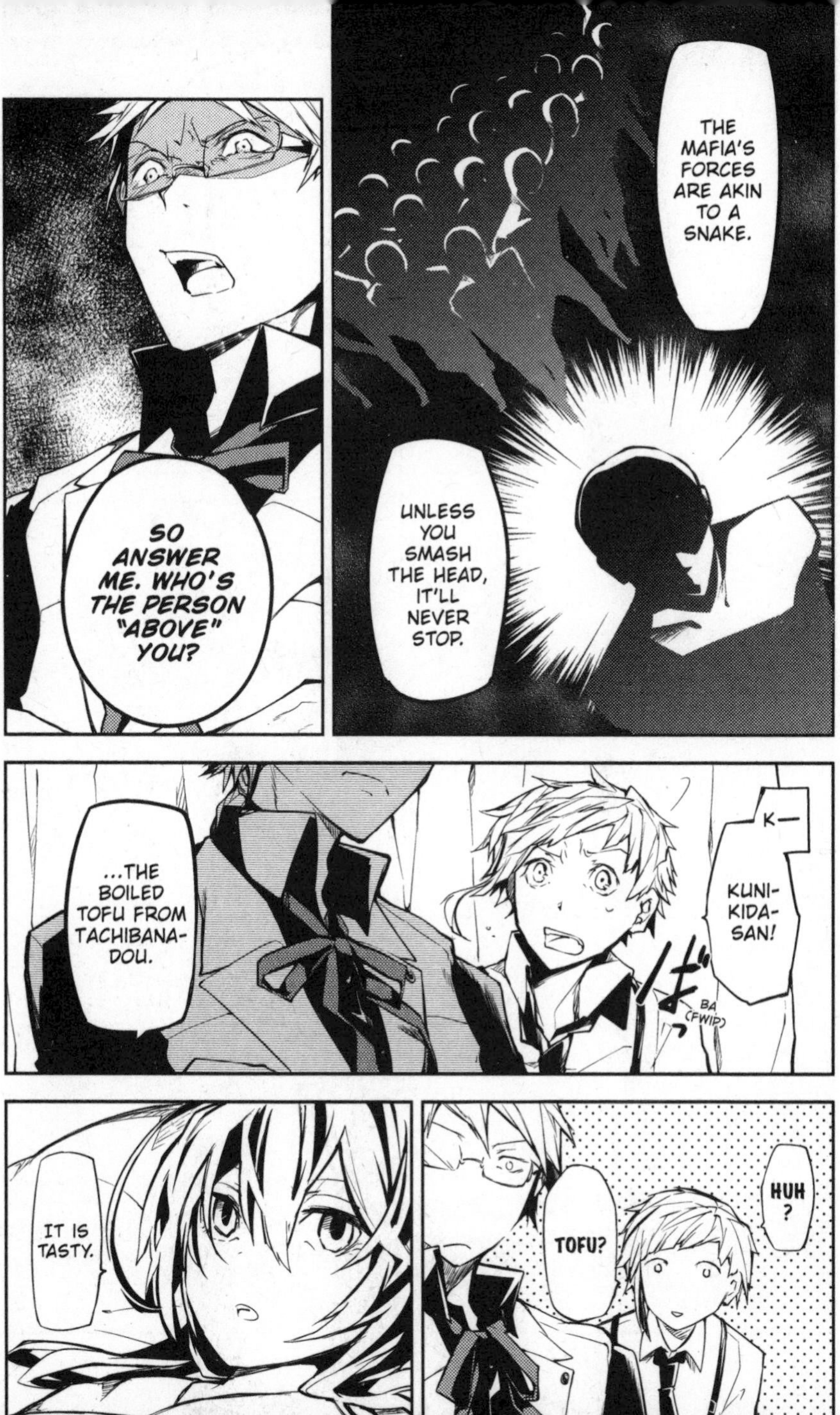
THE MAFIA'S FORCES ARE AKIN TO A SNAKE.
UNLESS YOU SMASH THE HEAD, IT'LL NEVER STOP.
SO ANSWER ME. WHO'S THE PERSON "ABOVE" YOU?
K—
KUNI-KIDA-SAN!
ば
BA (FWIP)
...THE BOILED TOFU FROM TACHIBANA-DOU.
HUH?
TOFU?
IT IS TASTY.

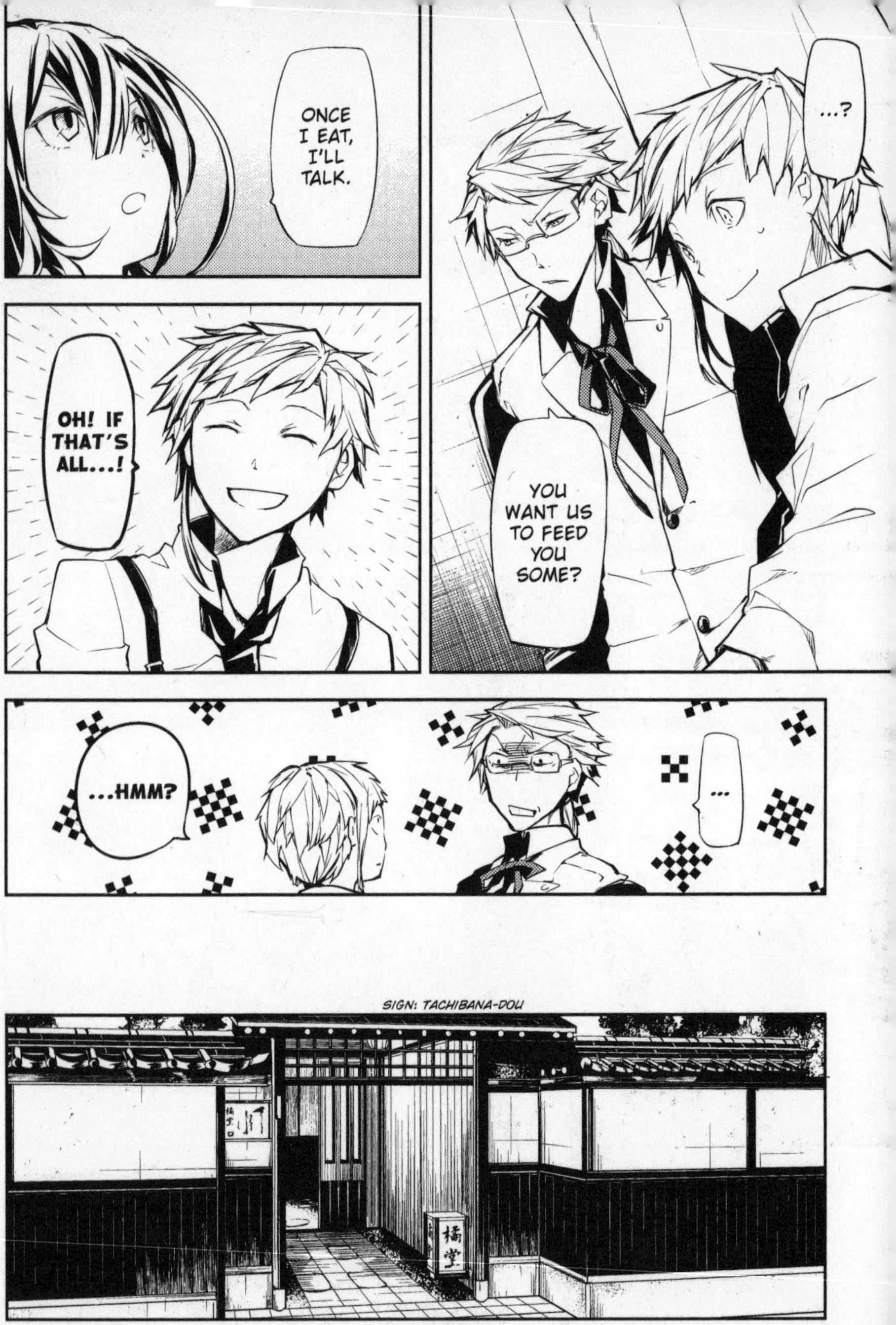
...?
YOU WANT US TO FEED YOU SOME?
ONCE I EAT, I'LL TALK.
OH! IF THAT'S ALL...!
...
...HMM?
SIGN: TACHIBANA-DOU
橘堂

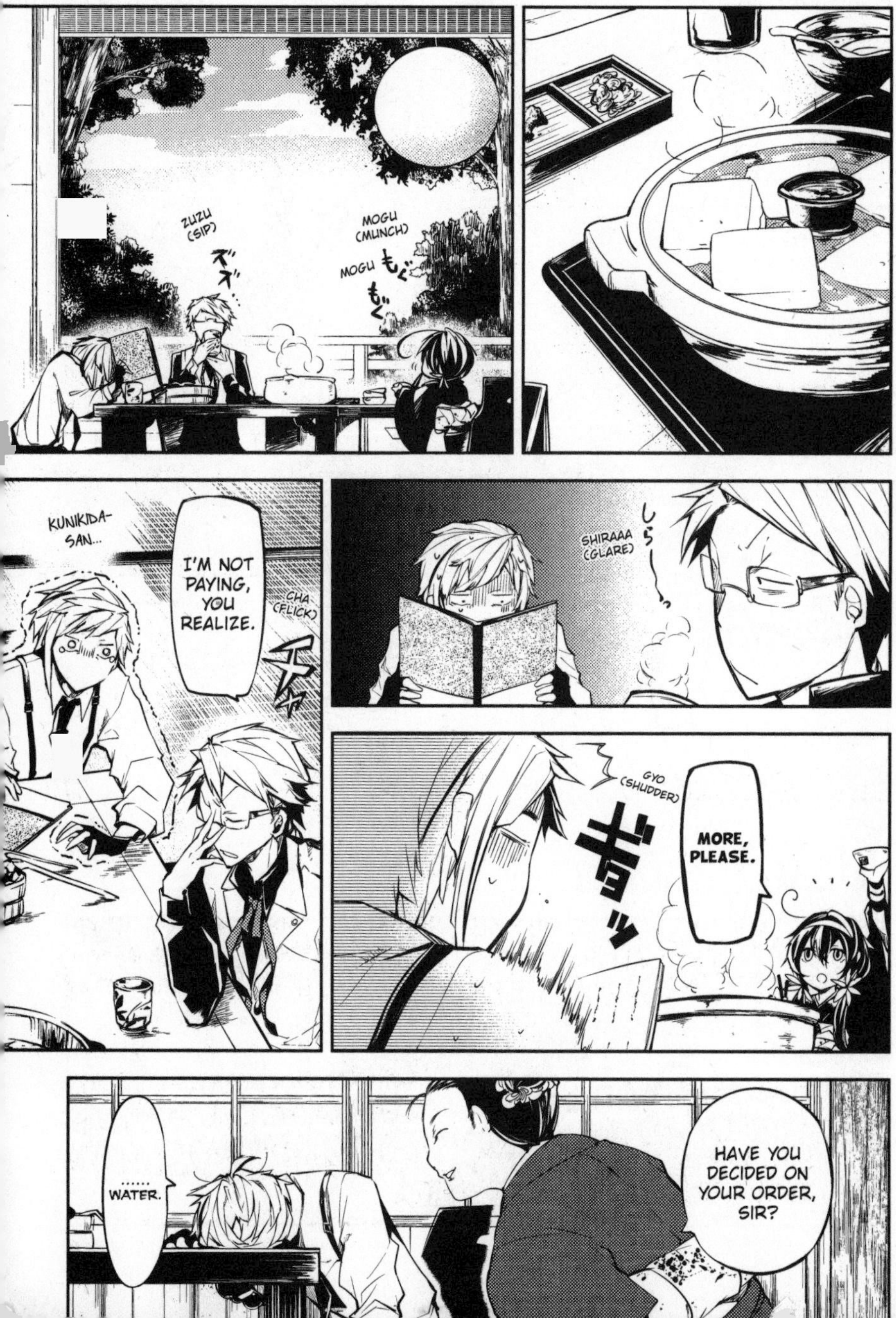
MOGU (MUNCH)
MOGU
もぐもぐ
ZUZU (SIP)
ズズ…
SHIRAAA (GLARE)
MORE, PLEASE.
GYO (SHUDDER)
I'M NOT PAYING, YOU REALIZE.
KUNIKIDA-SAN...
CHA (FLICK)
HAVE YOU DECIDED ON YOUR ORDER, SIR?
......WATER.

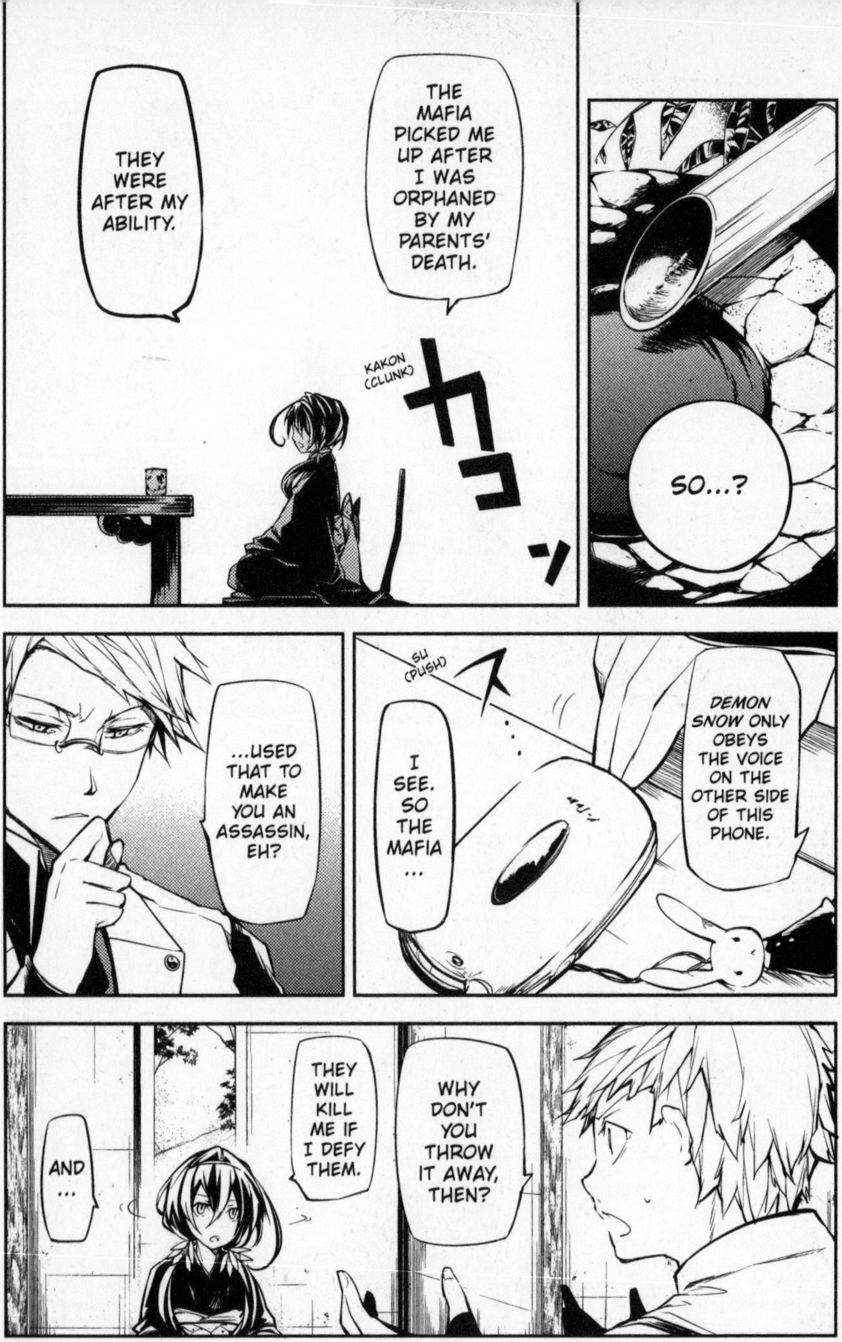
SO...?
THE MAFIA PICKED ME UP AFTER I WAS ORPHANED BY MY PARENTS' DEATH.
THEY WERE AFTER MY ABILITY.
KAKON (CLUNK)
カコッ
SU (PUSH)
ス
DEMON SNOW ONLY OBEYS THE VOICE ON THE OTHER SIDE OF THIS PHONE.
I SEE. SO THE MAFIA ...
...USED THAT TO MAKE YOU AN ASSASSIN, EH?
WHY DON'T YOU THROW IT AWAY, THEN?
THEY WILL KILL ME IF I DEFY THEM.
AND ...

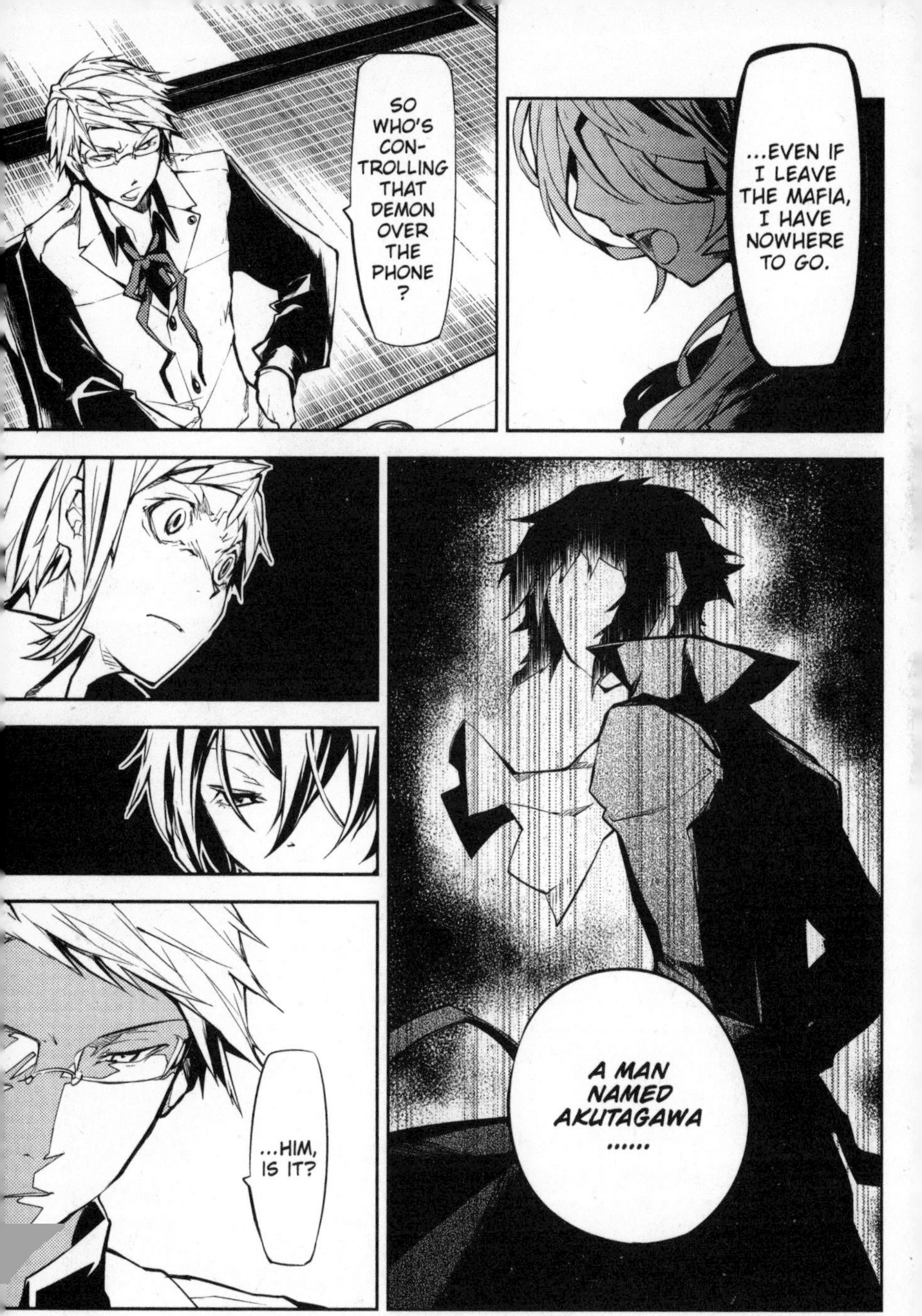
...EVEN IF I LEAVE THE MAFIA, I HAVE NOWHERE TO GO.
SO WHO'S CON-TROLLING THAT DEMON OVER THE PHONE?
A MAN NAMED AKUTAGAWA ......
...HIM, IS IT?

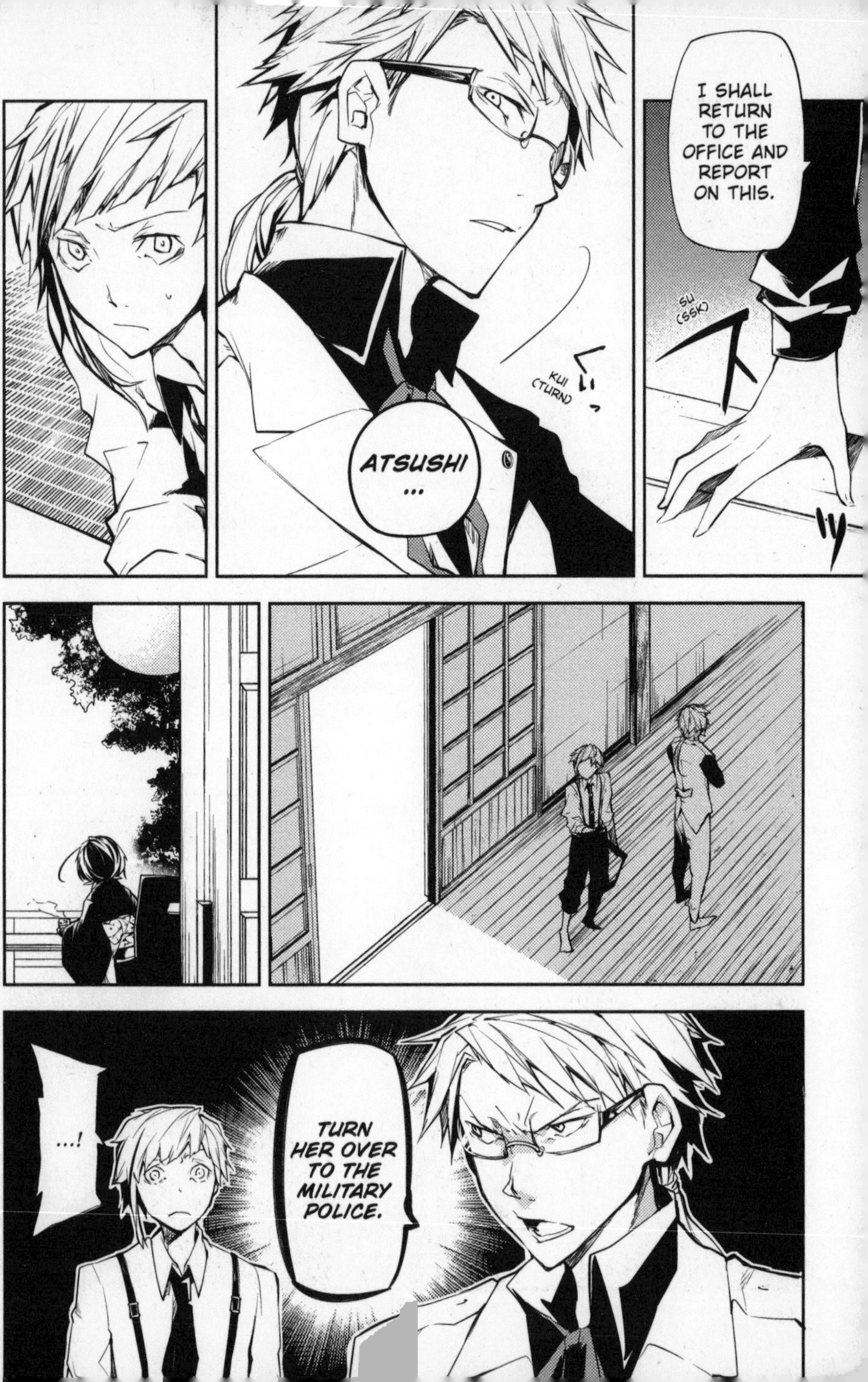
I SHALL RETURN TO THE OFFICE AND REPORT ON THIS.
SU (SSK)
KUI (TURN)
ATSUSHI ...
TURN HER OVER TO THE MILITARY POLICE.
...!

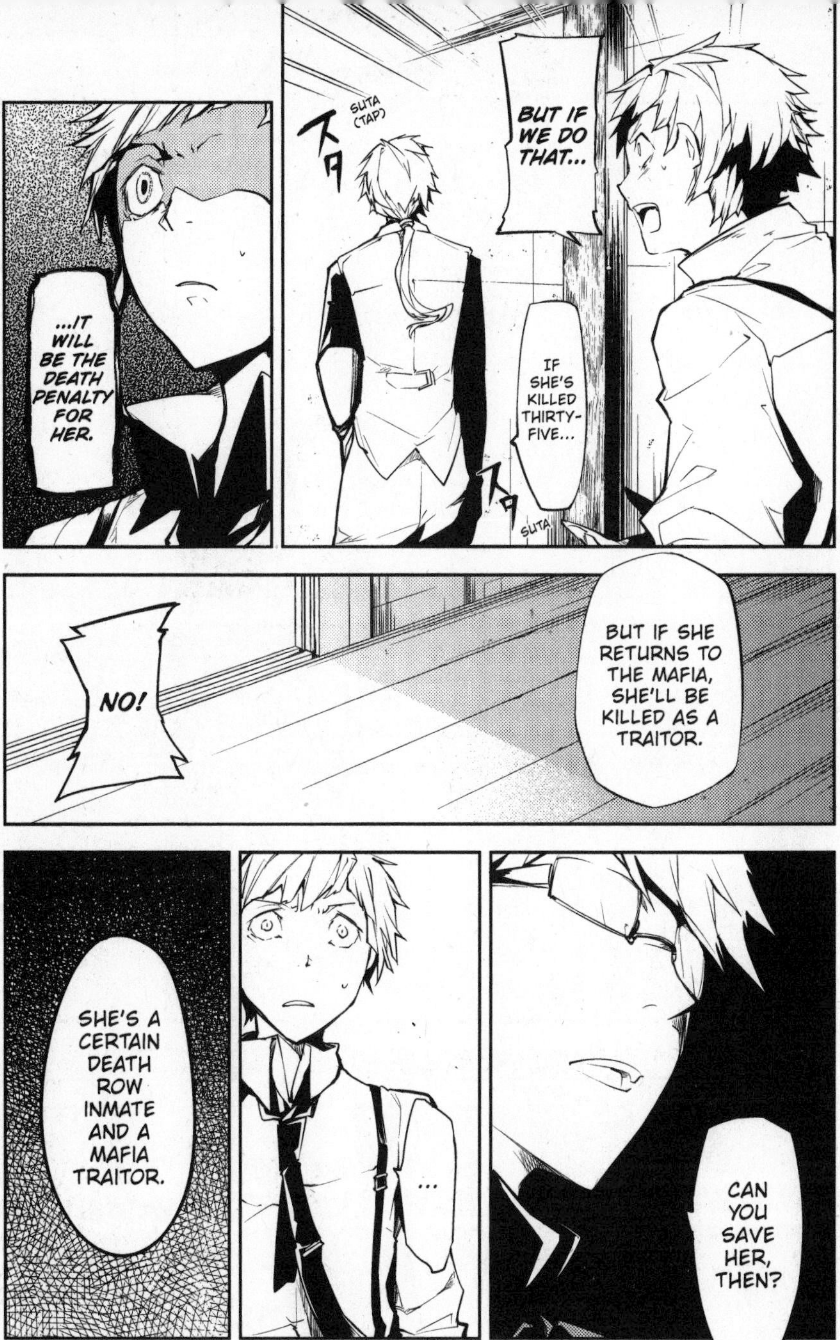
BUT IF WE DO THAT...
スタ
SUTA (TAP)
IF SHE'S KILLED THIRTY-FIVE...
スタ
SUTA
...IT WILL BE THE DEATH PENALTY FOR HER.
BUT IF SHE RETURNS TO THE MAFIA, SHE'LL BE KILLED AS A TRAITOR.
NO!
CAN YOU SAVE HER, THEN?
...
SHE'S A CERTAIN DEATH ROW INMATE AND A MAFIA TRAITOR.

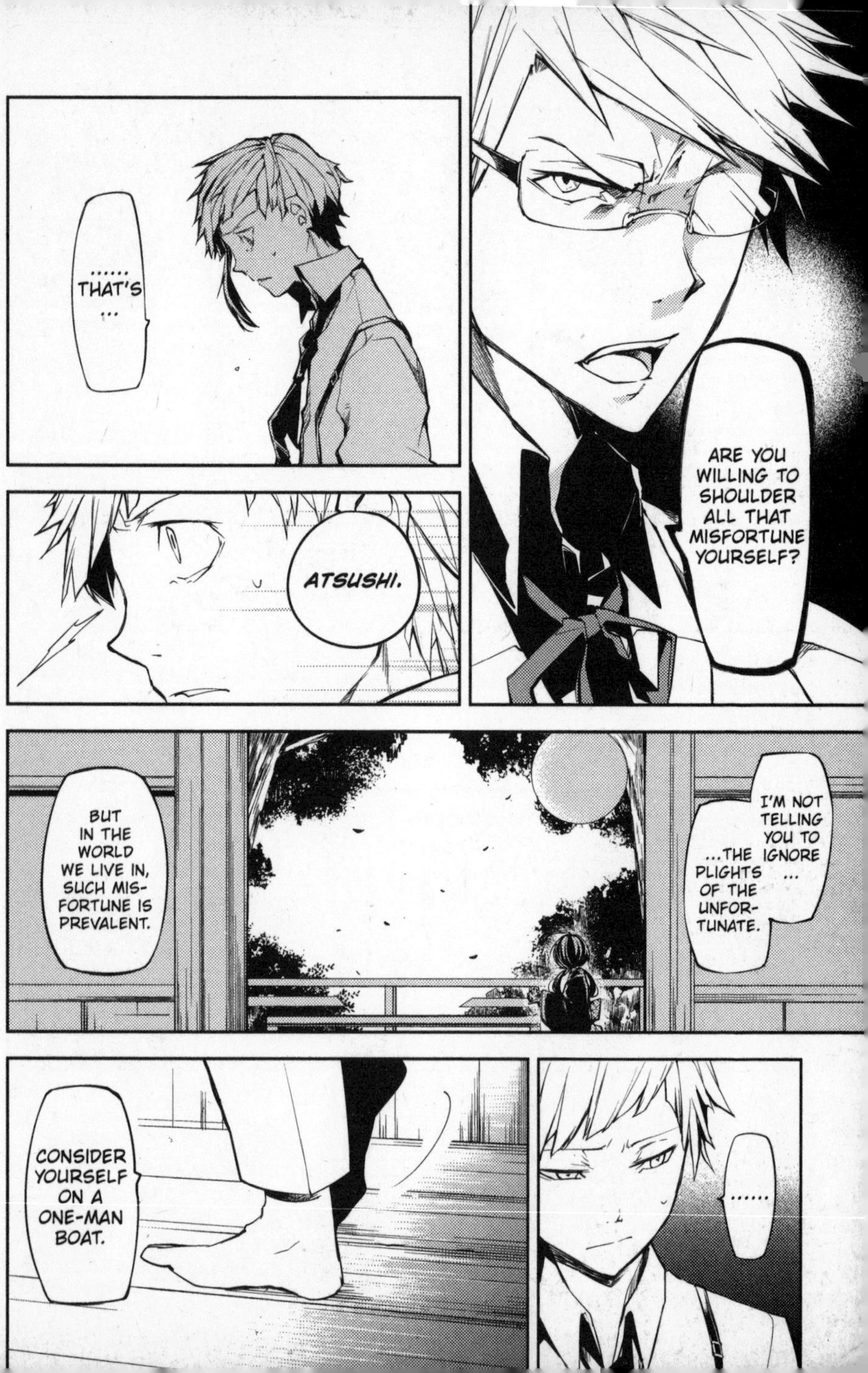

ARE YOU WILLING TO SHOULDER ALL THAT MISFORTUNE YOURSELF?
......THAT'S...
ATSUSHI.
I'M NOT TELLING YOU TO IGNORE...
...THE PLIGHTS OF THE UNFORTUNATE.
BUT IN THE WORLD WE LIVE IN, SUCH MISFORTUNE IS PREVALENT.
......
CONSIDER YOURSELF ON A ONE-MAN BOAT.

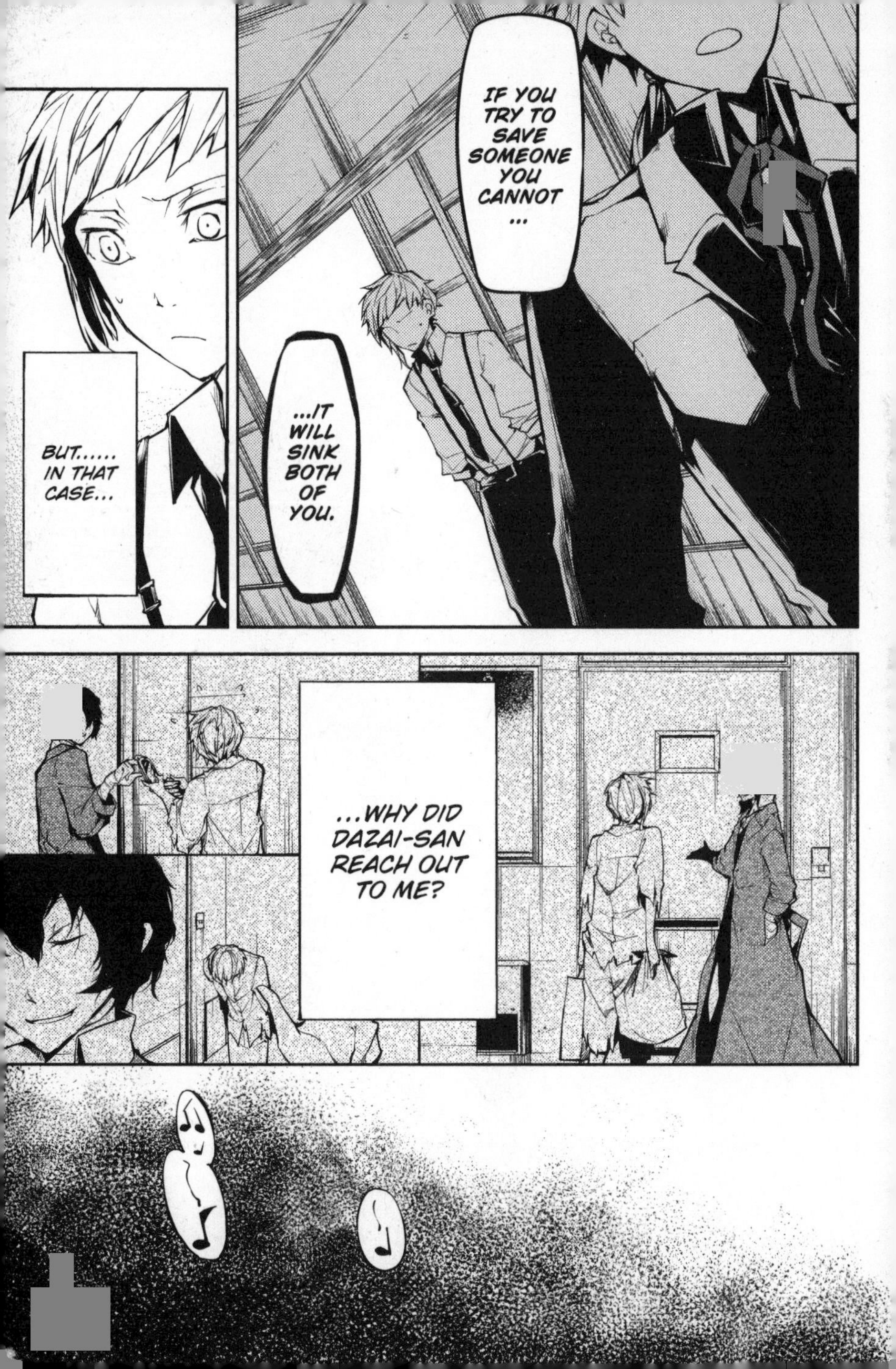
IF YOU TRY TO SAVE SOMEONE YOU CANNOT ...
...IT WILL SINK BOTH OF YOU.
BUT...... IN THAT CASE...
...WHY DID DAZAI-SAN REACH OUT TO ME?

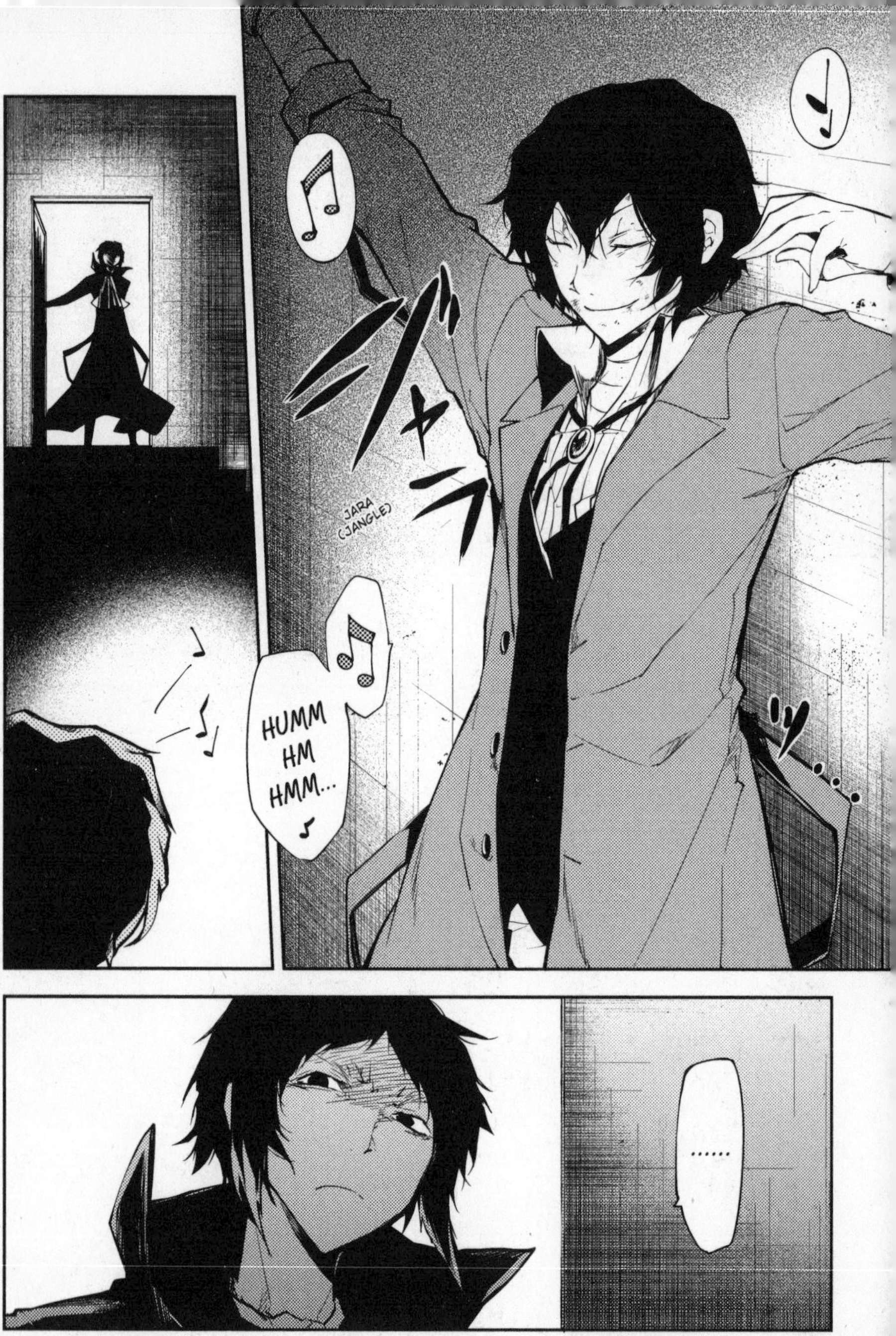

JARA (JANGLE)
HUMM HM HMM...
......

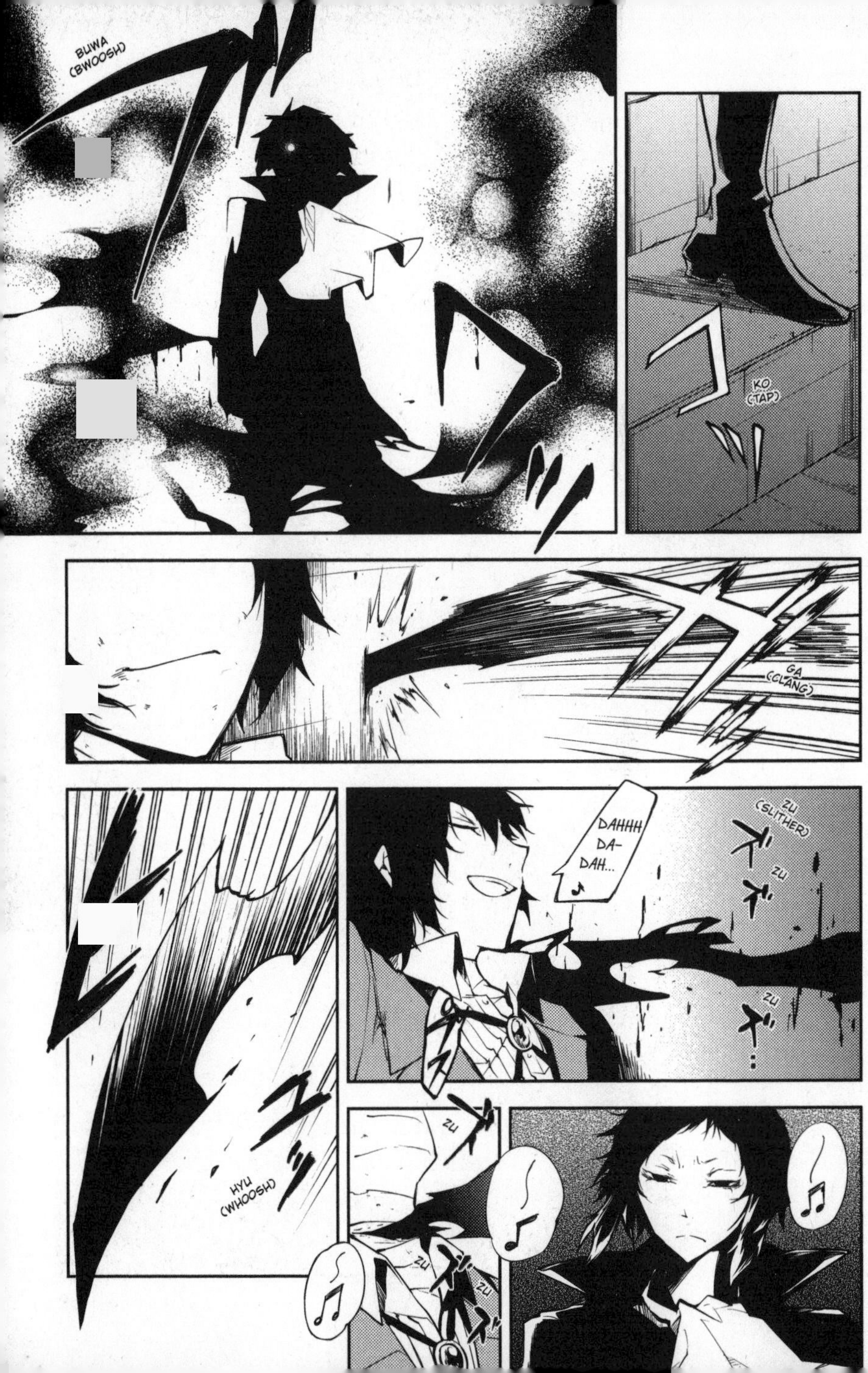
KO (TAP)
BUWA (BWOOSH)
GA (CLANG)
DAHHH DA-DAH... ♪
ZU (SLITHER)
ZU
ZU...
ZU
ZU
ZU
HYU (WHOOSH)

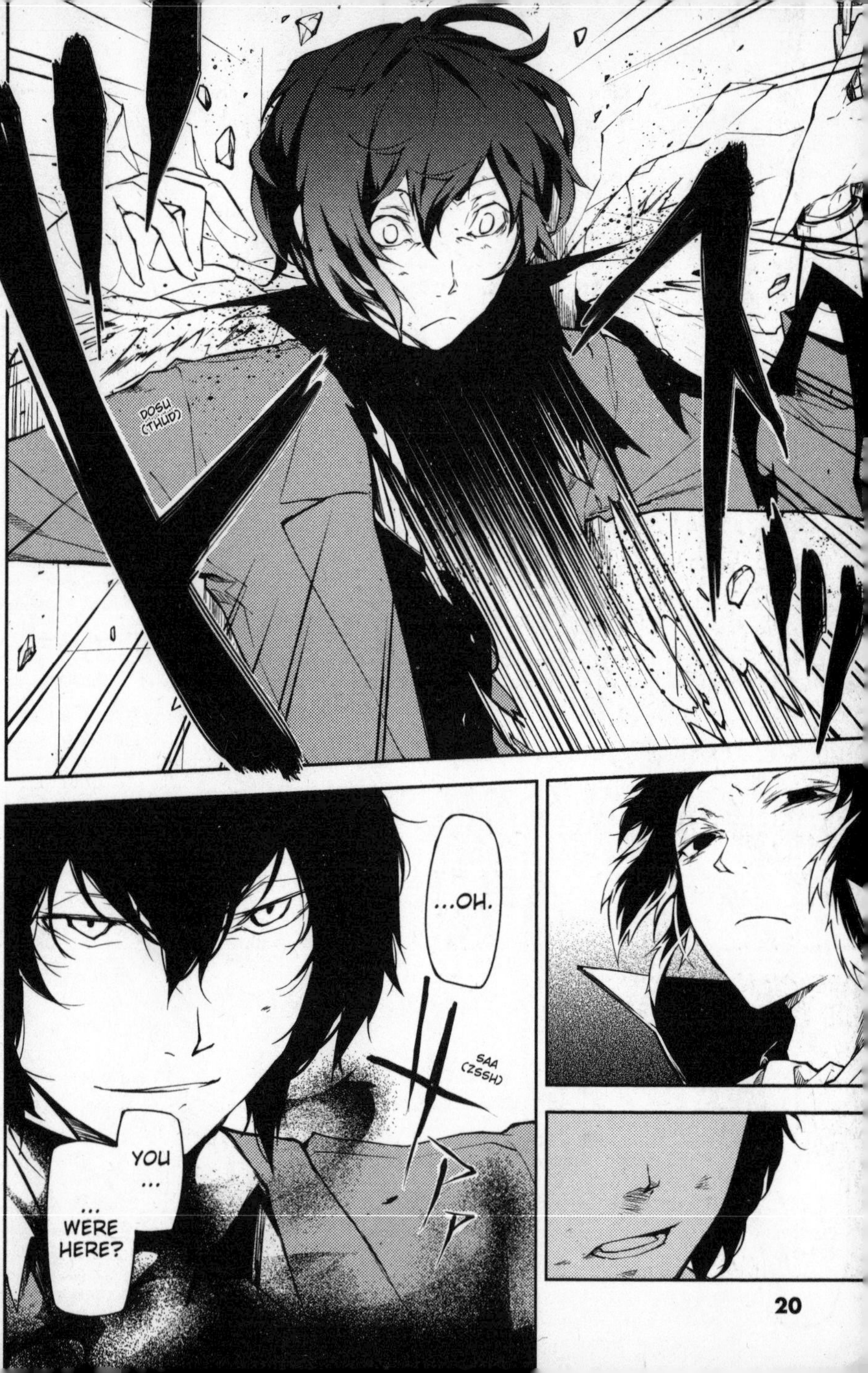
DOSU (THUD)
...OH.
SAA (ZSSH)
YOU... ...WERE HERE?

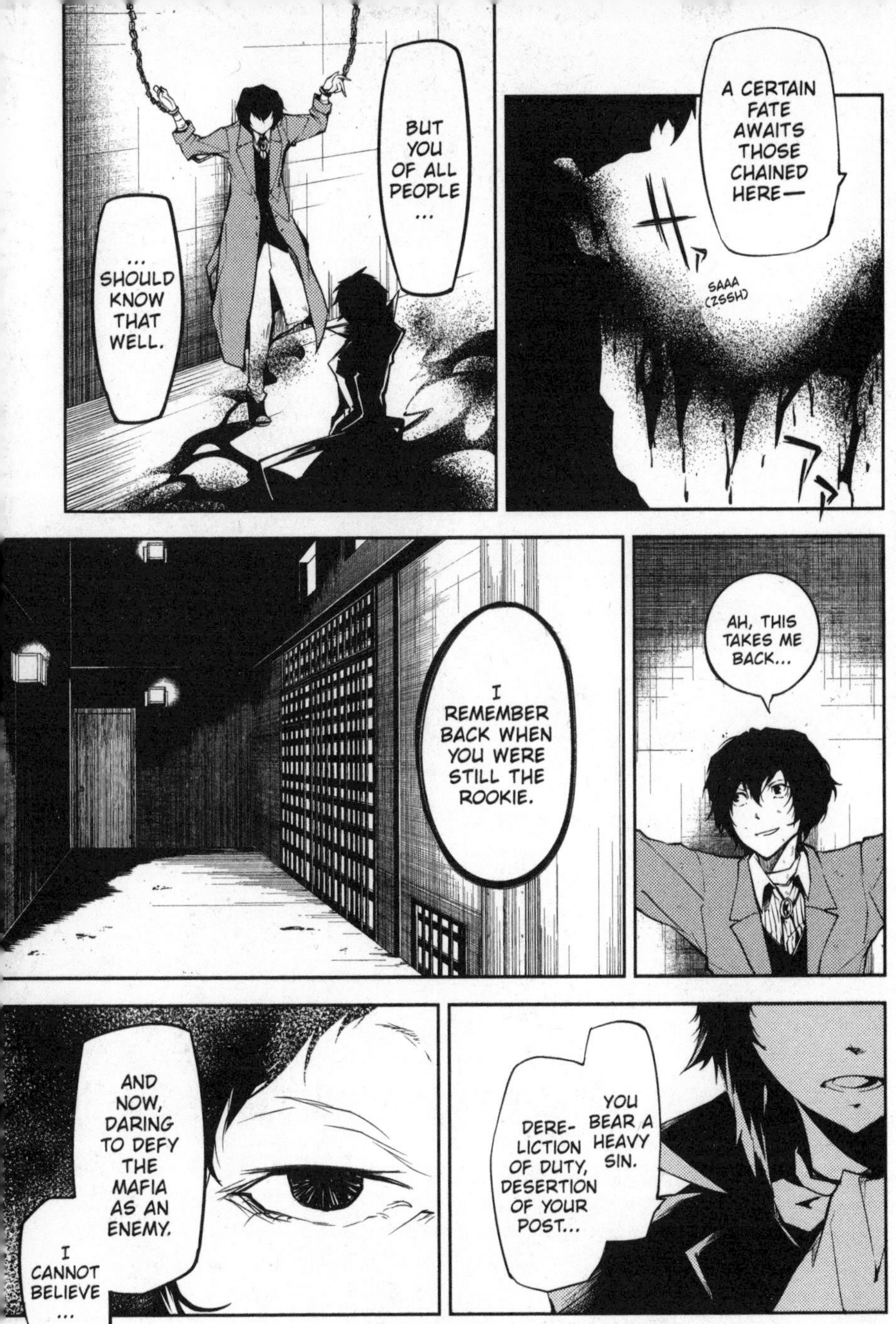
A CERTAIN FATE AWAITS THOSE CHAINED HERE—
SAAA (ZSSH)
BUT YOU OF ALL PEOPLE ...
... SHOULD KNOW THAT WELL.
AH, THIS TAKES ME BACK...
I REMEMBER BACK WHEN YOU WERE STILL THE ROOKIE.
YOU BEAR A HEAVY SIN.
DERE-LICTION OF DUTY, DESERTION OF YOUR POST...
AND NOW, DARING TO DEFY THE MAFIA AS AN ENEMY.
I CANNOT BELIEVE ...

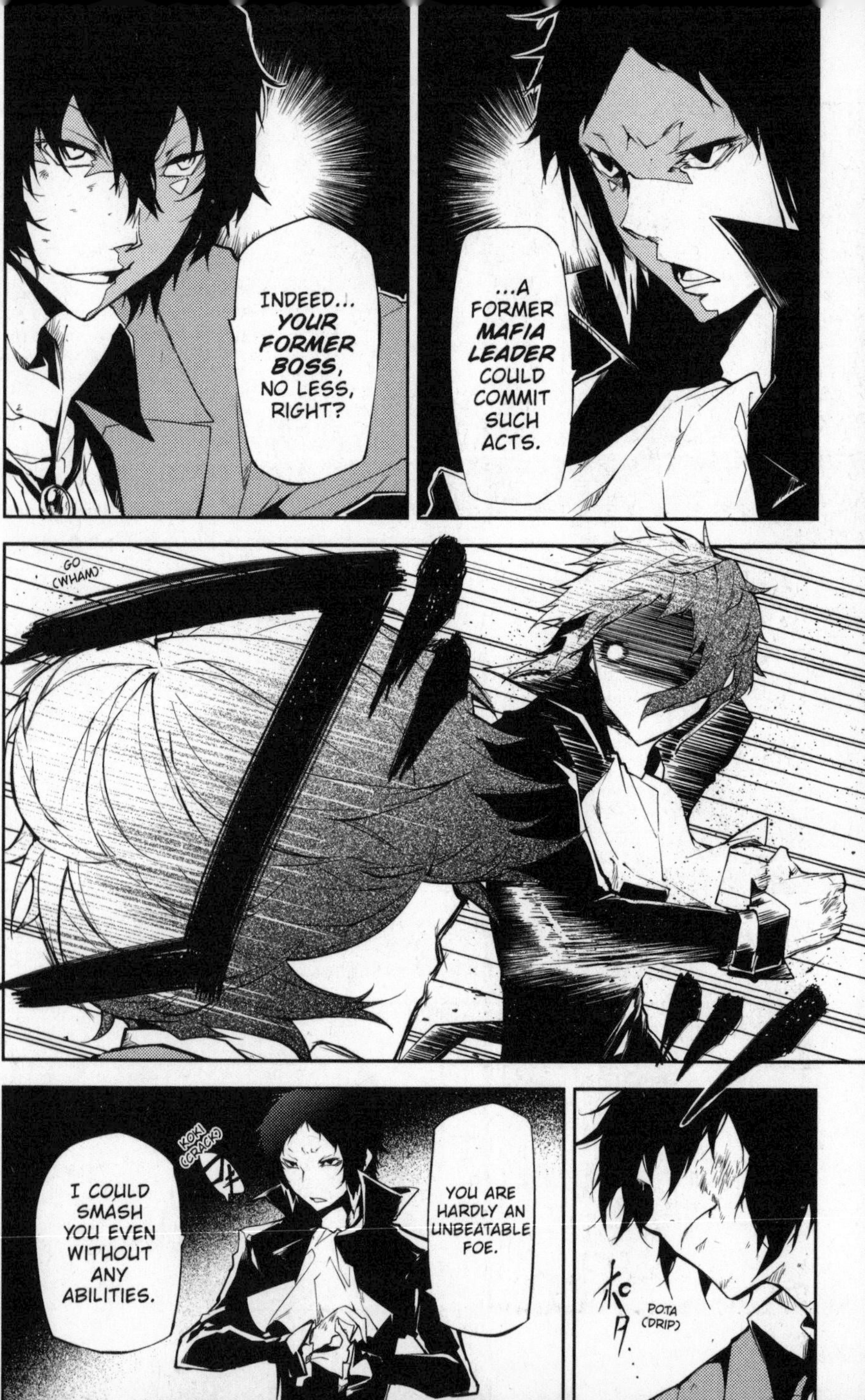
...A FORMER MAFIA LEADER COULD COMMIT SUCH ACTS.
INDEED... YOUR FORMER BOSS, NO LESS, RIGHT?
GO (WHAM)
POTA (DRIP)
KOKI (CRACK)
YOU ARE HARDLY AN UNBEATABLE FOE.
I COULD SMASH YOU EVEN WITHOUT ANY ABILITIES.

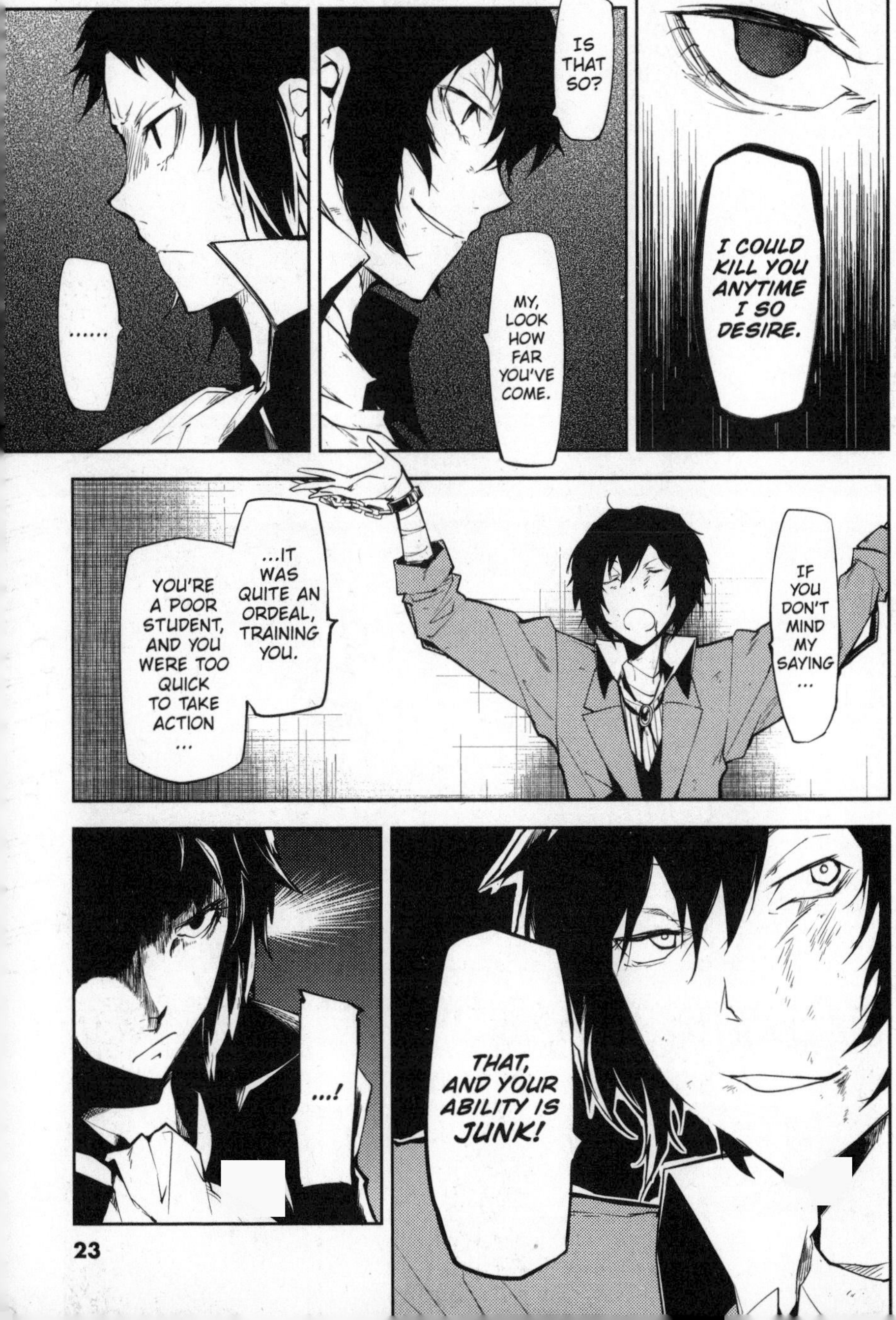
I COULD KILL YOU ANYTIME I SO DESIRE.
IS THAT SO?
MY, LOOK HOW FAR YOU'VE COME.
......
IF YOU DON'T MIND MY SAYING...
...IT WAS QUITE AN ORDEAL, TRAINING YOU.
YOU'RE A POOR STUDENT, AND YOU WERE TOO QUICK TO TAKE ACTION...
THAT, AND YOUR ABILITY IS JUNK!
...!

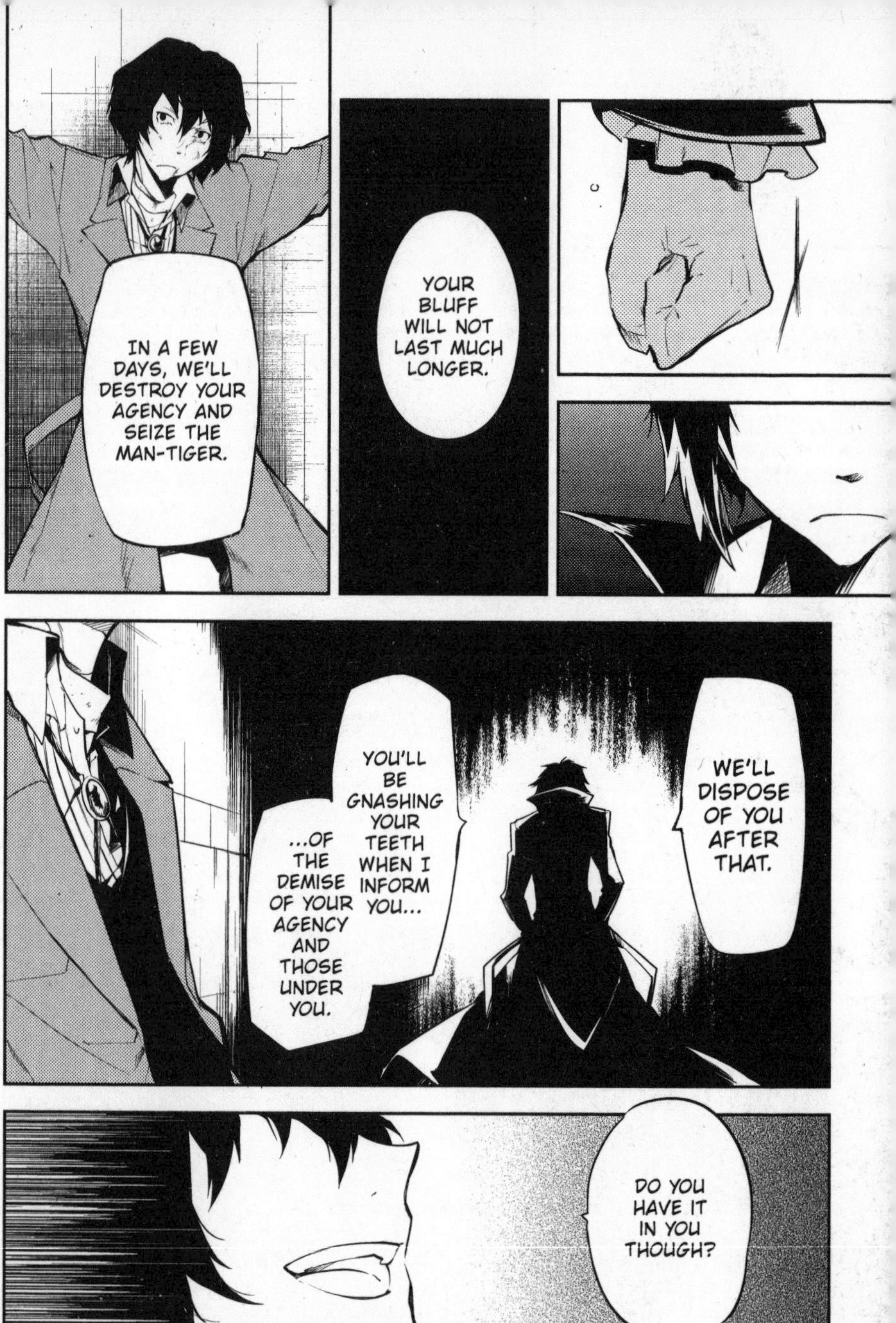
YOUR BLUFF WILL NOT LAST MUCH LONGER.
IN A FEW DAYS, WE'LL DESTROY YOUR AGENCY AND SEIZE THE MAN-TIGER.
WE'LL DISPOSE OF YOU AFTER THAT.
YOU'LL BE GNASHING YOUR TEETH WHEN I INFORM YOU...
...OF THE DEMISE OF YOUR AGENCY AND THOSE UNDER YOU.
DO YOU HAVE IT IN YOU THOUGH?

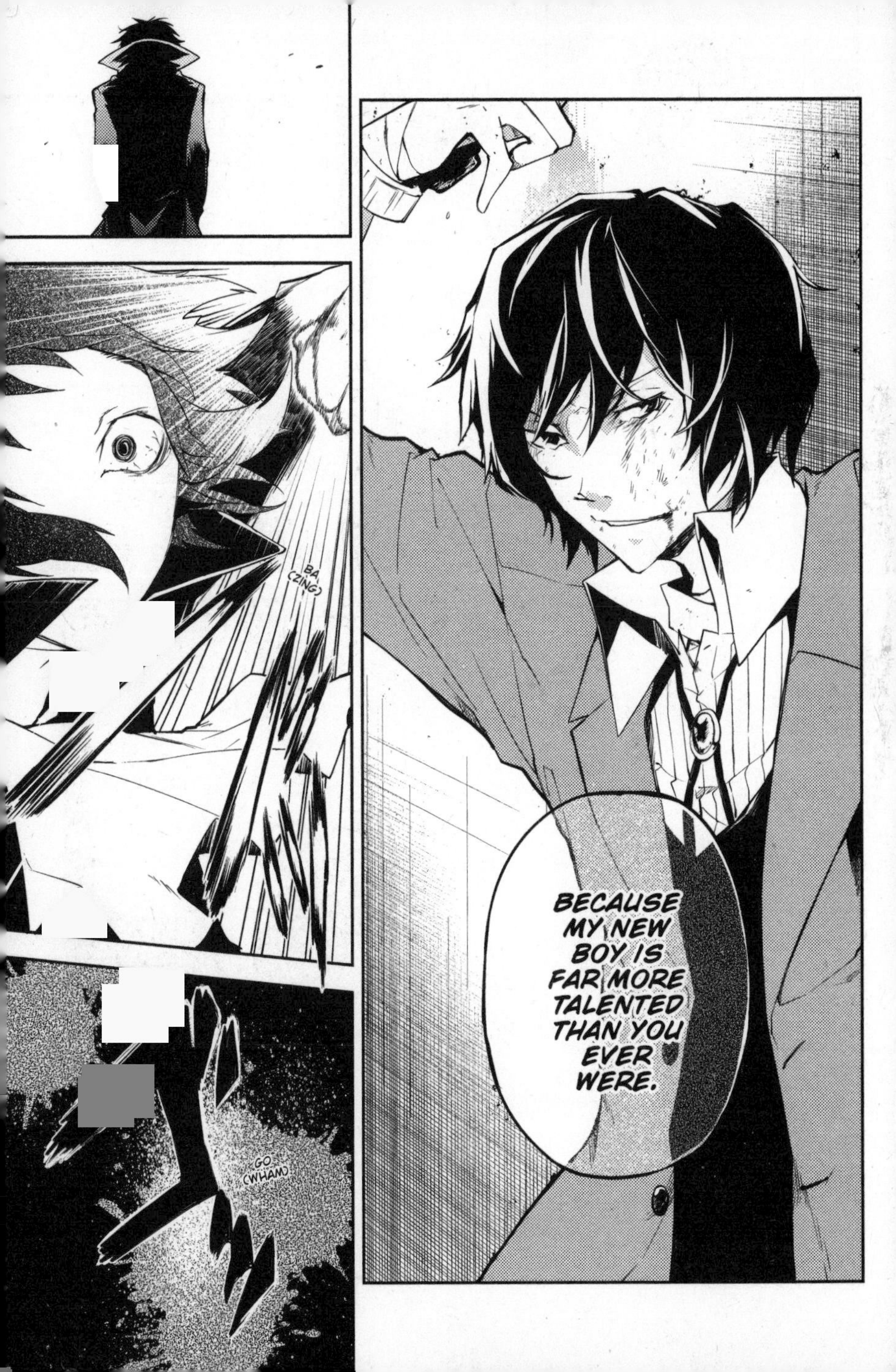
BECAUSE MY NEW BOY IS FAR MORE TALENTED THAN YOU EVER WERE.
BA (ZING)
GO (WHAM)

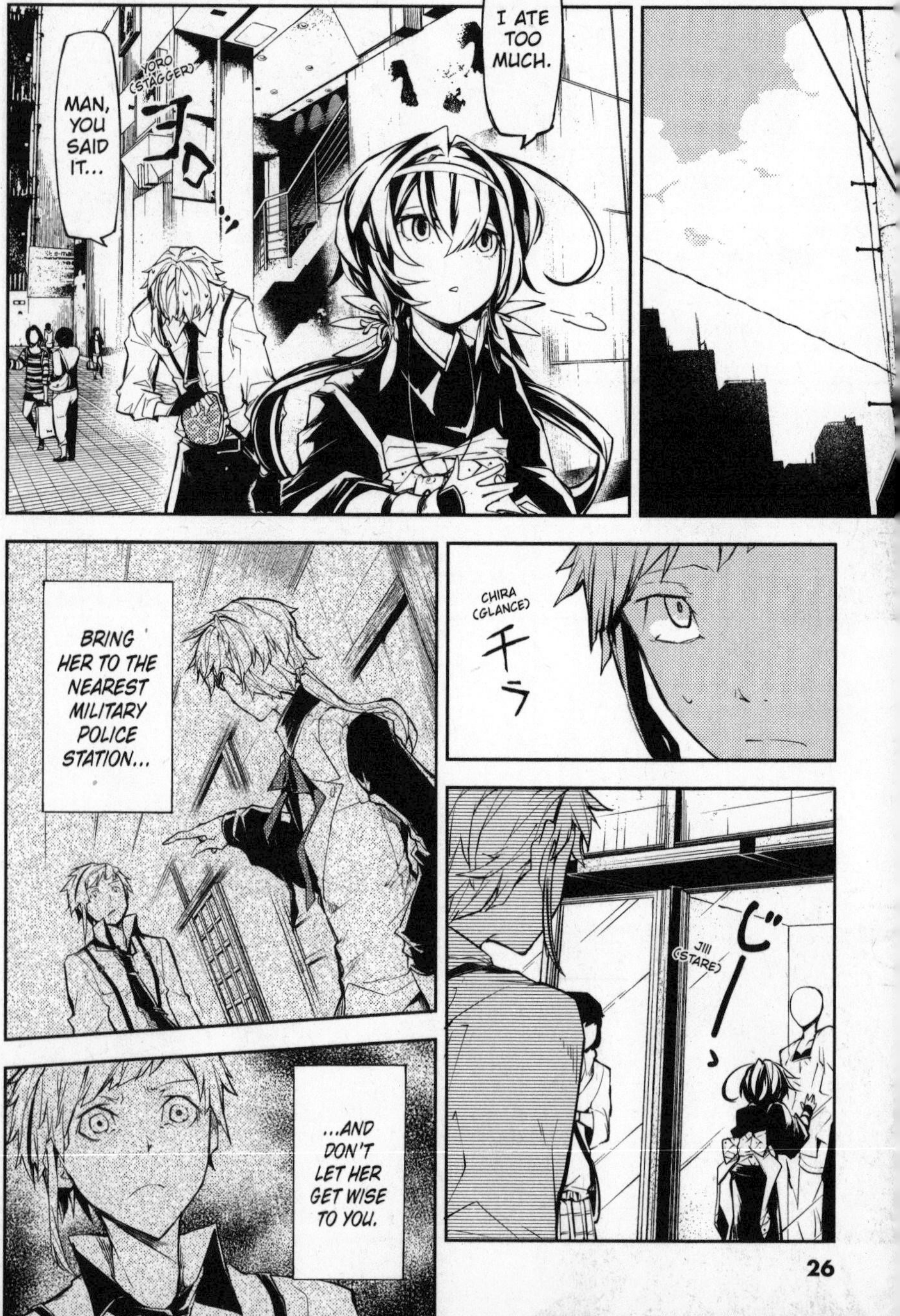
I ATE TOO MUCH.
YORO (STAGGER)
ヨロ
MAN, YOU SAID IT...
CHIRA (GLANCE)
チラ
JIII (STARE)
じー
BRING HER TO THE NEAREST MILITARY POLICE STATION...
...AND DON'T LET HER GET WISE TO YOU.

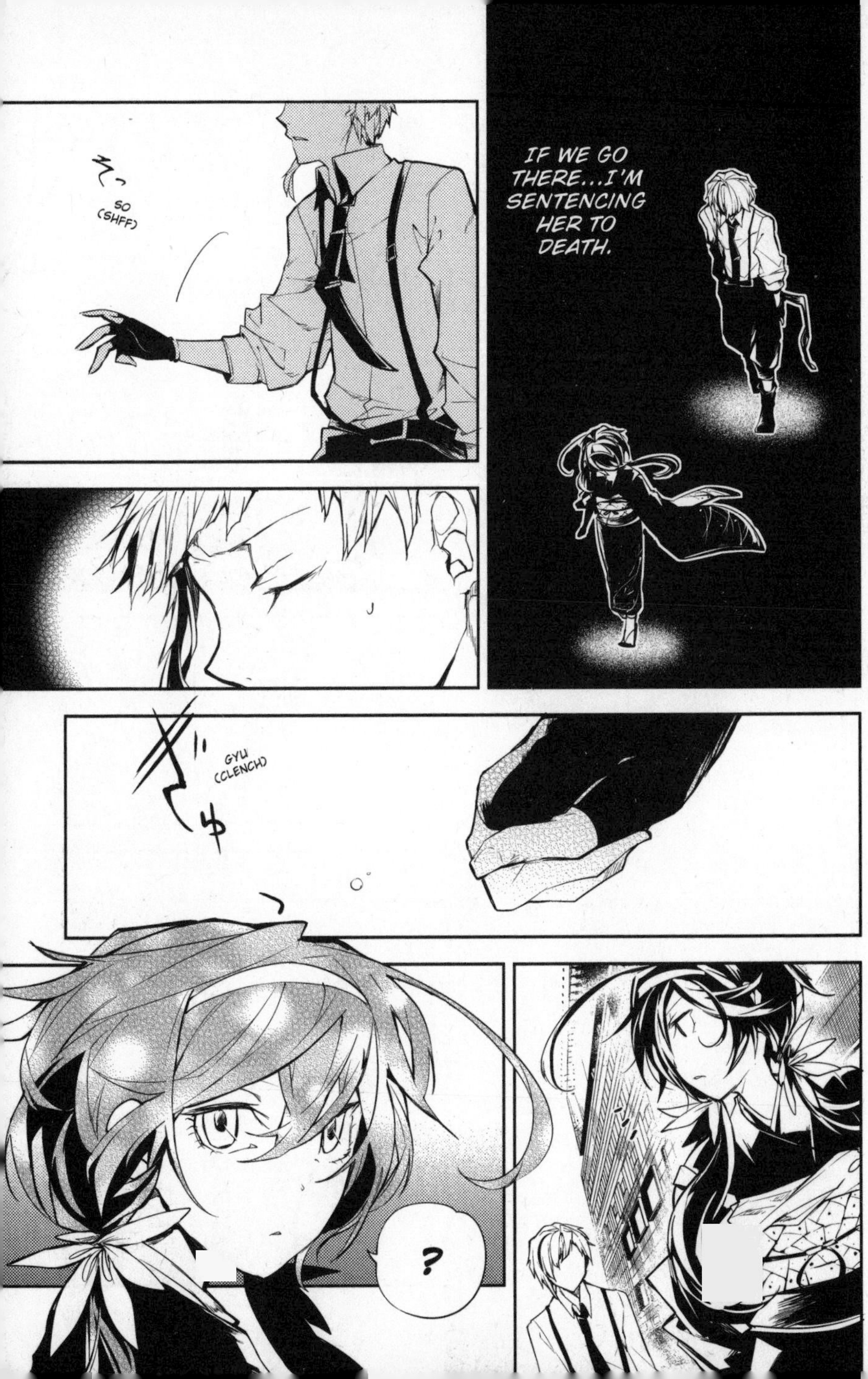
IF WE GO THERE...I'M SENTENCING HER TO DEATH.
SO (SHFF)
GYU (CLENCH)
?

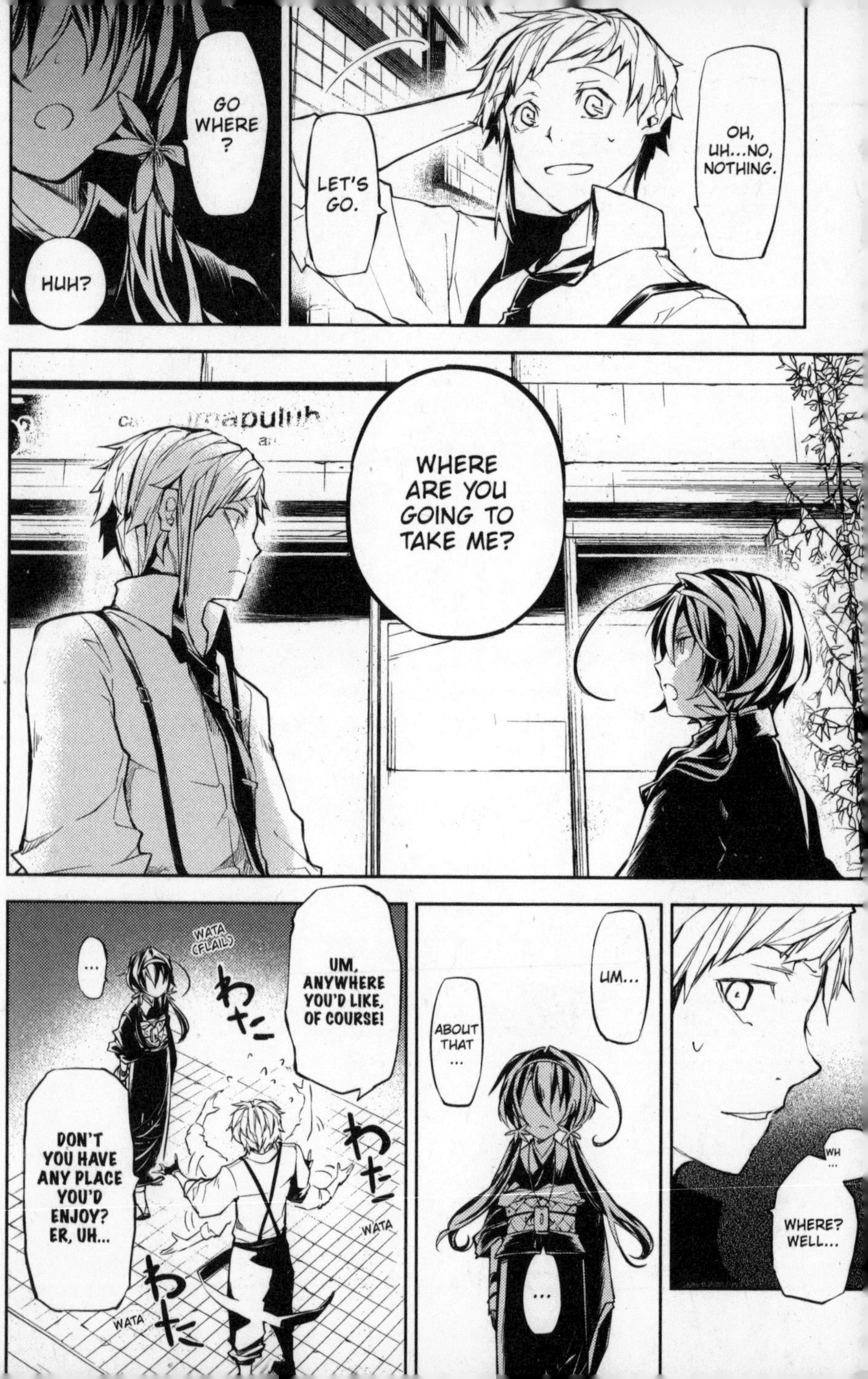
OH, UH...NO, NOTHING.
LET'S GO.
GO WHERE?
HUH?
WHERE ARE YOU GOING TO TAKE ME?
WH...
WHERE? WELL...
UM...
ABOUT THAT...
...
UM, ANYWHERE YOU'D LIKE, OF COURSE!
WATA (FLAIL)
わた
...
わた
WATA
DON'T YOU HAVE ANY PLACE YOU'D ENJOY? ER, UH...
わた
WATA

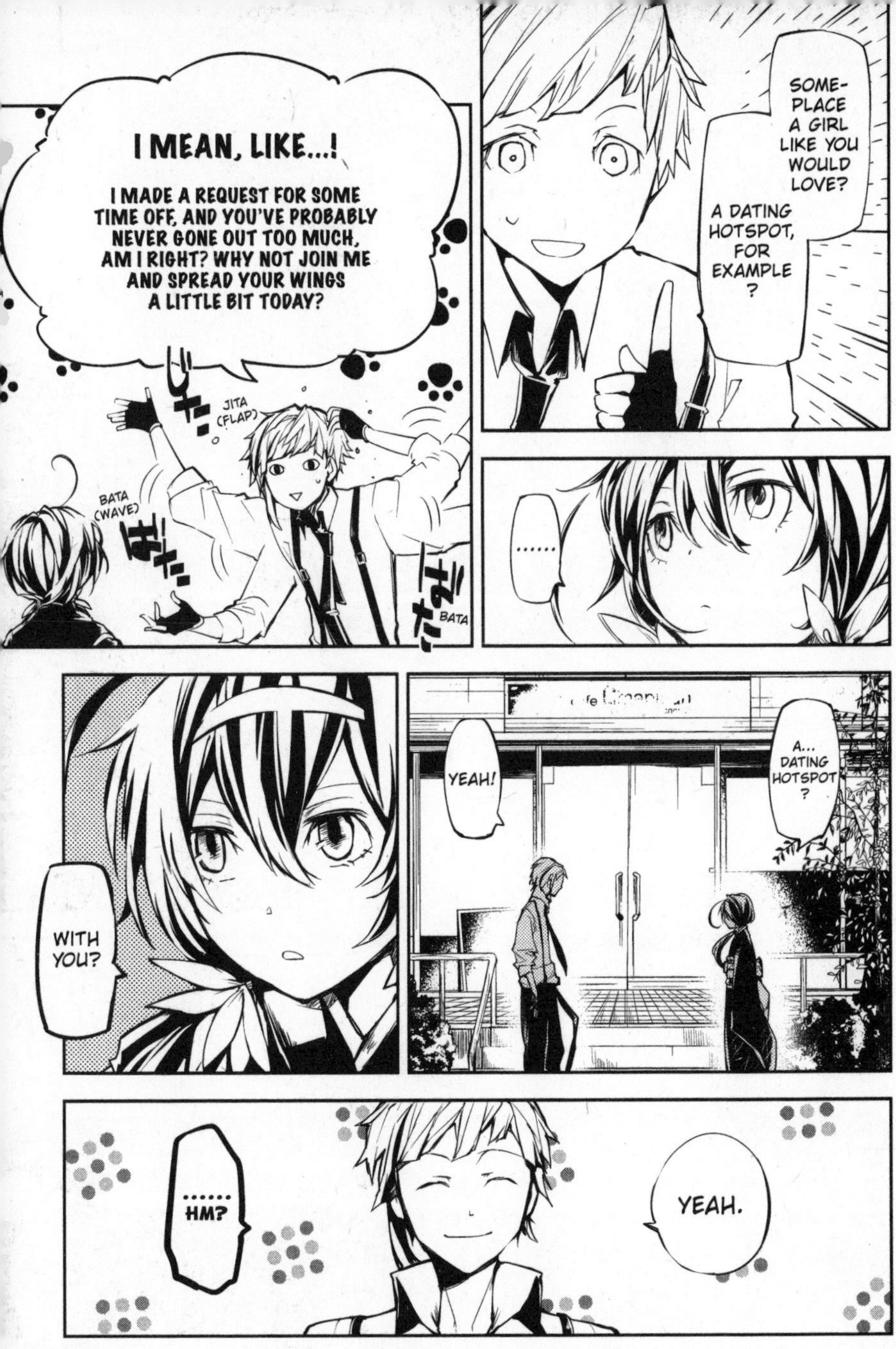
SOME-PLACE A GIRL LIKE YOU WOULD LOVE?
A DATING HOTSPOT, FOR EXAMPLE?
......
I MEAN, LIKE...!
I MADE A REQUEST FOR SOME TIME OFF, AND YOU'VE PROBABLY NEVER GONE OUT TOO MUCH, AM I RIGHT? WHY NOT JOIN ME AND SPREAD YOUR WINGS A LITTLE BIT TODAY?
JITA (FLAP)
BATA
BATA (WAVE)
A... DATING HOTSPOT?
YEAH!
WITH YOU?
YEAH.
......HM?

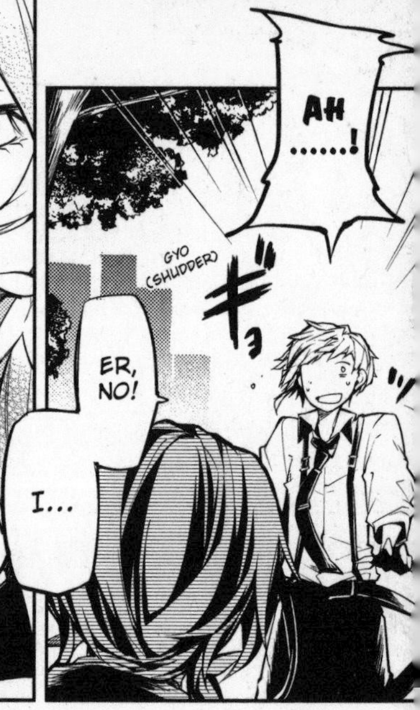
AH ......!
GYO (SHUDDER)
ER, NO!
I...

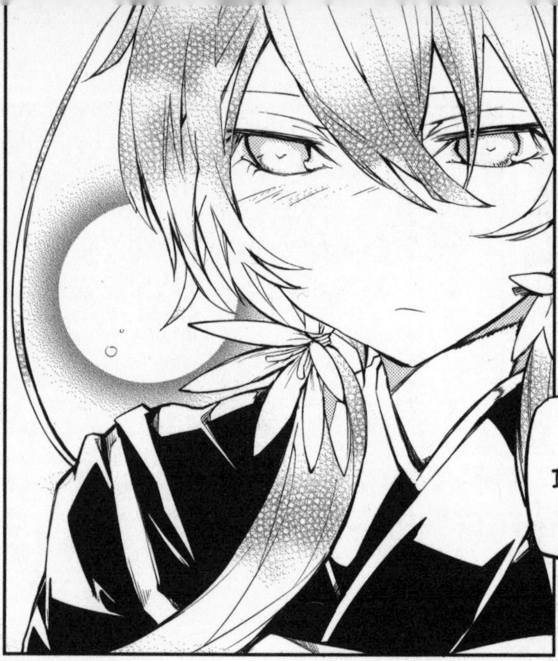

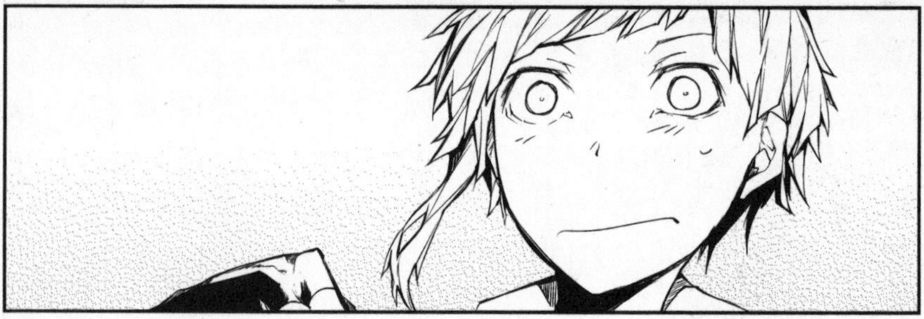

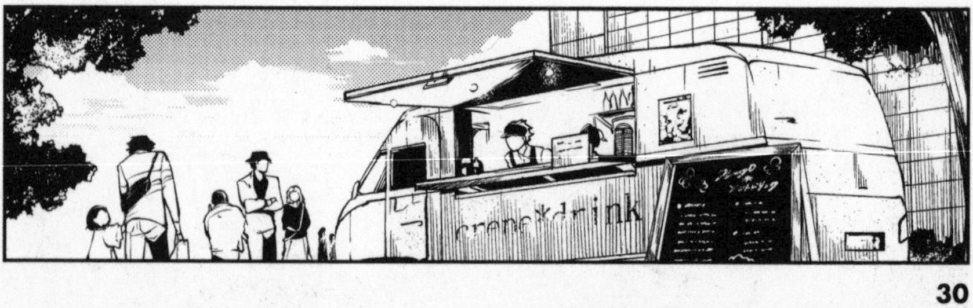

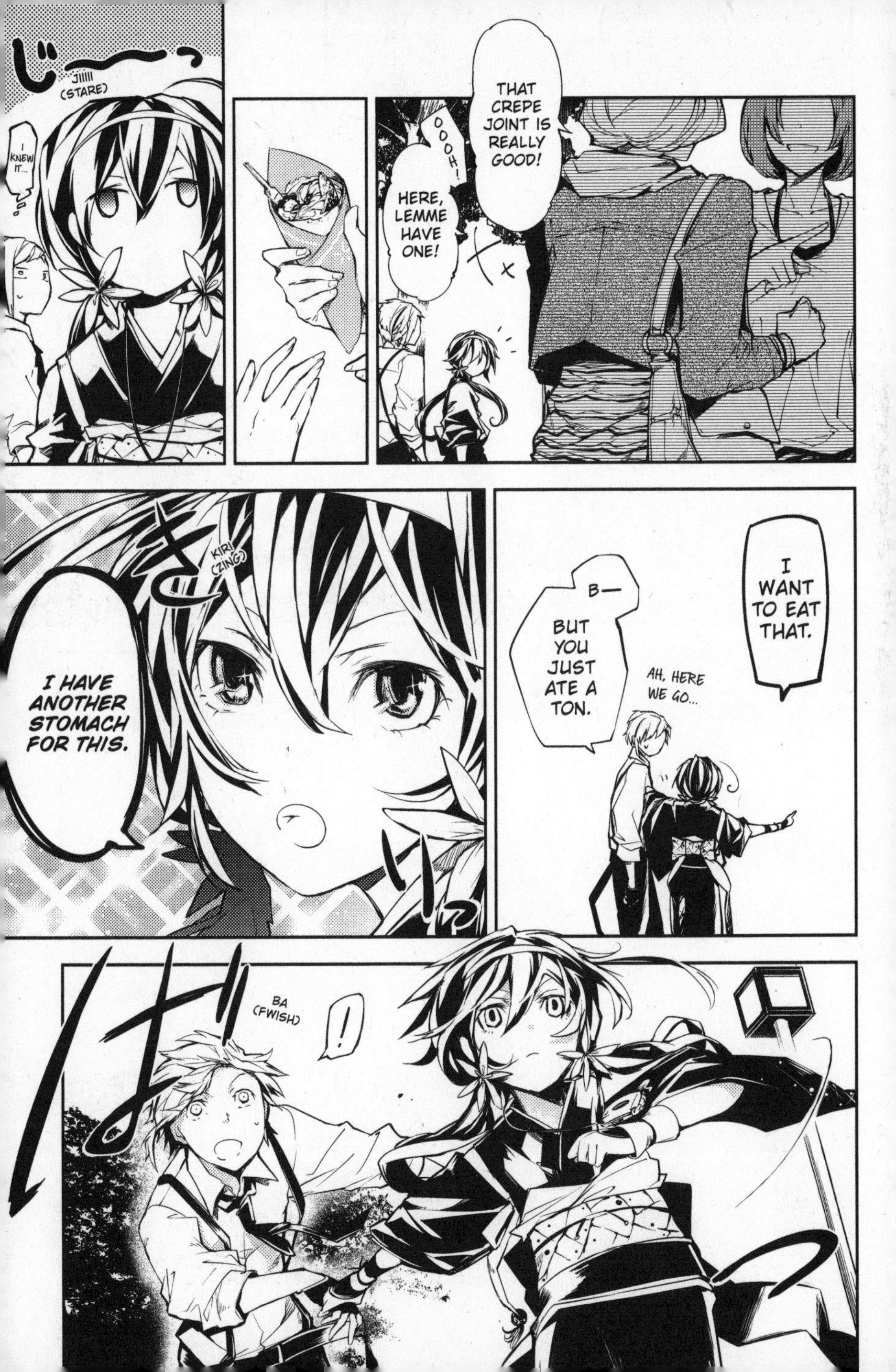
THAT CREPE JOINT IS REALLY GOOD!
OOOH!
HERE, LEMME HAVE ONE!
JIIIII (STARE)
I KNEW IT...
I WANT TO EAT THAT.
B—
BUT YOU JUST ATE A TON.
AH, HERE WE GO...
KIRI (ZING)
I HAVE ANOTHER STOMACH FOR THIS.
BA (FWISH)
!

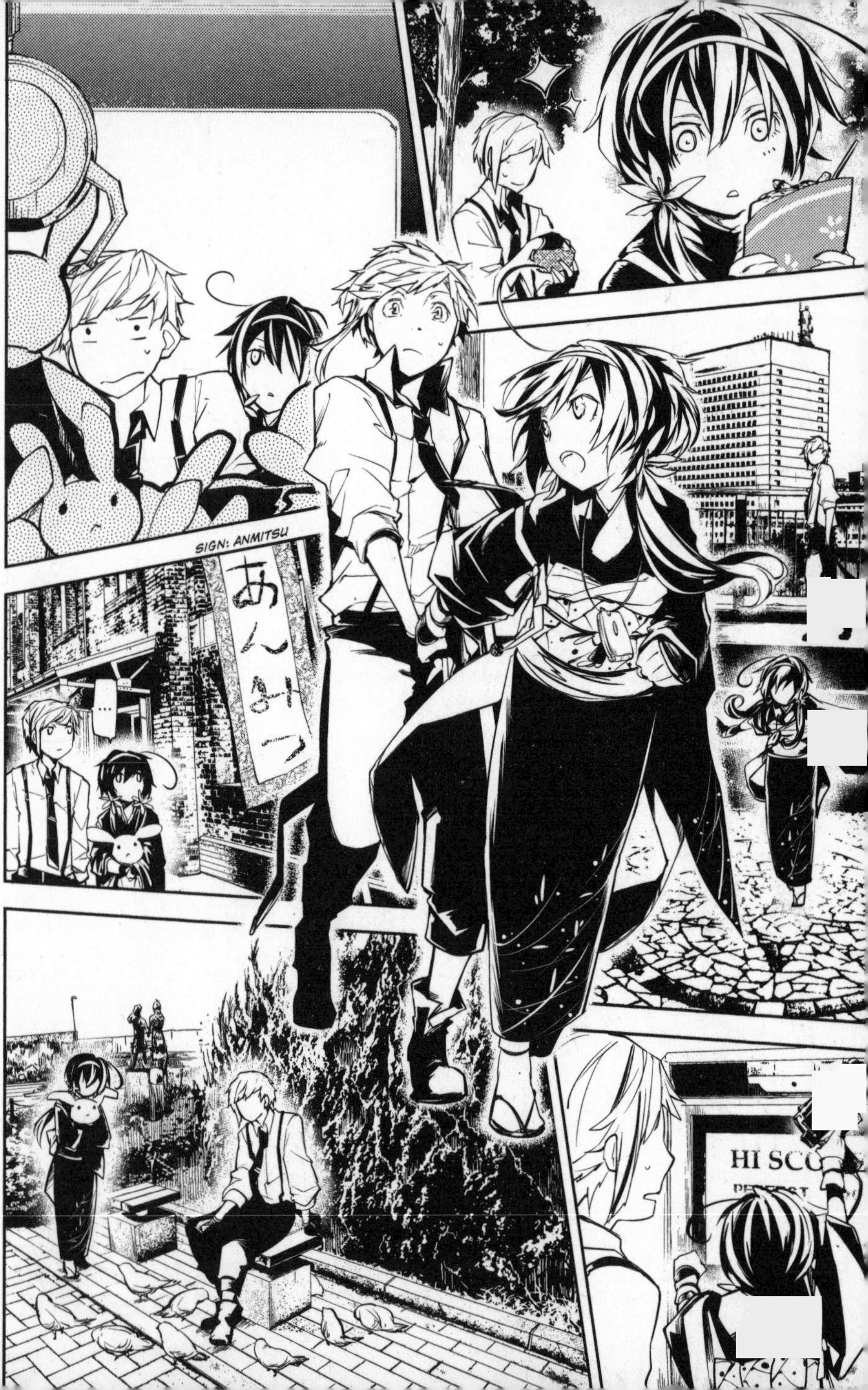
SIGN: ANMITSU
あんみつ
…

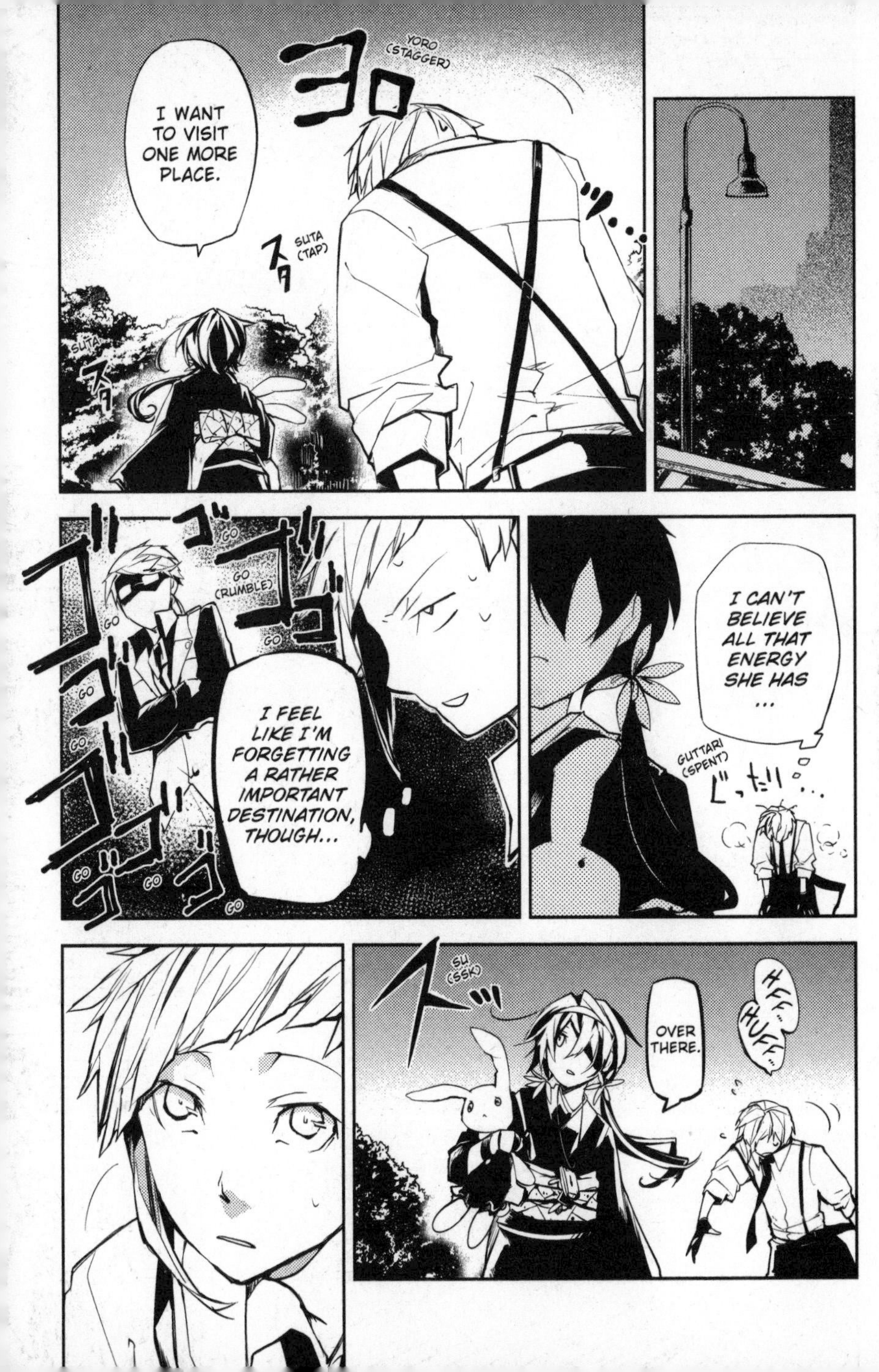
YORO (STAGGER)
I WANT TO VISIT ONE MORE PLACE.
SUTA (TAP)
SUTA
I CAN'T BELIEVE ALL THAT ENERGY SHE HAS...
GUTTARI (SPENT)
GO
GO (RUMBLE)
GO
GO
GO
I FEEL LIKE I'M FORGETTING A RATHER IMPORTANT DESTINATION, THOUGH...
GO
GO
GO
HUFF... HUFF...
OVER THERE.
SU (SSK)

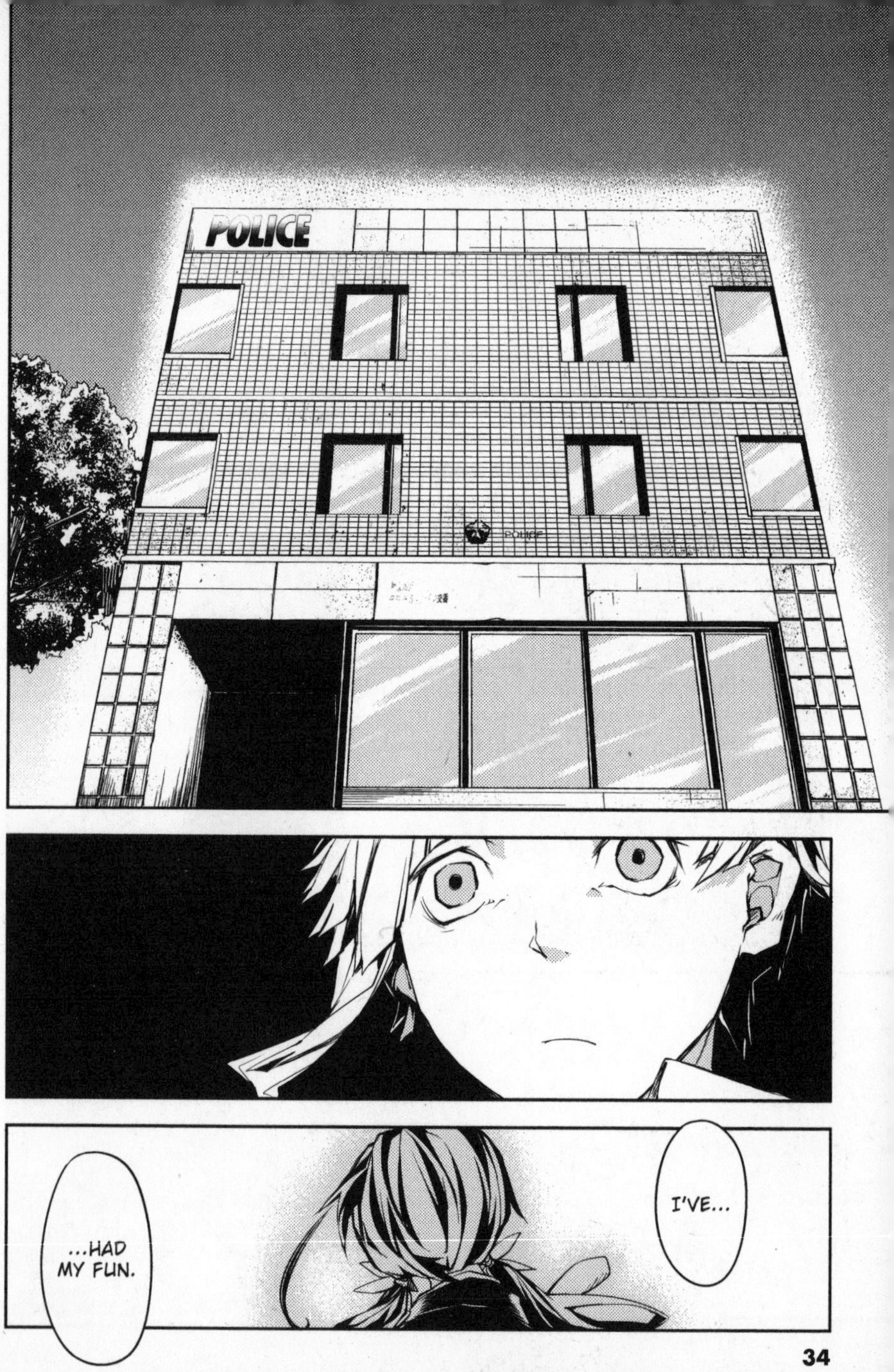
POLICE
I'VE...
...HAD MY FUN.

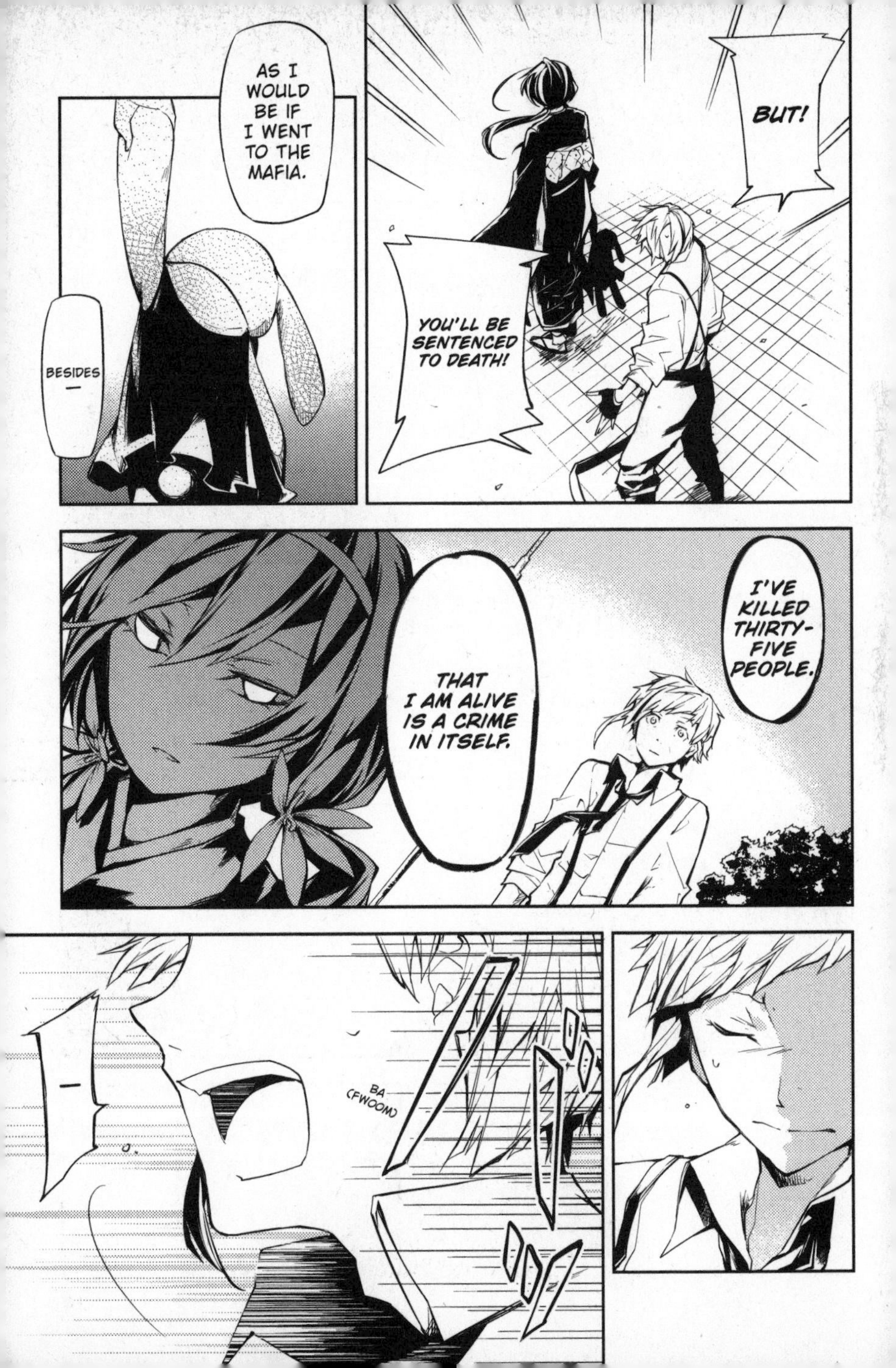
BUT!
YOU'LL BE SENTENCED TO DEATH!
AS I WOULD BE IF I WENT TO THE MAFIA.
BESIDES —
I'VE KILLED THIRTY-FIVE PEOPLE.
THAT I AM ALIVE IS A CRIME IN ITSELF.
BA (FWOOM)
—

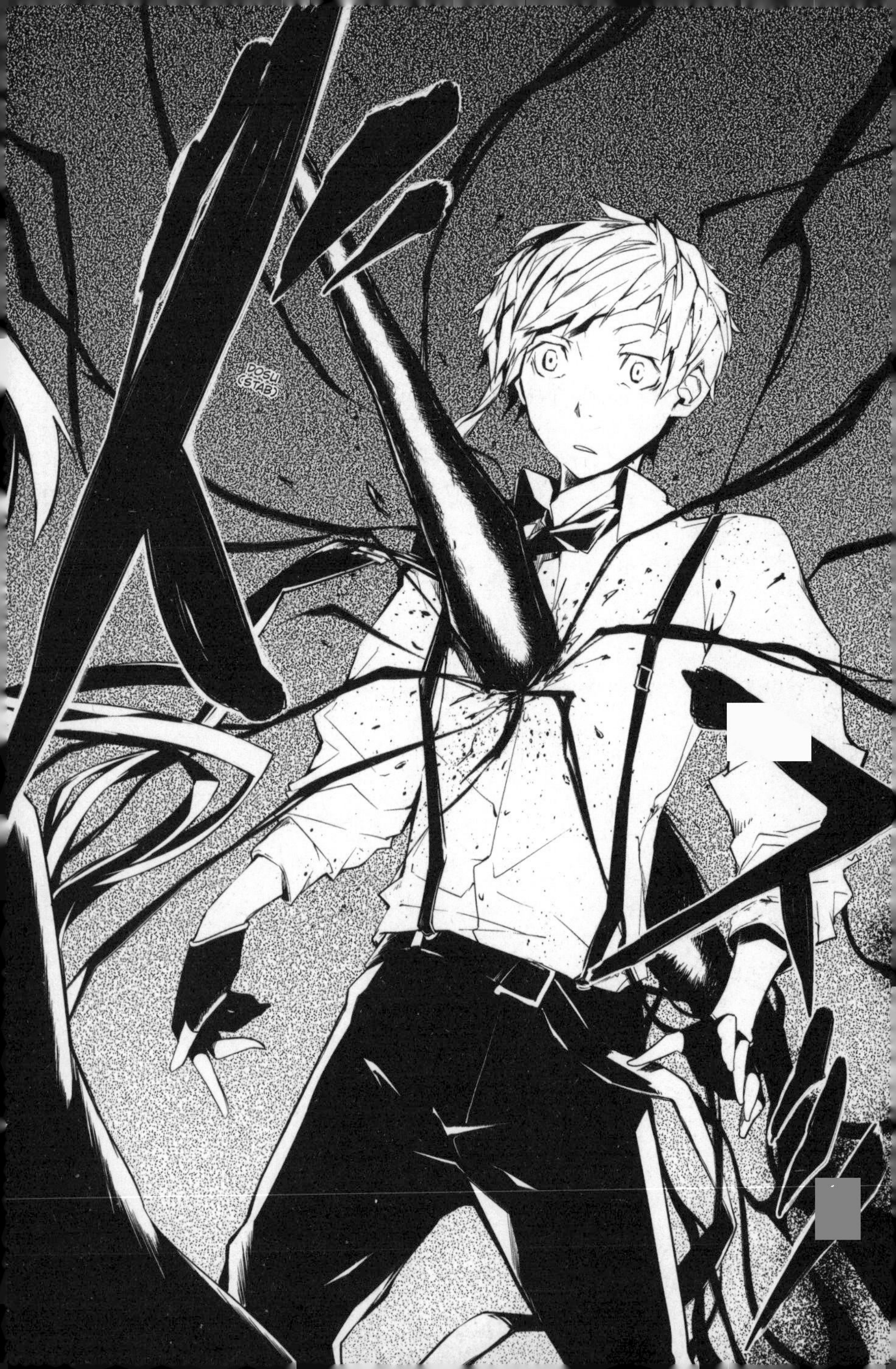
DOSU (STAB)

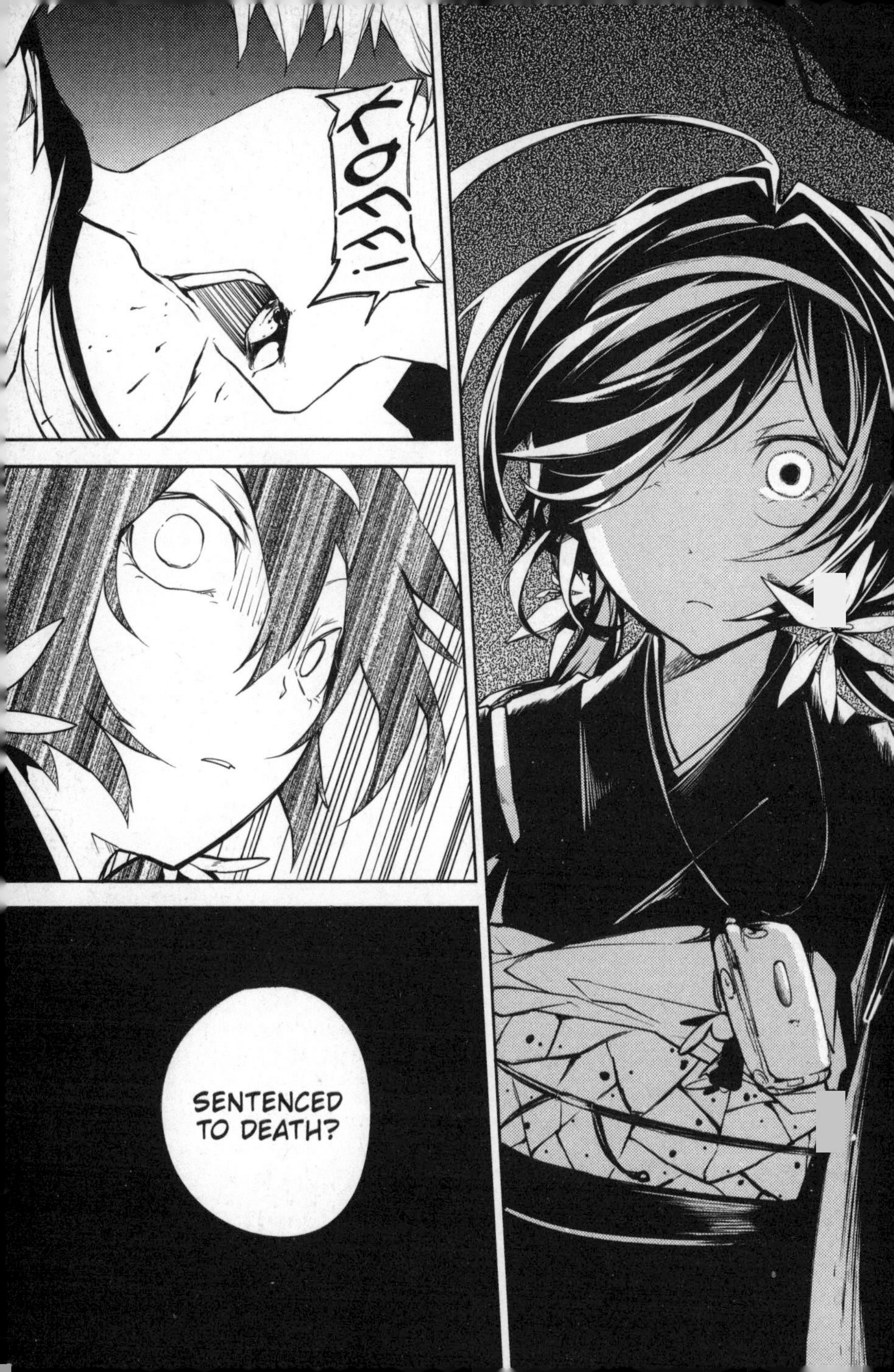
KOFF!
SENTENCED TO DEATH?

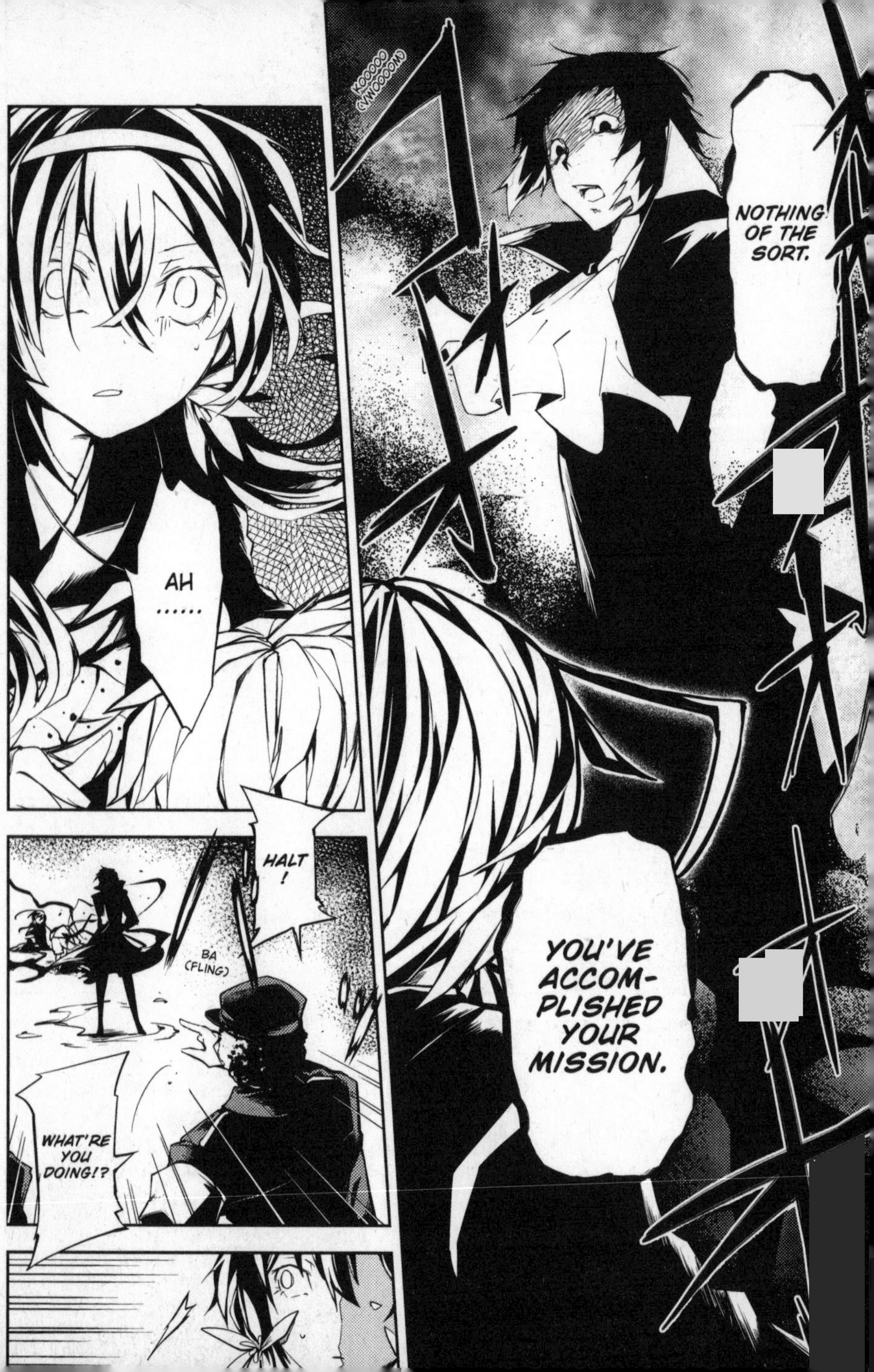
KOOOOO (VWOOOOM)
NOTHING OF THE SORT.
YOU'VE ACCOM-PLISHED YOUR MISSION.
AH ......
HALT!
BA (FLING)
WHAT'RE YOU DOING!?

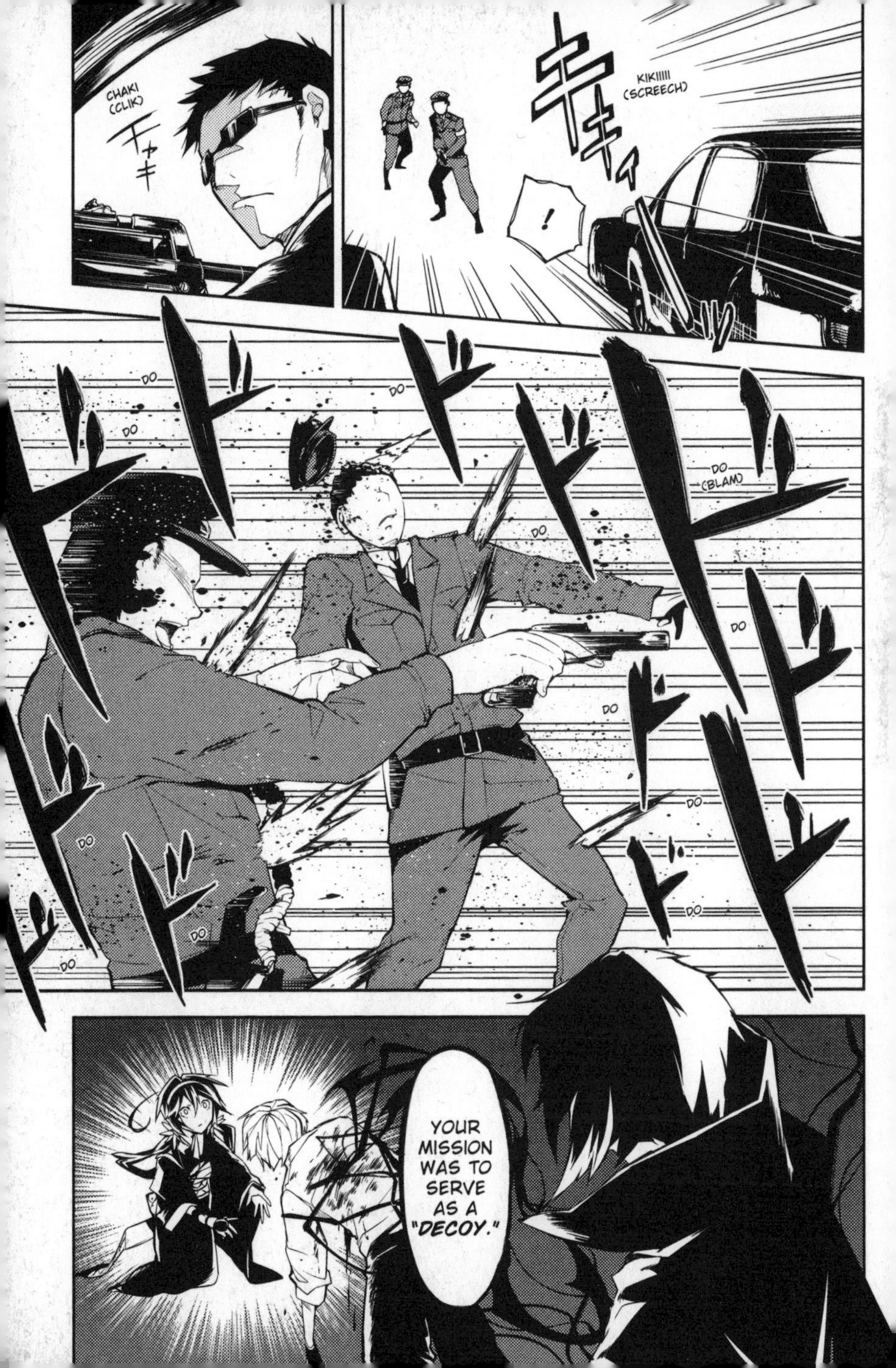
KIKIIIII
(SCREECH)
!
CHAKI
(CLIK)
DO
(BLAM)
DO
DO
DO
DO
DO
DO
DO
DO
DO
DO
DO
YOUR MISSION WAS TO SERVE AS A "DECOY."

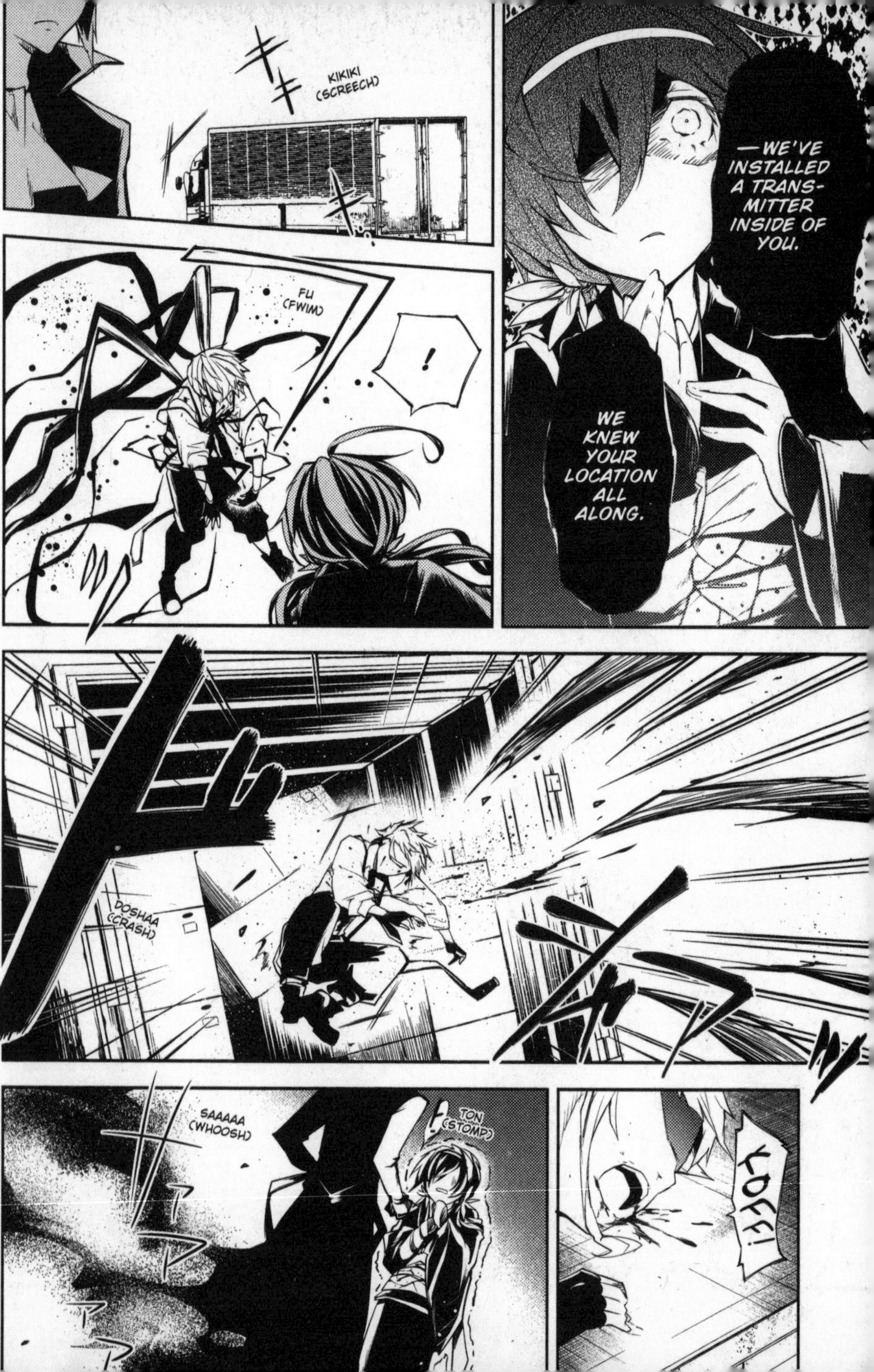
—WE'VE INSTALLED A TRANS-MITTER INSIDE OF YOU.
WE KNEW YOUR LOCATION ALL ALONG.
KIKIKI (SCREECH)
FU (FWIM)
!
DOSHAA (CRASH)
KOFF!
TON (STOMP)
SAAAAA (WHOOSH)

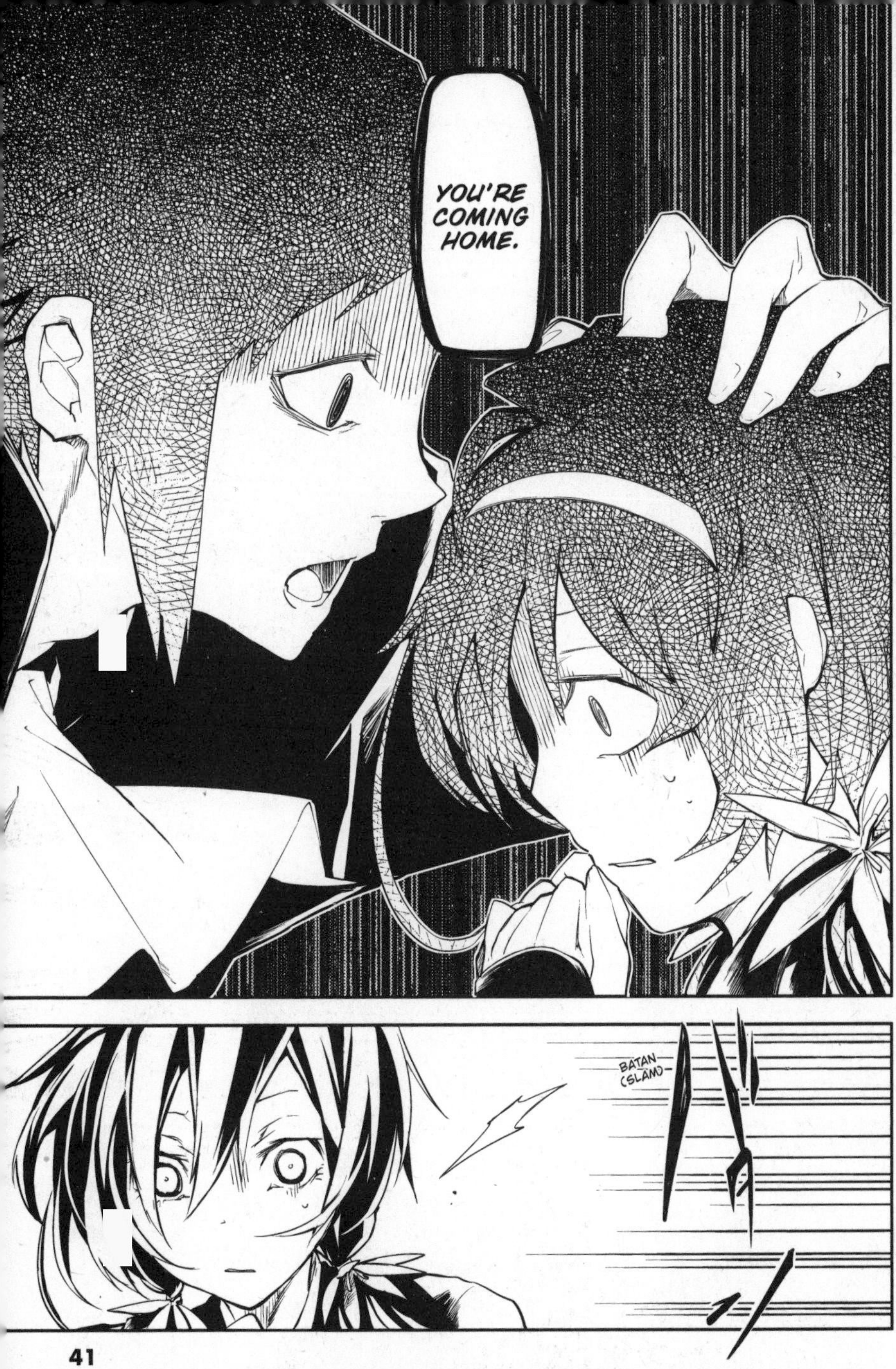
YOU'RE COMING HOME.
BATAN (SLAM)

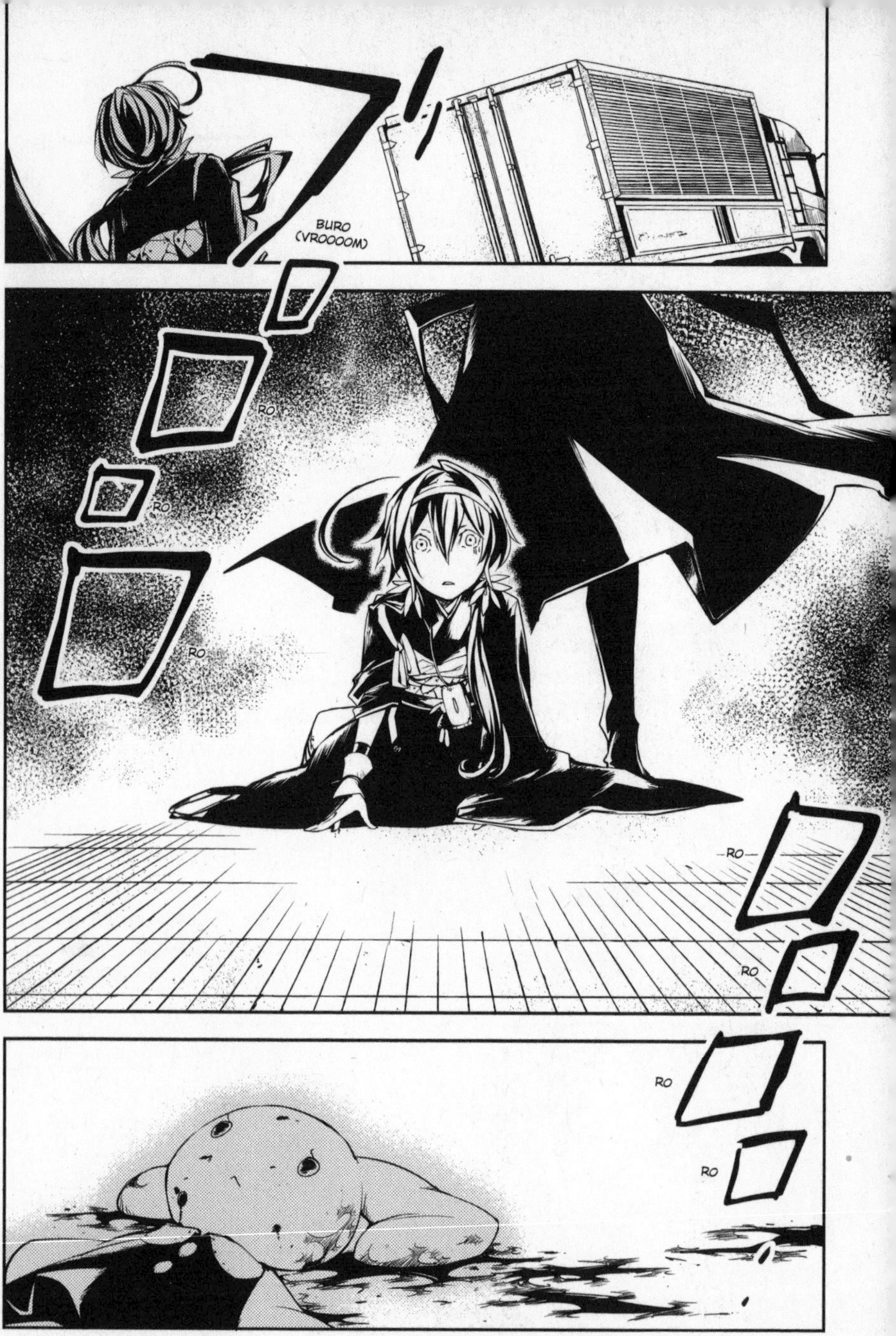
BURO
(VROOOOM)
RO
RO
RO
RO
RO
RO
RO

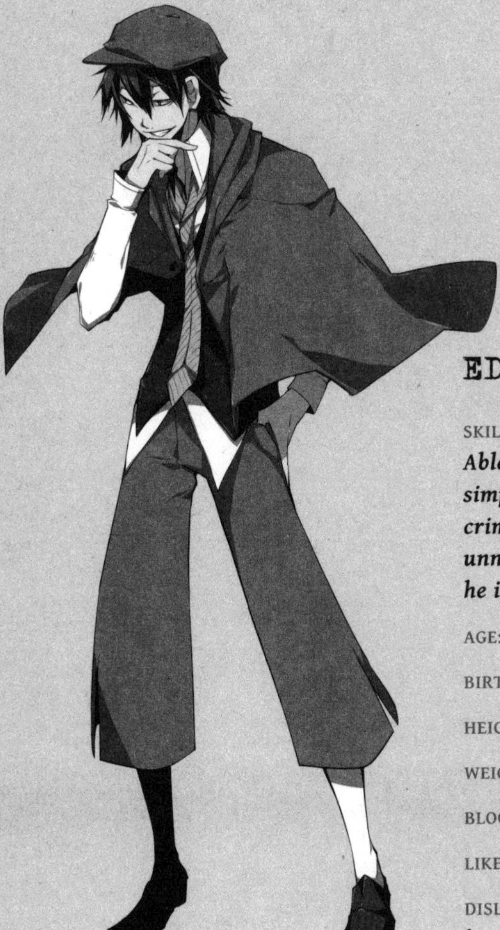

EDOGAWA RANPO

SKILL: **Super Deduction**
Able to instantly solve mysteries simply by viewing the scene of the crime. He believes it to be an unnatural "ability," but in actuality he is simply intelligent.

AGE: ***26***

BIRTH DATE: ***October 21***

HEIGHT: ***168cm***

WEIGHT: ***57kg***

BLOOD TYPE: ***O***

LIKES: ***Logical thinking, fantastic tales***

DISLIKES: ***Common sense, useless knowledge***

BUNGO
STRAY DOGS

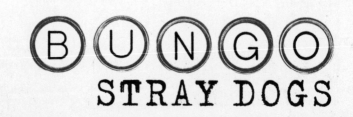

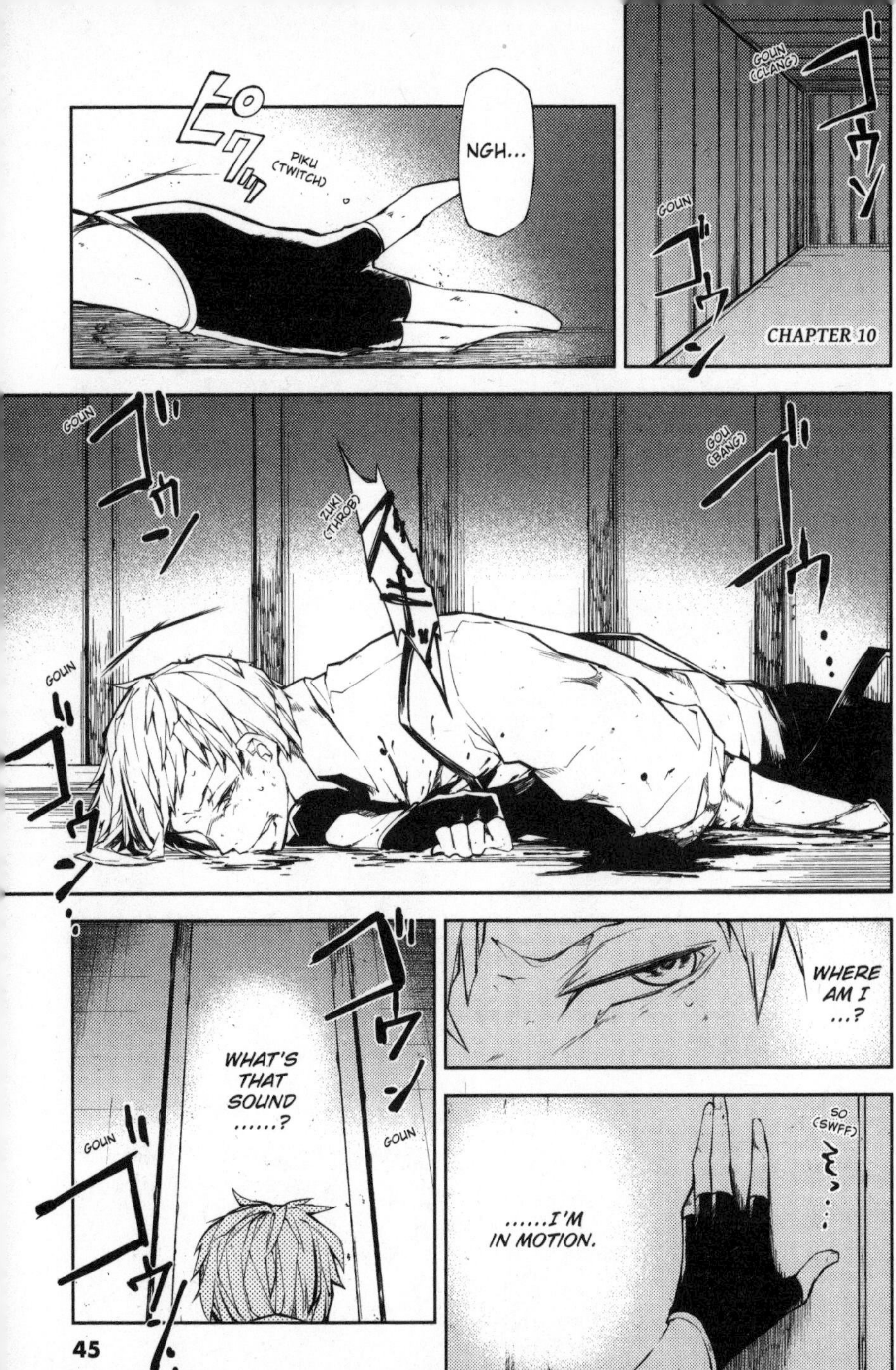
GOUN (CLANG)
GOUN
CHAPTER 10
PIKU (TWITCH)
NGH...
GOU (BANG)
ZUKI (THROB)
GOUN
GOUN
WHERE AM I ...?
SO (SWFF)
......I'M IN MOTION.
GOUN
WHAT'S THAT SOUND ......?
GOUN

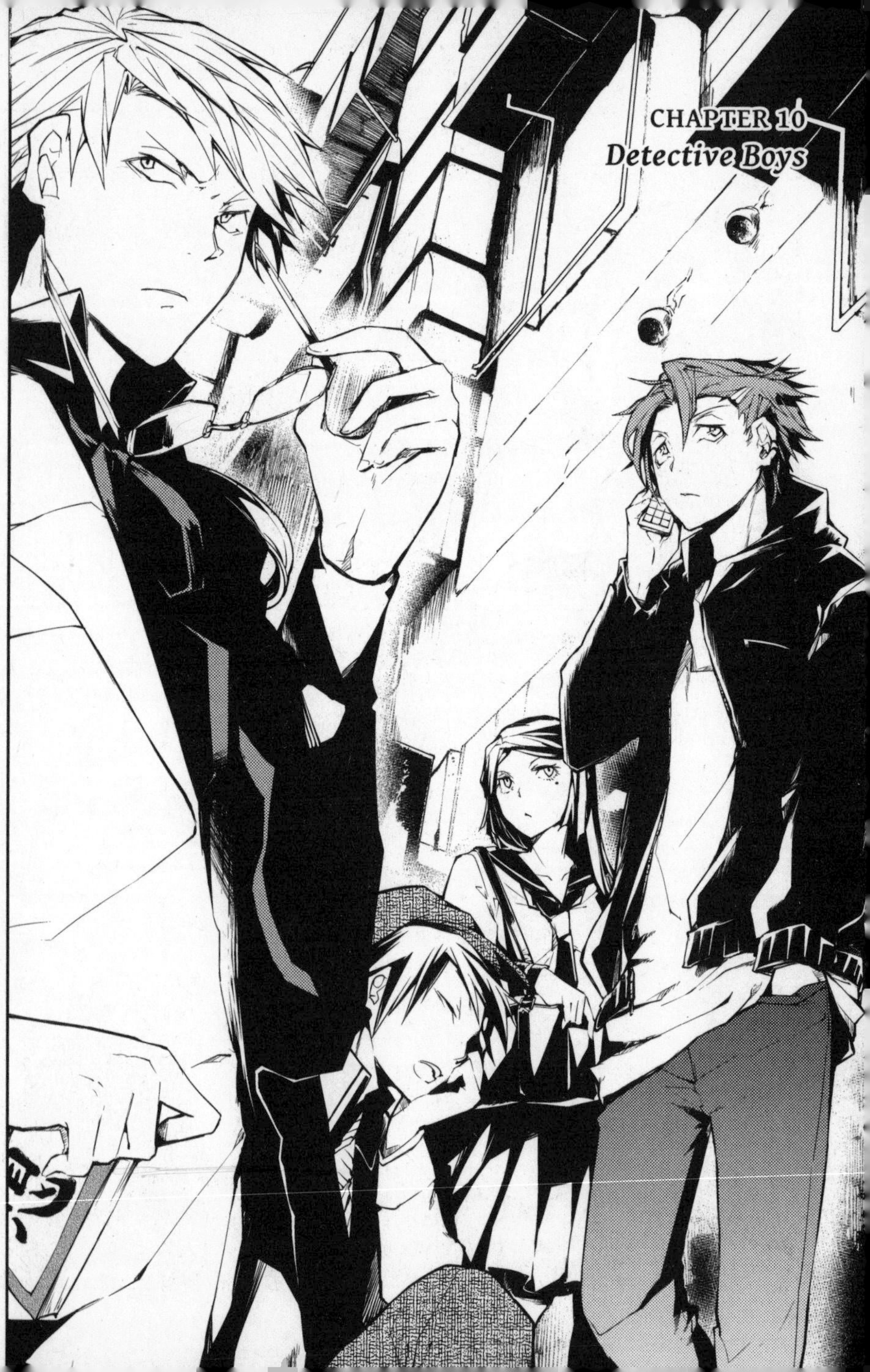
CHAPTER 10
Detective Boys

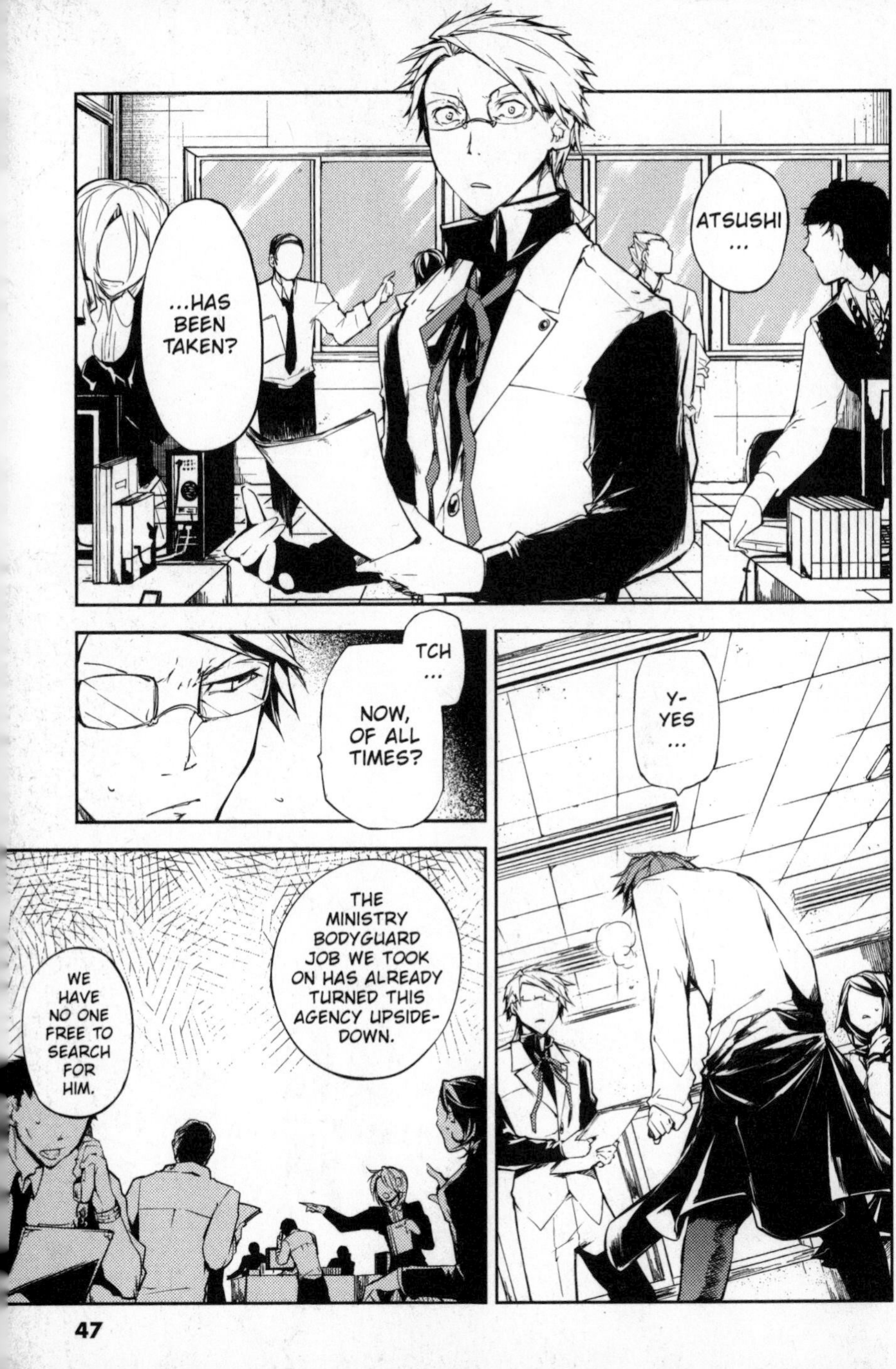
ATSUSHI ...
...HAS BEEN TAKEN?
Y-YES ...
TCH ...
NOW, OF ALL TIMES?
THE MINISTRY BODYGUARD JOB WE TOOK ON HAS ALREADY TURNED THIS AGENCY UPSIDE-DOWN.
WE HAVE NO ONE FREE TO SEARCH FOR HIM.

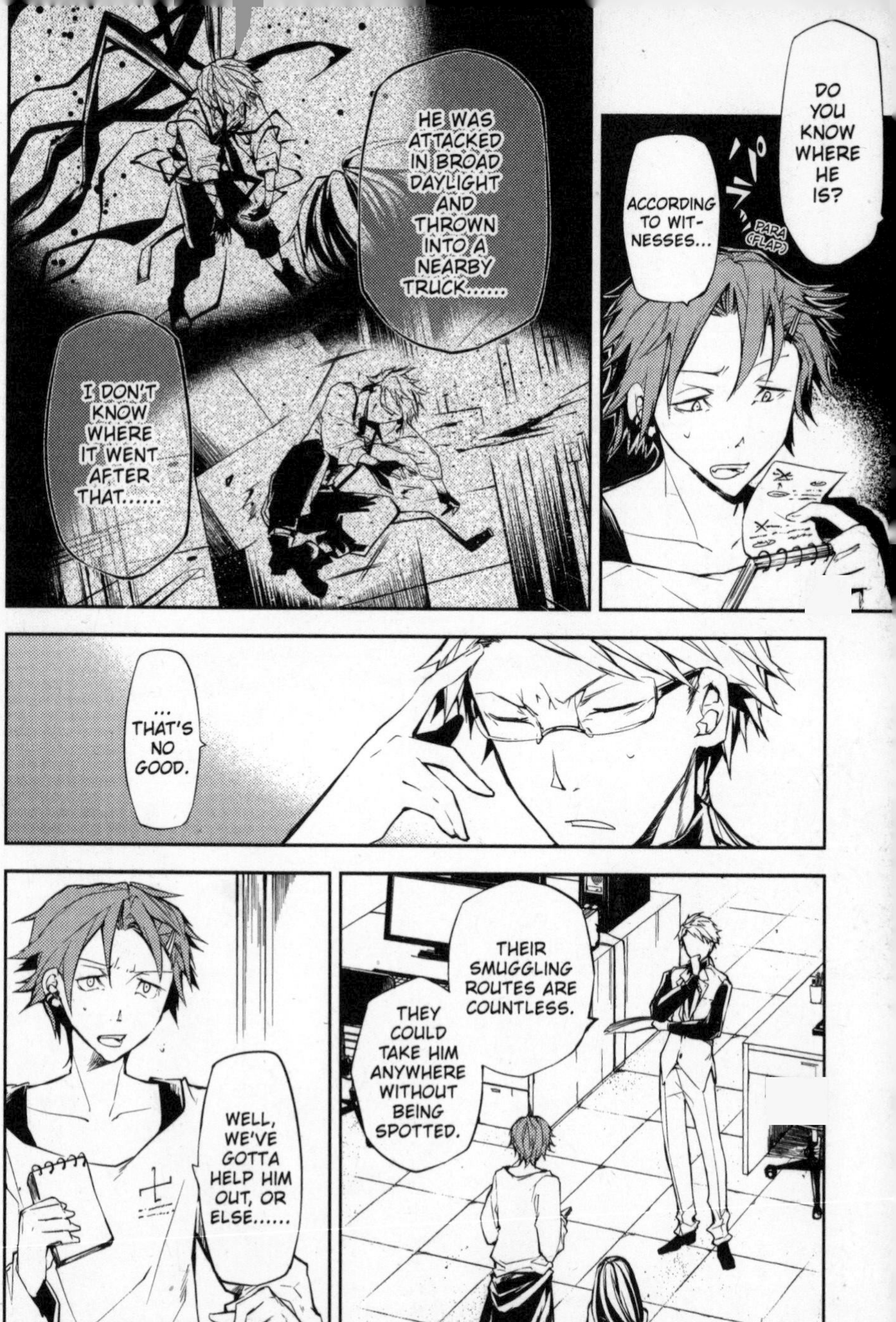
DO YOU KNOW WHERE HE IS?
PARA (FLAP)
ACCORDING TO WIT-NESSES...
HE WAS ATTACKED IN BROAD DAYLIGHT AND THROWN INTO A NEARBY TRUCK......
I DON'T KNOW WHERE IT WENT AFTER THAT......
...THAT'S NO GOOD.
THEIR SMUGGLING ROUTES ARE COUNTLESS.
THEY COULD TAKE HIM ANYWHERE WITHOUT BEING SPOTTED.
WELL, WE'VE GOTTA HELP HIM OUT, OR ELSE......

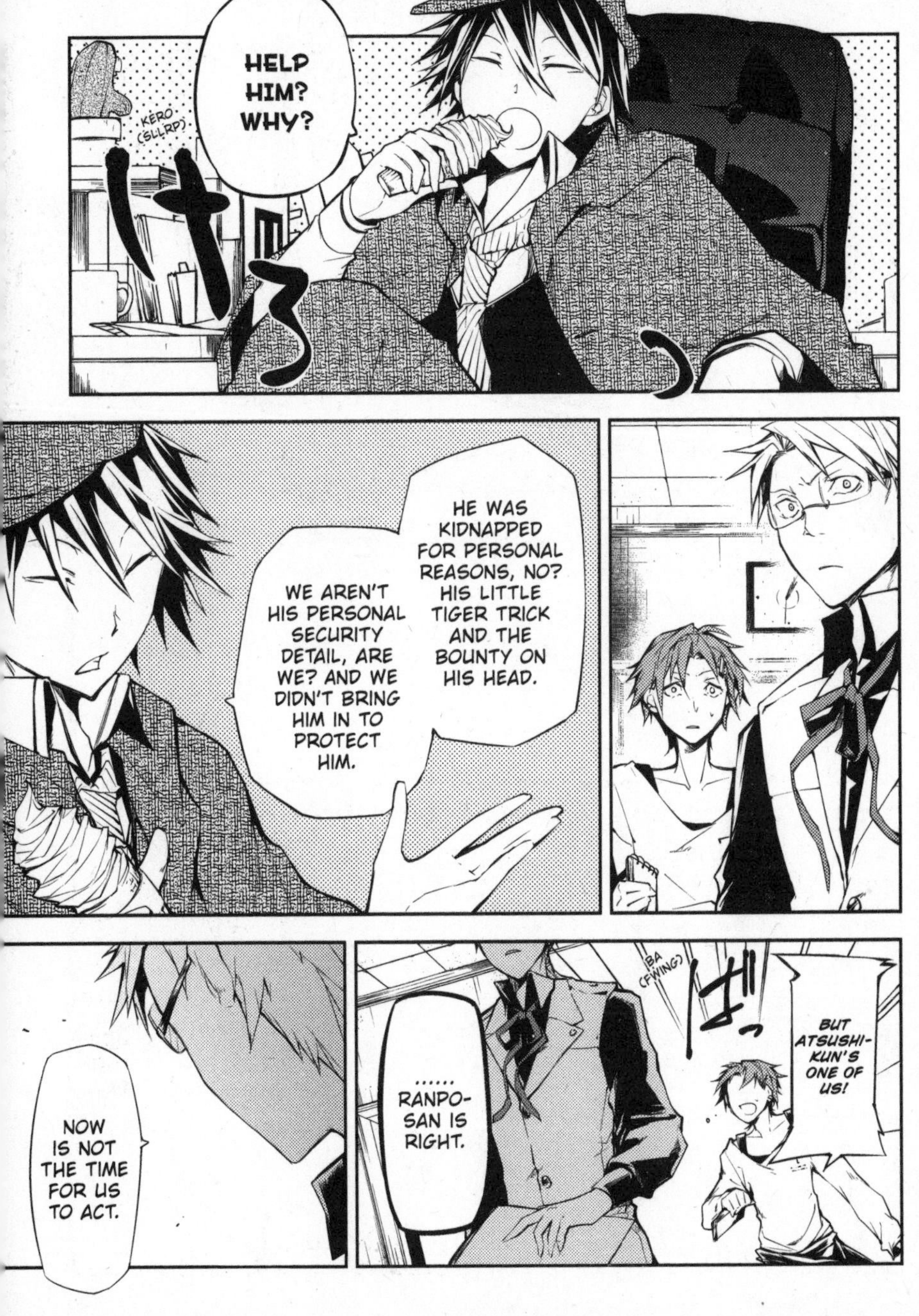
HELP HIM? WHY?
KERO (SLLRP)
HE WAS KIDNAPPED FOR PERSONAL REASONS, NO? HIS LITTLE TIGER TRICK AND THE BOUNTY ON HIS HEAD.
WE AREN'T HIS PERSONAL SECURITY DETAIL, ARE WE? AND WE DIDN'T BRING HIM IN TO PROTECT HIM.
BA (FWING)
BUT ATSUSHI-KUN'S ONE OF US!
...... RANPO-SAN IS RIGHT.
NOW IS NOT THE TIME FOR US TO ACT.

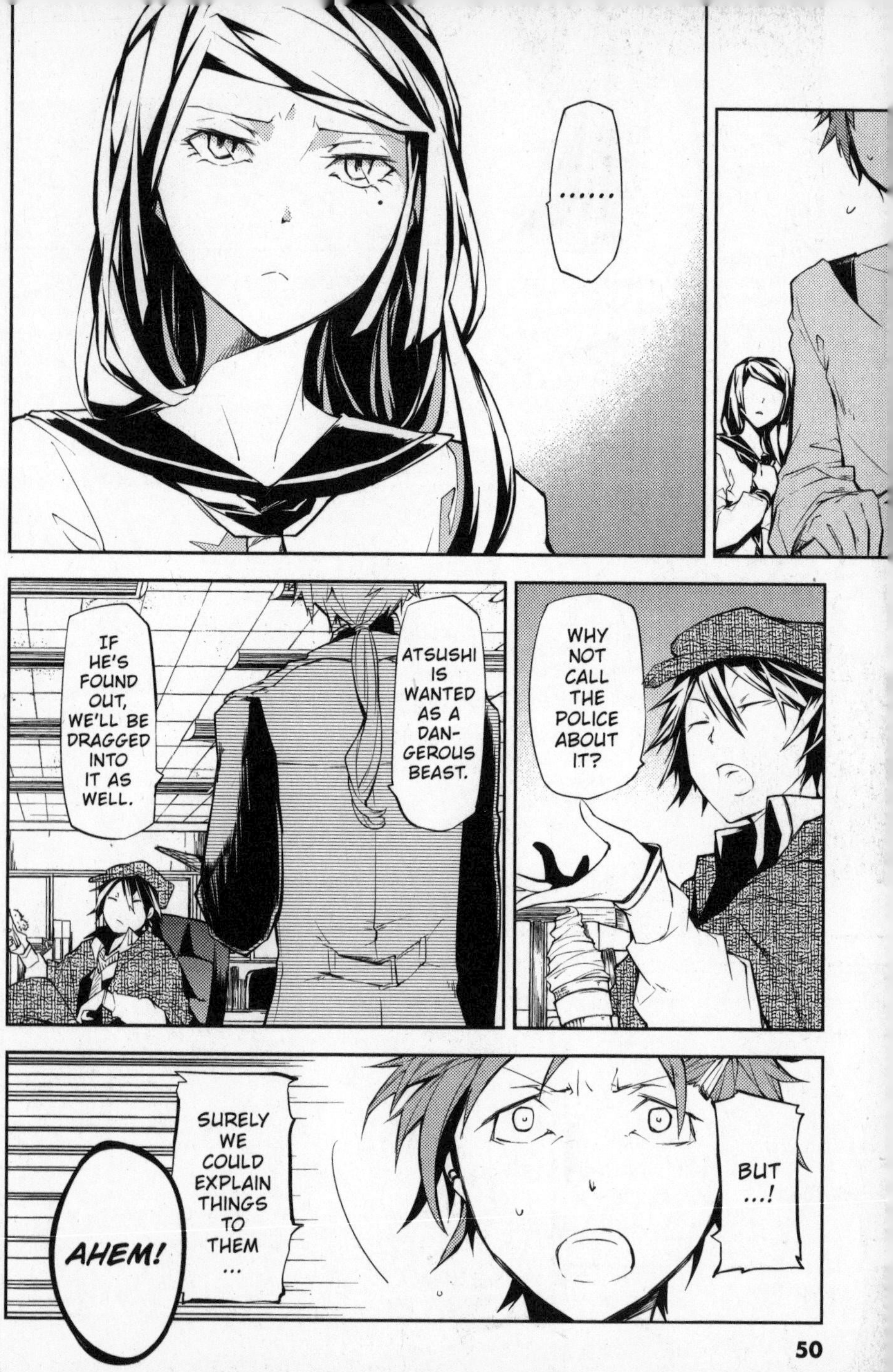
……
WHY NOT CALL THE POLICE ABOUT IT?
ATSUSHI IS WANTED AS A DAN-GEROUS BEAST.
IF HE'S FOUND OUT, WE'LL BE DRAGGED INTO IT AS WELL.
BUT ...!
SURELY WE COULD EXPLAIN THINGS TO THEM ...
AHEM!

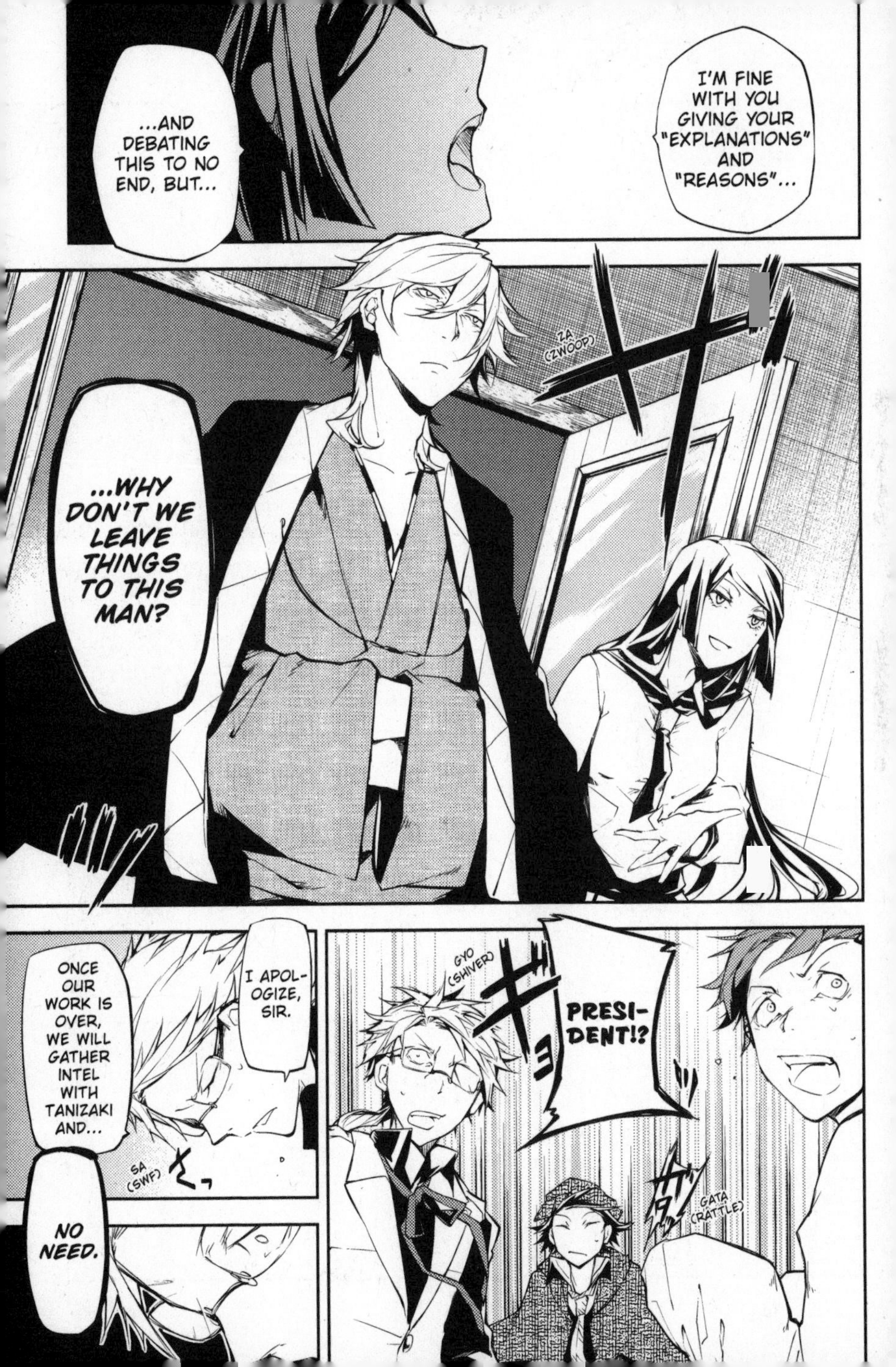
I'M FINE WITH YOU GIVING YOUR "EXPLANATIONS" AND "REASONS"...
...AND DEBATING THIS TO NO END, BUT...
ZA (ZWOOP)
...WHY DON'T WE LEAVE THINGS TO THIS MAN?
PRESI-DENT!?
GYO (SHIVER)
GATA (RATTLE)
I APOLOGIZE, SIR.
ONCE OUR WORK IS OVER, WE WILL GATHER INTEL WITH TANIZAKI AND...
SA (SWF)
NO NEED.

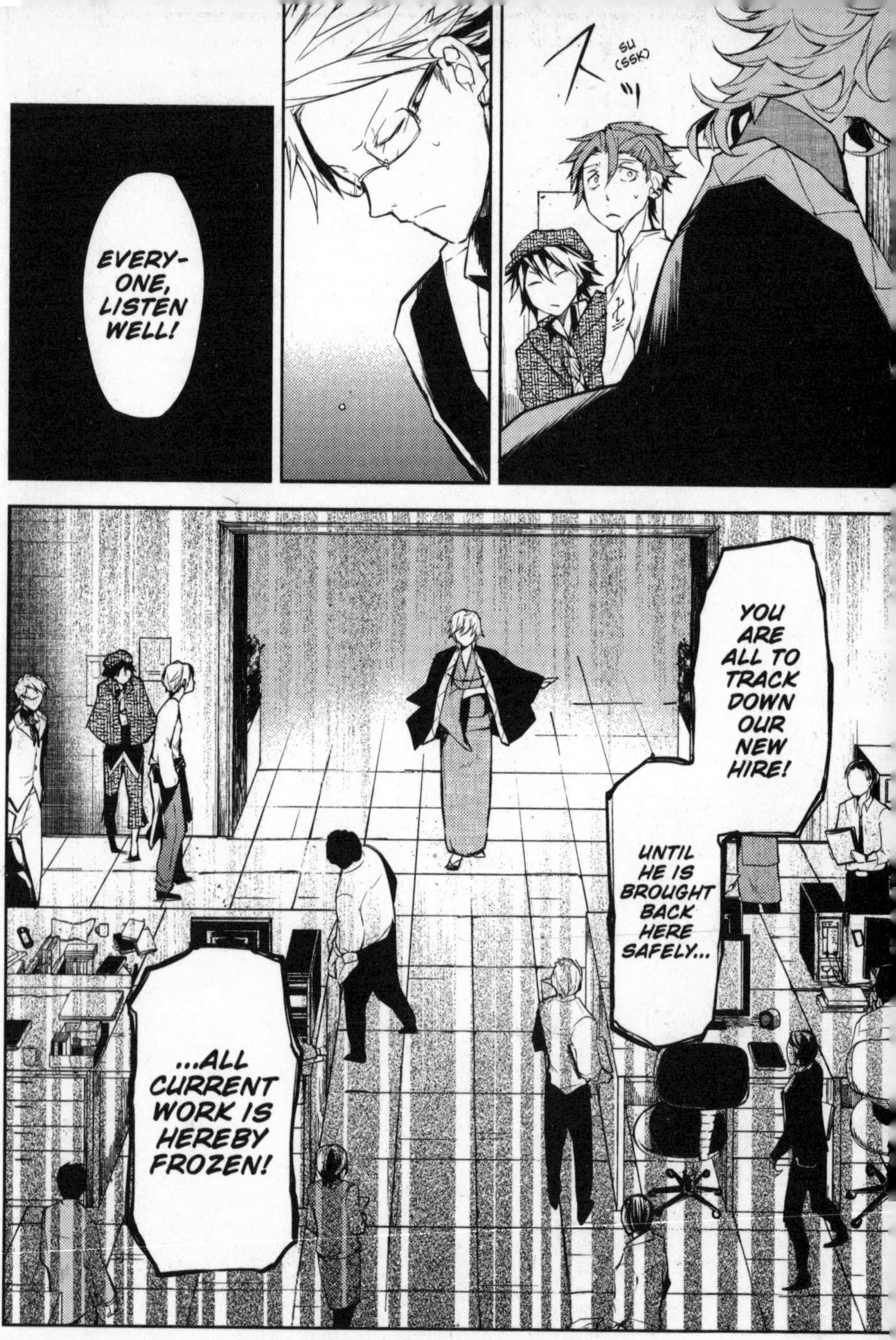
SU (SSK)
EVERY-ONE, LISTEN WELL!
YOU ARE ALL TO TRACK DOWN OUR NEW HIRE!
UNTIL HE IS BROUGHT BACK HERE SAFELY...
...ALL CURRENT WORK IS HEREBY FROZEN!

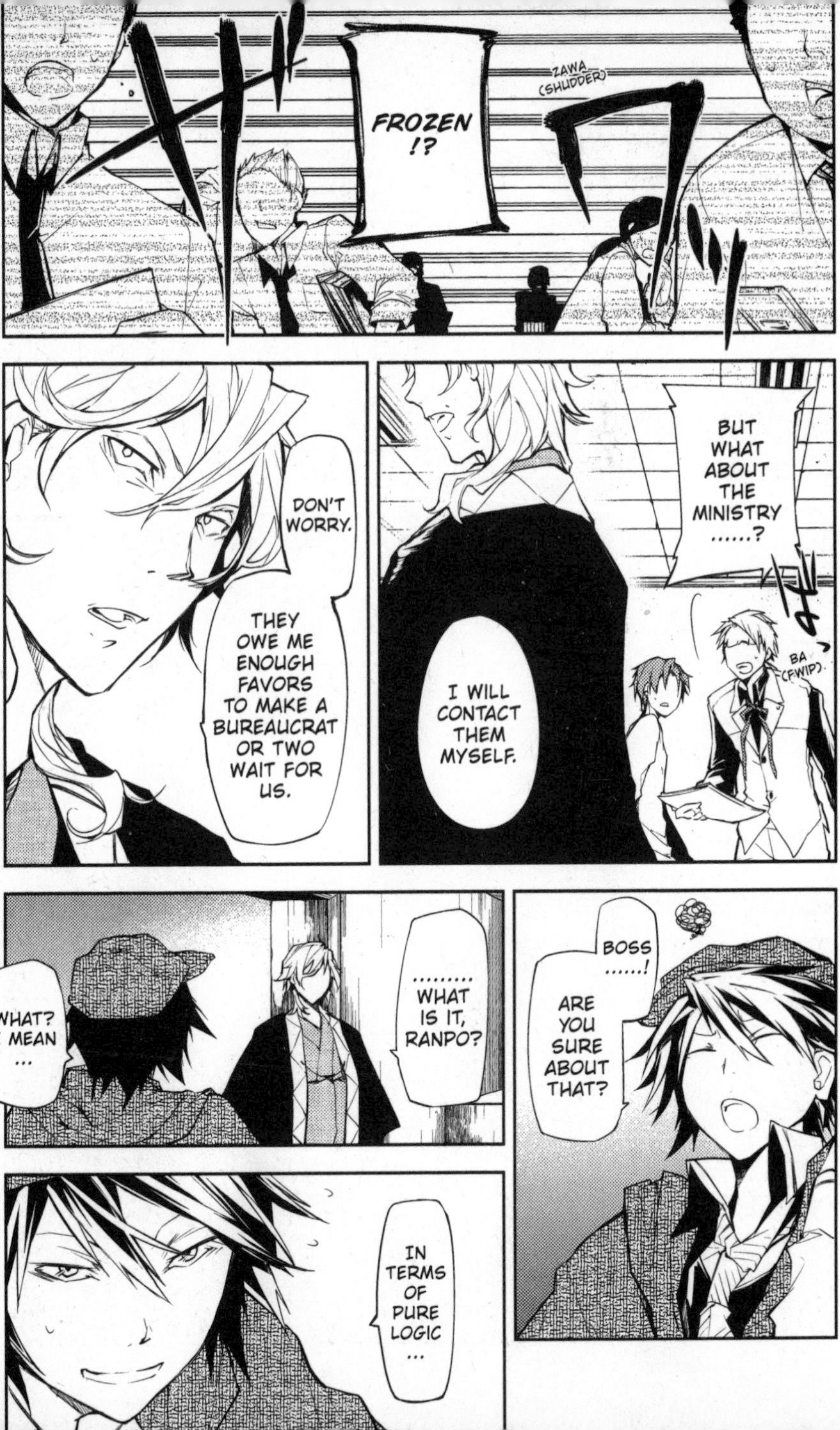
ZAWA (SHUDDER)
FROZEN !?
BUT WHAT ABOUT THE MINISTRY ......?
BA (FWIP)
I WILL CONTACT THEM MYSELF.
DON'T WORRY.
THEY OWE ME ENOUGH FAVORS TO MAKE A BUREAUCRAT OR TWO WAIT FOR US.
BOSS ......!
ARE YOU SURE ABOUT THAT?
.... WHAT IS IT, RANPO?
WHAT? I MEAN ...
IN TERMS OF PURE LOGIC ...

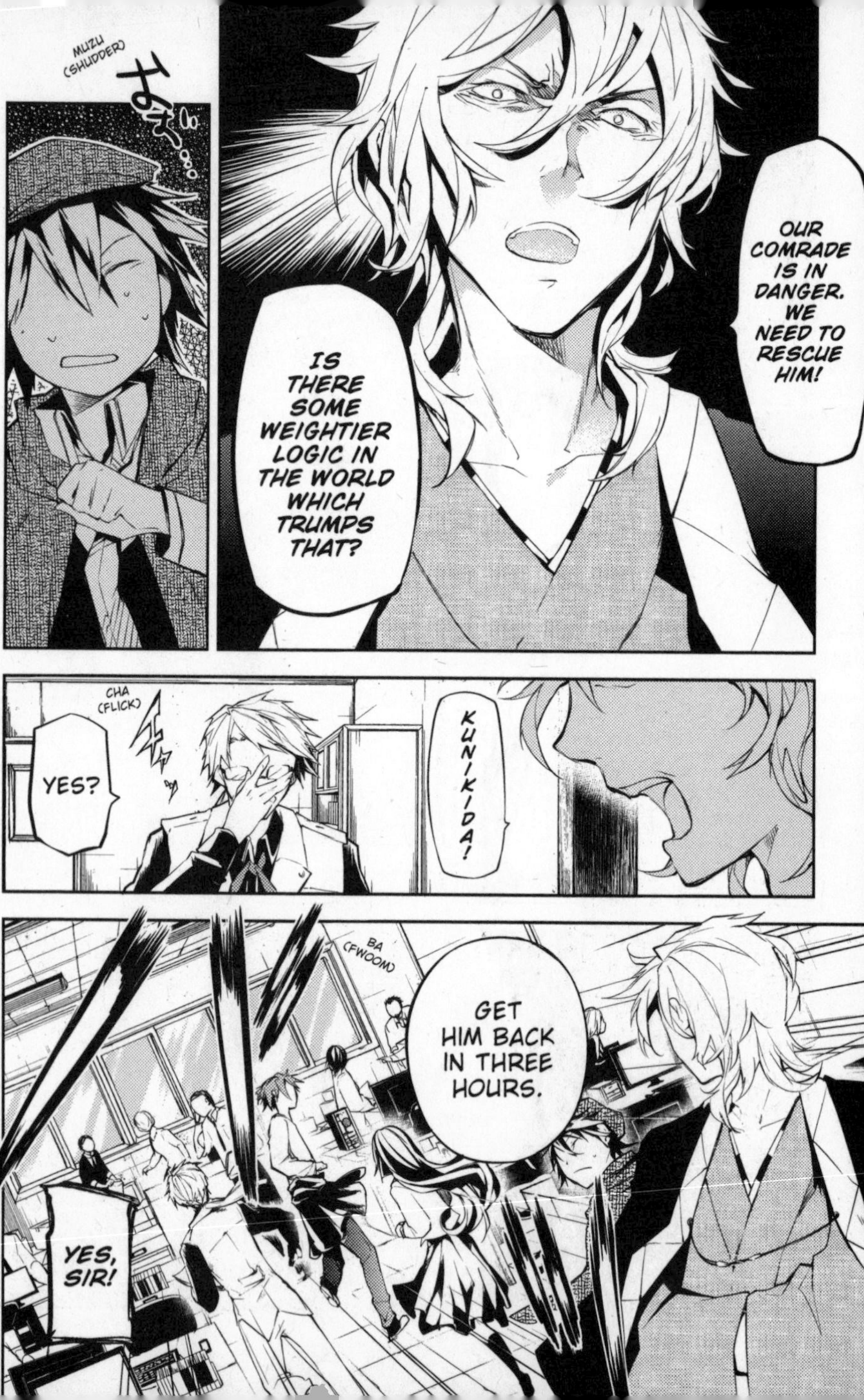
OUR COMRADE IS IN DANGER. WE NEED TO RESCUE HIM!
IS THERE SOME WEIGHTIER LOGIC IN THE WORLD WHICH TRUMPS THAT?
MUZU (SHUDDER)
KUNIKIDA!
CHA (FLICK)
YES?
GET HIM BACK IN THREE HOURS.
BA (FWOOM)
YES, SIR!

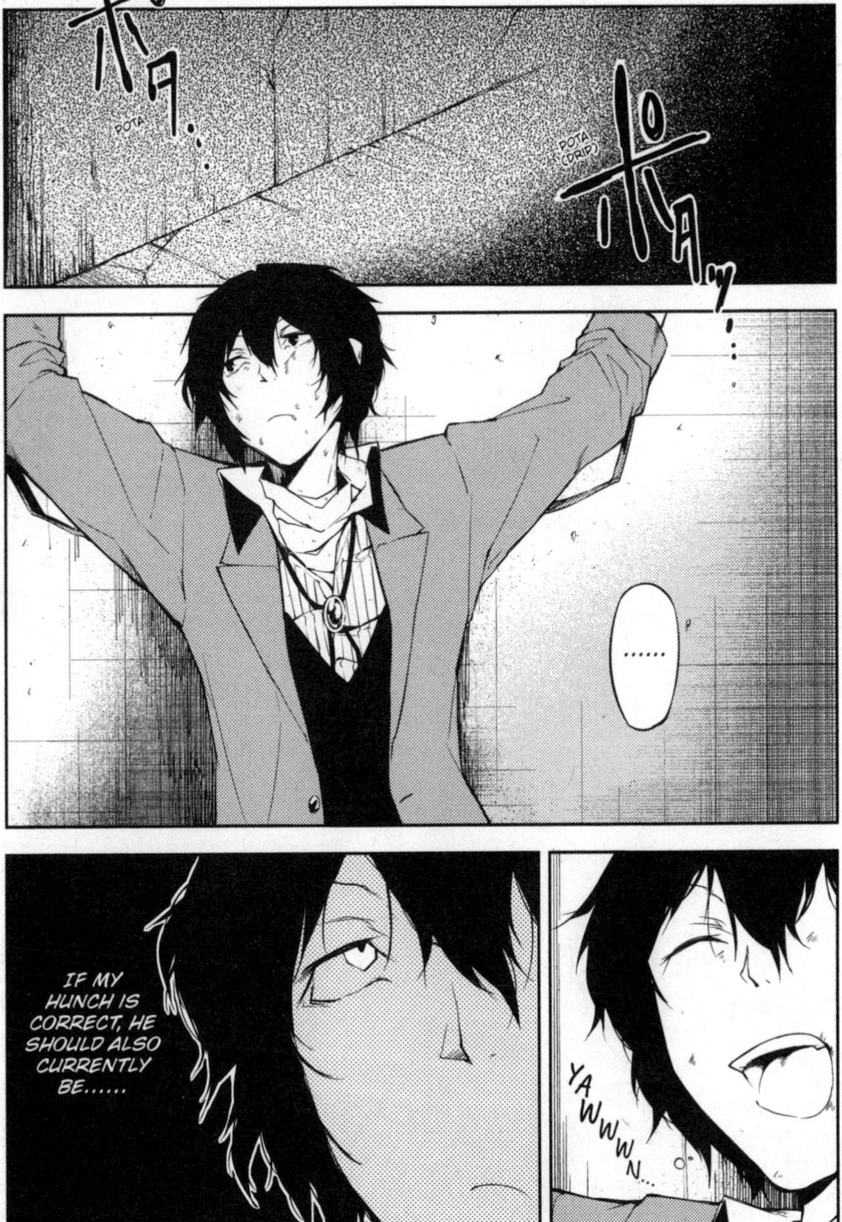
POTA (DRIP)
ポタッ…
POTA
ポタ…
......
YAWWWN...
IF MY HUNCH IS CORRECT, HE SHOULD ALSO CURRENTLY BE......

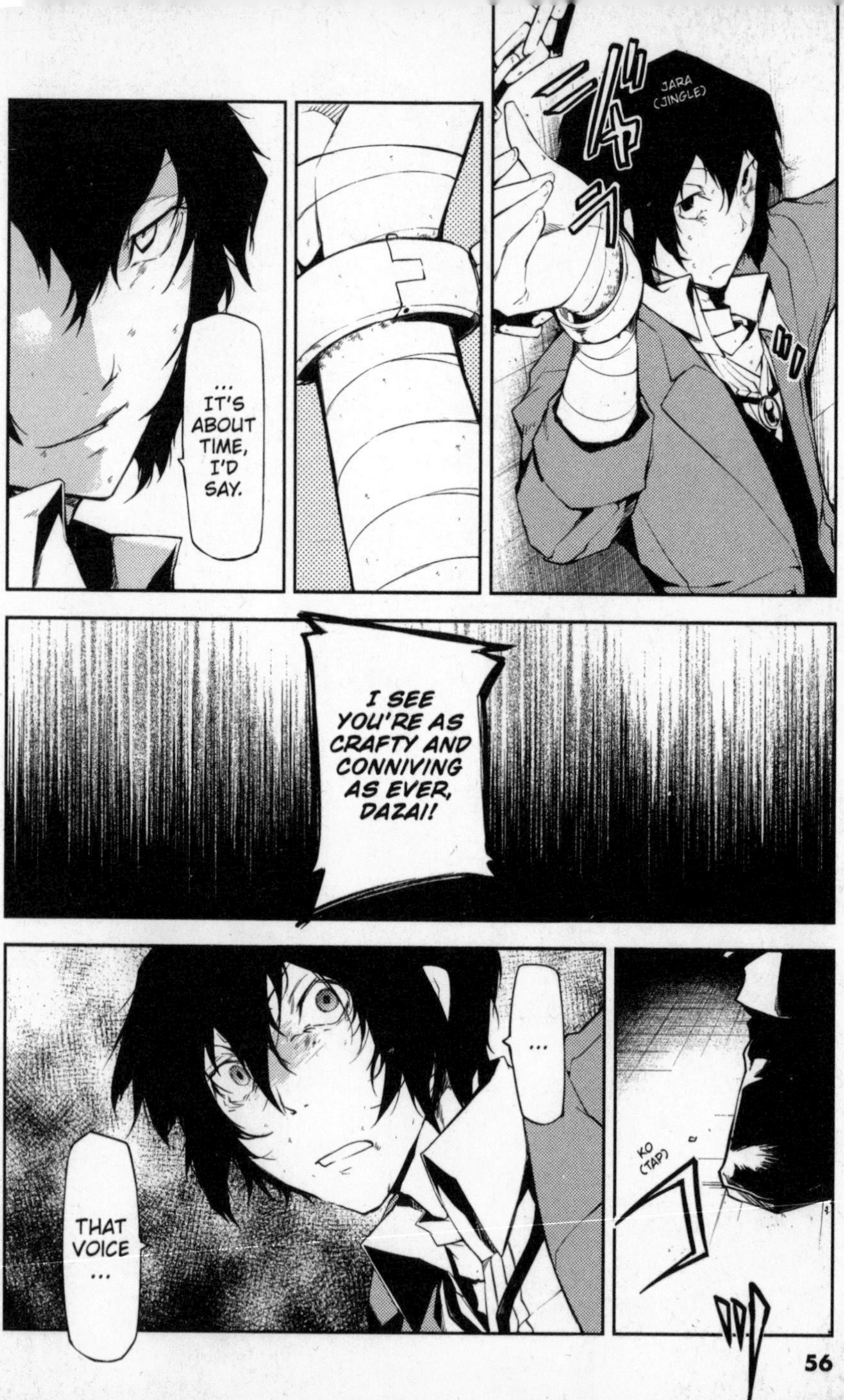
JARA (JINGLE)
... IT'S ABOUT TIME, I'D SAY.
I SEE YOU'RE AS CRAFTY AND CONNIVING AS EVER, DAZAI!
KO (TAP)
...
THAT VOICE ...

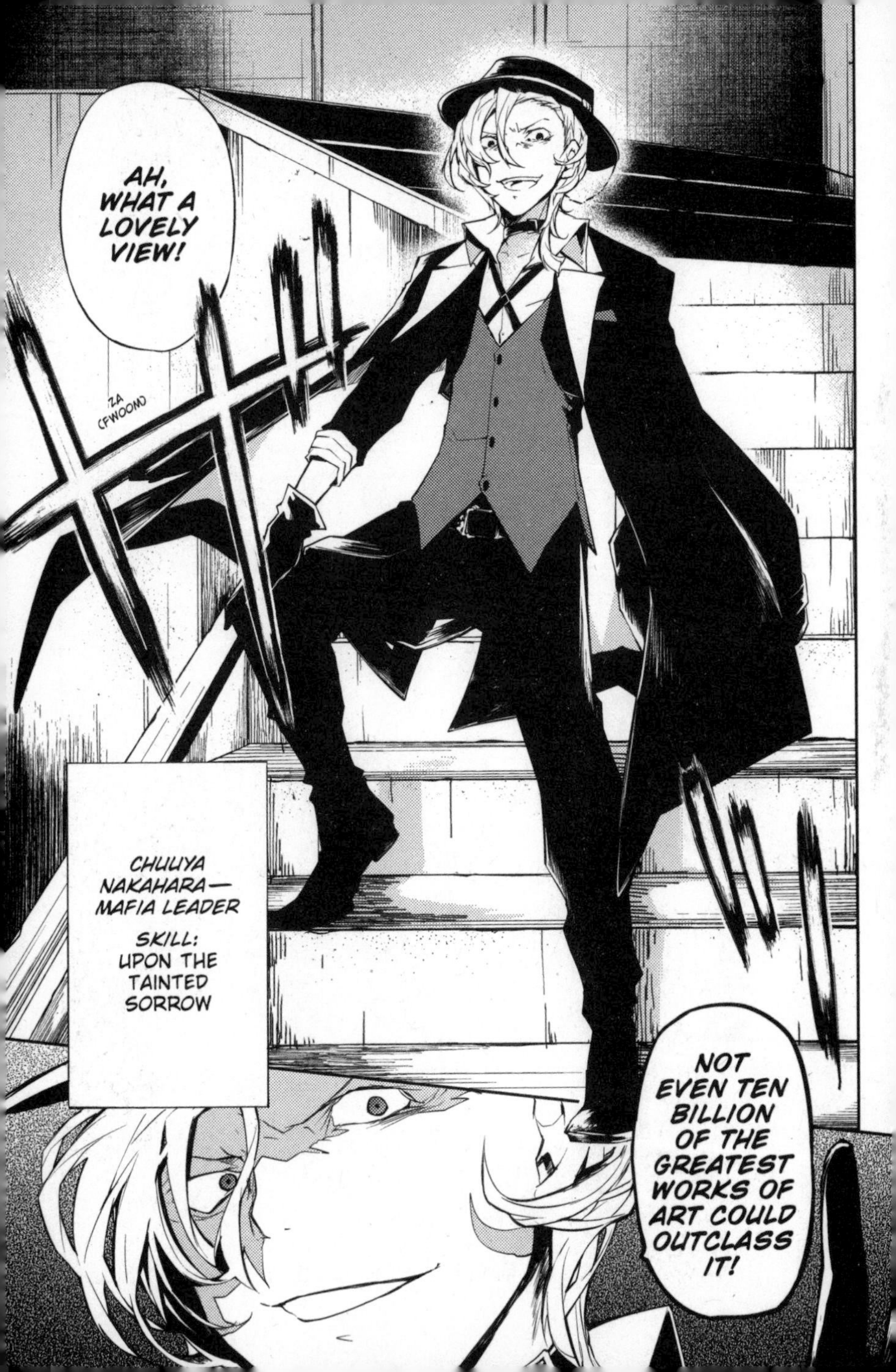
AH, WHAT A LOVELY VIEW!
ZA (FWOOM)
CHUUYA NAKAHARA—MAFIA LEADER
SKILL: UPON THE TAINTED SORROW
NOT EVEN TEN BILLION OF THE GREATEST WORKS OF ART COULD OUTCLASS IT!

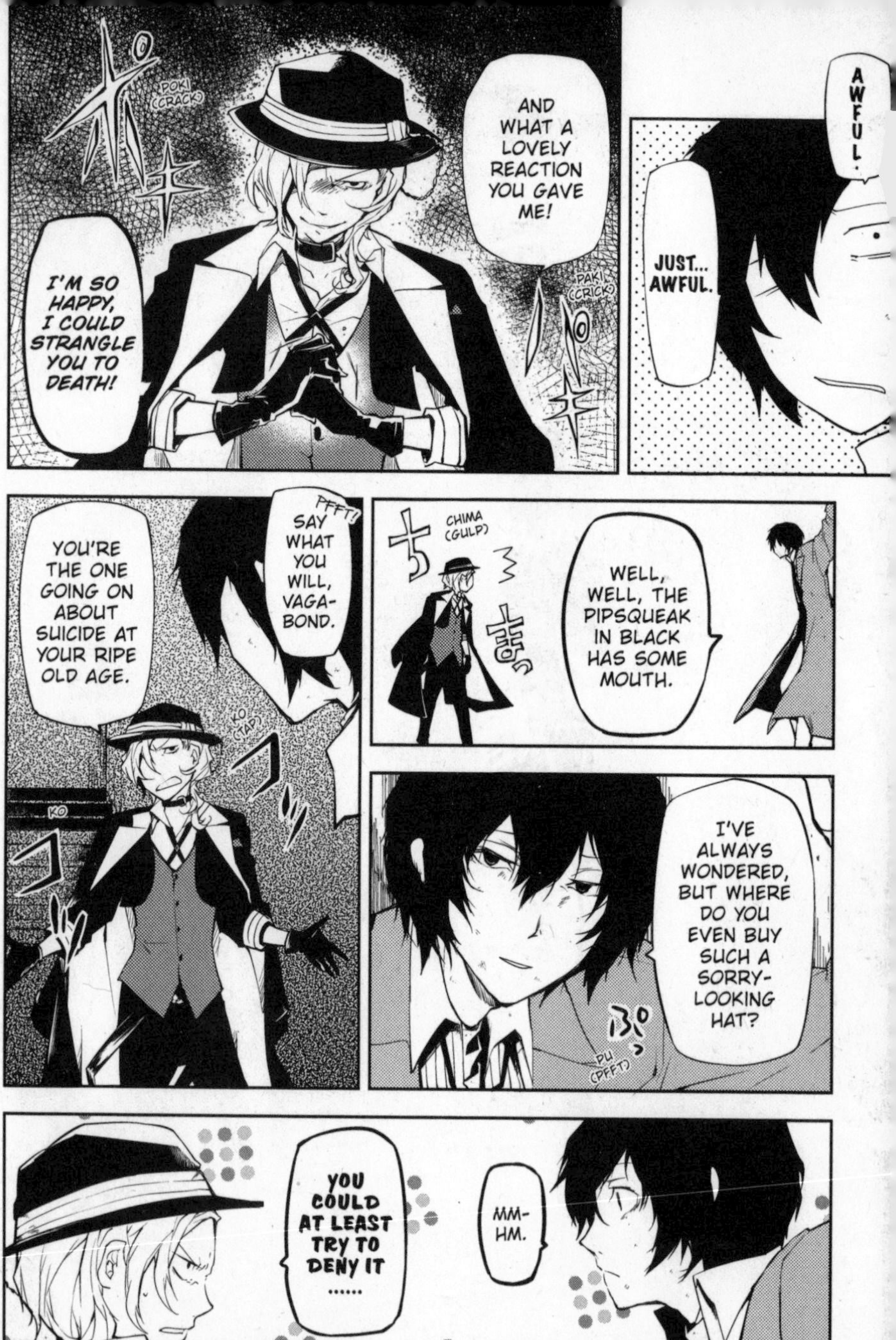
AWFUL.
JUST... AWFUL.
AND WHAT A LOVELY REACTION YOU GAVE ME!
POKI (CRACK)
PAKI (CRICK)
I'M SO HAPPY, I COULD STRANGLE YOU TO DEATH!
WELL, WELL, THE PIPSQUEAK IN BLACK HAS SOME MOUTH.
CHIMA (GULP)
I'VE ALWAYS WONDERED, BUT WHERE DO YOU EVEN BUY SUCH A SORRY-LOOKING HAT?
PU (PFFFT)
PFFT!
SAY WHAT YOU WILL, VAGABOND.
YOU'RE THE ONE GOING ON ABOUT SUICIDE AT YOUR RIPE OLD AGE.
KO (TAP)
KO
MM-HM.
YOU COULD AT LEAST TRY TO DENY IT ......

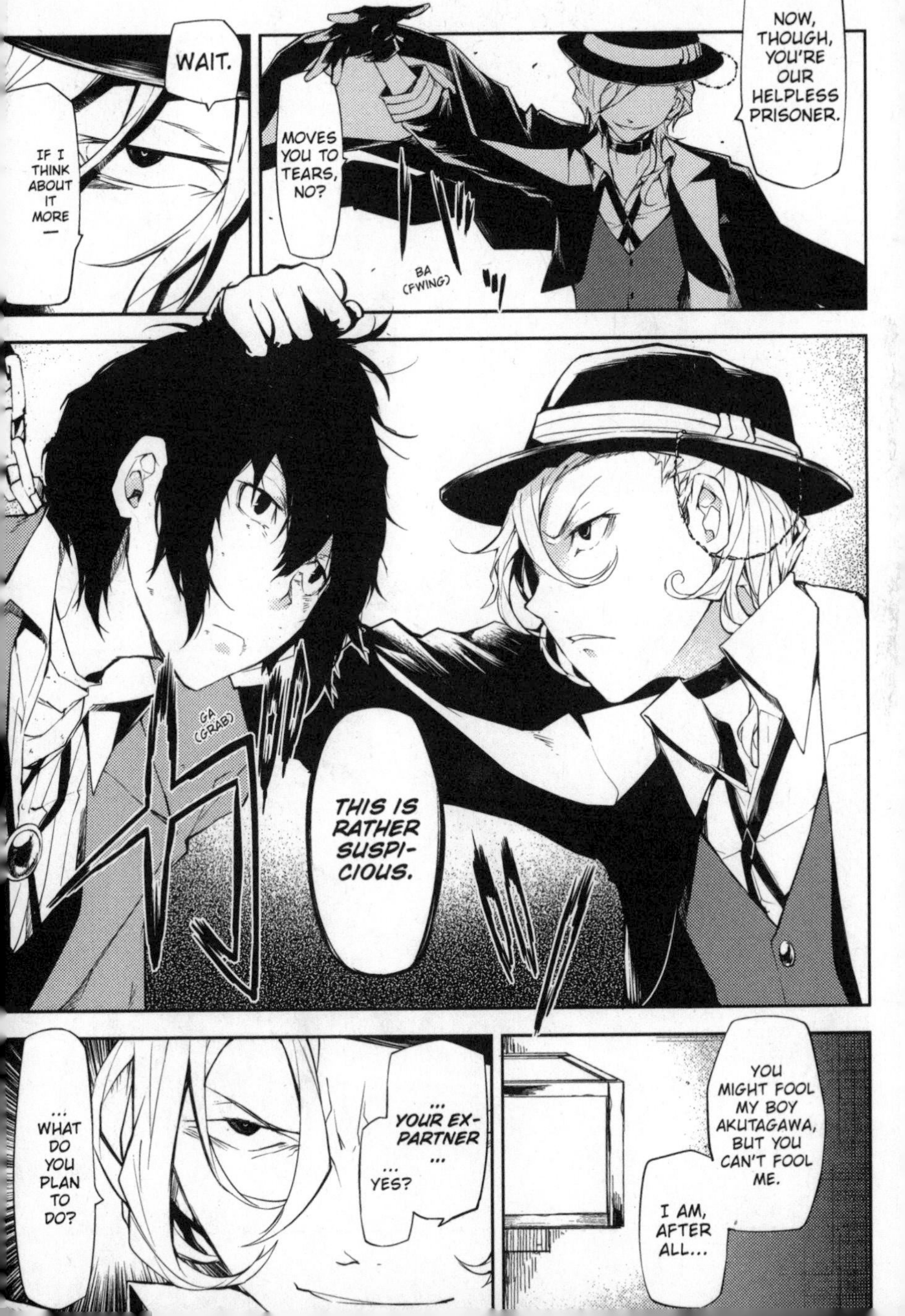
NOW, THOUGH, YOU'RE OUR HELPLESS PRISONER.
MOVES YOU TO TEARS, NO?
BA (FWING)
WAIT.
IF I THINK ABOUT IT MORE—
GA (GRAB)
THIS IS RATHER SUSPICIOUS.
YOU MIGHT FOOL MY BOY AKUTAGAWA, BUT YOU CAN'T FOOL ME.
I AM, AFTER ALL...
...YOUR EX-PARTNER...
...YES?
...WHAT DO YOU PLAN TO DO?

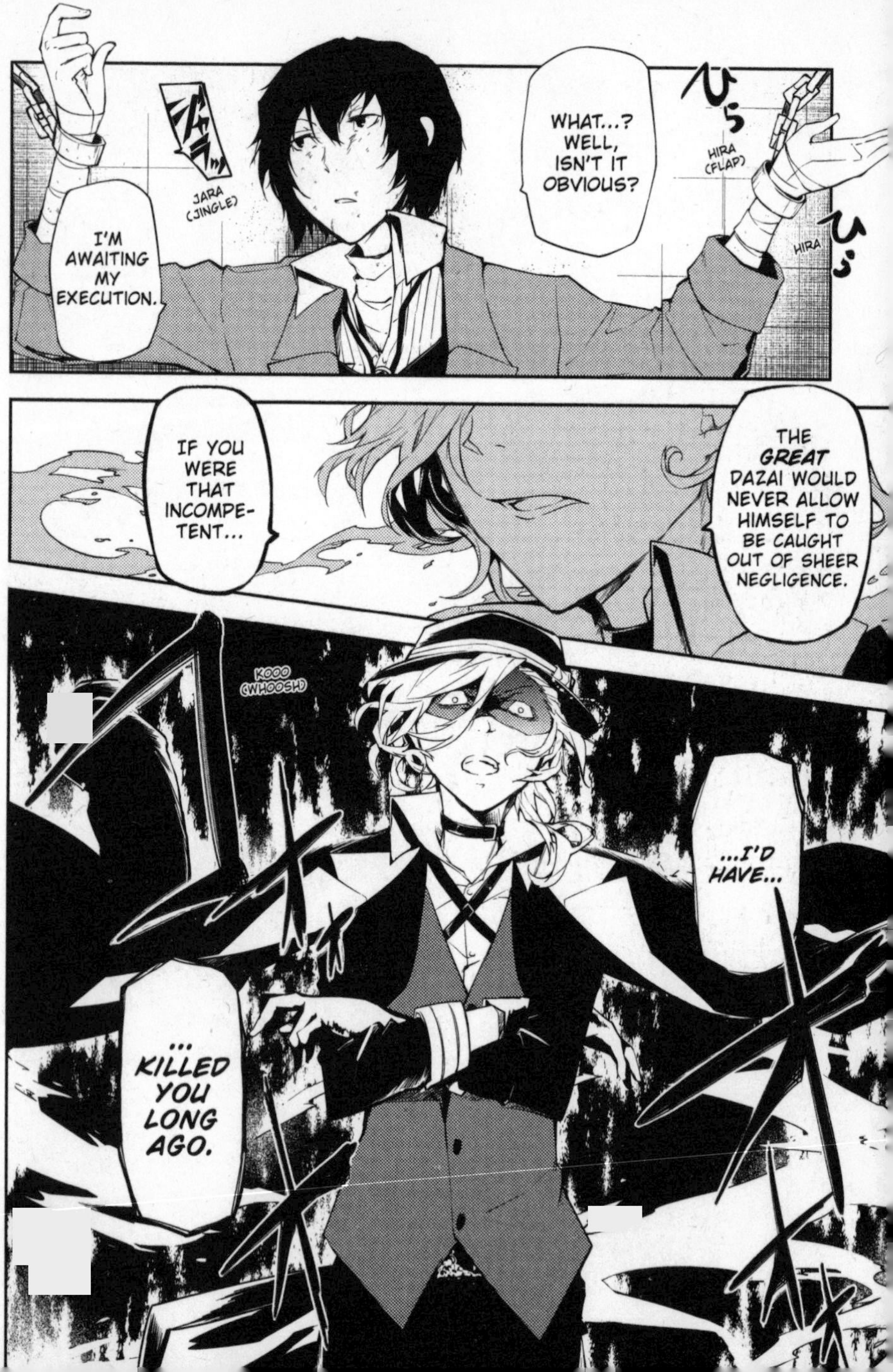
ひら
HIRA (FLAP)
WHAT...? WELL, ISN'T IT OBVIOUS?
ひら
HIRA
JARA (JINGLE)
I'M AWAITING MY EXECUTION.
THE *GREAT* DAZAI WOULD NEVER ALLOW HIMSELF TO BE CAUGHT OUT OF SHEER NEGLIGENCE.
IF YOU WERE THAT INCOMPETENT...
KOOO (WHOOSH)
...I'D HAVE...
...KILLED YOU LONG AGO.

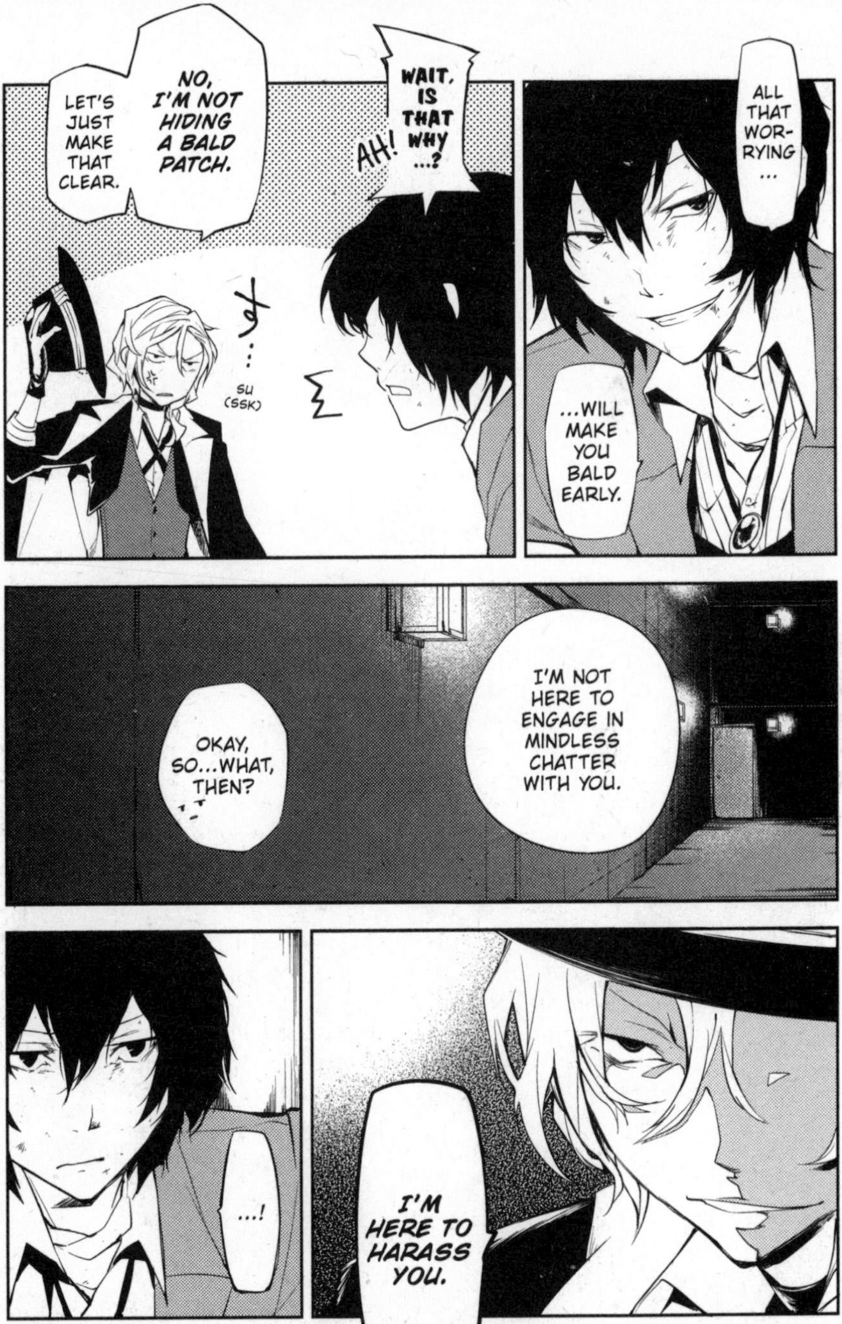
ALL THAT WOR-RYING...
...WILL MAKE YOU BALD EARLY.
WAIT, IS THAT WHY...?
AH!
NO, I'M NOT HIDING A BALD PATCH.
LET'S JUST MAKE THAT CLEAR.
SU (SSK)
I'M NOT HERE TO ENGAGE IN MINDLESS CHATTER WITH YOU.
OKAY, SO...WHAT, THEN?
I'M HERE TO HARASS YOU.
...!

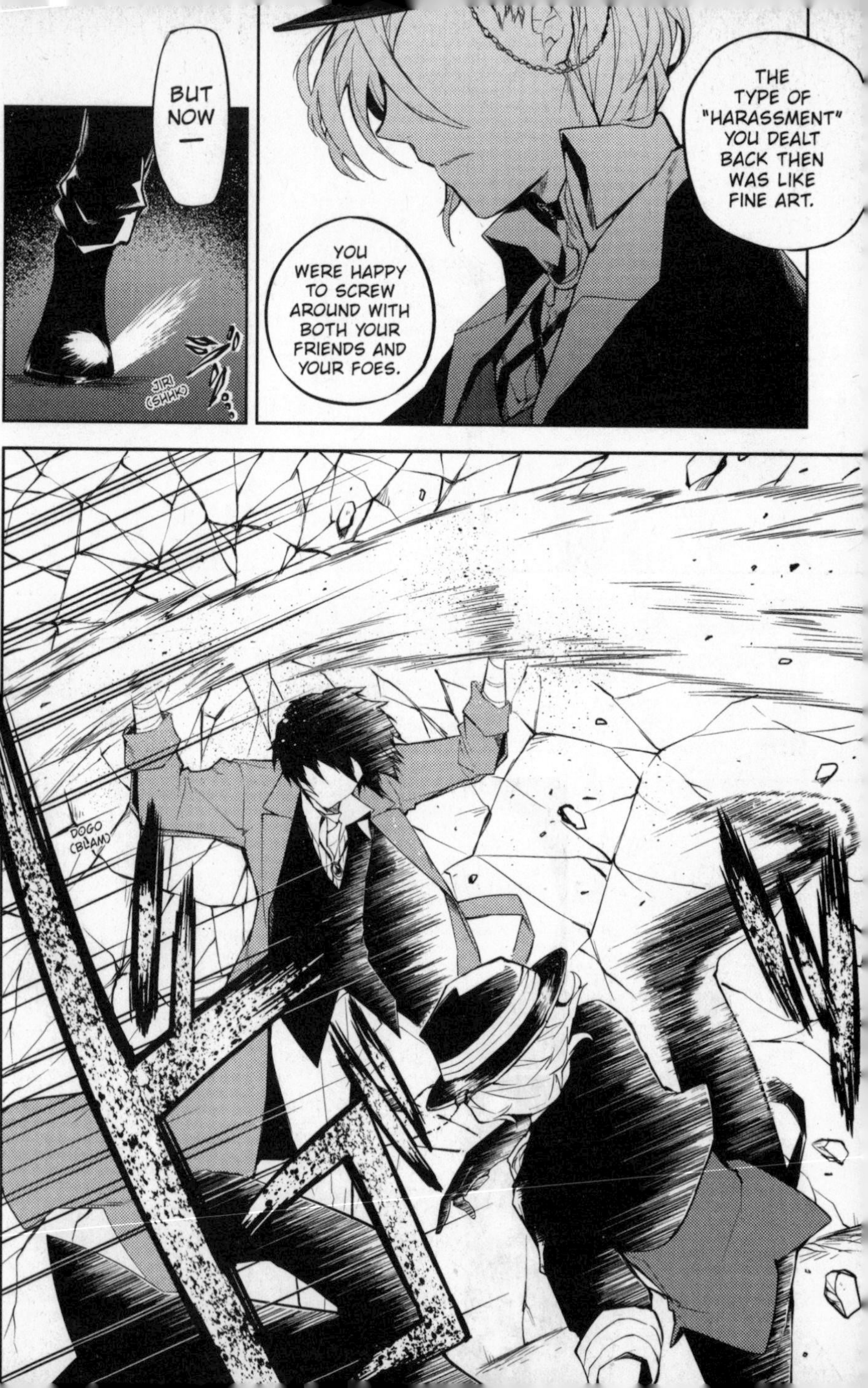
THE TYPE OF "HARASSMENT" YOU DEALT BACK THEN WAS LIKE FINE ART.
YOU WERE HAPPY TO SCREW AROUND WITH BOTH YOUR FRIENDS AND YOUR FOES.
BUT NOW —
JIRI (SHHK)
DOGO (BLAM)

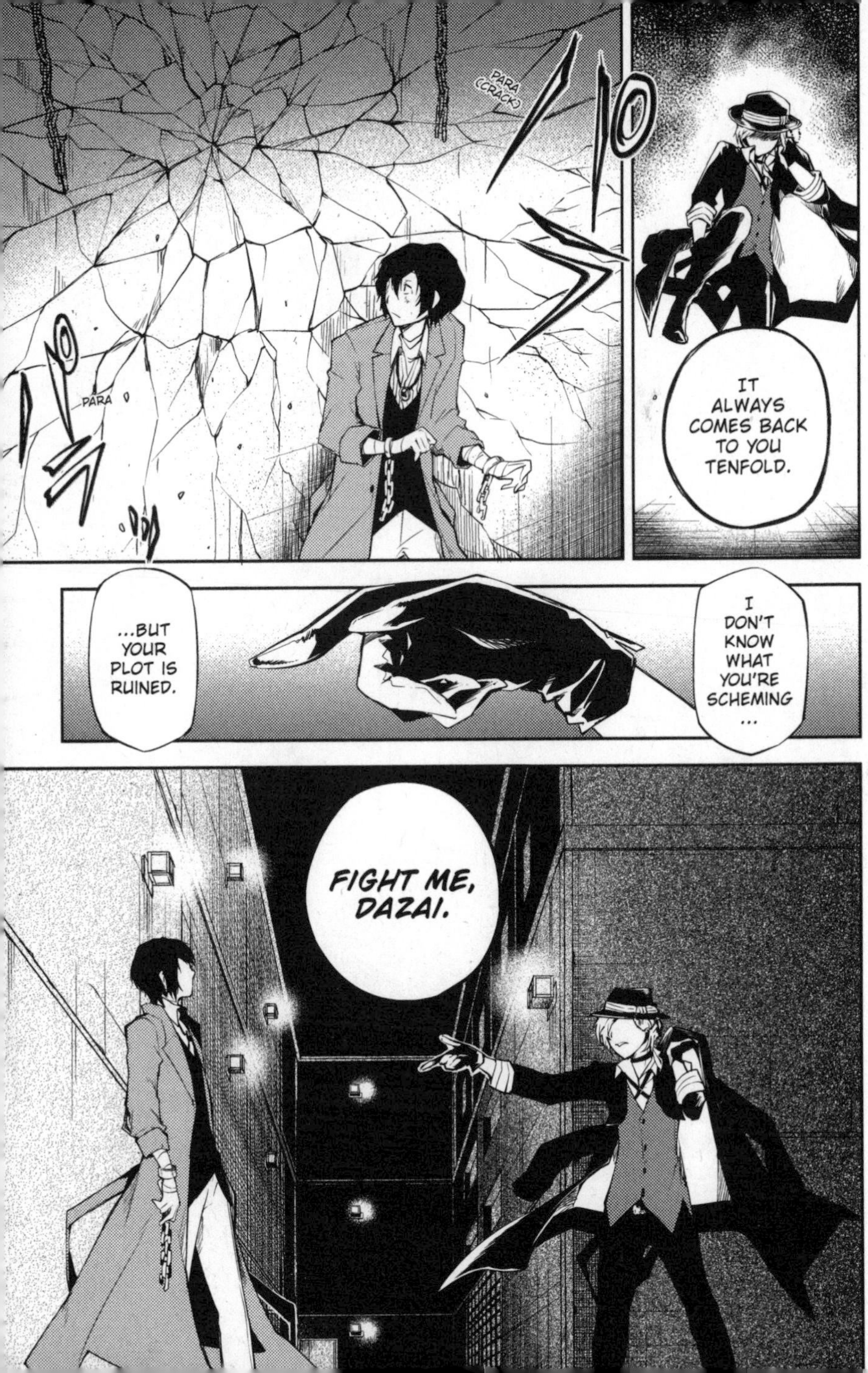
IT ALWAYS COMES BACK TO YOU TENFOLD.
PARA (CRACK)
PARA
I DON'T KNOW WHAT YOU'RE SCHEMING ...
...BUT YOUR PLOT IS RUINED.
FIGHT ME, DAZAI.

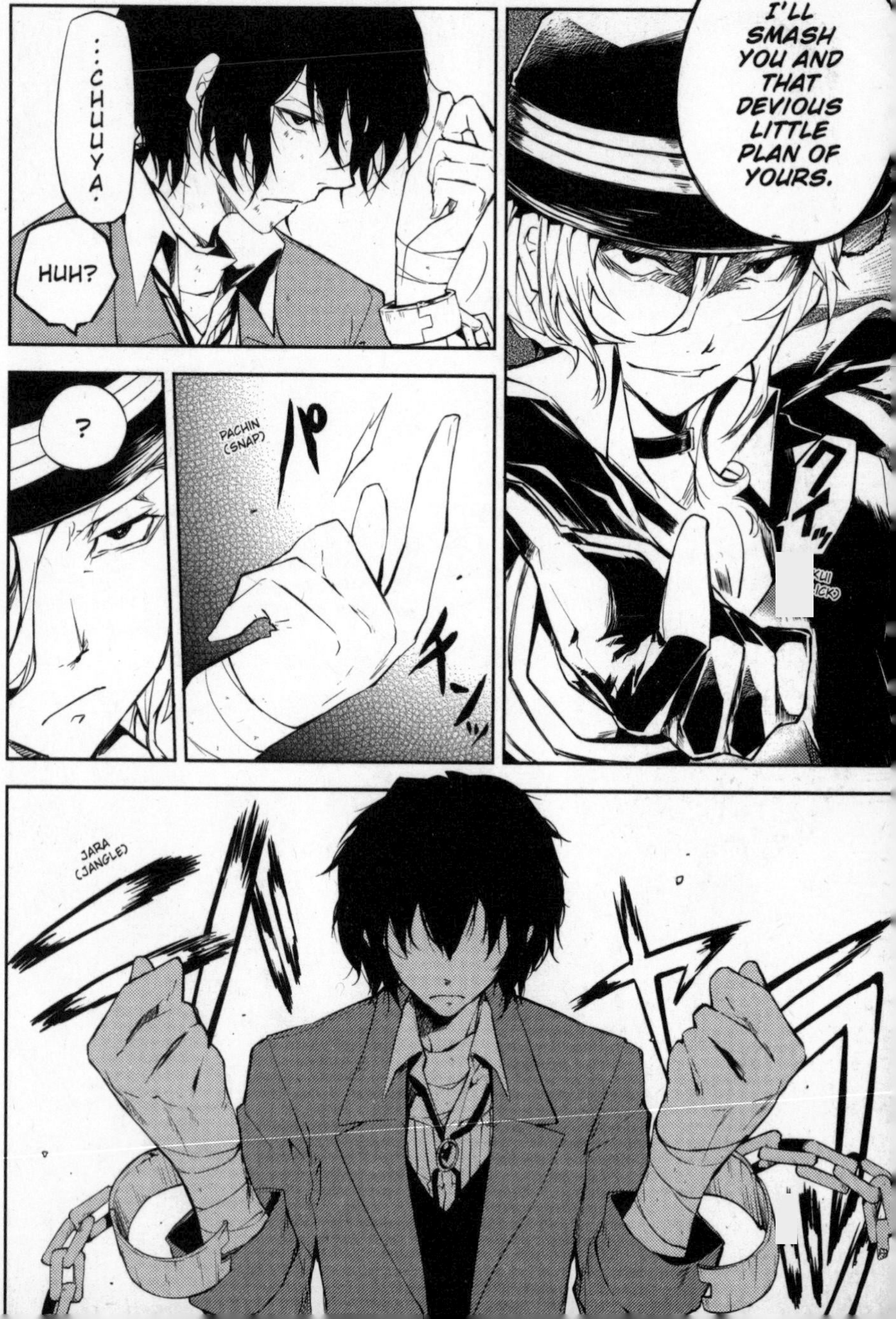
I'LL SMASH YOU AND THAT DEVIOUS LITTLE PLAN OF YOURS.
KUII
...CHUUYA.
HUH?
PACHIN (SNAP)
?
JARA (JANGLE)

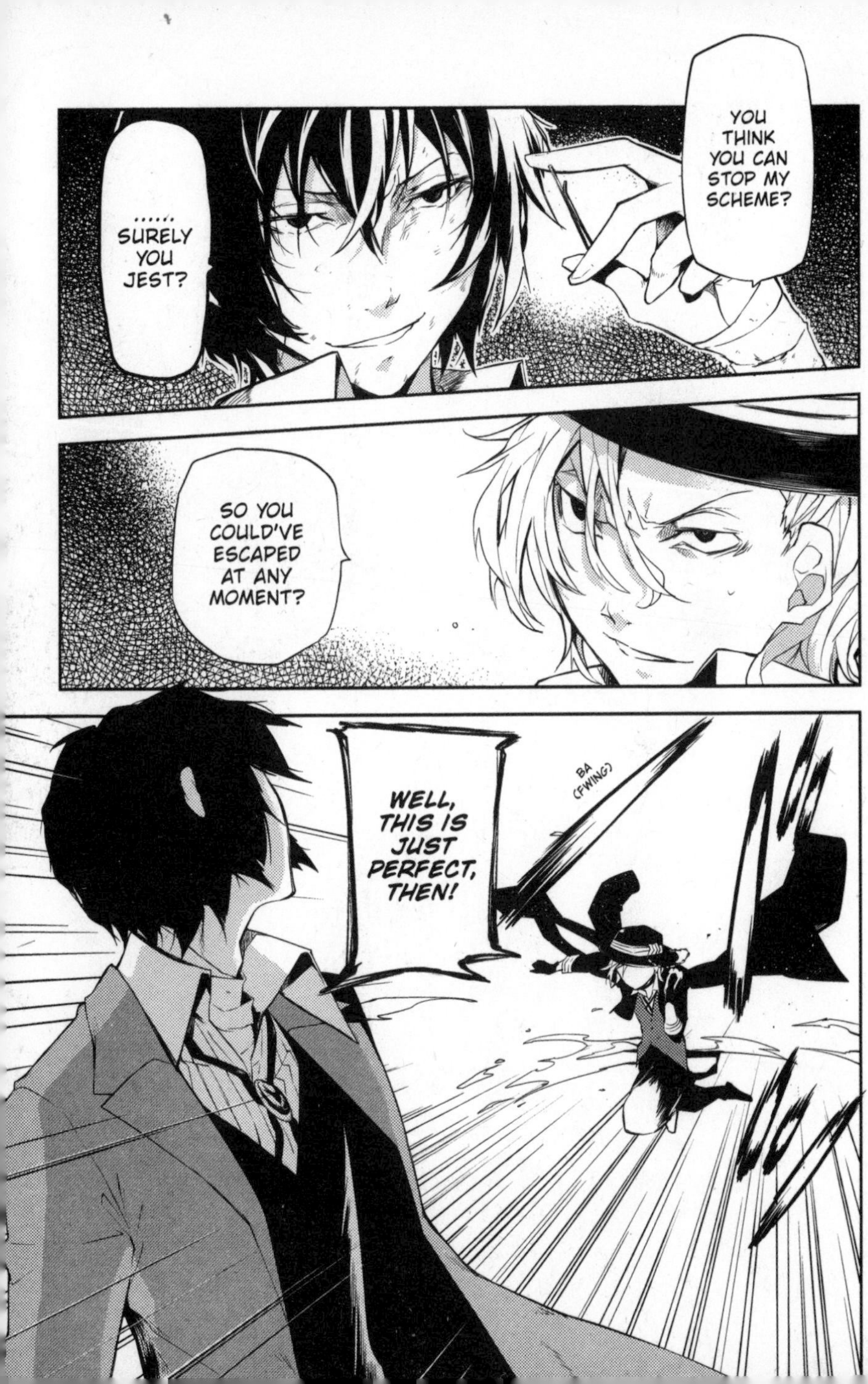
YOU THINK YOU CAN STOP MY SCHEME?
...... SURELY YOU JEST?
SO YOU COULD'VE ESCAPED AT ANY MOMENT?
BA (FWING)
WELL, THIS IS JUST PERFECT, THEN!

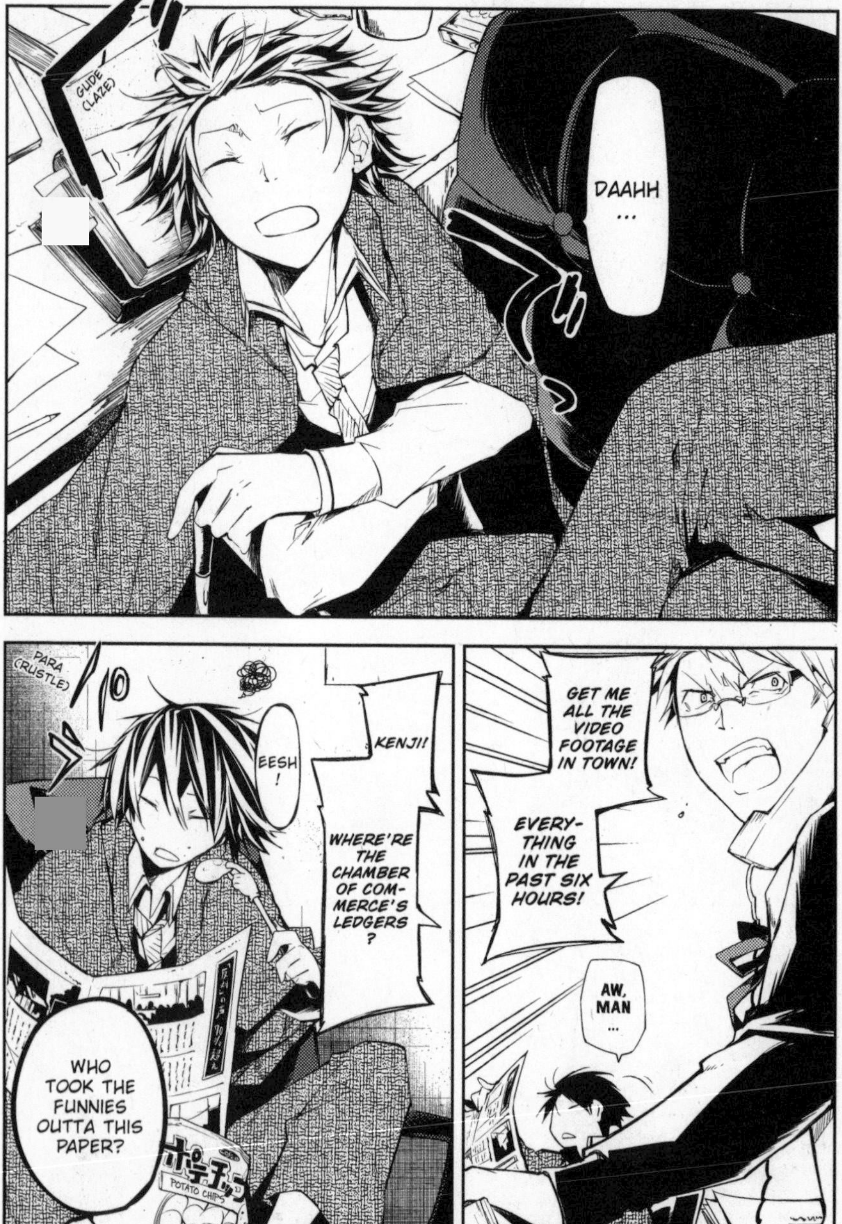
DAAHH ...
GUDE (LAZE)
GET ME ALL THE VIDEO FOOTAGE IN TOWN!
EVERYTHING IN THE PAST SIX HOURS!
AW, MAN ...
KENJI!
WHERE'RE THE CHAMBER OF COMMERCE'S LEDGERS?
EESH!
PARA (RUSTLE)
WHO TOOK THE FUNNIES OUTTA THIS PAPER?
POTATO CHIPS

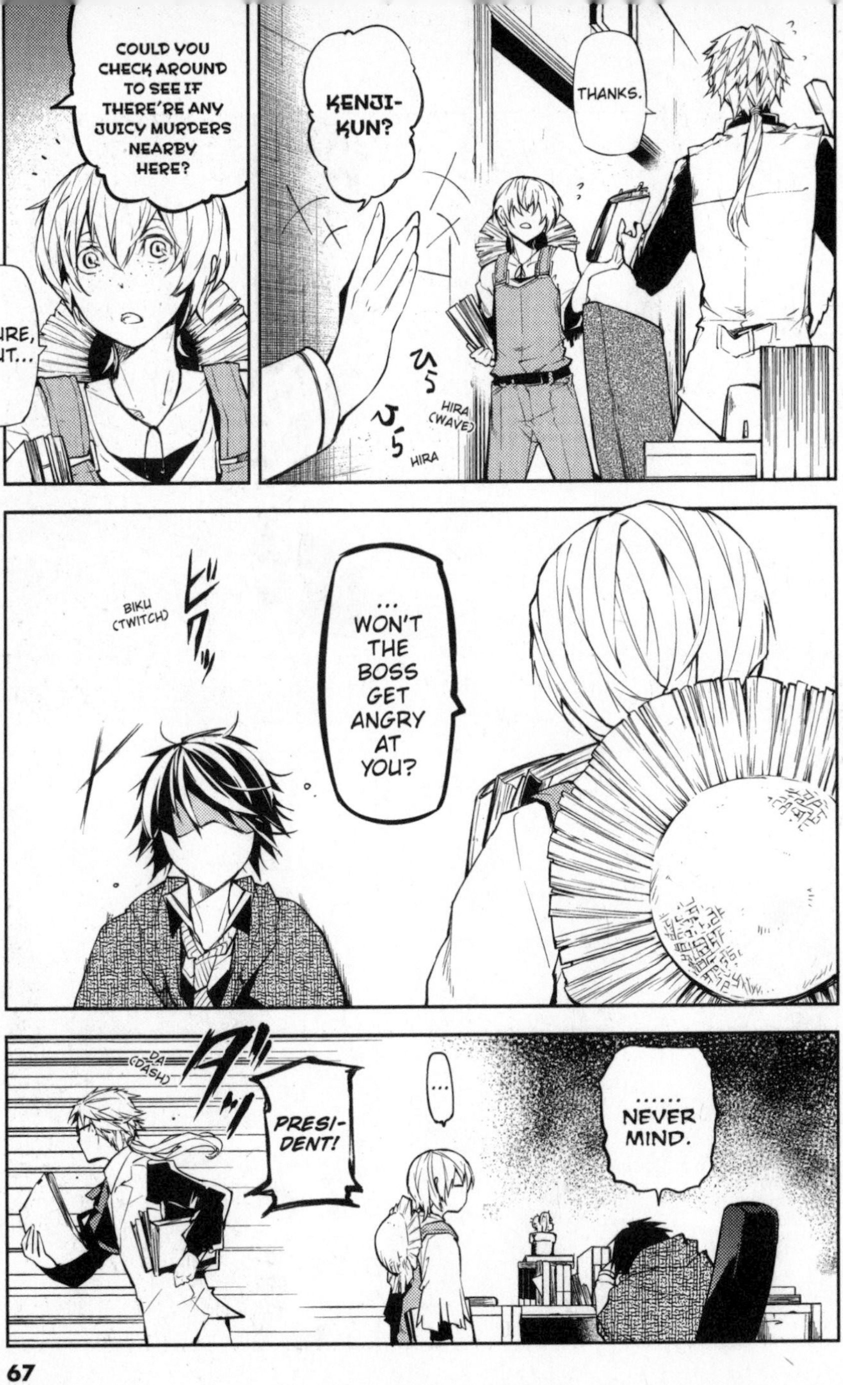
THANKS.
KENJI-KUN?
HIRA (WAVE)
HIRA
COULD YOU CHECK AROUND TO SEE IF THERE'RE ANY JUICY MURDERS NEARBY HERE?
SURE, BUT...
... WON'T THE BOSS GET ANGRY AT YOU?
BIKU (TWITCH)
...... NEVER MIND.
...
PRESI-DENT!
DA (DASH)

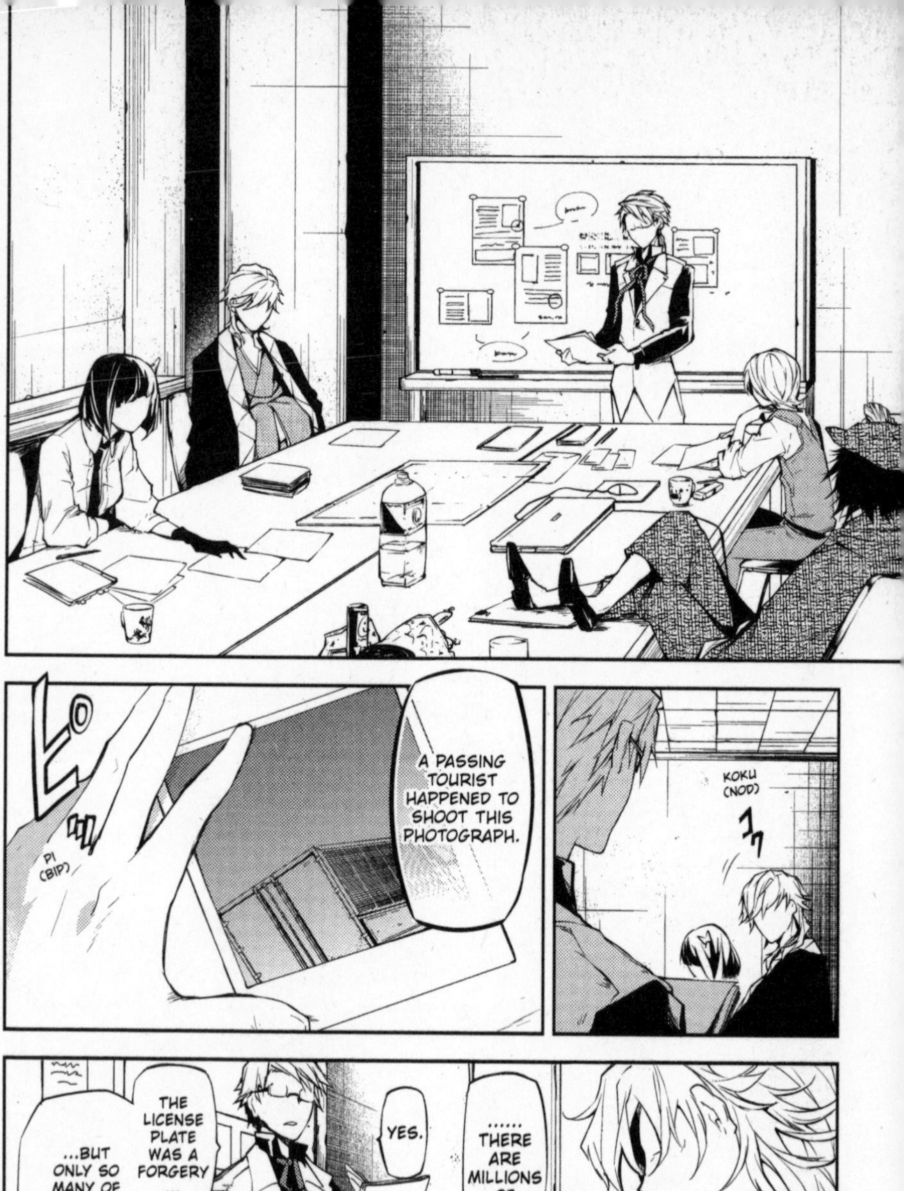
KOKU (NOD)
A PASSING TOURIST HAPPENED TO SHOOT THIS PHOTOGRAPH.
PI (BIP)
...... THERE ARE MILLIONS OF THESE.
YES.
THE LICENSE PLATE WAS A FORGERY ...
...BUT ONLY SO MANY OF THESE FORGERS EXIST IN YOKOHAMA.

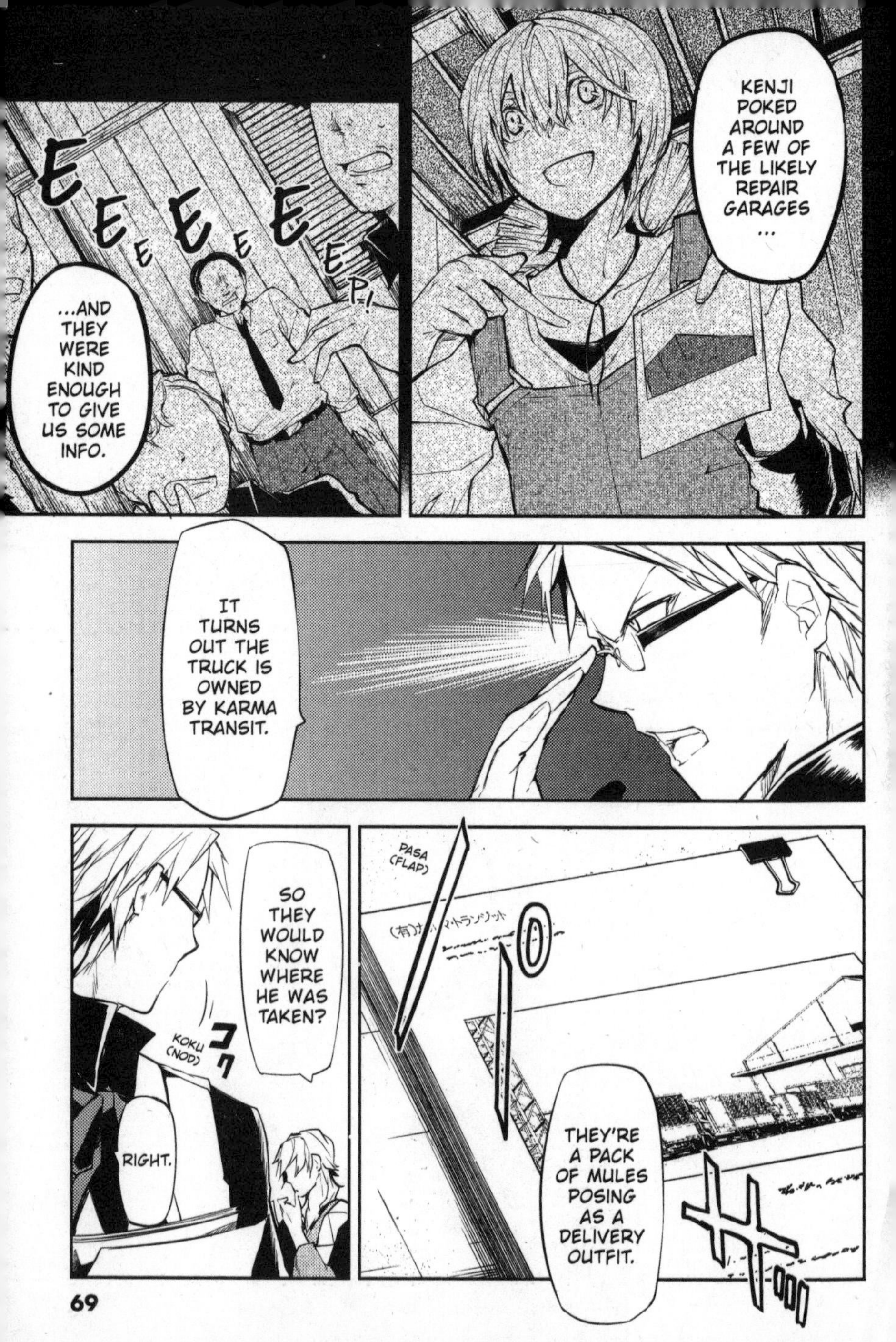
KENJI POKED AROUND A FEW OF THE LIKELY REPAIR GARAGES ...
EEEEEEEEEP!
...AND THEY WERE KIND ENOUGH TO GIVE US SOME INFO.
IT TURNS OUT THE TRUCK IS OWNED BY KARMA TRANSIT.
PASA (FLAP)
THEY'RE A PACK OF MULES POSING AS A DELIVERY OUTFIT.
SO THEY WOULD KNOW WHERE HE WAS TAKEN?
KOKU (NOD)
RIGHT.

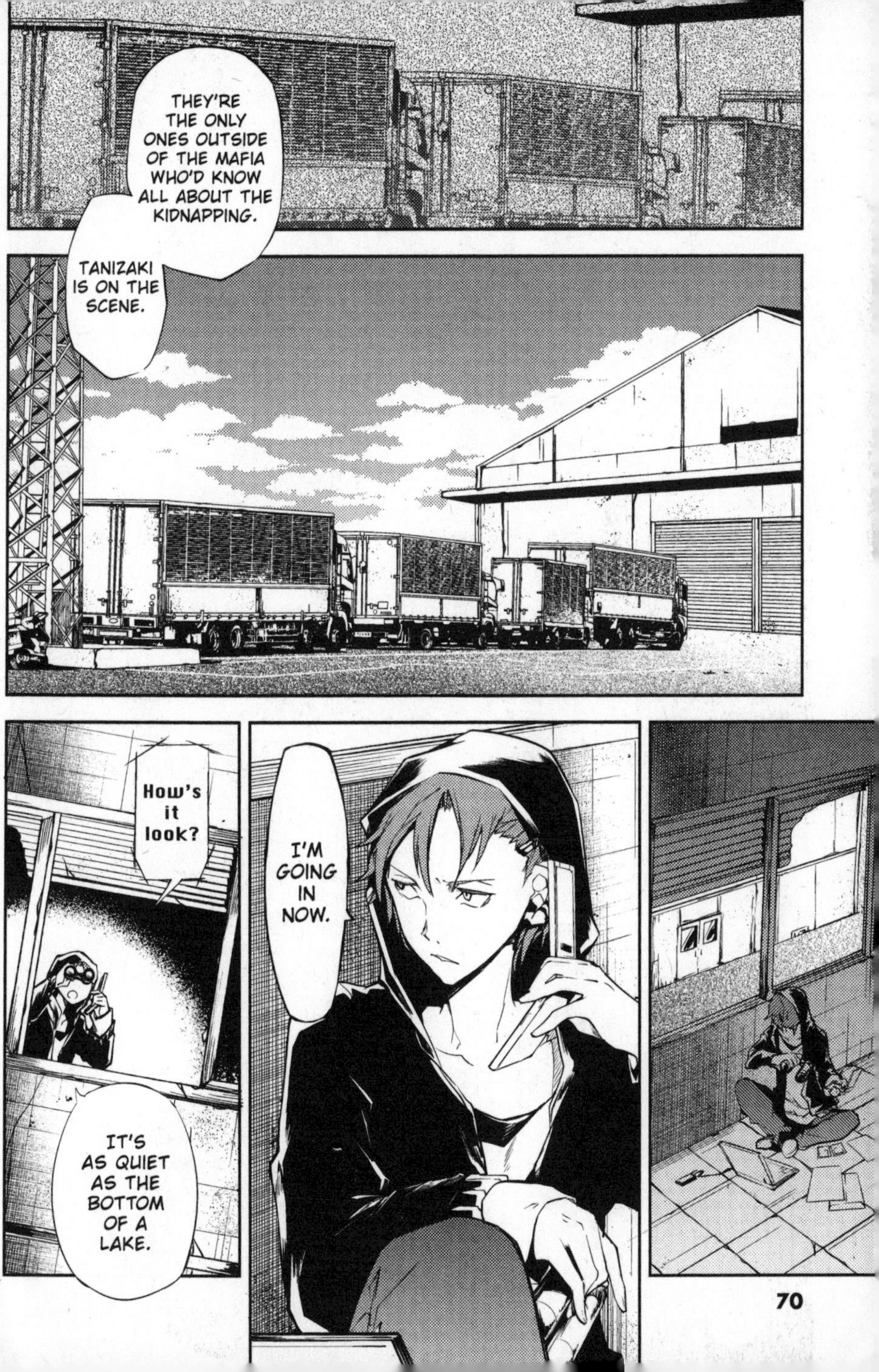
THEY'RE THE ONLY ONES OUTSIDE OF THE MAFIA WHO'D KNOW ALL ABOUT THE KIDNAPPING.
TANIZAKI IS ON THE SCENE.
I'M GOING IN NOW.
How's it look?
IT'S AS QUIET AS THE BOTTOM OF A LAKE.

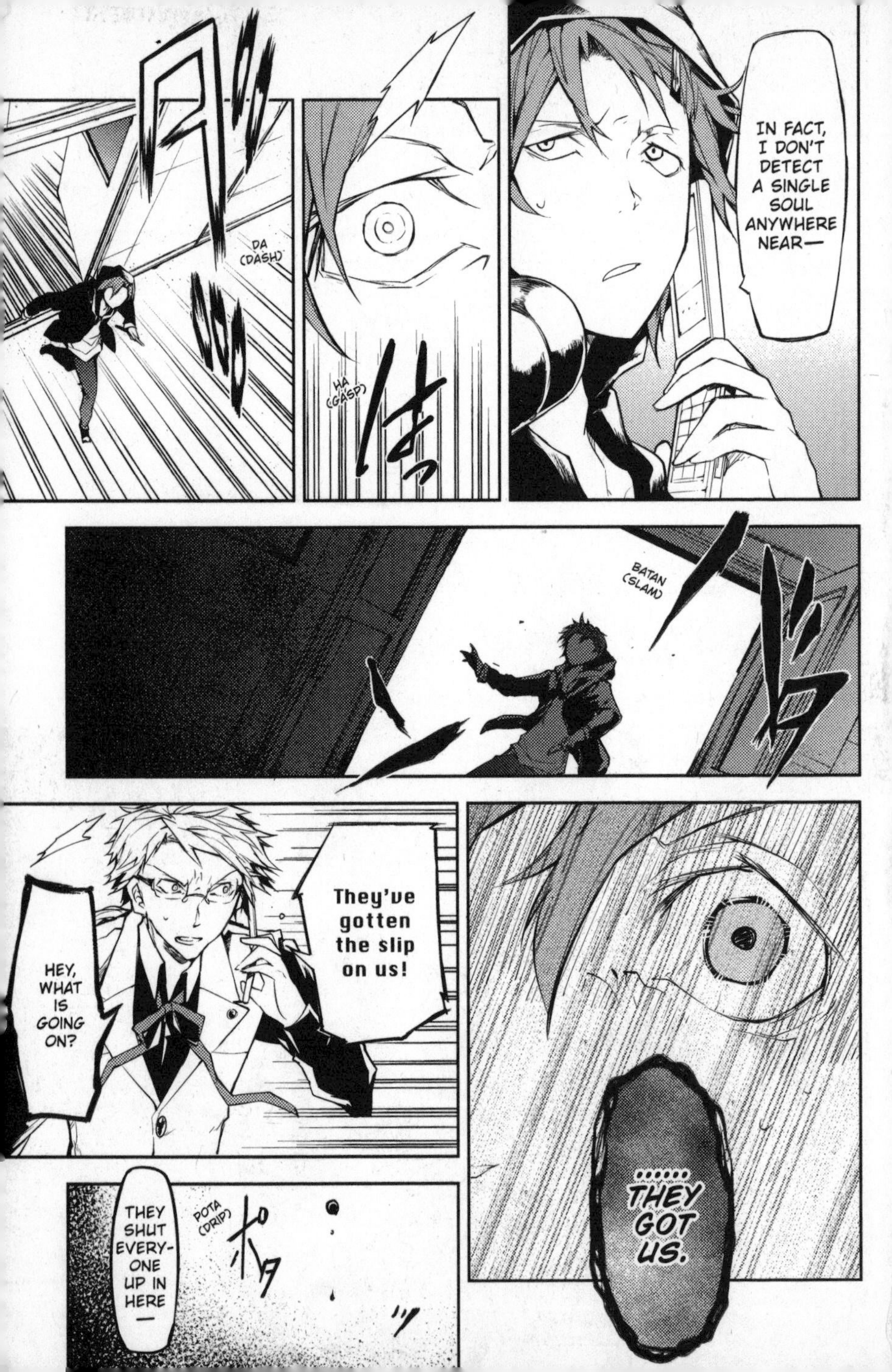
IN FACT, I DON'T DETECT A SINGLE SOUL ANYWHERE NEAR—
HA (GASP)
DA (DASH)
BATAN (SLAM)
......THEY GOT US.
They've gotten the slip on us!
HEY, WHAT IS GOING ON?
POTA (DRIP)
THEY SHUT EVERY-ONE UP IN HERE—

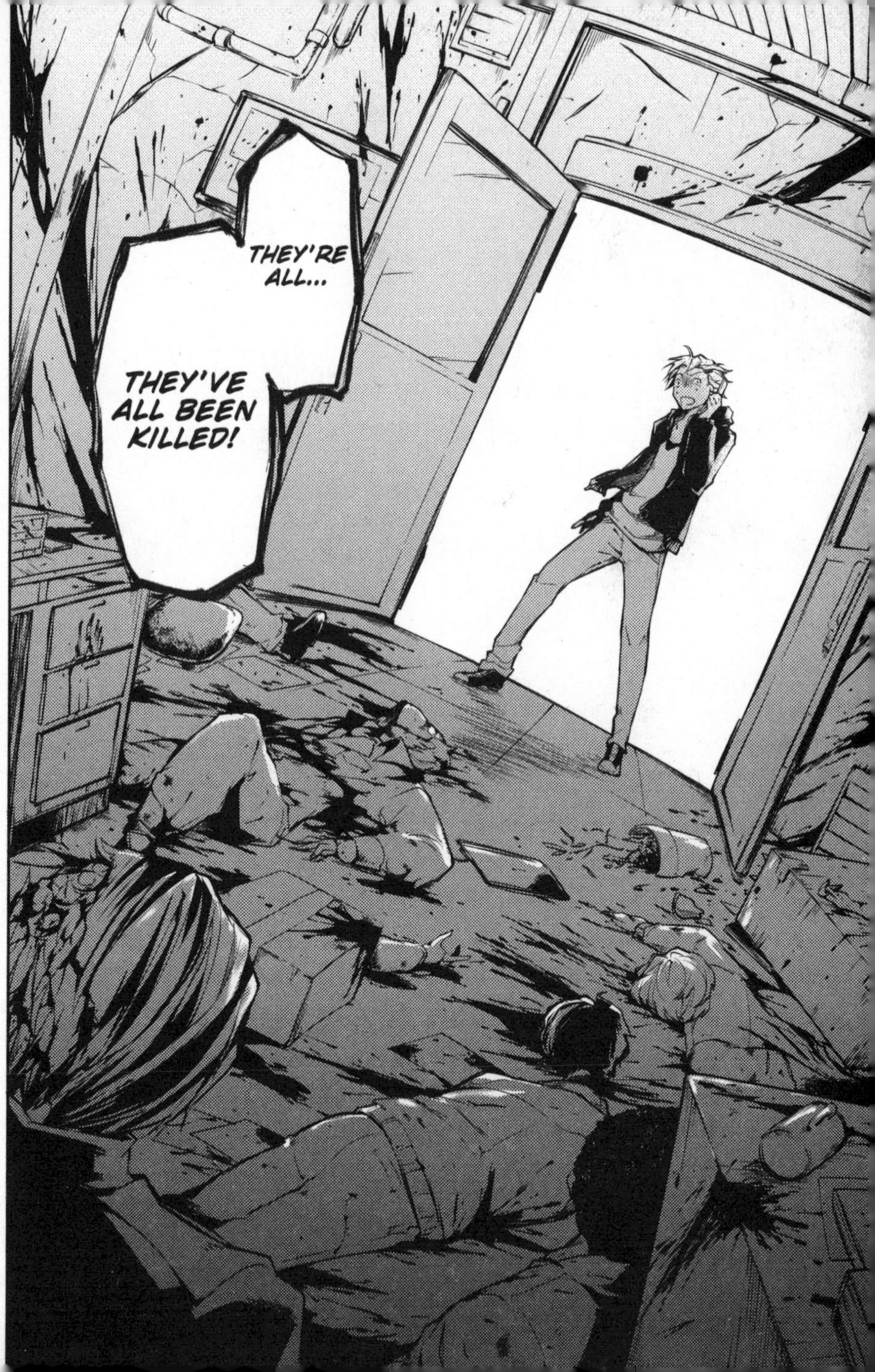
THEY'RE ALL...
THEY'VE ALL BEEN KILLED!

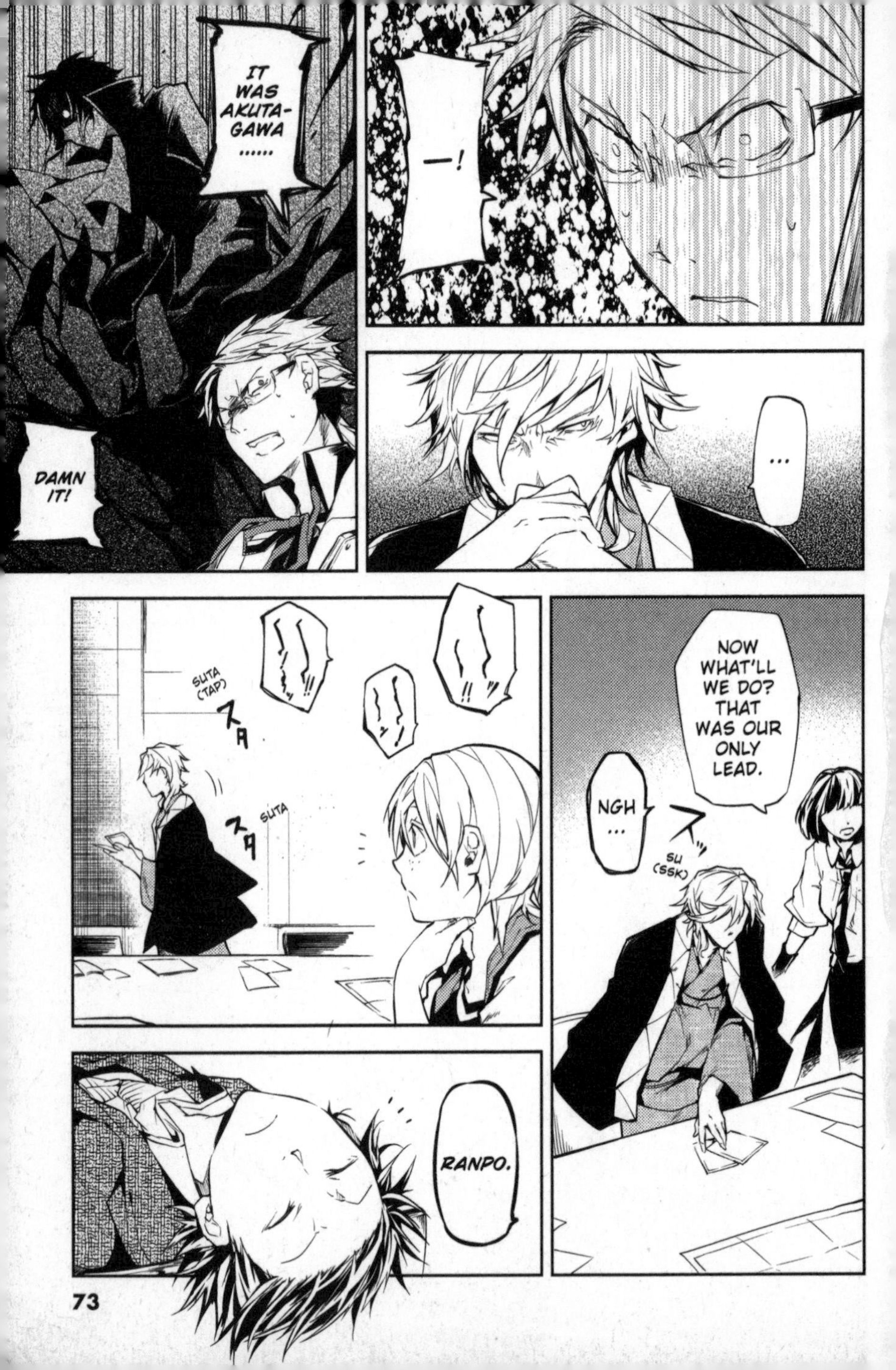
—!
...
IT WAS AKUTAGAWA......
DAMN IT!
NOW WHAT'LL WE DO? THAT WAS OUR ONLY LEAD.
NGH...
SU (SSK)
!!
!
!!
SUTA (TAP)
SUTA
RANPO.

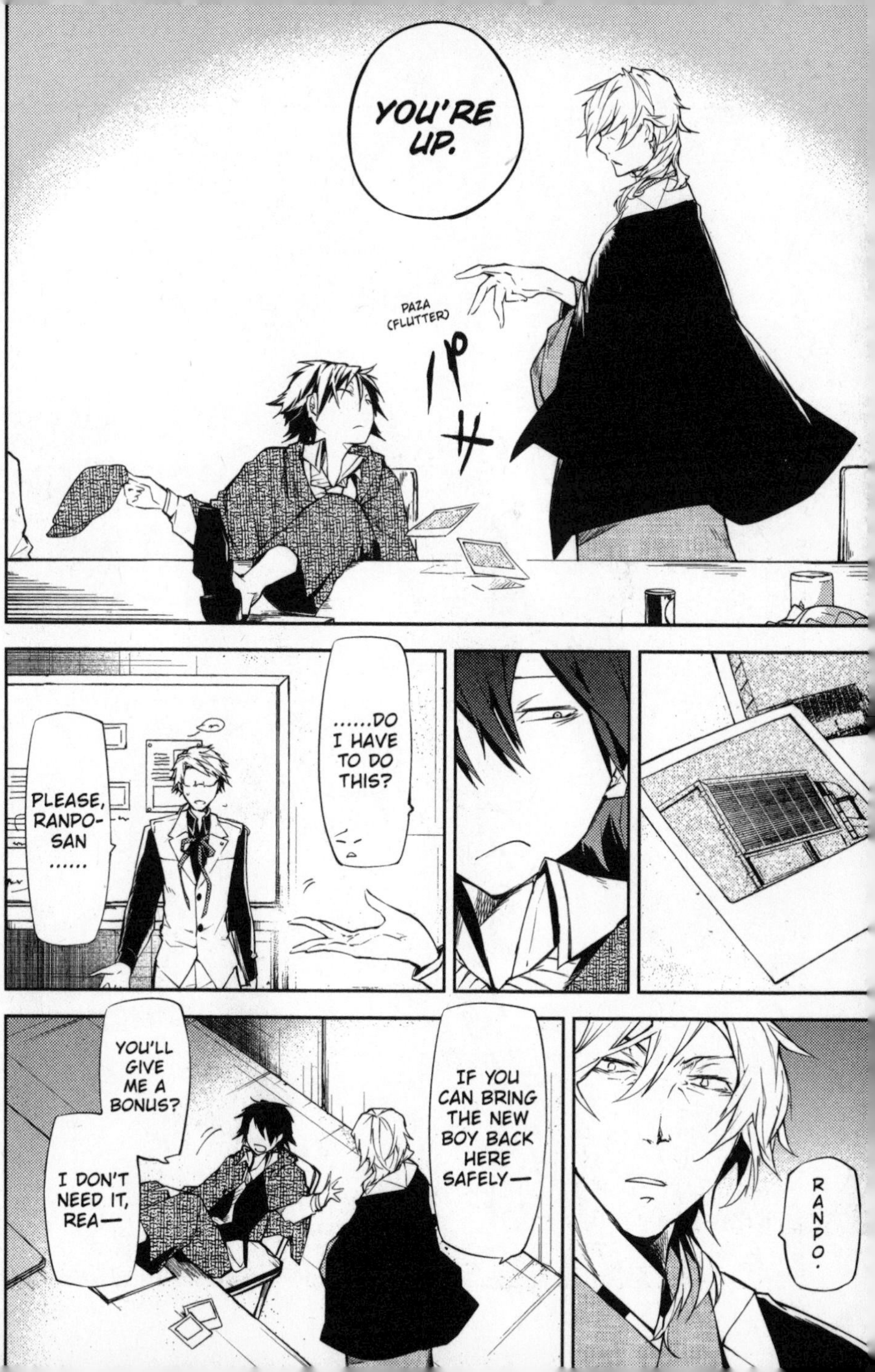
YOU'RE UP.
PAZA (FLUTTER)
......DO I HAVE TO DO THIS?
PLEASE, RANPO-SAN ......
RANPO.
IF YOU CAN BRING THE NEW BOY BACK HERE SAFELY—
YOU'LL GIVE ME A BONUS?
I DON'T NEED IT, REA—

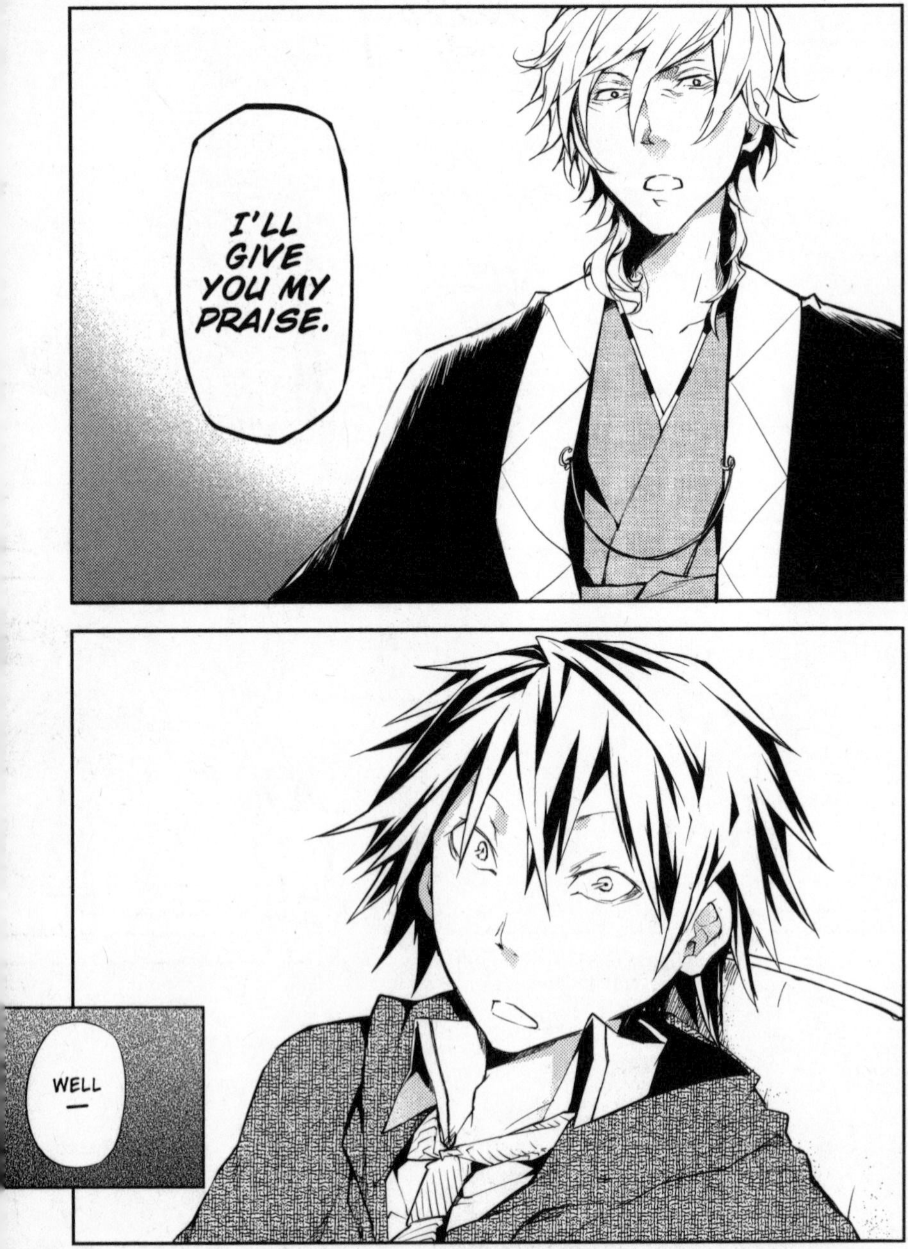
I'LL GIVE YOU MY PRAISE.
WELL —

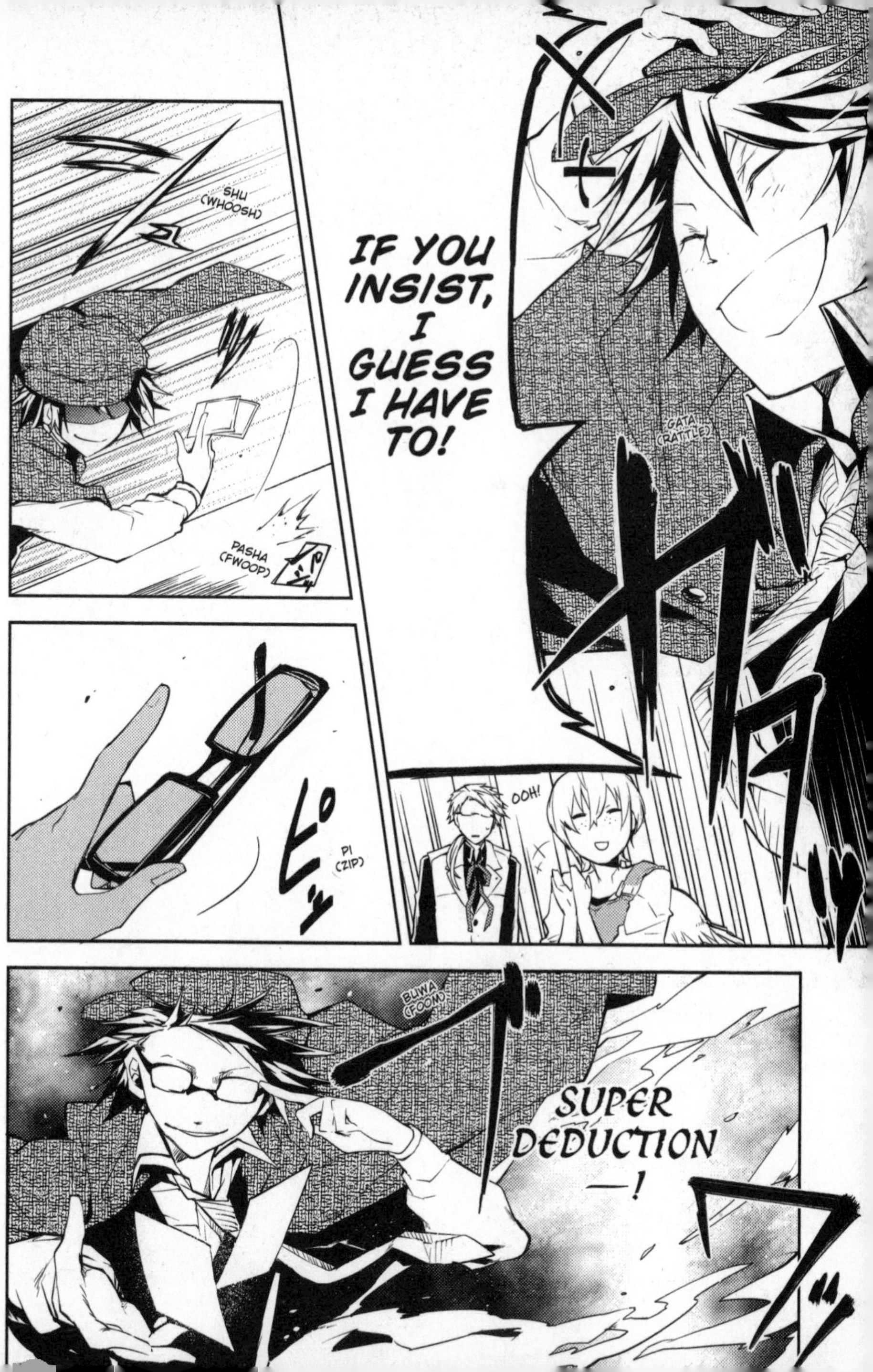
IF YOU INSIST, I GUESS I HAVE TO!
GATA (RATTLE)
SHU (WHOOSH)
PASHA (FWOOP)
PI (ZIP)
OOH!
BUWA (FOOM)
SUPER DEDUCTION —!

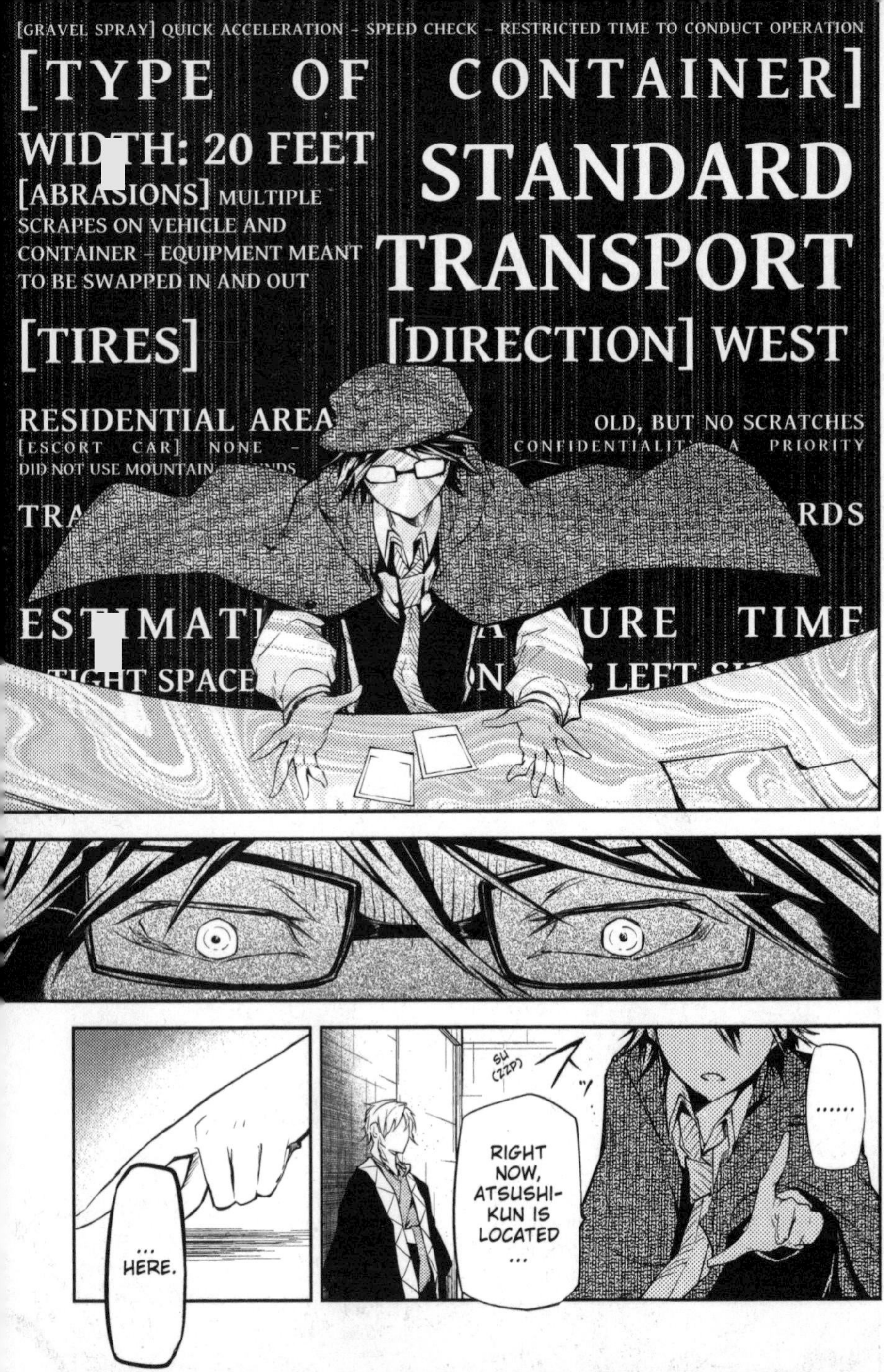

[GRAVEL SPRAY] QUICK ACCELERATION – SPEED CHECK – RESTRICTED TIME TO CONDUCT OPERATION
[TYPE OF CONTAINER]
WIDTH: 20 FEET
STANDARD TRANSPORT
[ABRASIONS] MULTIPLE SCRAPES ON VEHICLE AND CONTAINER – EQUIPMENT MEANT TO BE SWAPPED IN AND OUT
[TIRES]
[DIRECTION] WEST
RESIDENTIAL AREA
OLD, BUT NO SCRATCHES
[ESCORT CAR] NONE –
DID NOT USE MOUNTAIN
......
SU (ZZP)
RIGHT NOW, ATSUSHI-KUN IS LOCATED ...
... HERE.

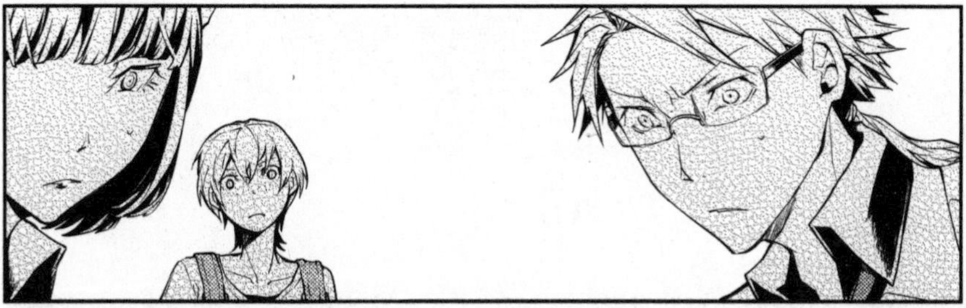

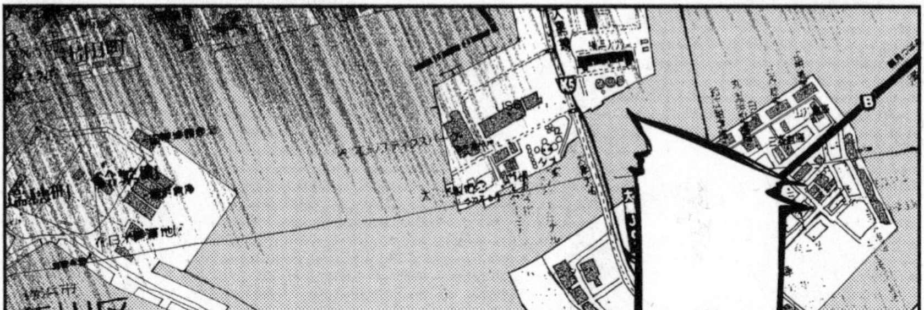
Kanagawa Ward
Kanagawa Prefectural Office
... IN THE OCEAN !?

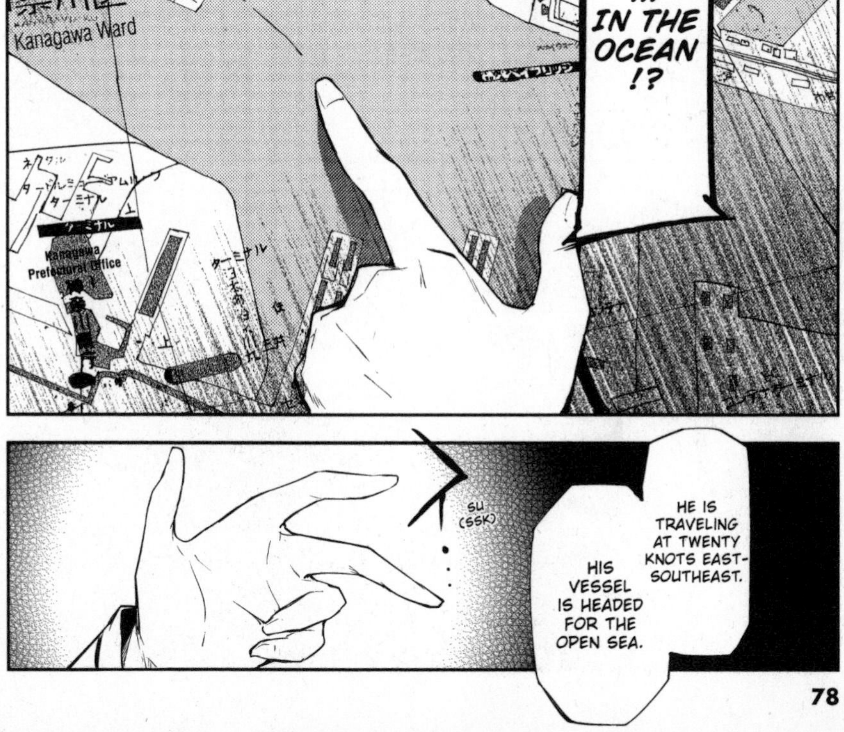
HE IS TRAVELING AT TWENTY KNOTS EAST-SOUTHEAST.
HIS VESSEL IS HEADED FOR THE OPEN SEA.
SU (SSK)

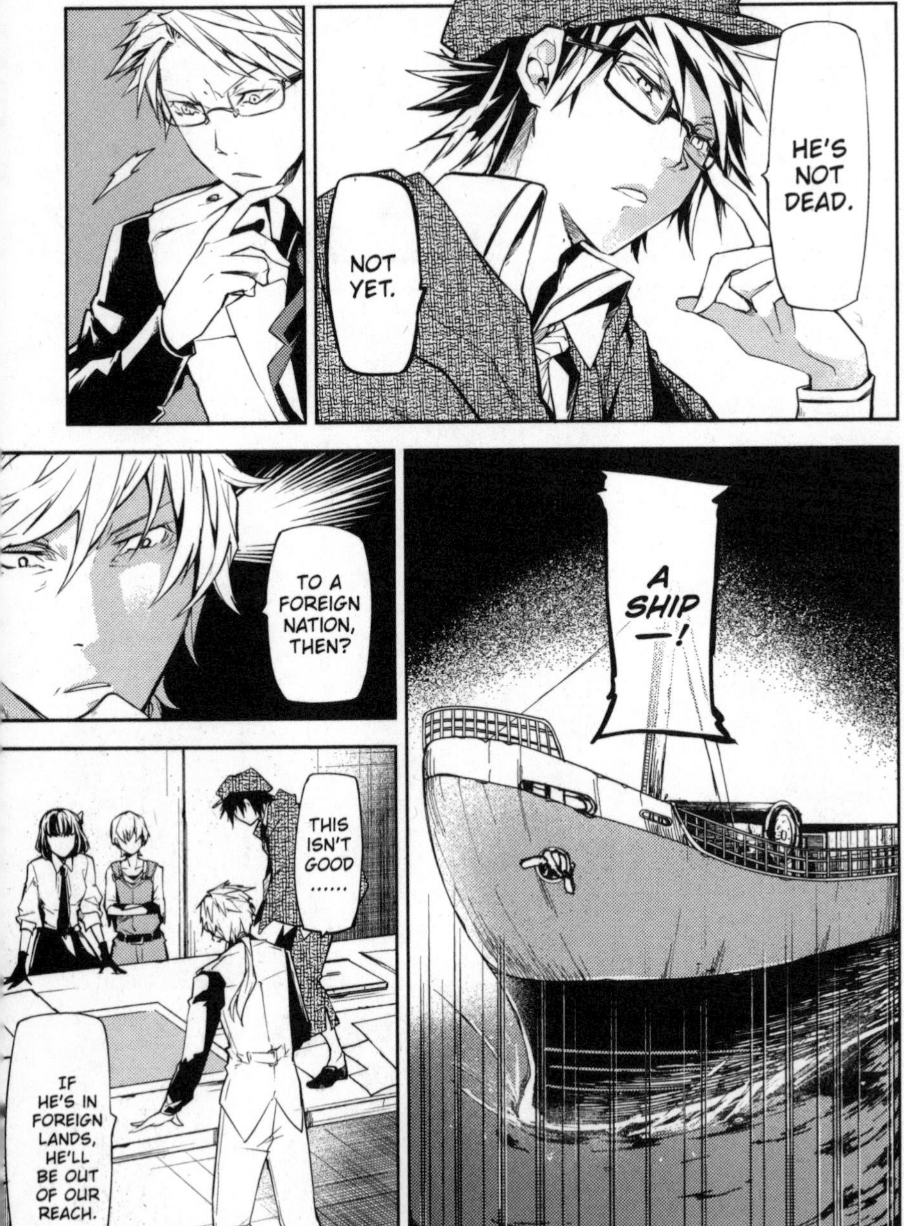
HE'S NOT DEAD.
NOT YET.
A SHIP—!
TO A FOREIGN NATION, THEN?
THIS ISN'T GOOD......
IF HE'S IN FOREIGN LANDS, HE'LL BE OUT OF OUR REACH.

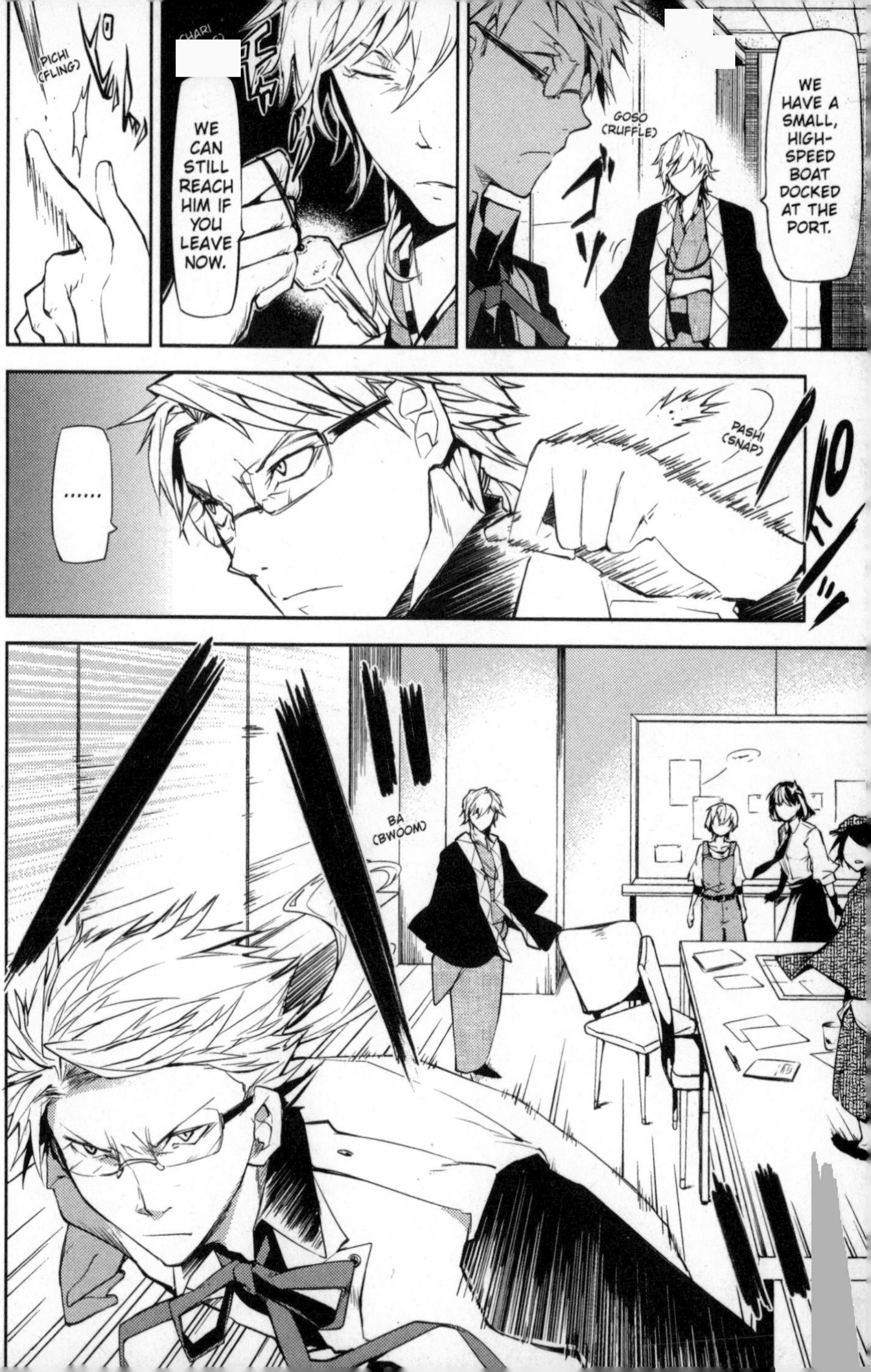
WE HAVE A SMALL, HIGH-SPEED BOAT DOCKED AT THE PORT.
GOSO (RUFFLE)
CHARI
WE CAN STILL REACH HIM IF YOU LEAVE NOW.
PICHI (FLING)
PASHI (SNAP)
......
BA (BWOOM)

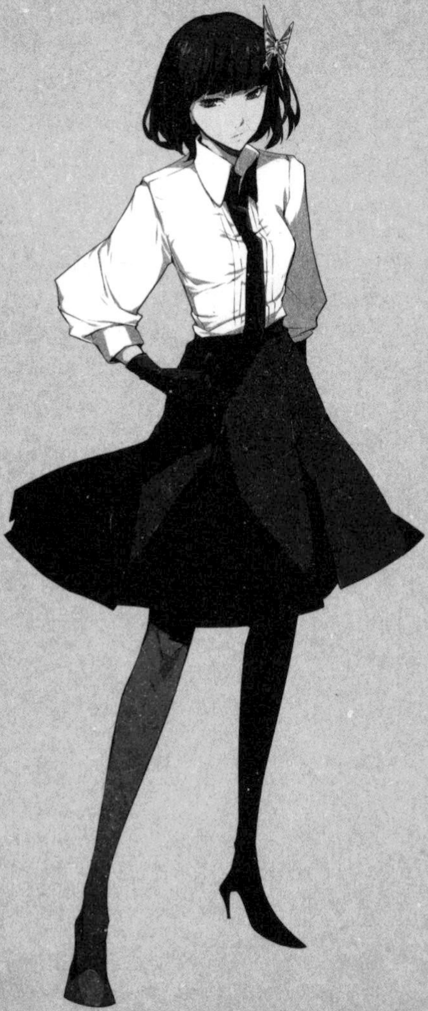

AKIKO YOSANO

SKILL: Thou Shalt Not Die
One of the rare healing-type skills among the agency staff. However, it only works on those near death, forcing her to half-kill her patients first.

AGE: *25*

BIRTH DATE: *December 7*

HEIGHT: *166cm*

WEIGHT: *52kg*

BLOOD TYPE: *O*

LIKES: *Flowers, Japanese sweets, eel, sake*

DISLIKES: *Male chauvinism, weak men*

BUNGO
STRAY DOGS

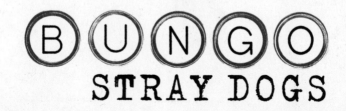

CHAPTER 11
Back in the Day...

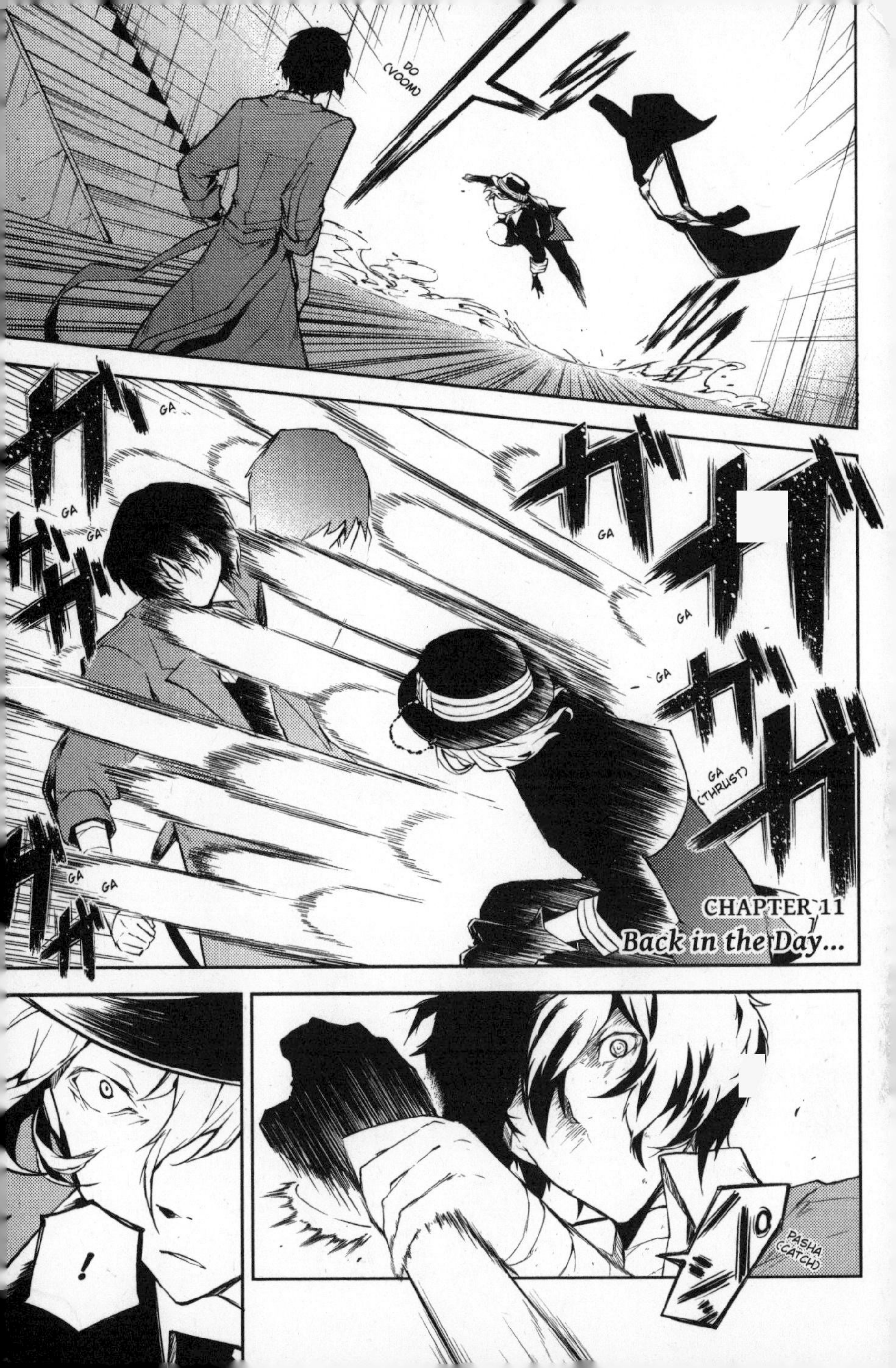
DO (VOOM)
GA
GA
GA
GA (THRUST)
GA
GA
GA
GA
GA
PASHA (CATCH)
!

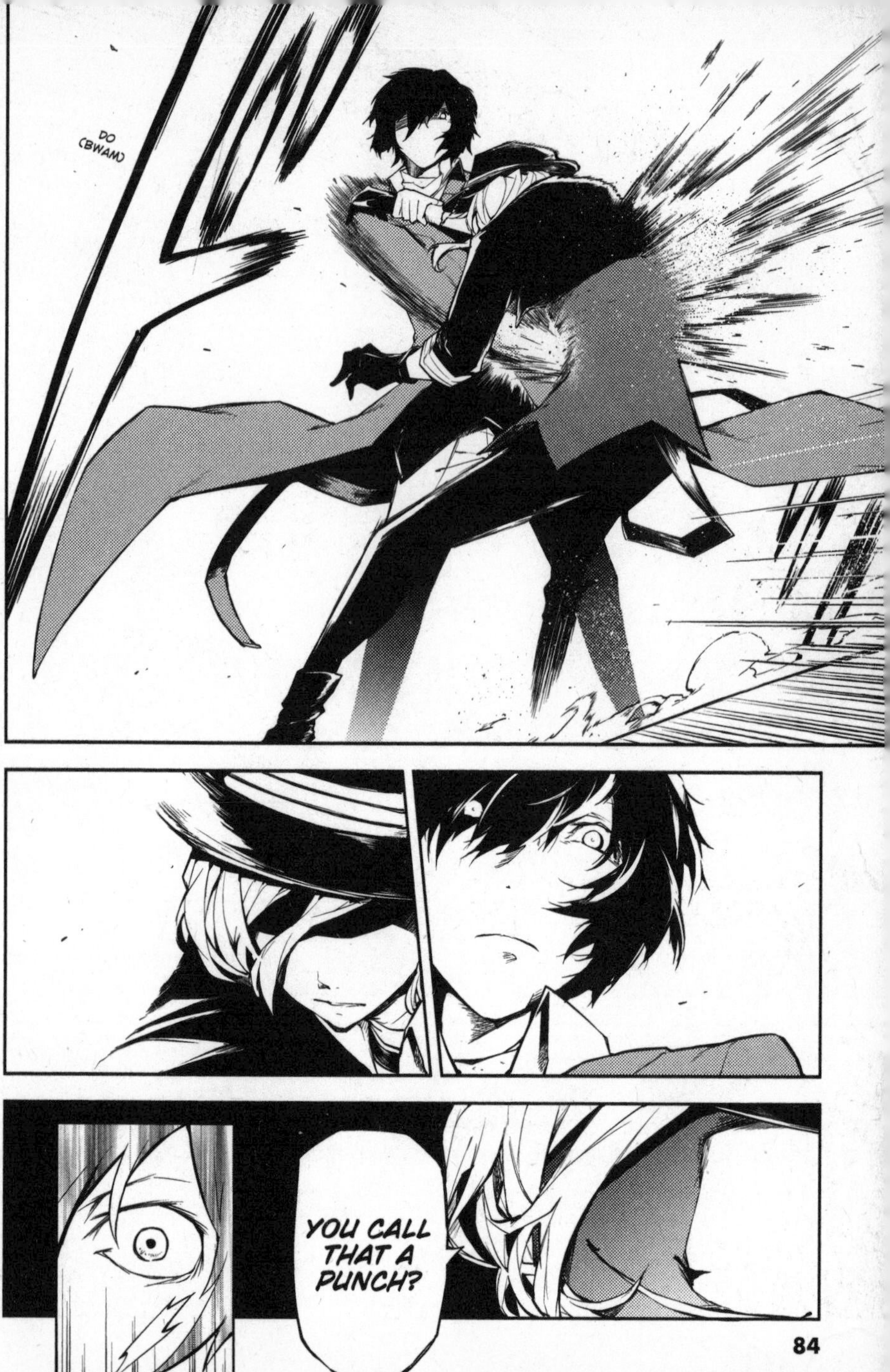
DO
(BWAM)
YOU CALL THAT A PUNCH?

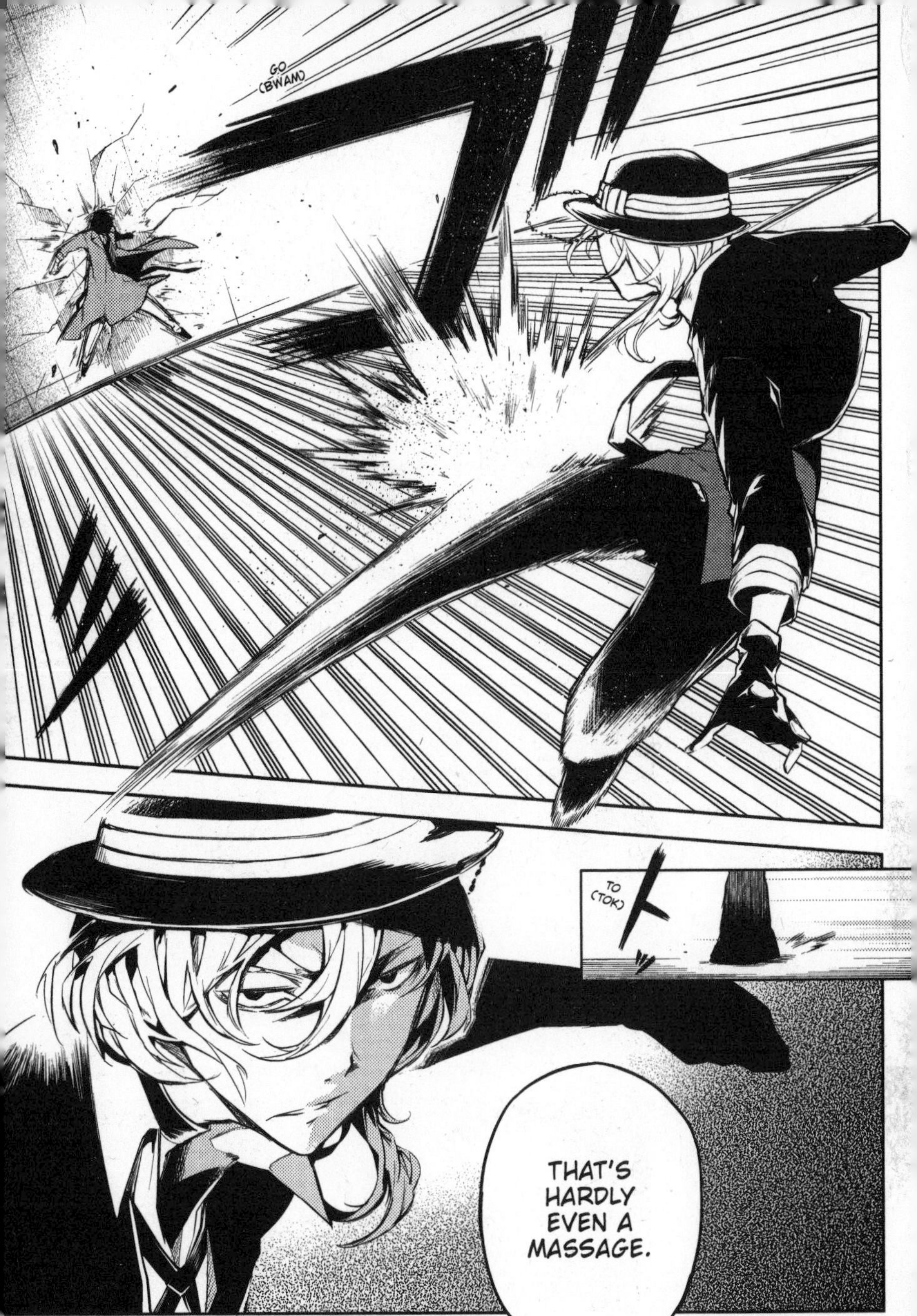
GO (BWAM)
TO (TOK)
THAT'S HARDLY EVEN A MASSAGE.

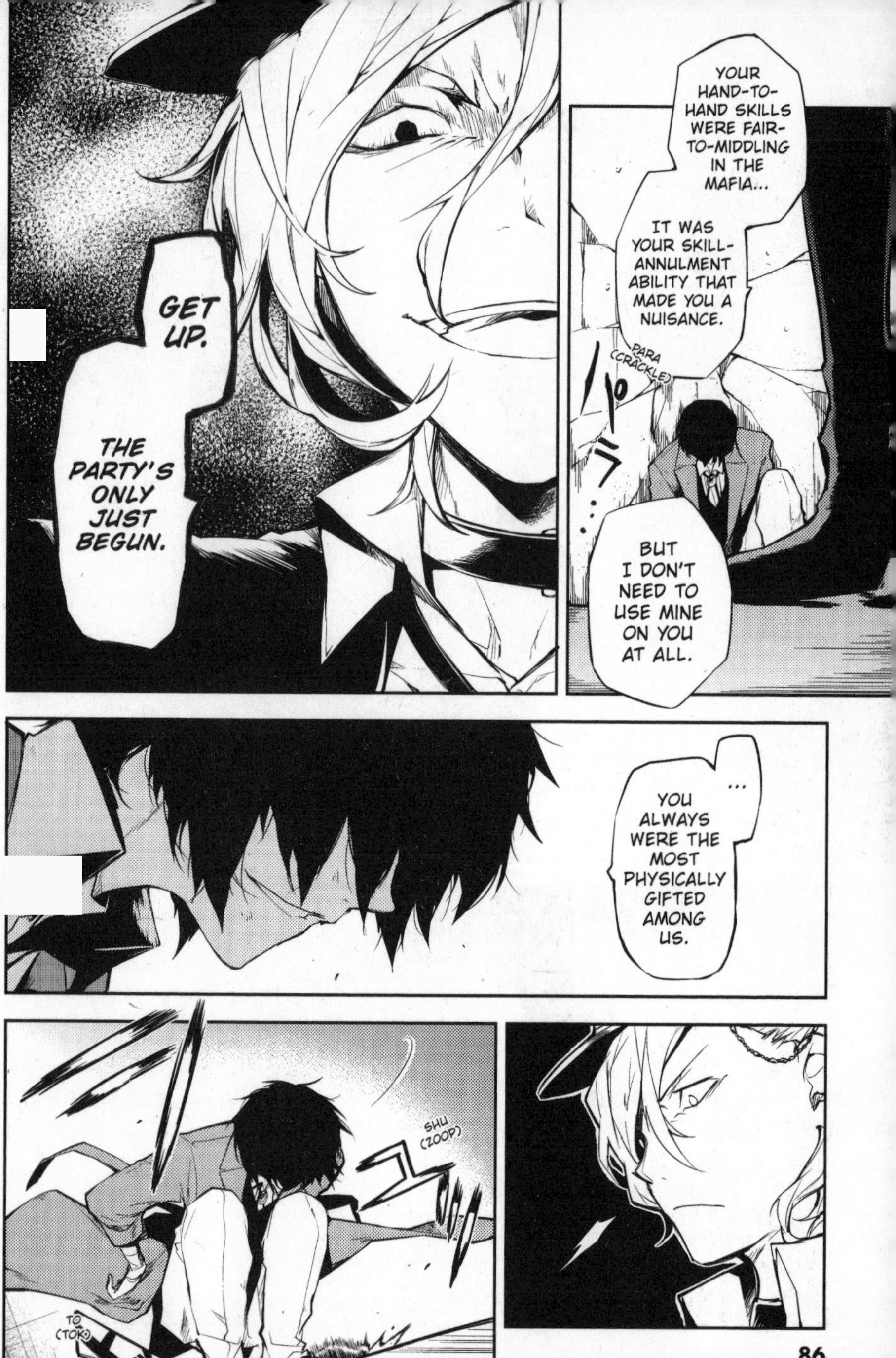
YOUR HAND-TO-HAND SKILLS WERE FAIR-TO-MIDDLING IN THE MAFIA...
IT WAS YOUR SKILL-ANNULMENT ABILITY THAT MADE YOU A NUISANCE.
PARA (CRACKLE)
BUT I DON'T NEED TO USE MINE ON YOU AT ALL.
GET UP.
THE PARTY'S ONLY JUST BEGUN.
... YOU ALWAYS WERE THE MOST PHYSICALLY GIFTED AMONG US.
SHU (ZOOP)
TO (TOK)

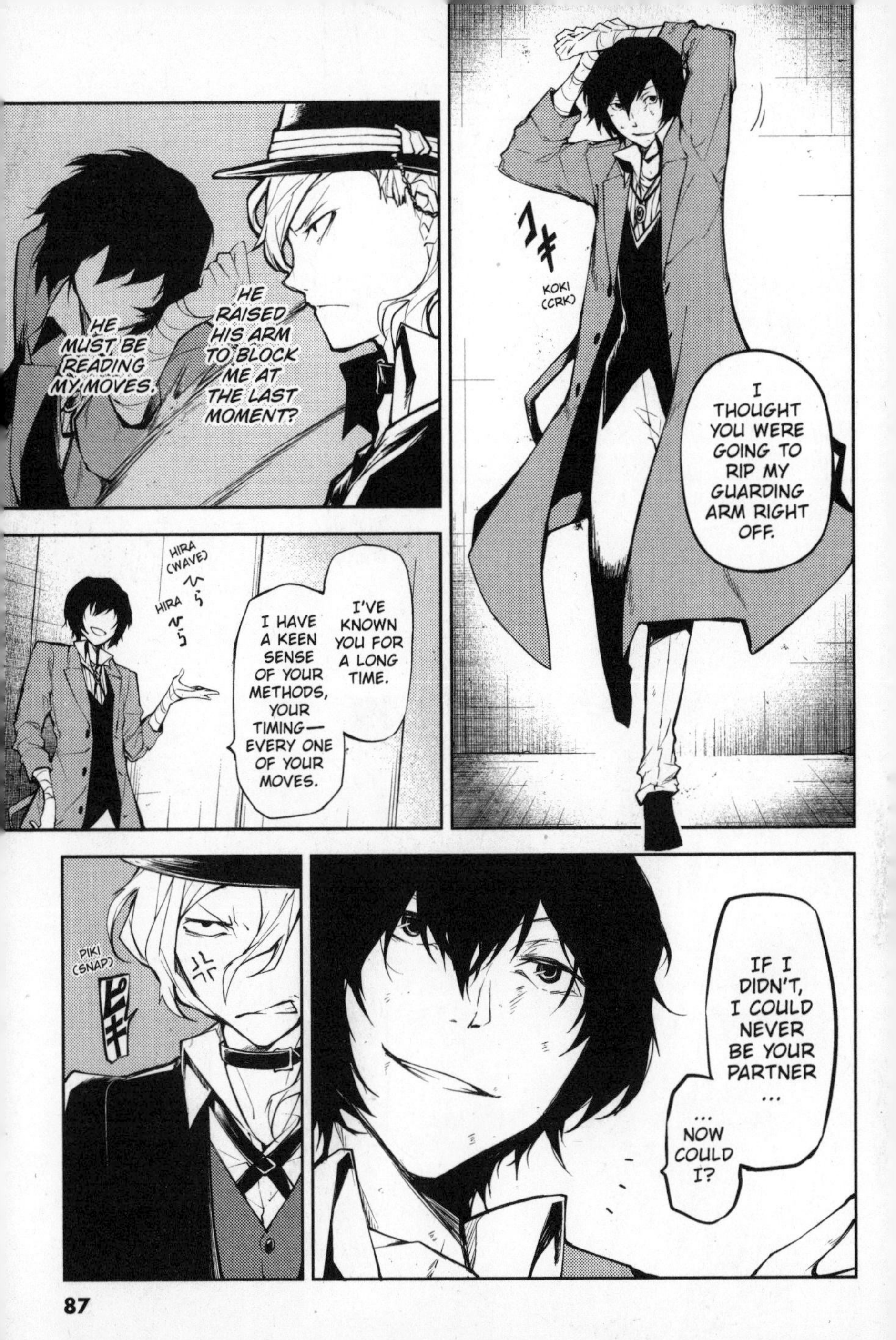
KOKI (CRK)
I THOUGHT YOU WERE GOING TO RIP MY GUARDING ARM RIGHT OFF.
HE RAISED HIS ARM TO BLOCK ME AT THE LAST MOMENT?
HE MUST BE READING MY MOVES.
HIRA (WAVE)
HIRA
I'VE KNOWN YOU FOR A LONG TIME.
I HAVE A KEEN SENSE OF YOUR METHODS, YOUR TIMING—EVERY ONE OF YOUR MOVES.
IF I DIDN'T, I COULD NEVER BE YOUR PARTNER...
...NOW COULD I?
PIKI (SNAP)

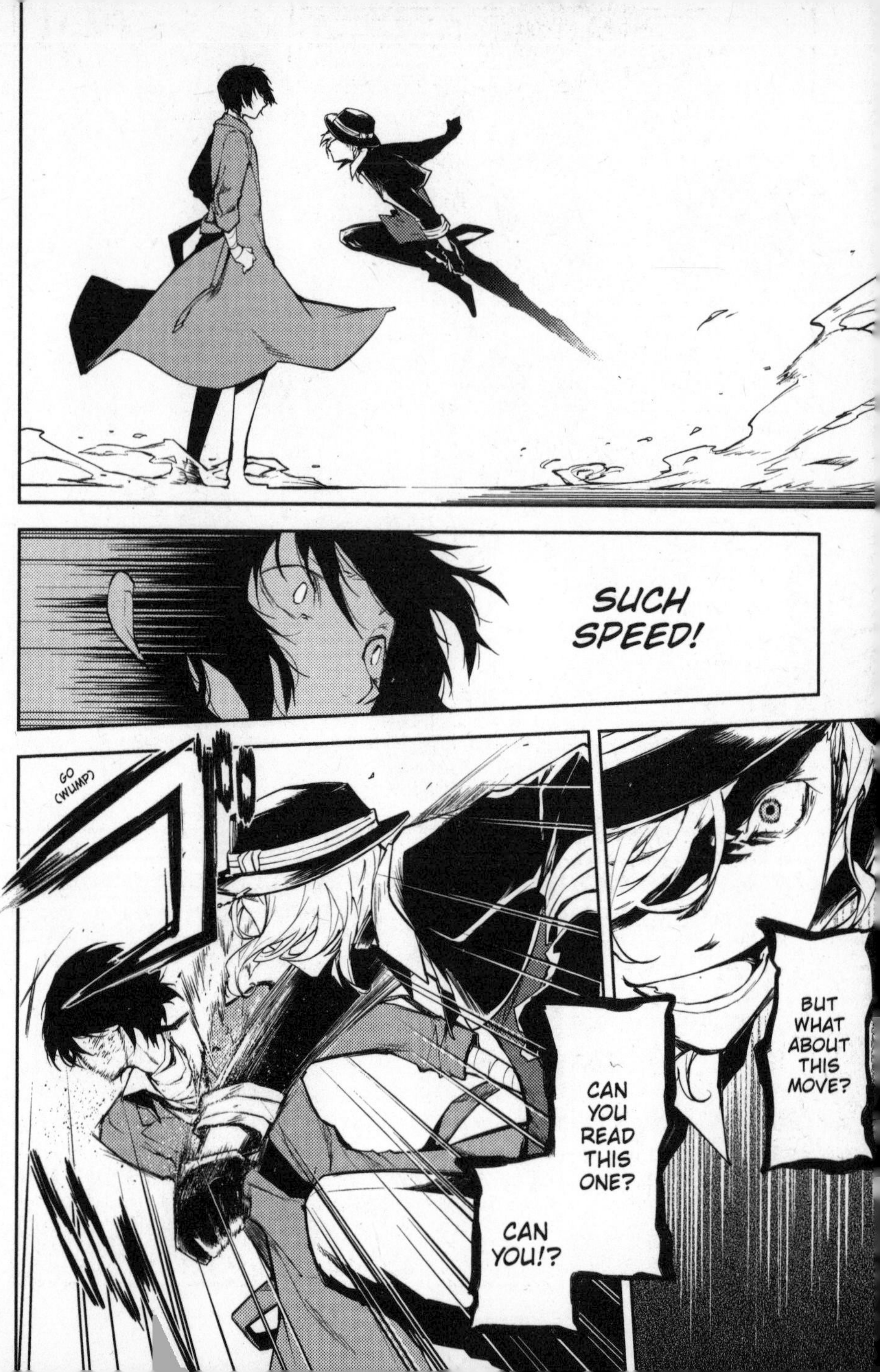
SUCH SPEED!
BUT WHAT ABOUT THIS MOVE?
CAN YOU READ THIS ONE?
CAN YOU!?
GO (WUMP)

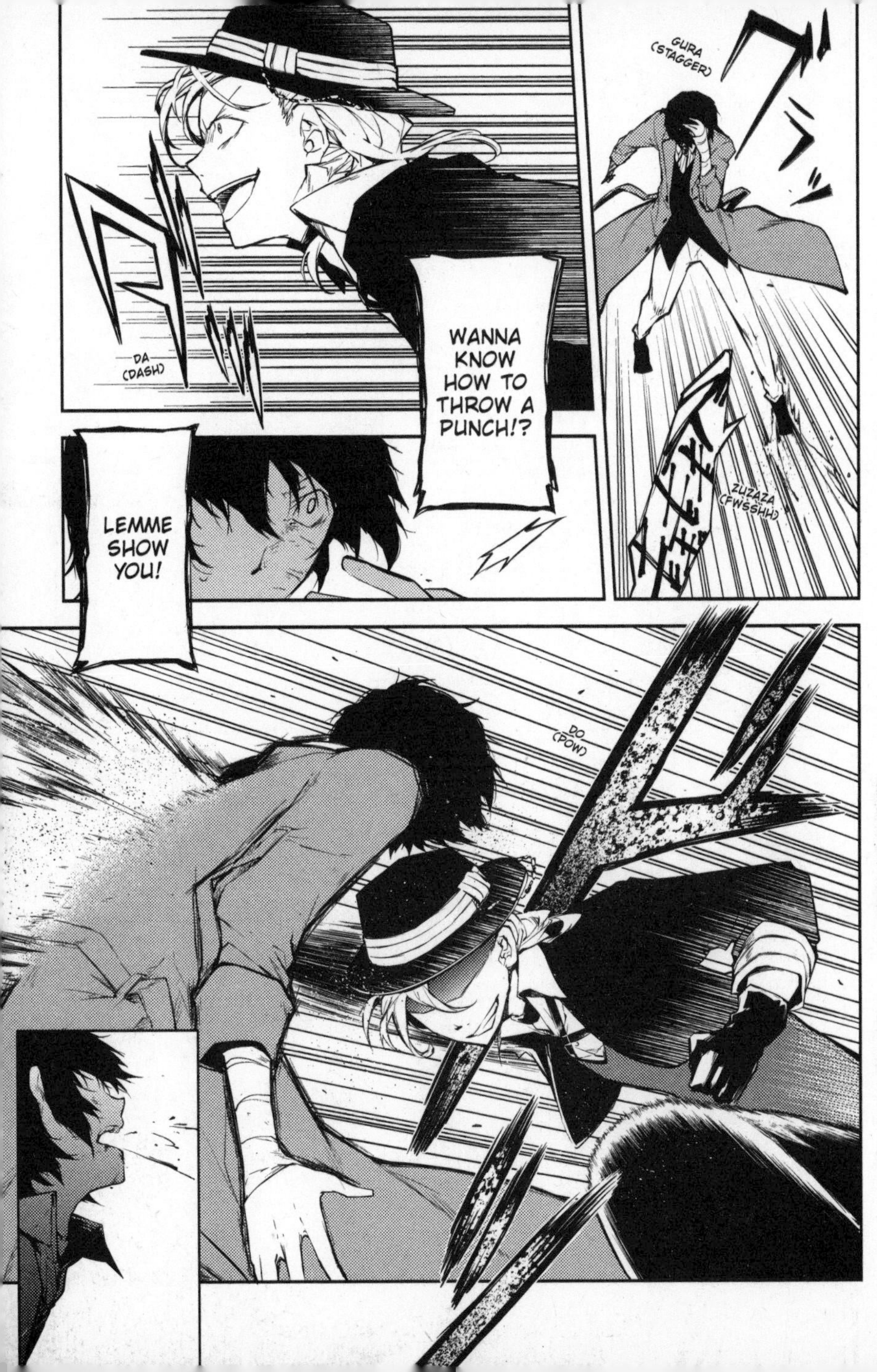
GURA
(STAGGER)
ZUZAZA
(FWSSHH)
DA
(DASH)
WANNA KNOW HOW TO THROW A PUNCH!?
LEMME SHOW YOU!
DO
(POW)

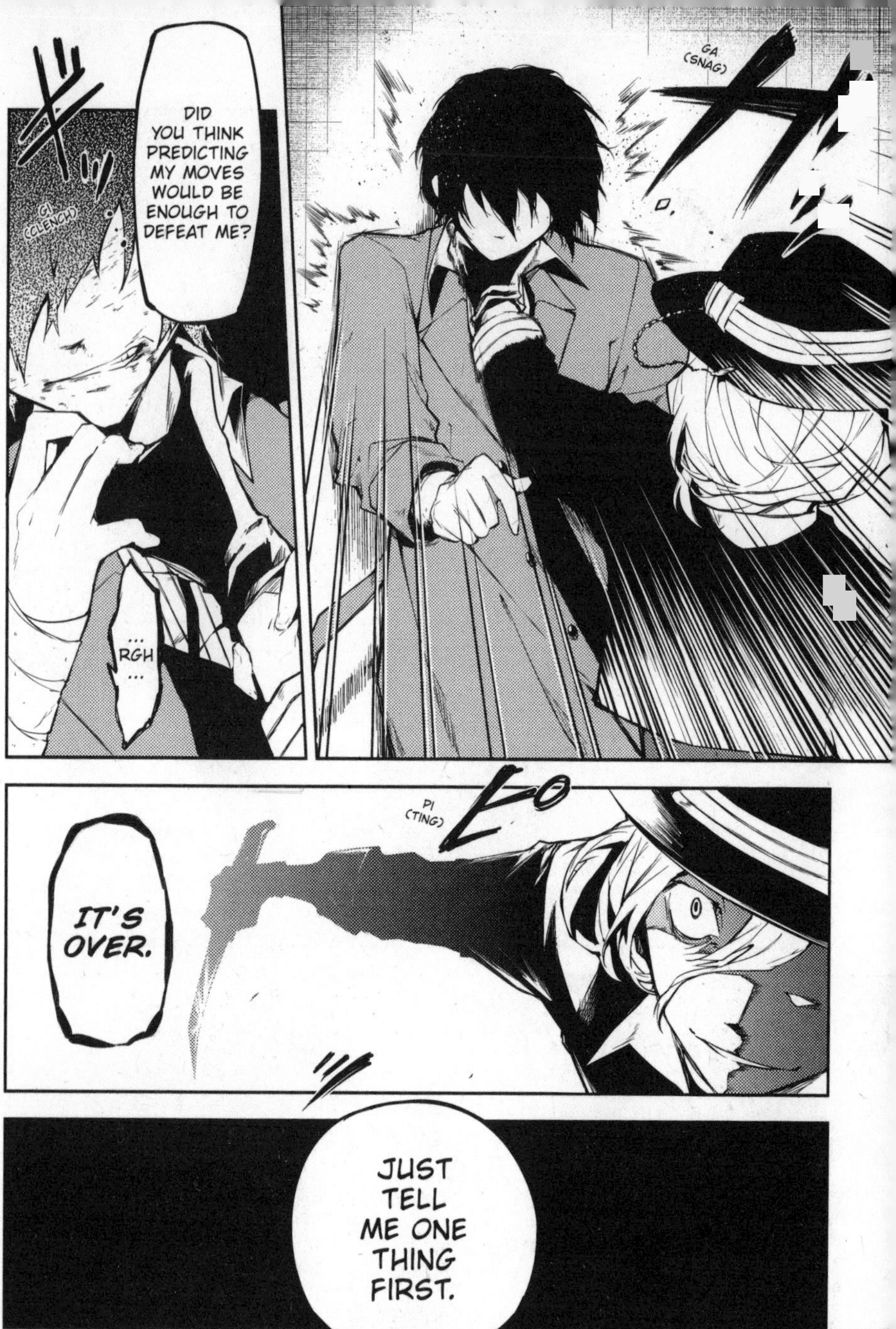
GA (SNAG)
DID YOU THINK PREDICTING MY MOVES WOULD BE ENOUGH TO DEFEAT ME?
GI (CLENCH)
...RGH...
PI (TING)
IT'S OVER.
JUST TELL ME ONE THING FIRST.

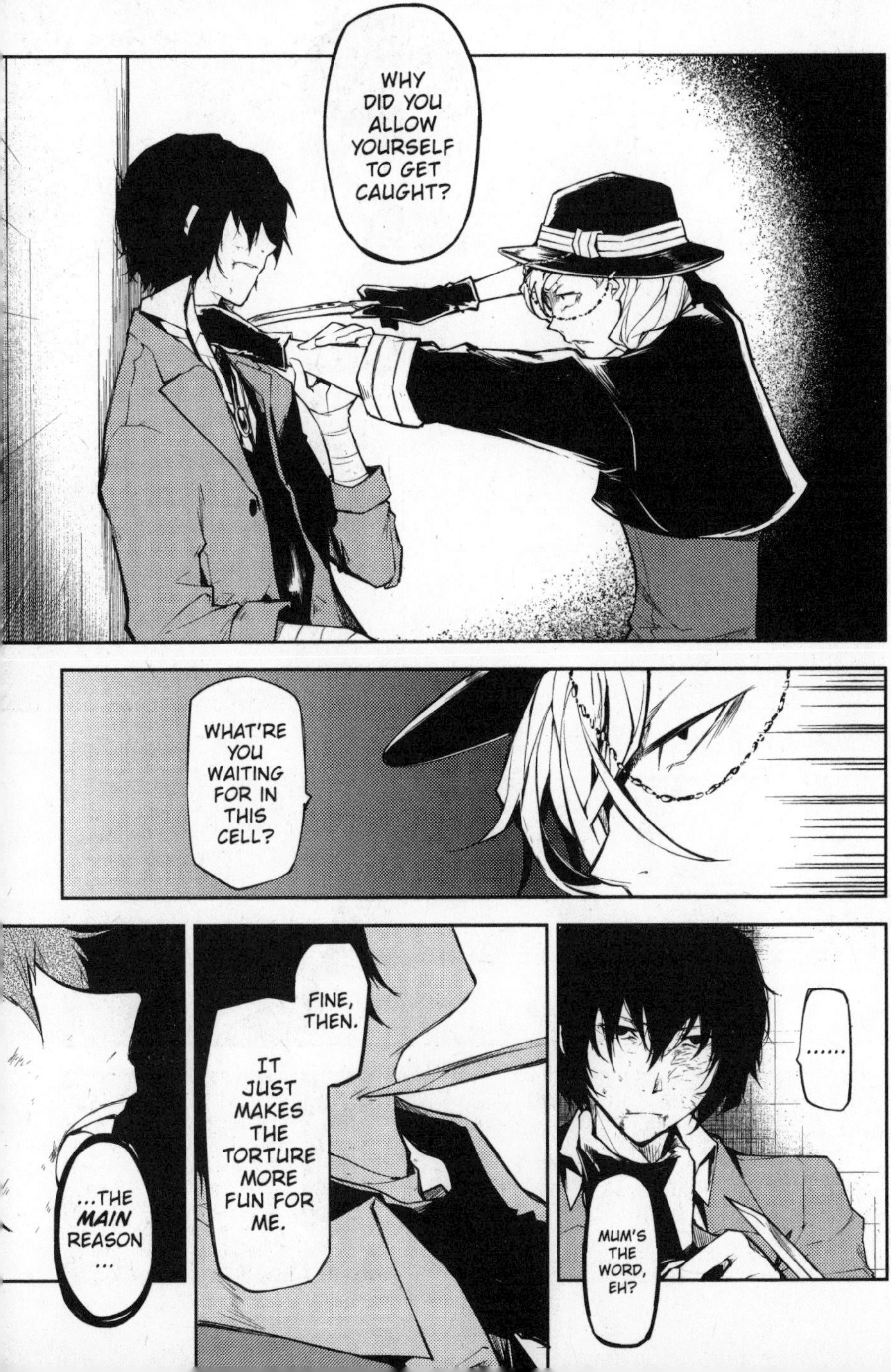
WHY DID YOU ALLOW YOURSELF TO GET CAUGHT?
WHAT'RE YOU WAITING FOR IN THIS CELL?
......
MUM'S THE WORD, EH?
FINE, THEN.
IT JUST MAKES THE TORTURE MORE FUN FOR ME.
...THE *MAIN* REASON ...

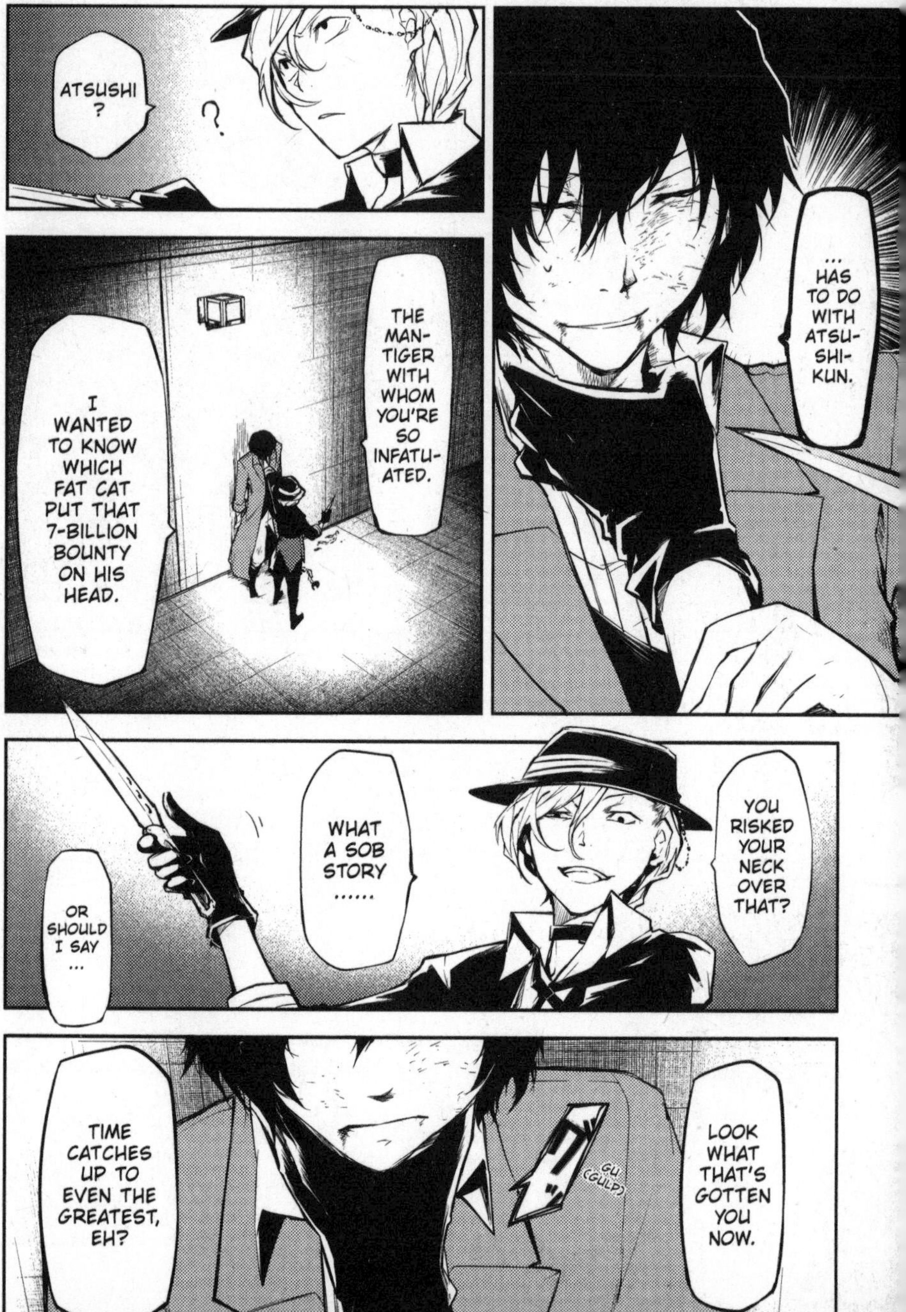
... HAS TO DO WITH ATSU-SHI-KUN.
ATSUSHI ?
?
THE MAN-TIGER WITH WHOM YOU'RE SO INFATUATED.
I WANTED TO KNOW WHICH FAT CAT PUT THAT 7-BILLION BOUNTY ON HIS HEAD.
YOU RISKED YOUR NECK OVER THAT?
WHAT A SOB STORY ......
OR SHOULD I SAY ...
LOOK WHAT THAT'S GOTTEN YOU NOW.
GU (GULP)
TIME CATCHES UP TO EVEN THE GREATEST, EH?

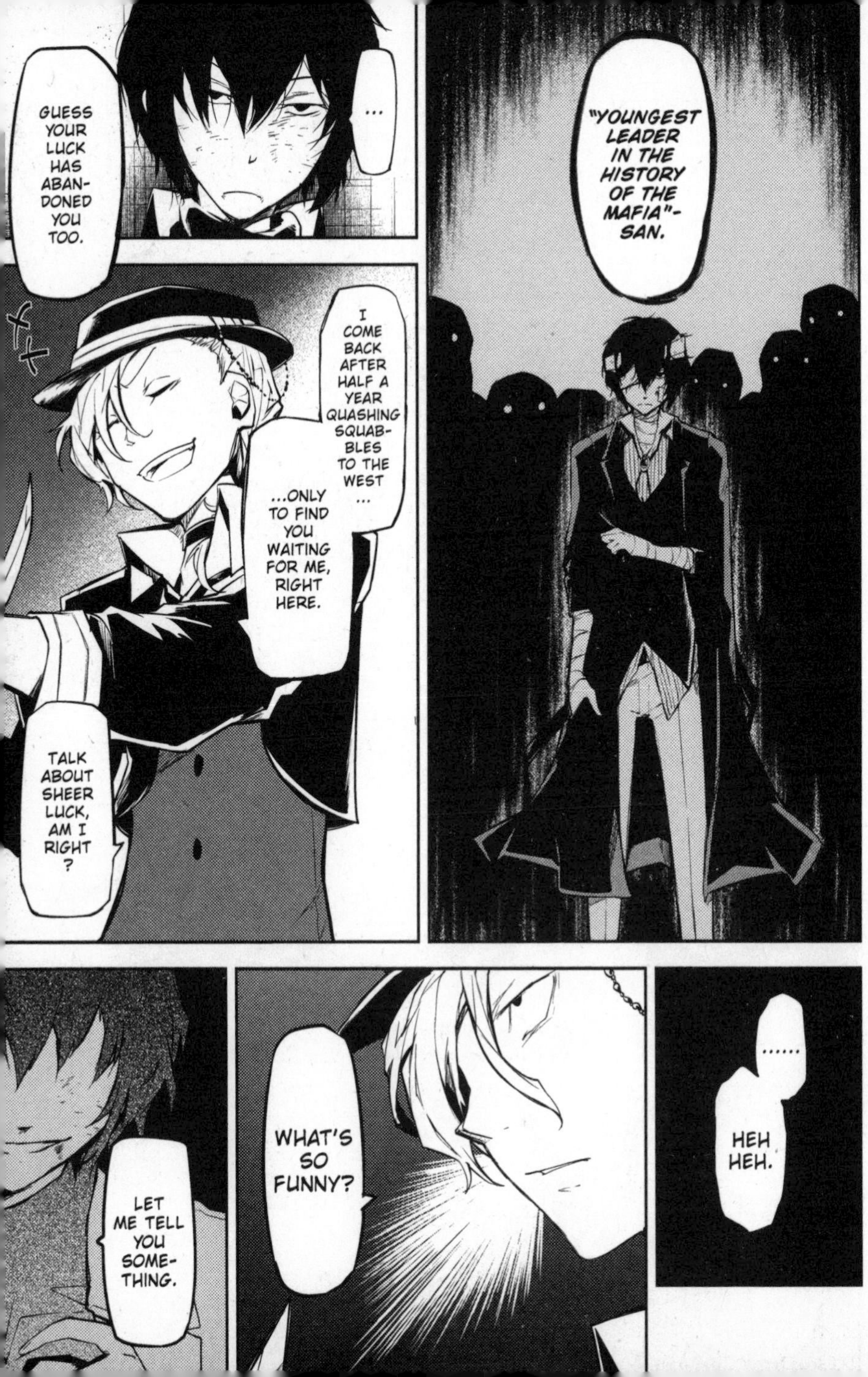
"YOUNGEST LEADER IN THE HISTORY OF THE MAFIA"-SAN.
...
GUESS YOUR LUCK HAS ABANDONED YOU TOO.
I COME BACK AFTER HALF A YEAR QUASHING SQUABBLES TO THE WEST...
...ONLY TO FIND YOU WAITING FOR ME, RIGHT HERE.
TALK ABOUT SHEER LUCK, AM I RIGHT?
......
HEH HEH.
WHAT'S SO FUNNY?
LET ME TELL YOU SOMETHING.

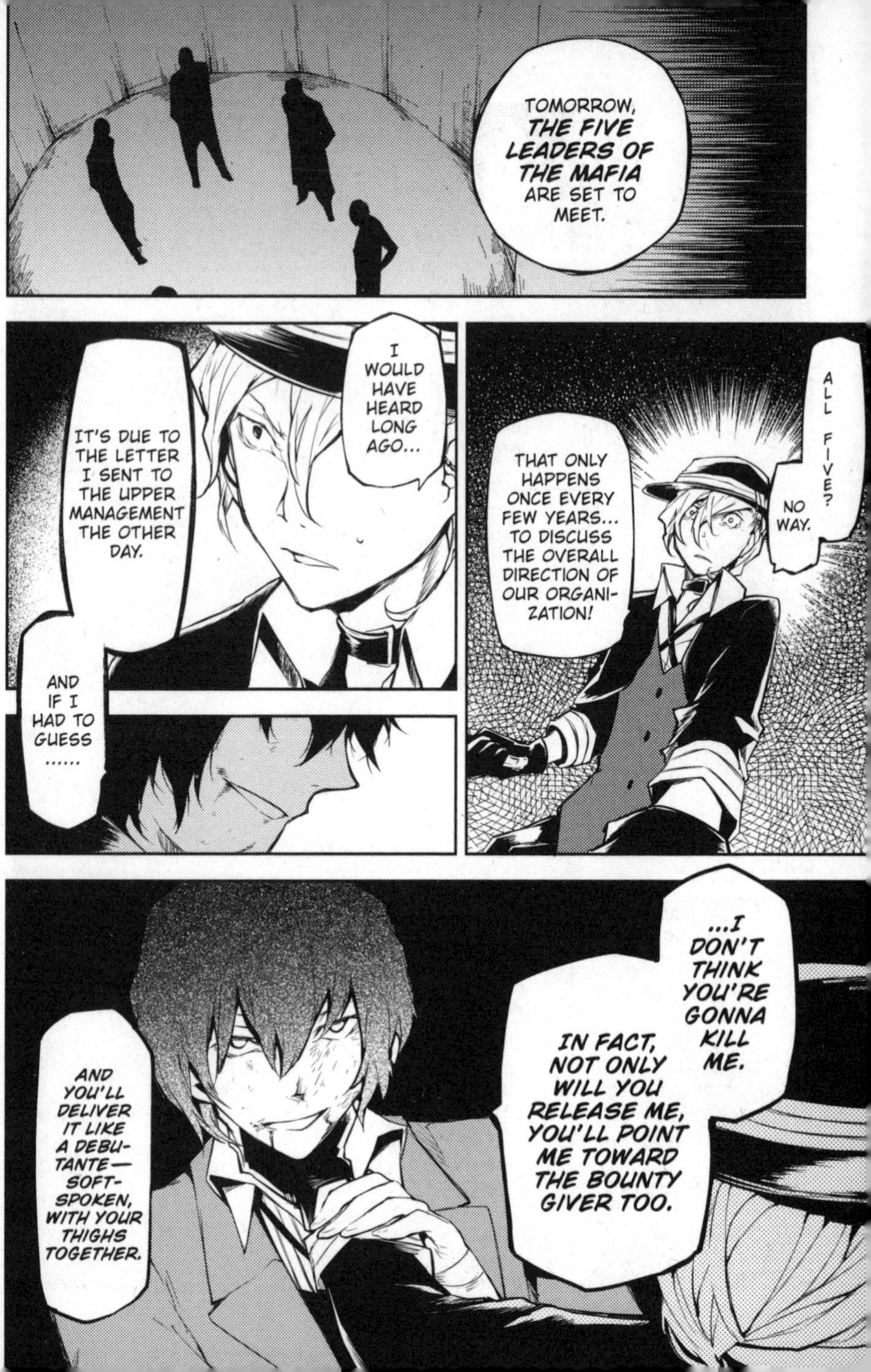
TOMORROW, THE FIVE LEADERS OF THE MAFIA ARE SET TO MEET.
ALL FIVE?
NO WAY.
THAT ONLY HAPPENS ONCE EVERY FEW YEARS... TO DISCUSS THE OVERALL DIRECTION OF OUR ORGANIZATION!
I WOULD HAVE HEARD LONG AGO...
IT'S DUE TO THE LETTER I SENT TO THE UPPER MANAGEMENT THE OTHER DAY.
AND IF I HAD TO GUESS ......
...I DON'T THINK YOU'RE GONNA KILL ME.
IN FACT, NOT ONLY WILL YOU RELEASE ME, YOU'LL POINT ME TOWARD THE BOUNTY GIVER TOO.
AND YOU'LL DELIVER IT LIKE A DEBUTANTE—SOFT-SPOKEN, WITH YOUR THIGHS TOGETHER.

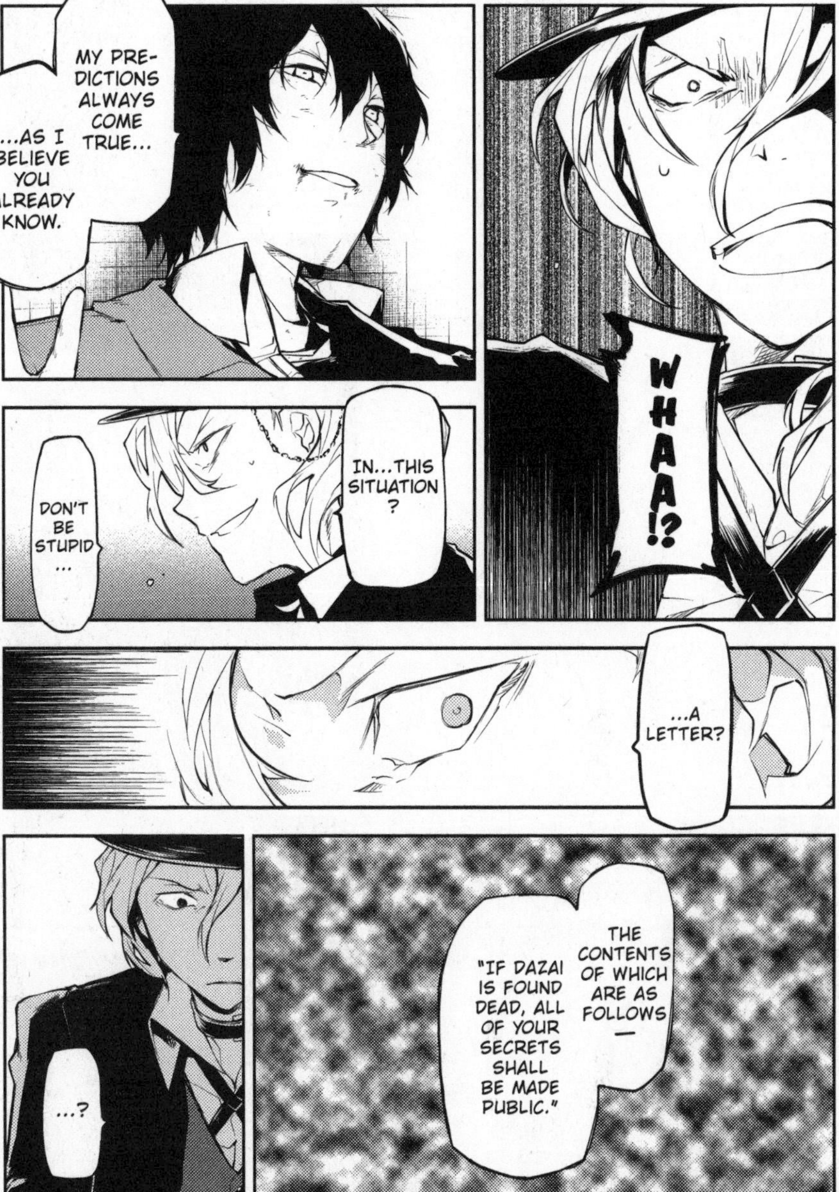
WHAA!?
MY PRE-DICTIONS ALWAYS COME TRUE...
...AS I BELIEVE YOU ALREADY KNOW.
IN...THIS SITUATION?
DON'T BE STUPID...
...A LETTER?
THE CONTENTS OF WHICH ARE AS FOLLOWS—
"IF DAZAI IS FOUND DEAD, ALL OF YOUR SECRETS SHALL BE MADE PUBLIC."
...?

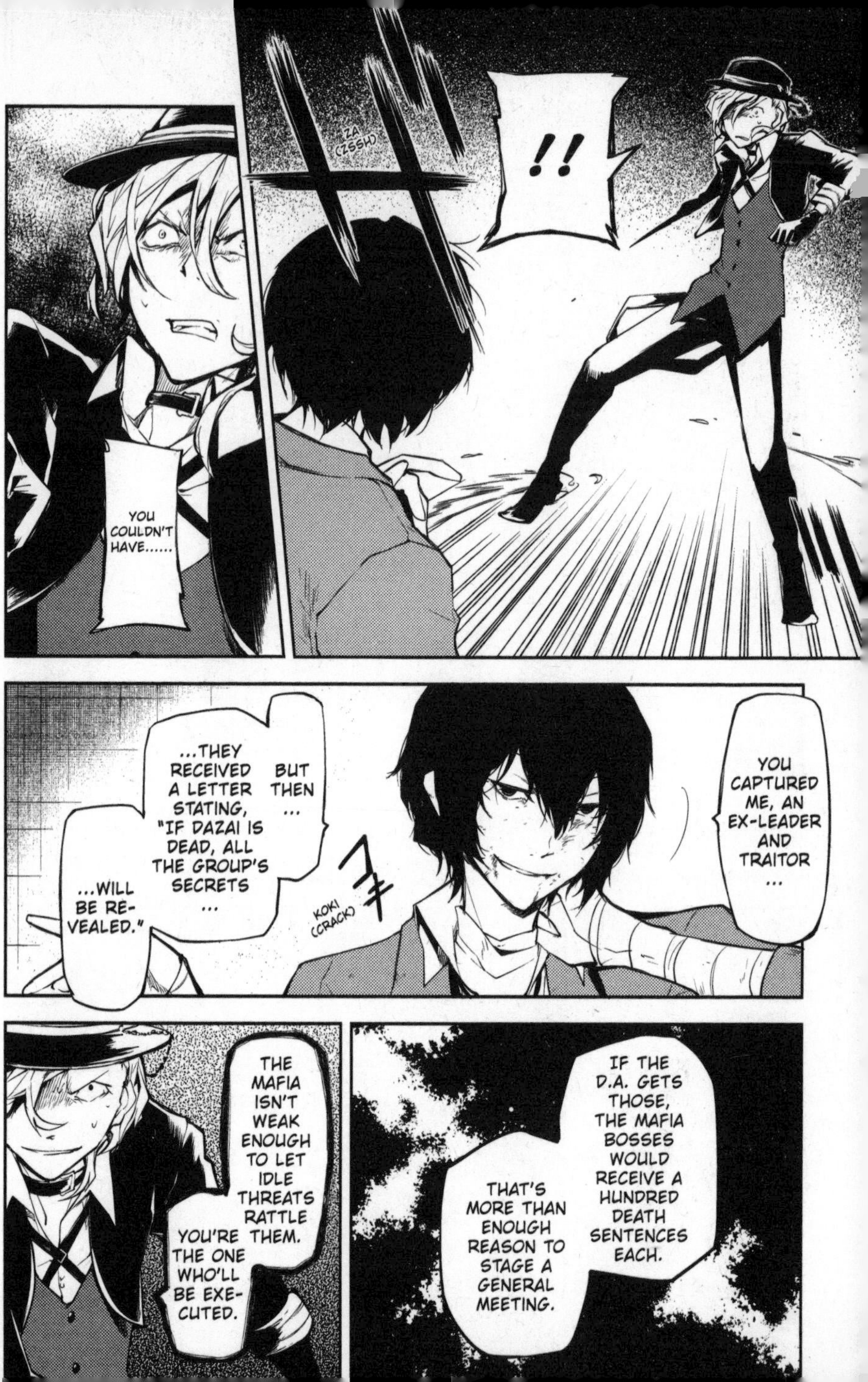
ZA (ZSSH)
!!
YOU COULDN'T HAVE......
YOU CAPTURED ME, AN EX-LEADER AND TRAITOR ...
KOKI (CRACK)
BUT THEN ...
...THEY RECEIVED A LETTER STATING, "IF DAZAI IS DEAD, ALL THE GROUP'S SECRETS ...
...WILL BE RE-VEALED."
IF THE D.A. GETS THOSE, THE MAFIA BOSSES WOULD RECEIVE A HUNDRED DEATH SENTENCES EACH.
THAT'S MORE THAN ENOUGH REASON TO STAGE A GENERAL MEETING.
THE MAFIA ISN'T WEAK ENOUGH TO LET IDLE THREATS RATTLE THEM.
YOU'RE THE ONE WHO'LL BE EXE-CUTED.

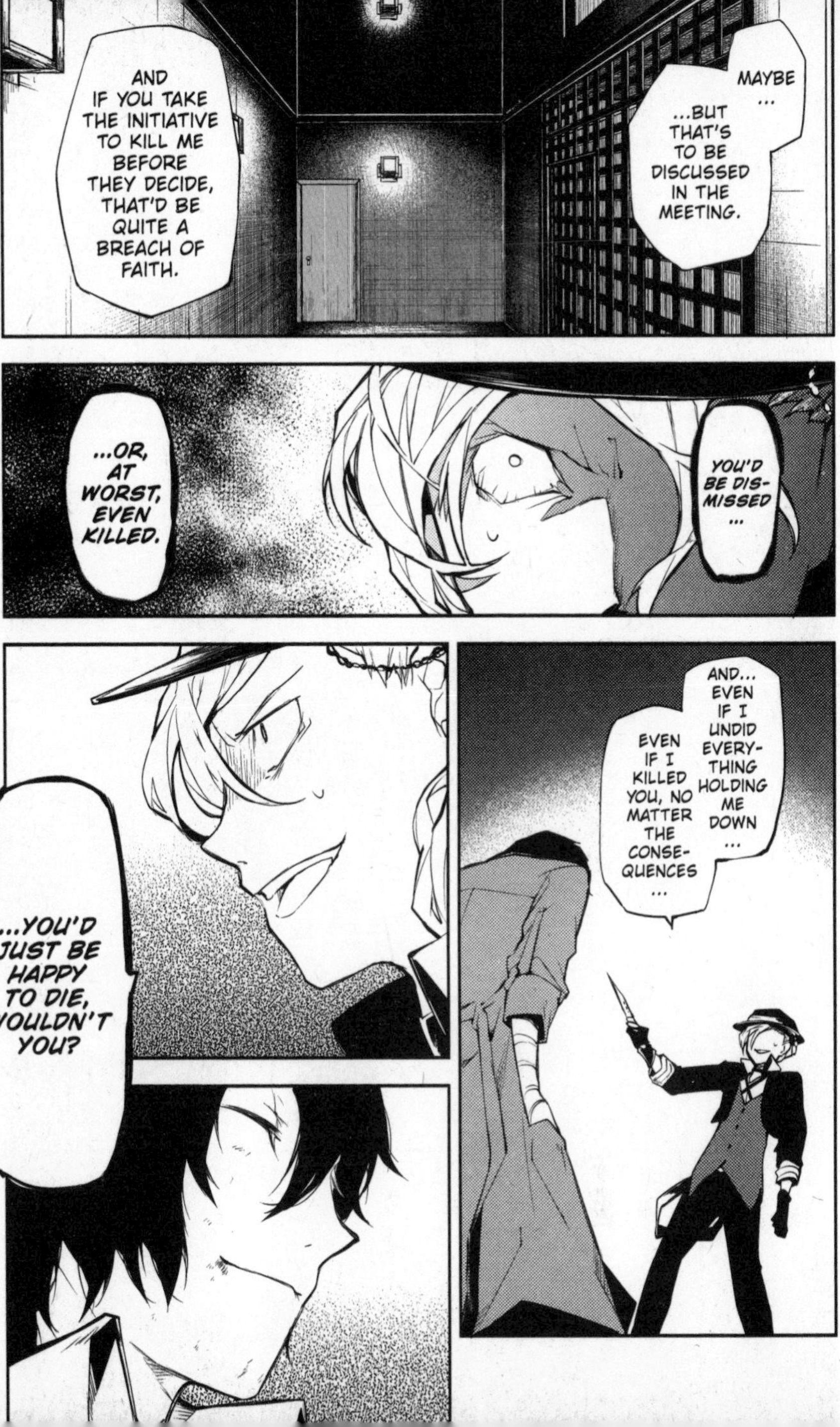
MAYBE ...BUT THAT'S TO BE DISCUSSED IN THE MEETING.
AND IF YOU TAKE THE INITIATIVE TO KILL ME BEFORE THEY DECIDE, THAT'D BE QUITE A BREACH OF FAITH.
YOU'D BE DIS-MISSED ...
...OR, AT WORST, EVEN KILLED.
AND... EVEN IF I UNDID EVERY-THING HOLDING ME DOWN ...
EVEN IF I KILLED YOU, NO MATTER THE CONSE-QUENCES ...
...YOU'D JUST BE HAPPY TO DIE, WOULDN'T YOU?

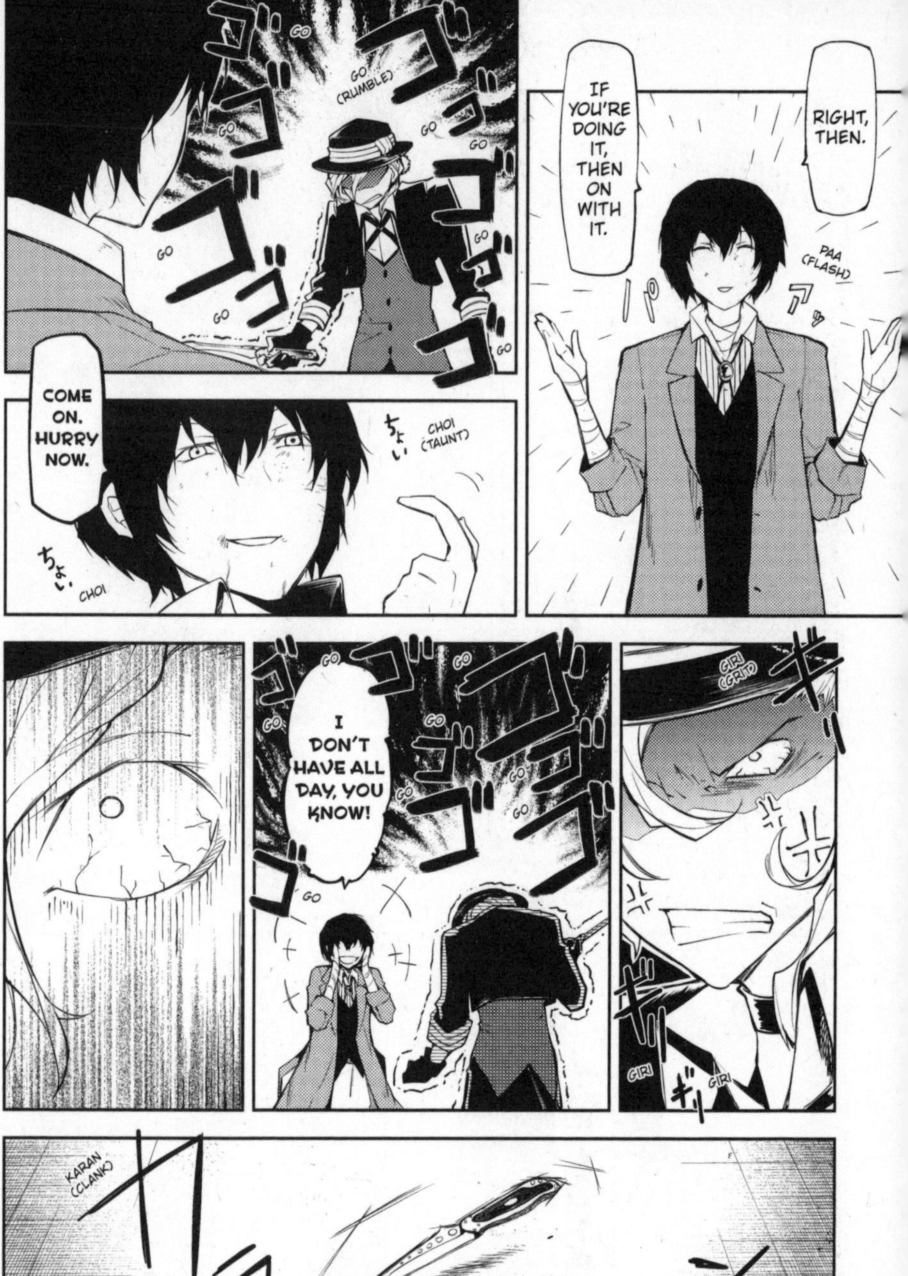
RIGHT, THEN.
IF YOU'RE DOING IT, THEN ON WITH IT.
PAA (FLASH)
GO (RUMBLE)
GO
GO
GO
GO
GO
GO
GO
ちょい
CHOI (TAUNT)
COME ON. HURRY NOW.
ちょい
CHOI
GIRI (GRIT)
GIRI
GIRI
GO
GO
GO
GO
GO
GO
I DON'T HAVE ALL DAY, YOU KNOW!
GO
KARAN (CLANK)

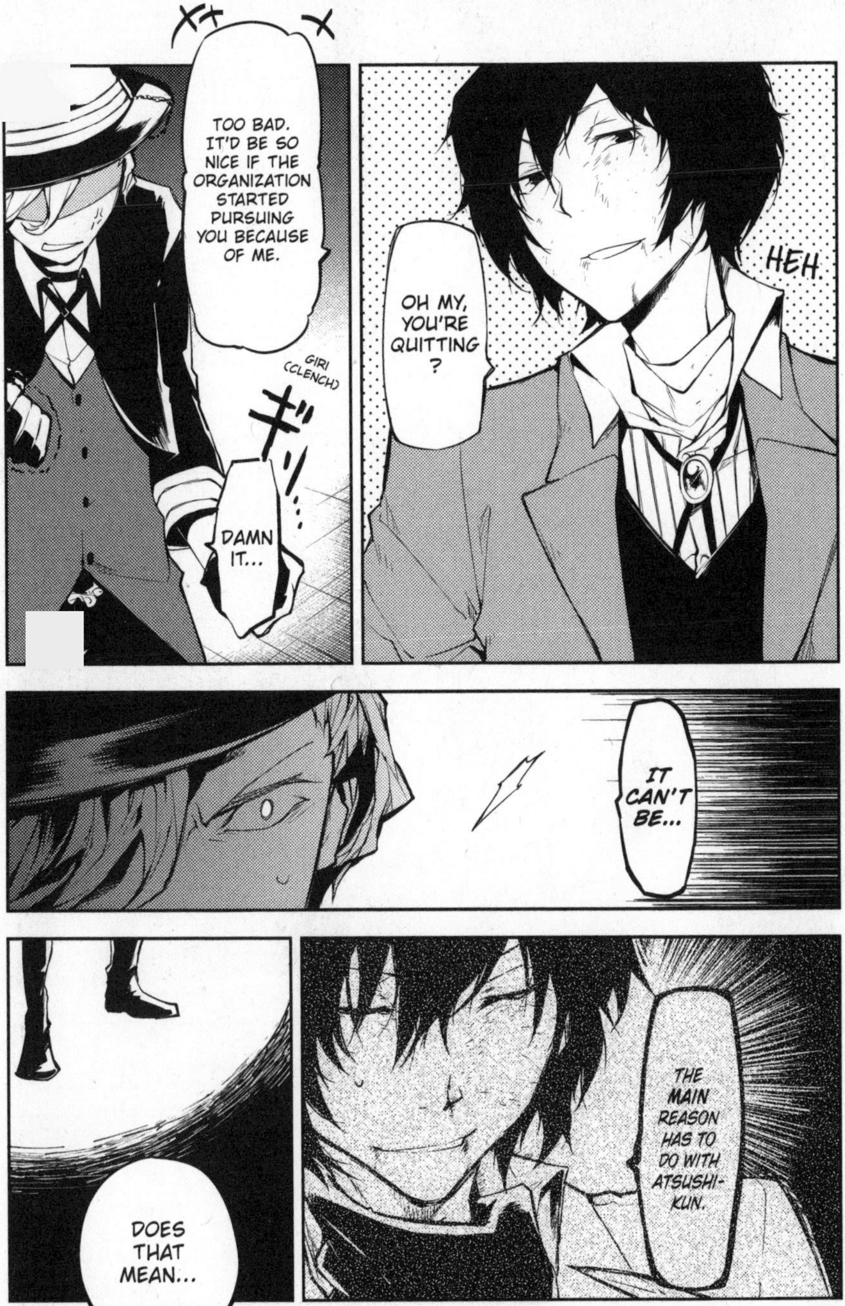

HEH.
OH MY, YOU'RE QUITTING?
TOO BAD. IT'D BE SO NICE IF THE ORGANIZATION STARTED PURSUING YOU BECAUSE OF ME.
GIRI (CLENCH)
DAMN IT...
IT CAN'T BE...
THE MAIN REASON HAS TO DO WITH ATSUSHI-KUN.
DOES THAT MEAN...

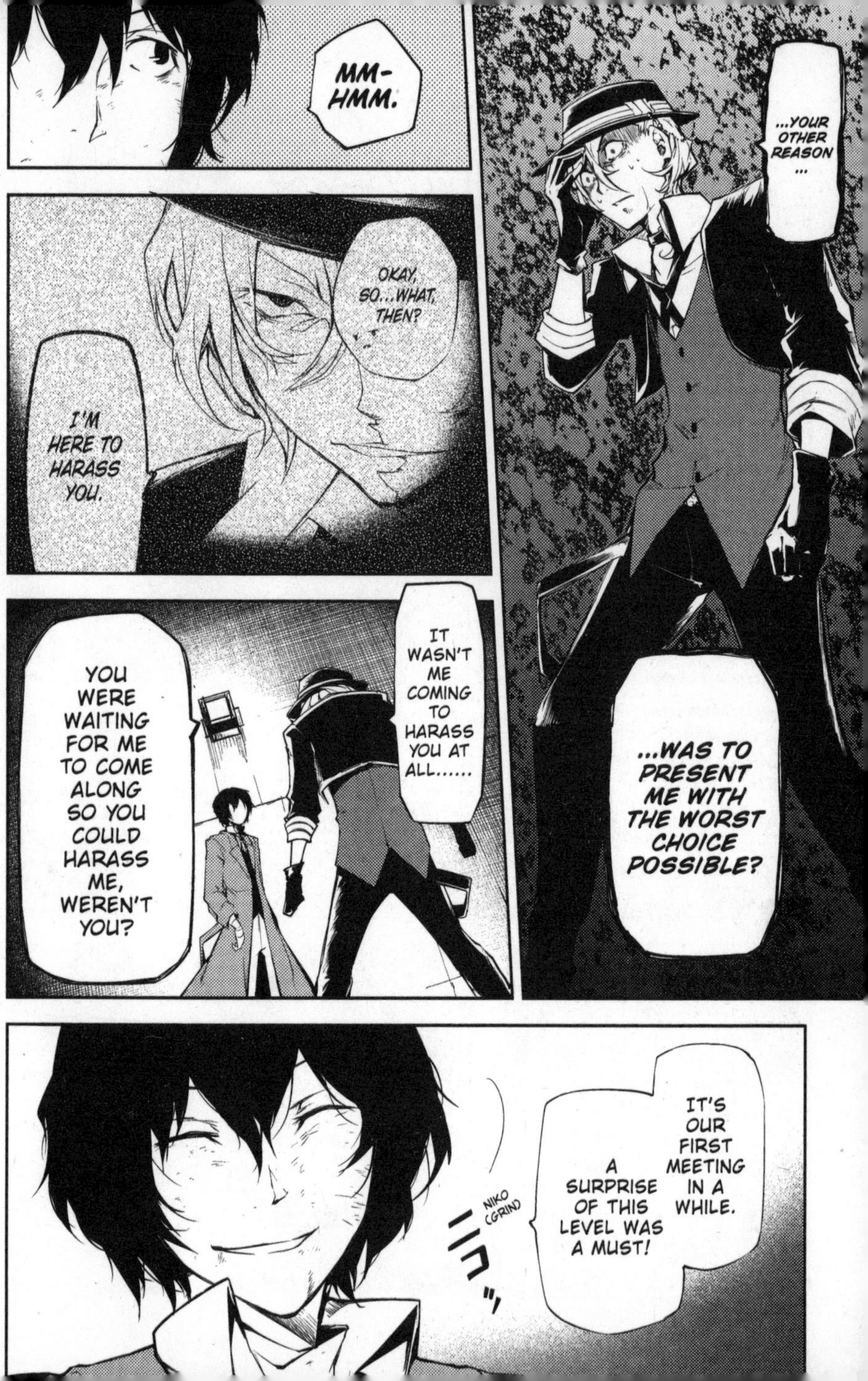
...YOUR OTHER REASON ...
...WAS TO PRESENT ME WITH THE WORST CHOICE POSSIBLE?
MM-HMM.
OKAY, SO...WHAT, THEN?
I'M HERE TO HARASS YOU.
IT WASN'T ME COMING TO HARASS YOU AT ALL......
YOU WERE WAITING FOR ME TO COME ALONG SO YOU COULD HARASS ME, WEREN'T YOU?
IT'S OUR FIRST MEETING IN A WHILE.
A SURPRISE OF THIS LEVEL WAS A MUST!
NIKO (GRIN)

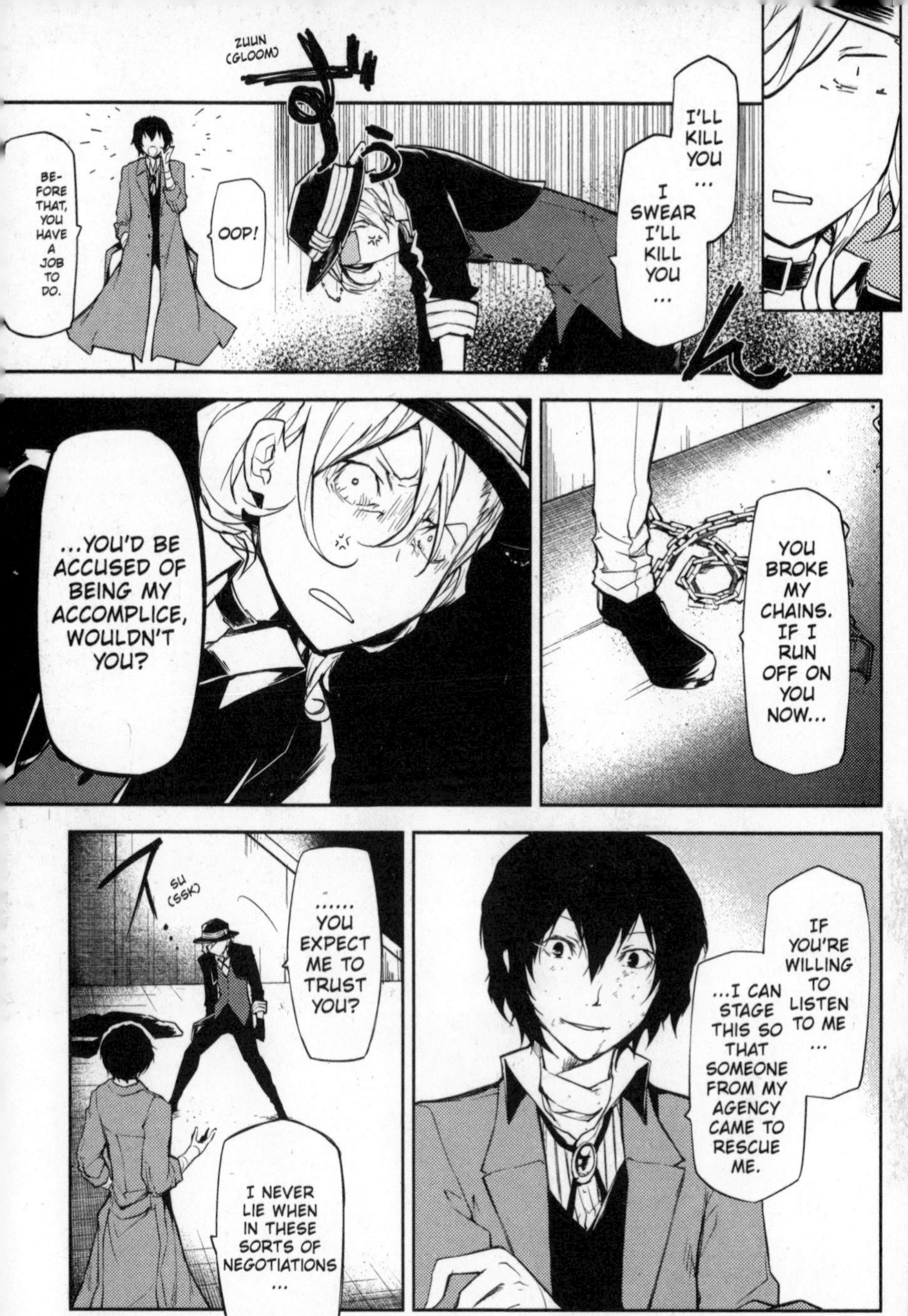
I'LL KILL YOU ... I SWEAR I'LL KILL YOU ...
ZUUN (GLOOM)
OOP!
BE-FORE THAT, YOU HAVE A JOB TO DO.
YOU BROKE MY CHAINS. IF I RUN OFF ON YOU NOW...
...YOU'D BE ACCUSED OF BEING MY ACCOMPLICE, WOULDN'T YOU?
IF YOU'RE WILLING TO LISTEN TO ME ...
...I CAN STAGE THIS SO THAT SOMEONE FROM MY AGENCY CAME TO RESCUE ME.
...... YOU EXPECT ME TO TRUST YOU?
SU (SSK)
I NEVER LIE WHEN IN THESE SORTS OF NEGOTIATIONS ...

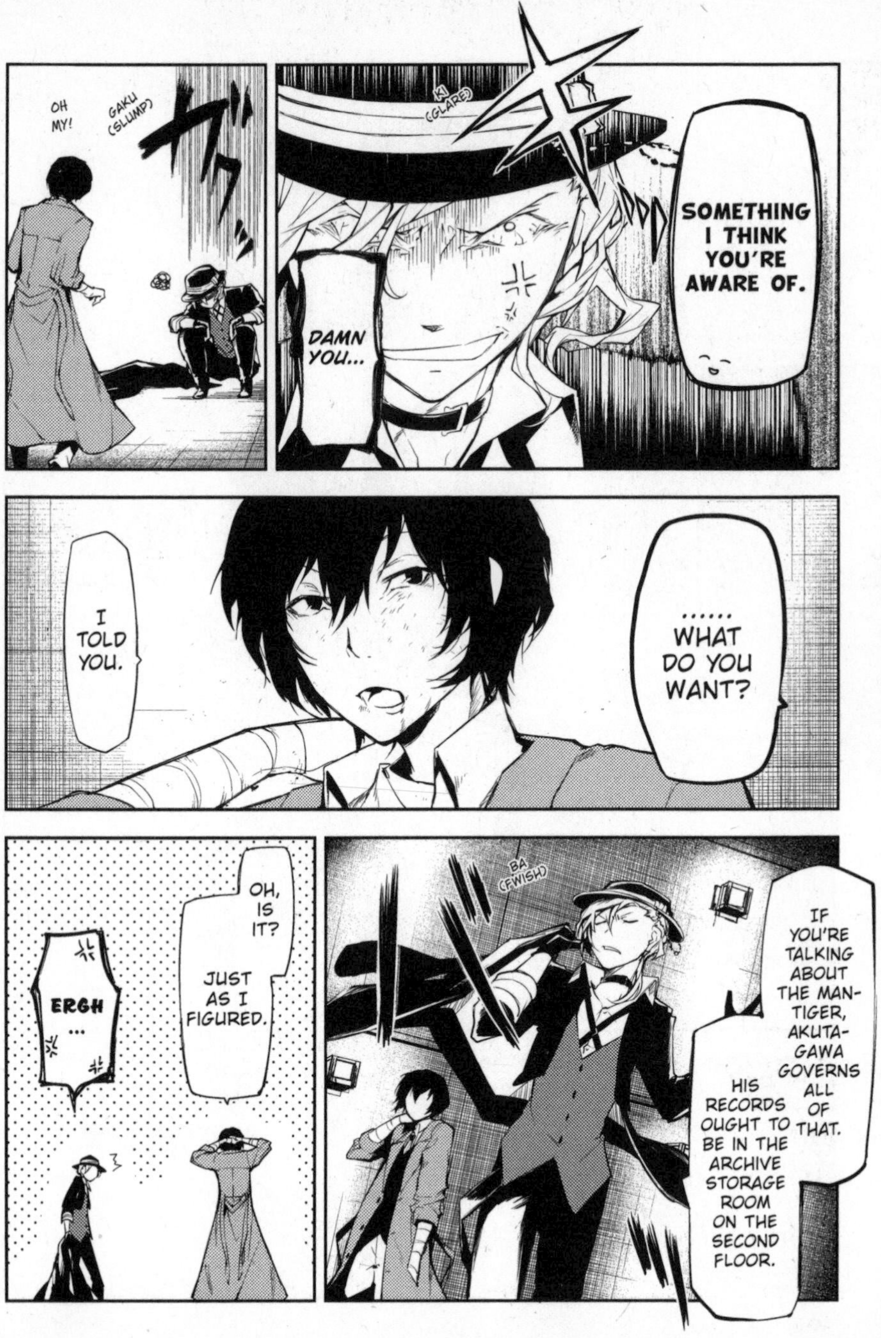
KI (GLARE)
SOMETHING I THINK YOU'RE AWARE OF.
DAMN YOU...
GAKU (SLUMP)
OH MY!
...... WHAT DO YOU WANT?
I TOLD YOU.
BA (FWISH)
IF YOU'RE TALKING ABOUT THE MAN-TIGER, AKUTAGAWA GOVERNS ALL OF THAT.
HIS RECORDS OUGHT TO BE IN THE ARCHIVE STORAGE ROOM ON THE SECOND FLOOR.
OH, IS IT?
JUST AS I FIGURED.
ERGH ...

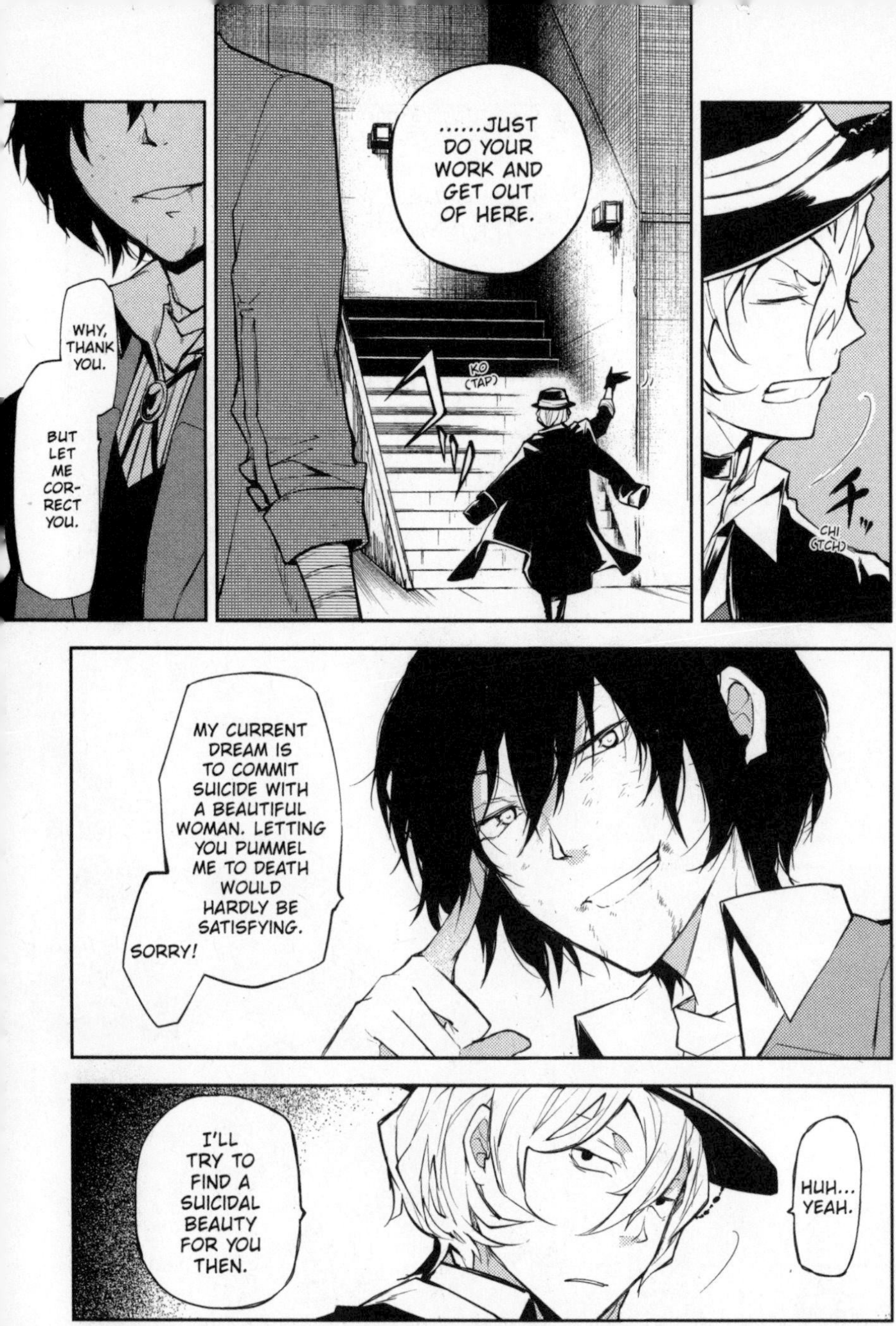
チッ
CHI (TCH)
......JUST DO YOUR WORK AND GET OUT OF HERE.
KO (TAP)
WHY, THANK YOU.
BUT LET ME CORRECT YOU.
MY CURRENT DREAM IS TO COMMIT SUICIDE WITH A BEAUTIFUL WOMAN. LETTING YOU PUMMEL ME TO DEATH WOULD HARDLY BE SATISFYING.
SORRY!
HUH... YEAH.
I'LL TRY TO FIND A SUICIDAL BEAUTY FOR YOU THEN.

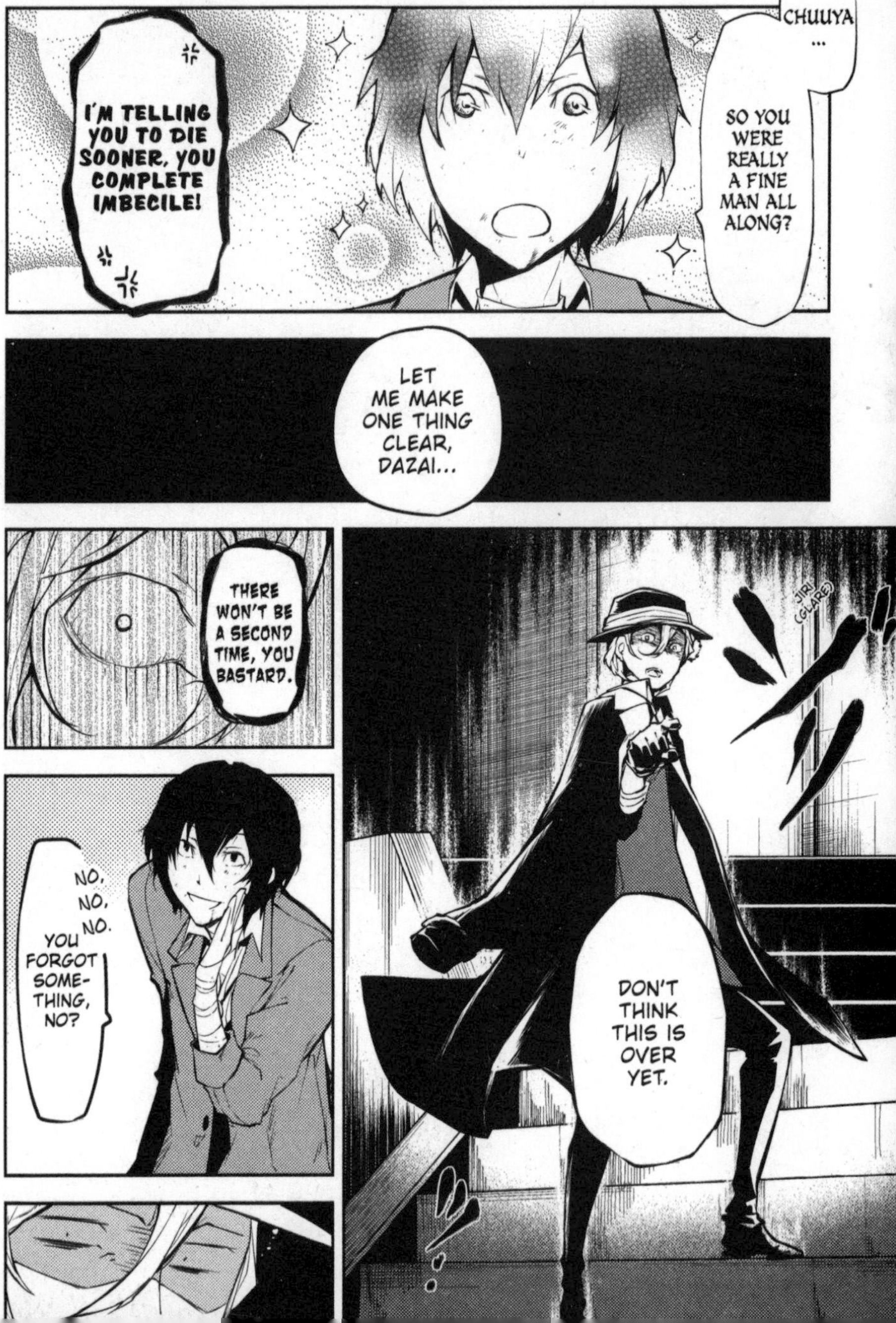
CHUUYA ...
SO YOU WERE REALLY A FINE MAN ALL ALONG?
I'M TELLING YOU TO DIE SOONER, YOU COMPLETE IMBECILE!
LET ME MAKE ONE THING CLEAR, DAZAI...
JIRI (GLARE)
DON'T THINK THIS IS OVER YET.
THERE WON'T BE A SECOND TIME, YOU BASTARD.
NO, NO, NO. YOU FORGOT SOME-THING, NO?

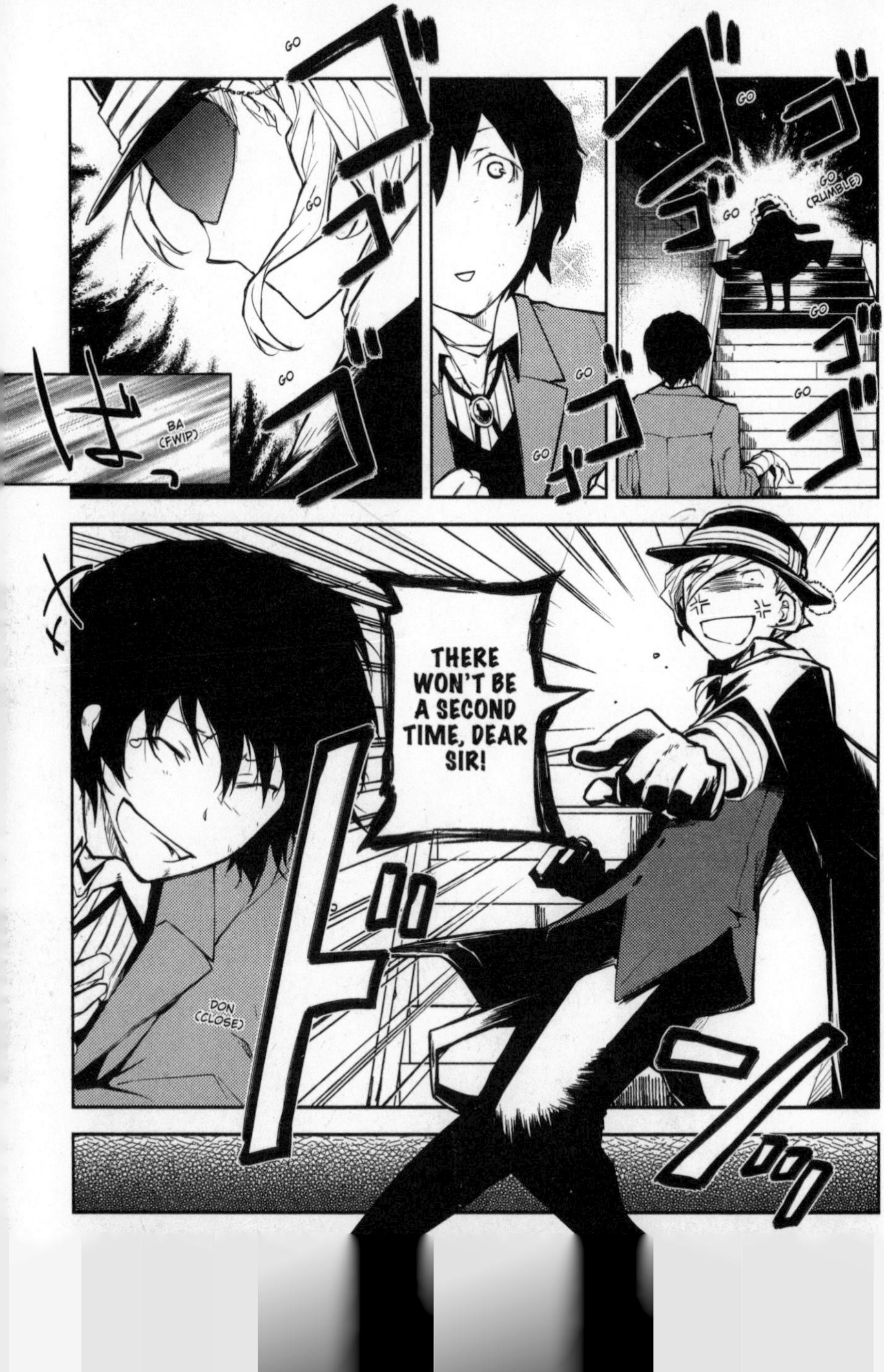
GO
GO (RUMBLE)
GO
GO
GO
GO
GO
GO
GO
GO
BA (FWIP)
THERE WON'T BE A SECOND TIME, DEAR SIR!
DON (CLOSE)

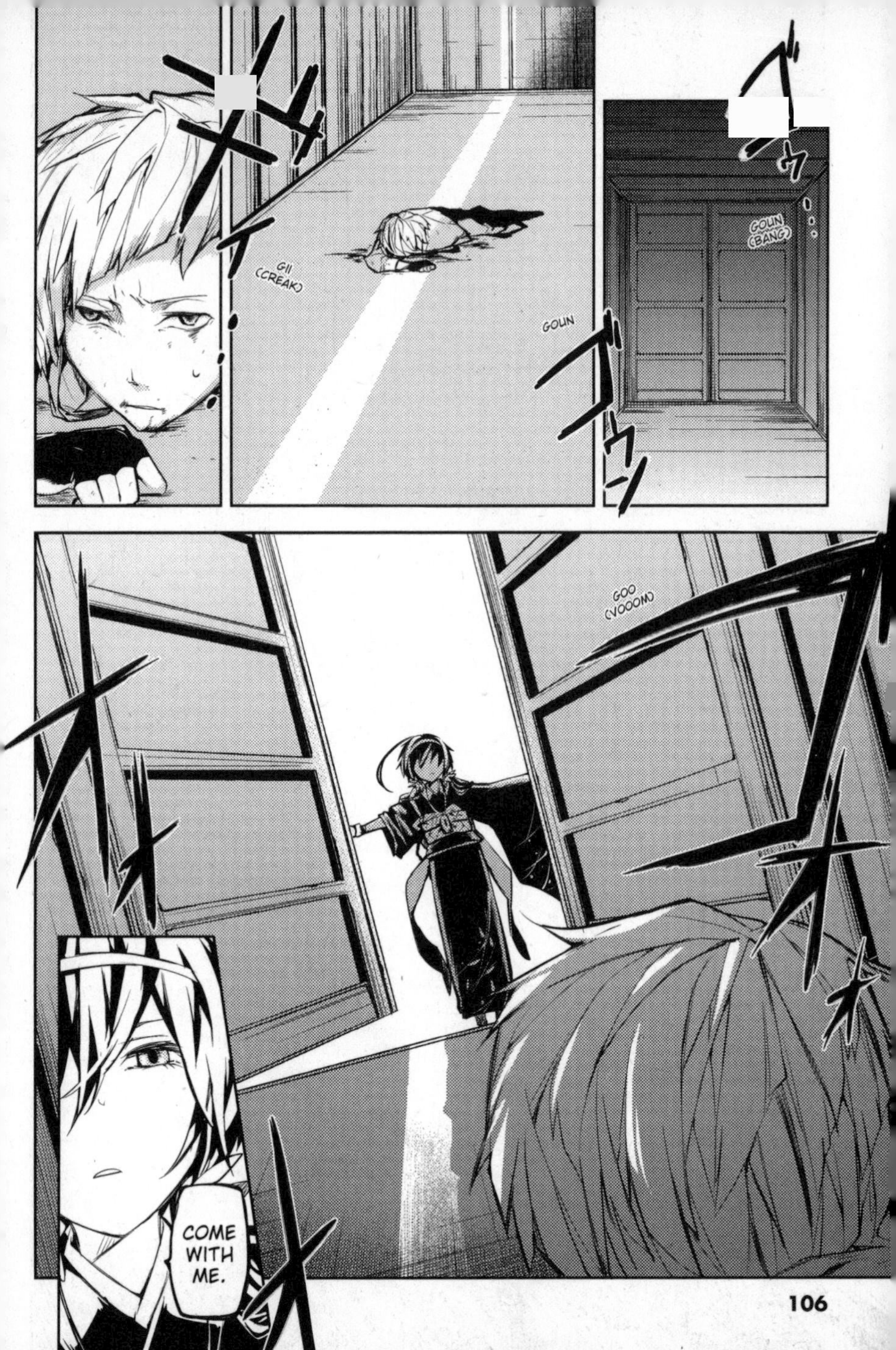
GOUN (BANG)
GOUN
GII (CREAK)
GOO (VOOOM)
COME WITH ME.

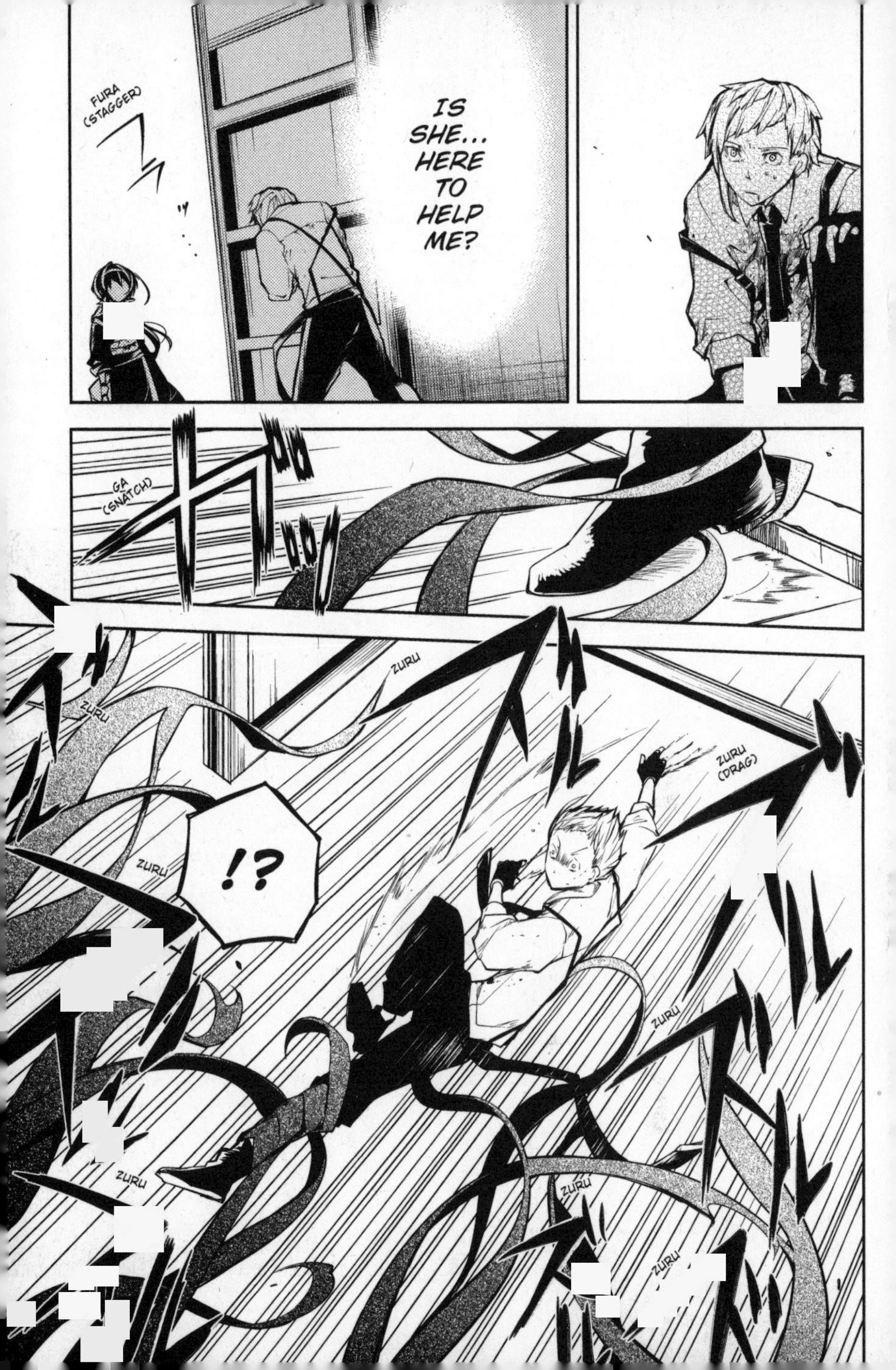
IS SHE... HERE TO HELP ME?
FURA (STAGGER)
GA (SNATCH)
ZURU (DRAG)
ZURU
ZURU
!?
ZURU
ZURU
ZURU
ZURU
ZURU

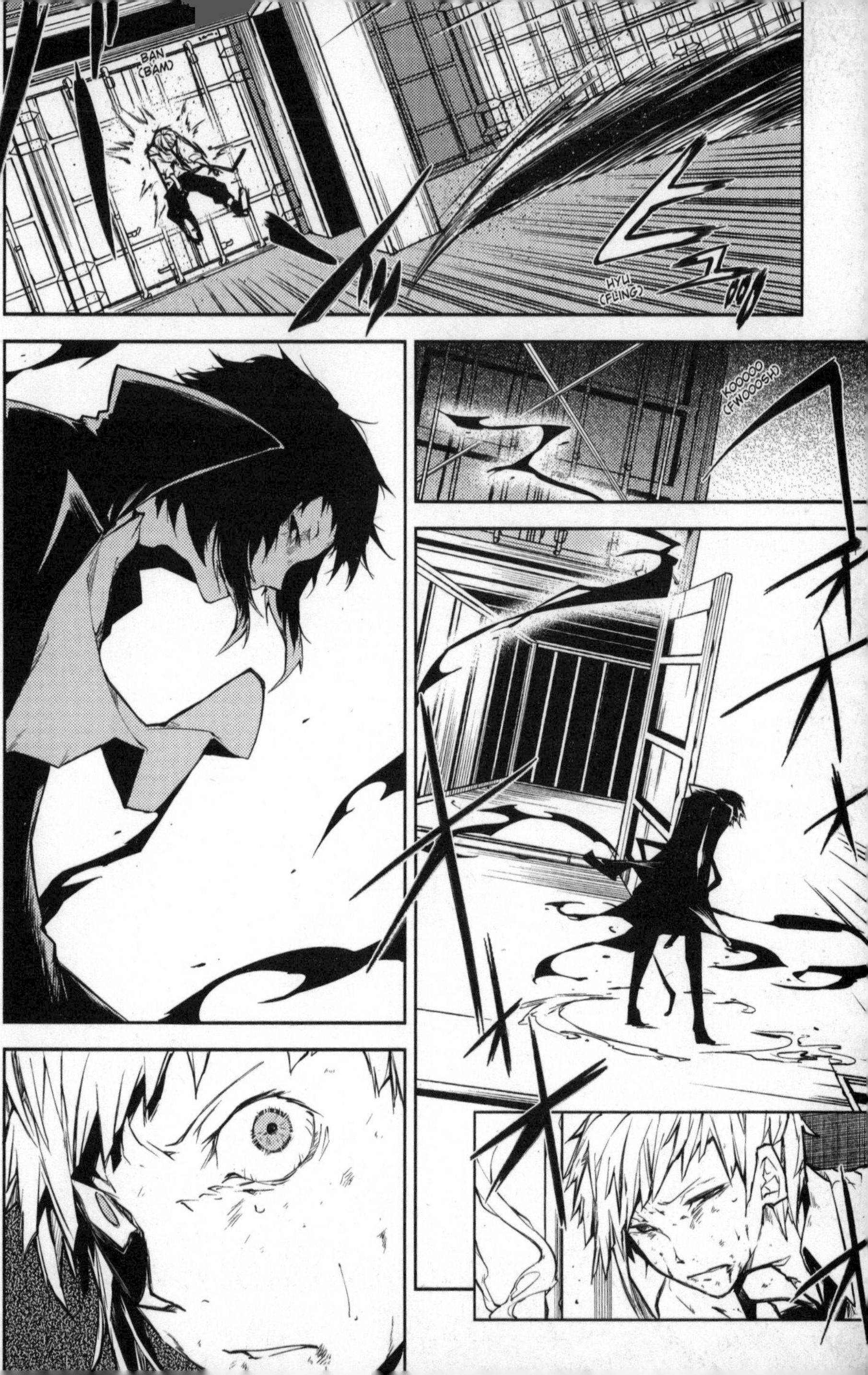
BAN
(BAM)
HYU
(FLING)
KOOOOO
(FWOOOSH)

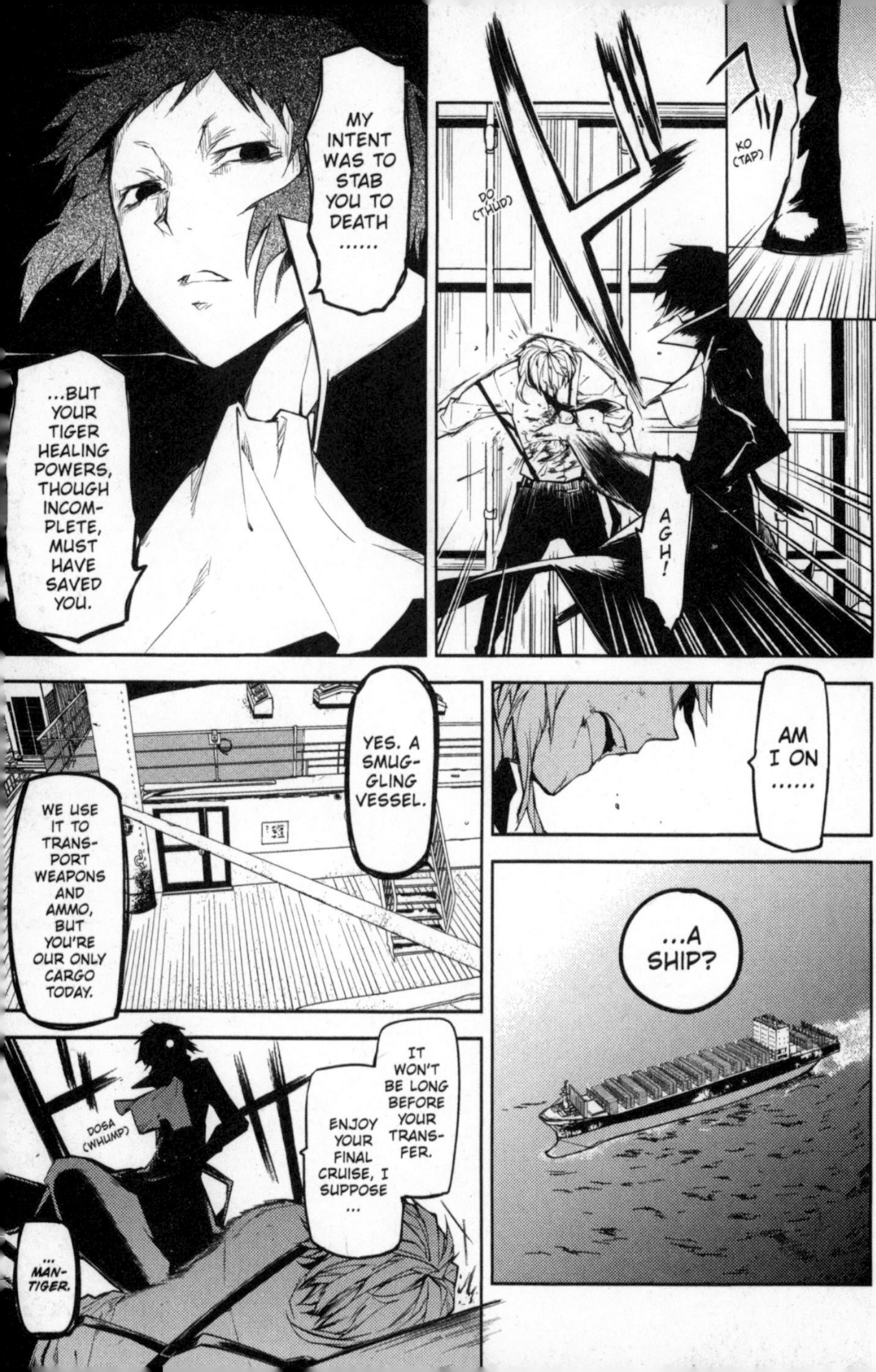
KO (TAP)
DO (THUD)
AGH!
MY INTENT WAS TO STAB YOU TO DEATH ......
...BUT YOUR TIGER HEALING POWERS, THOUGH INCOMPLETE, MUST HAVE SAVED YOU.
AM I ON ......
...A SHIP?
YES. A SMUGGLING VESSEL.
WE USE IT TO TRANSPORT WEAPONS AND AMMO, BUT YOU'RE OUR ONLY CARGO TODAY.
IT WON'T BE LONG BEFORE YOUR TRANSFER.
ENJOY YOUR FINAL CRUISE, I SUPPOSE ...
DOSA (WHUMP)
...MAN-TIGER.

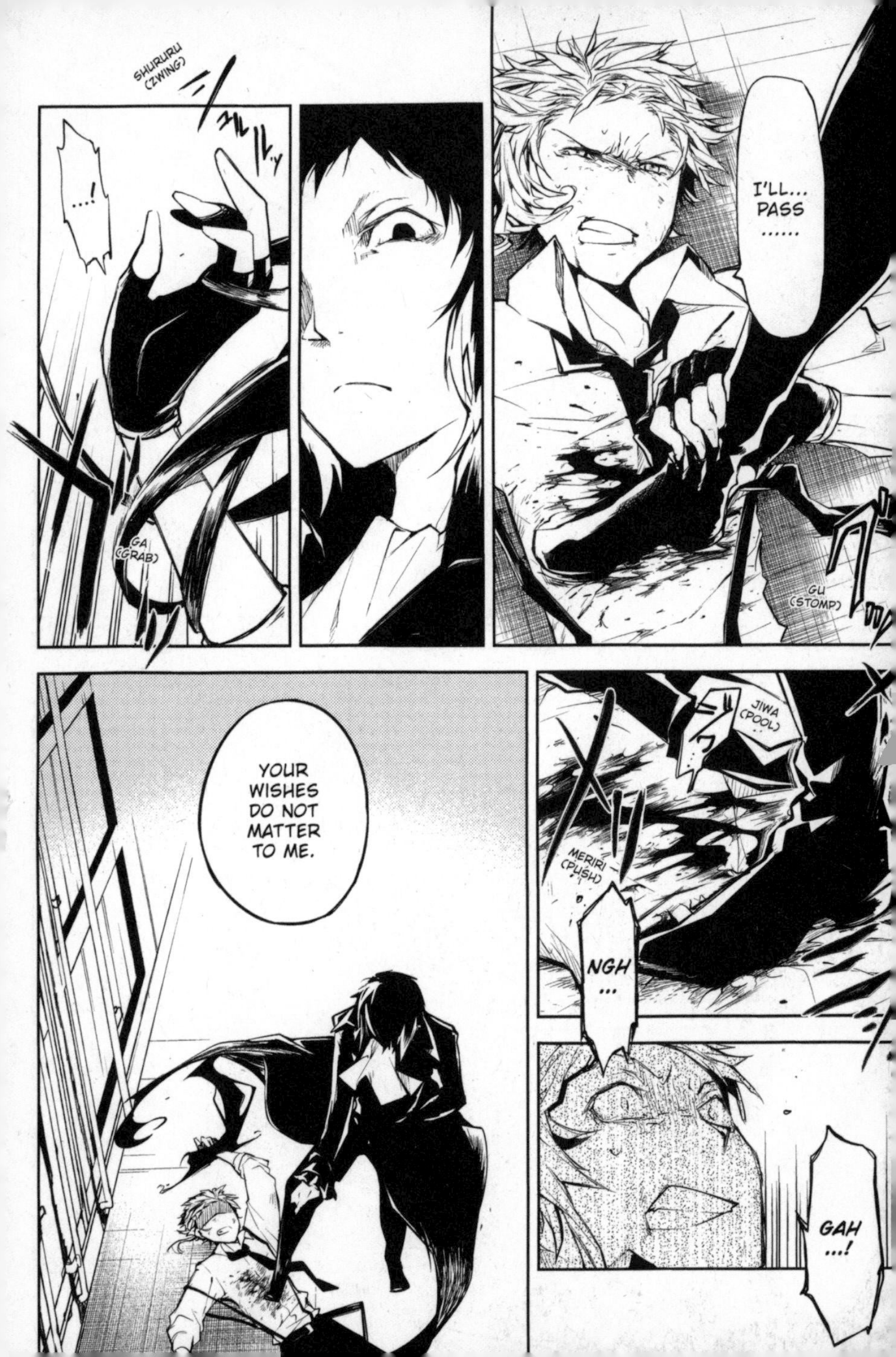
I'LL... PASS ......
GU (STOMP)
SHURURU (ZWING)
...!
GA (GRAB)
JIWA (POOL)
MERIRI (PUSH)
NGH ...
GAH ...!
YOUR WISHES DO NOT MATTER TO ME.

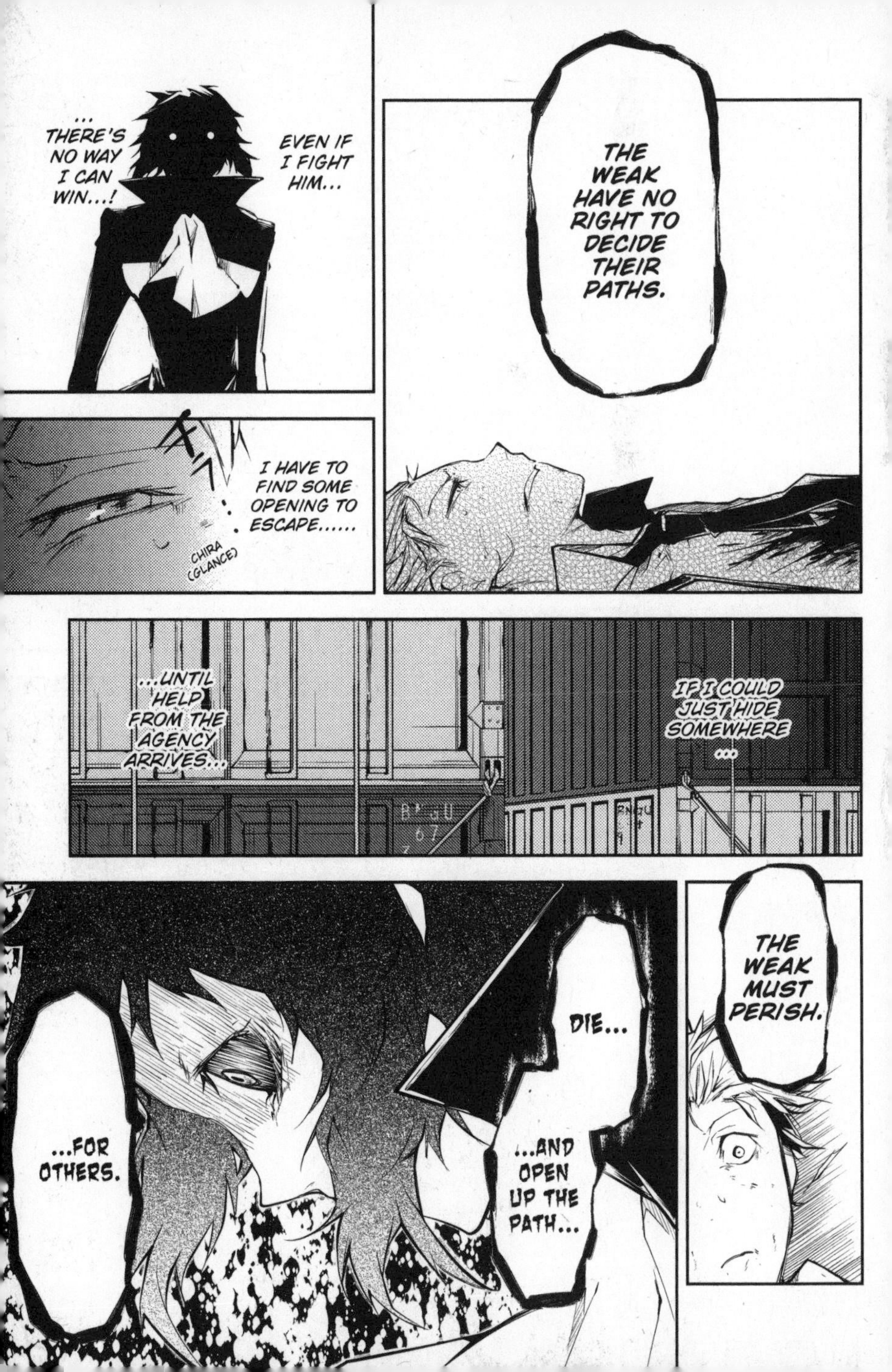
THE WEAK HAVE NO RIGHT TO DECIDE THEIR PATHS.
EVEN IF I FIGHT HIM...
...THERE'S NO WAY I CAN WIN...!
I HAVE TO FIND SOME OPENING TO ESCAPE......
CHIRA (GLANCE)
IF I COULD JUST HIDE SOMEWHERE...
...UNTIL HELP FROM THE AGENCY ARRIVES...
THE WEAK MUST PERISH.
DIE...
...AND OPEN UP THE PATH...
...FOR OTHERS.

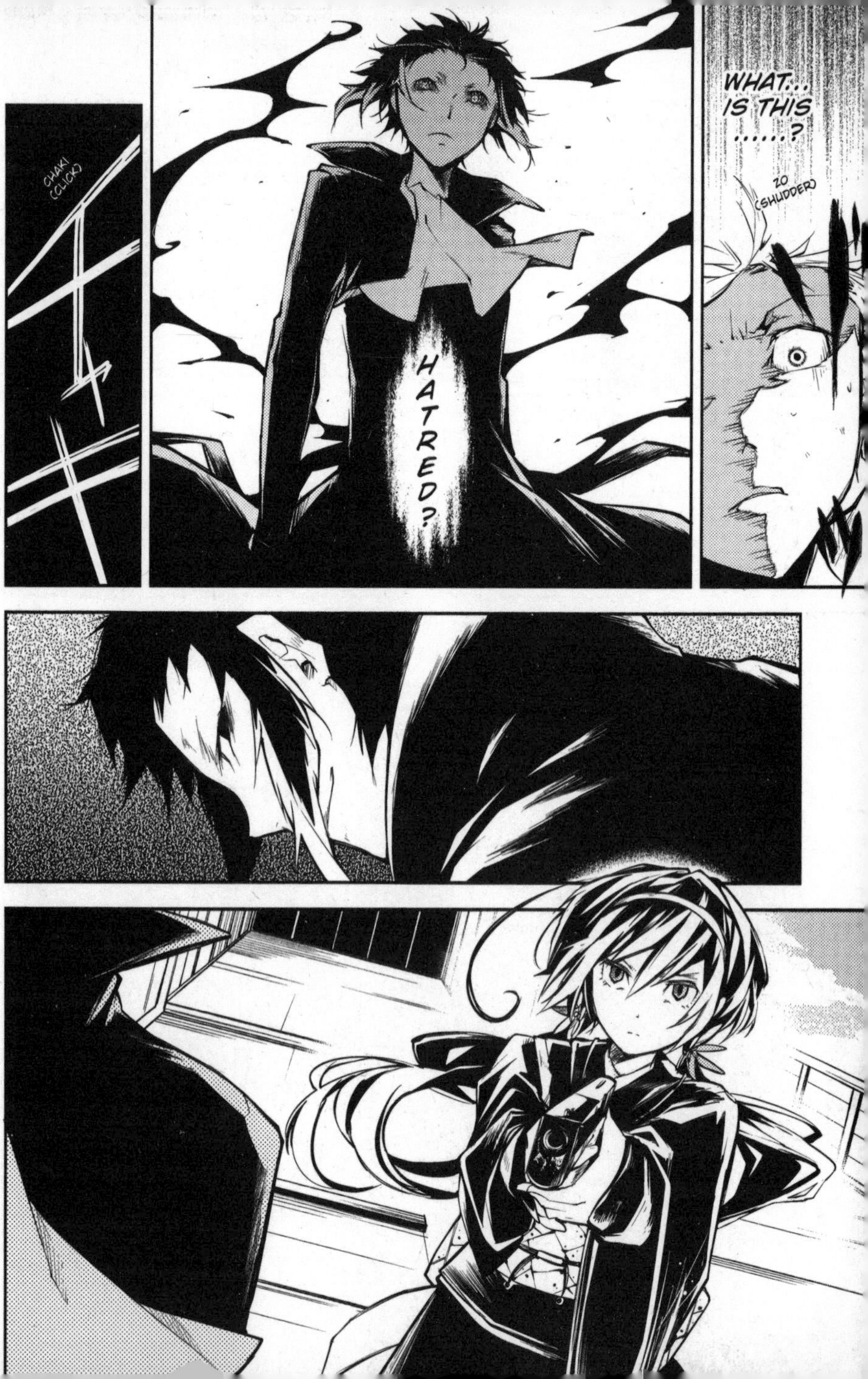
WHAT... IS THIS ......?
ZO (SHUDDER)
HATRED?
CHAKI (CLICK)

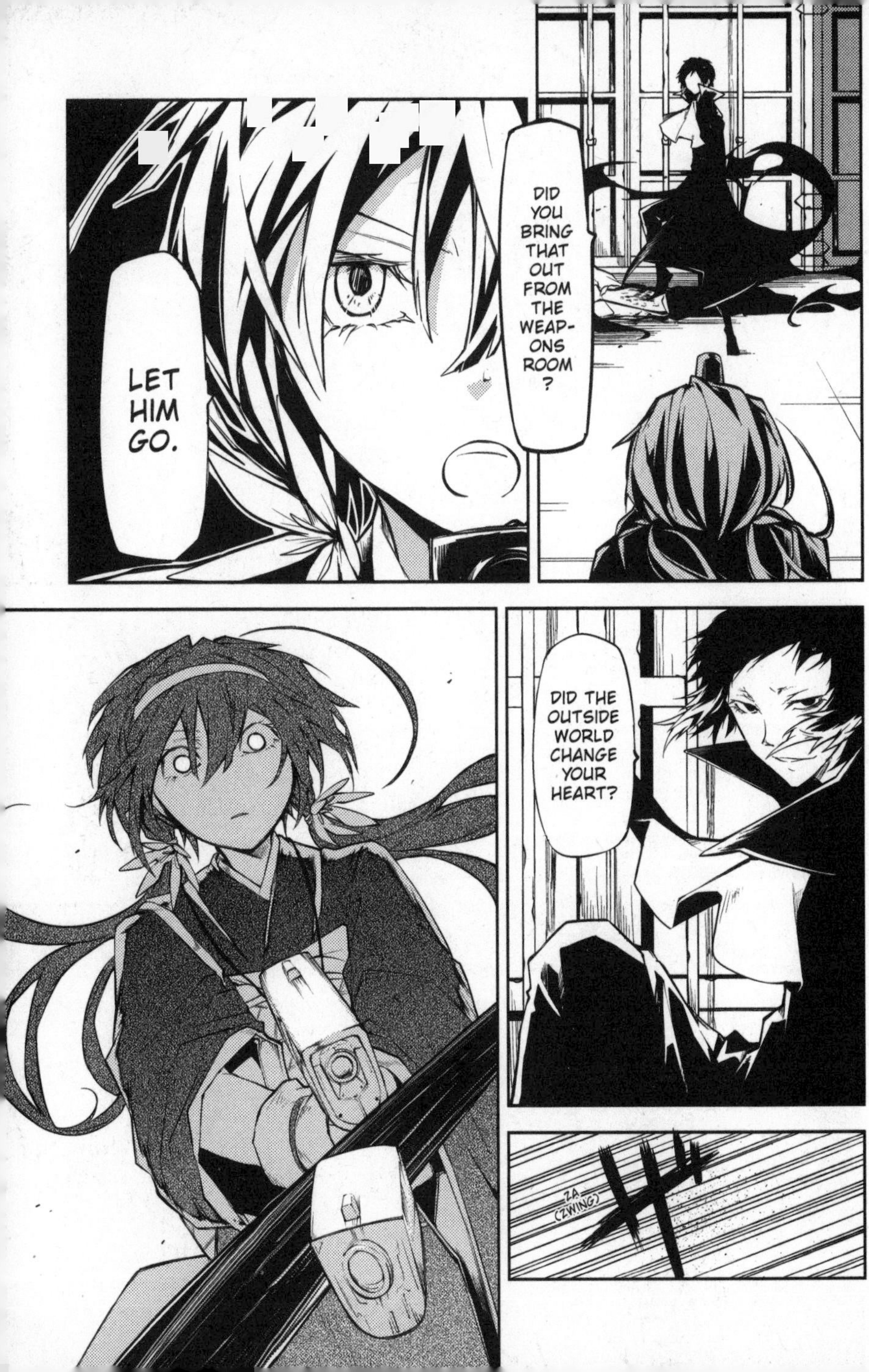
DID YOU BRING THAT OUT FROM THE WEAP-ONS ROOM ?
LET HIM GO.
DID THE OUTSIDE WORLD CHANGE YOUR HEART?
ZA (ZWING)

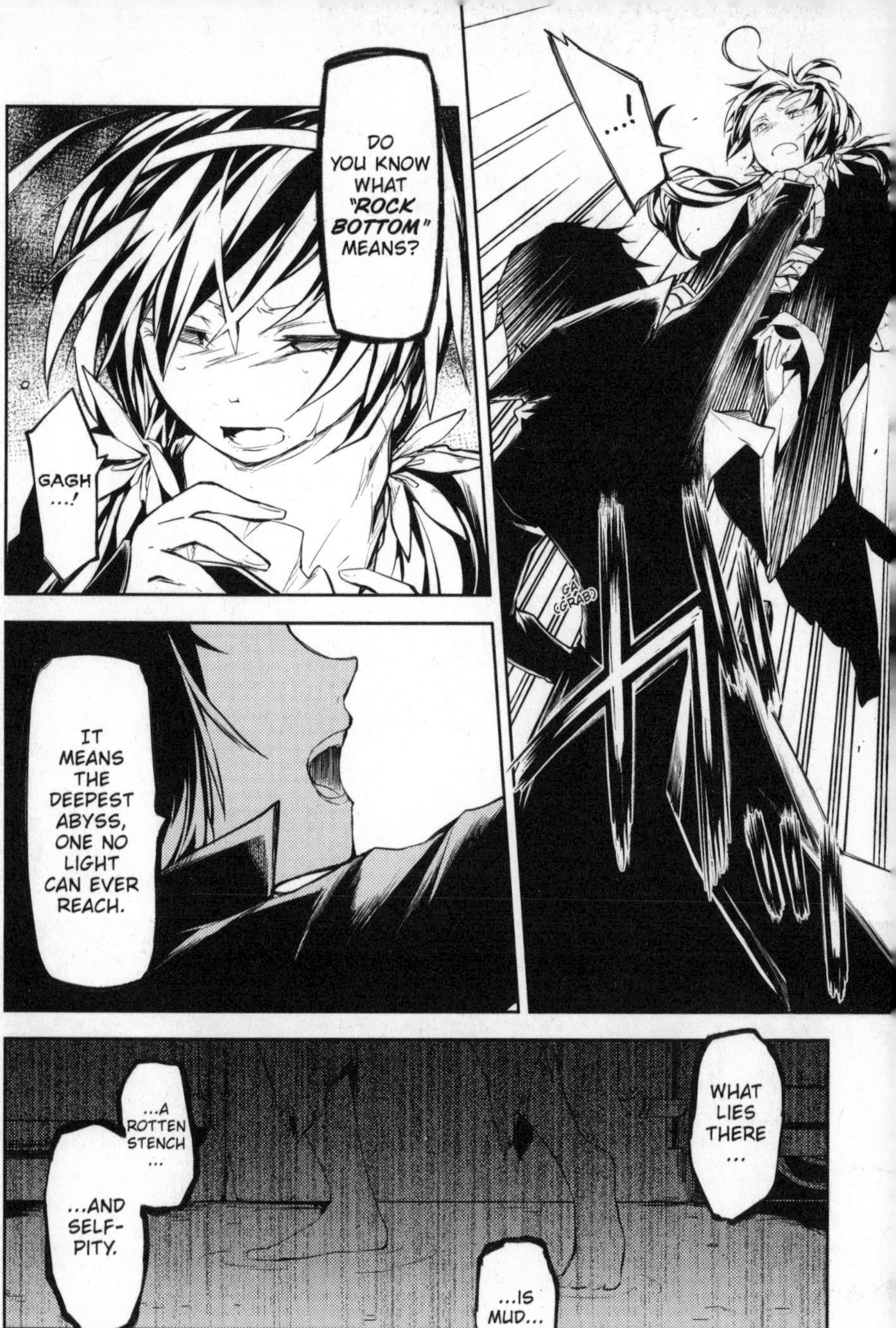
...!
GA (GRAB)
DO YOU KNOW WHAT "ROCK BOTTOM" MEANS?
GAGH ...!
IT MEANS THE DEEPEST ABYSS, ONE NO LIGHT CAN EVER REACH.
WHAT LIES THERE ...
...IS MUD...
...A ROTTEN STENCH ...
...AND SELF-PITY.

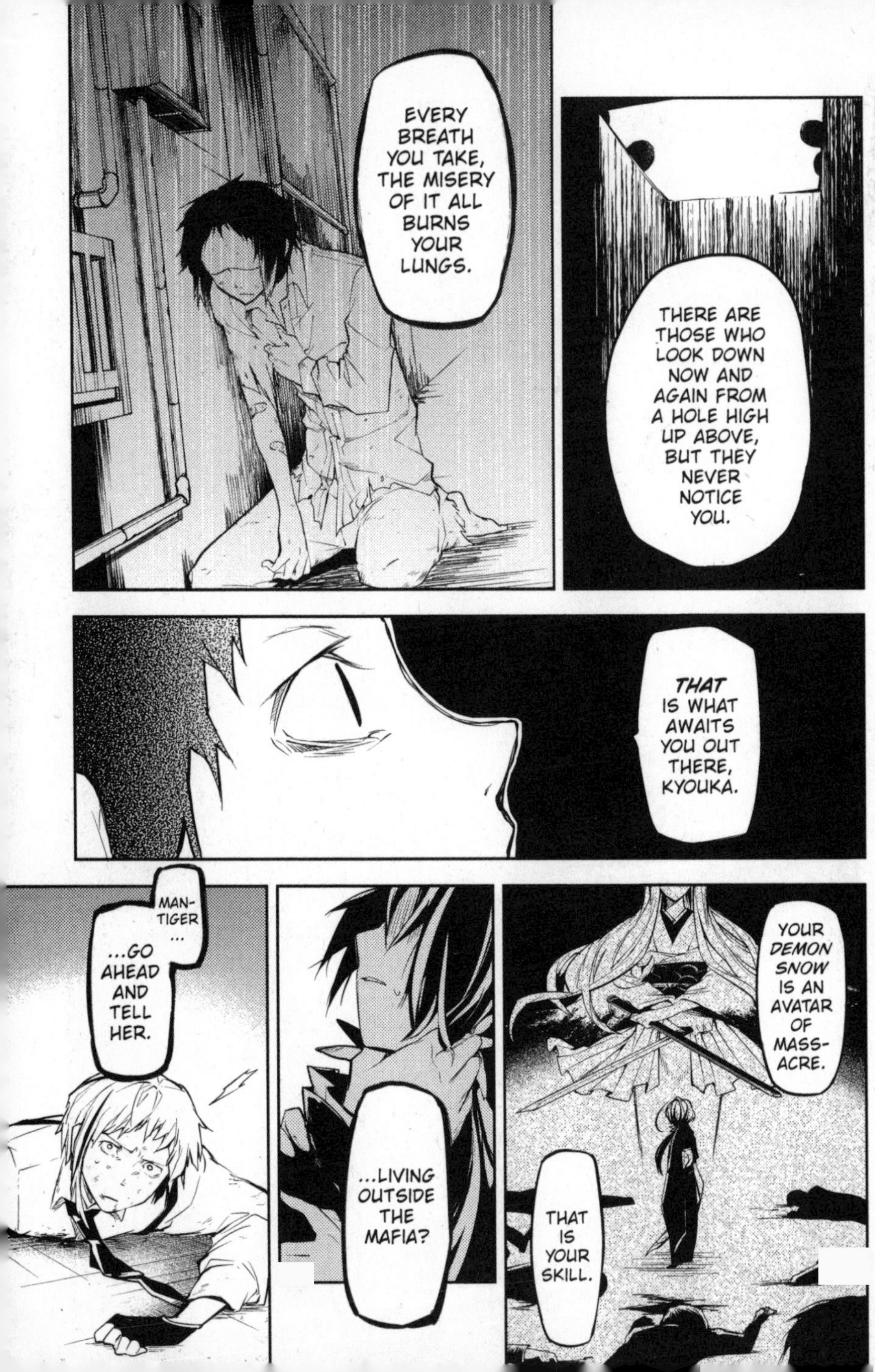
THERE ARE THOSE WHO LOOK DOWN NOW AND AGAIN FROM A HOLE HIGH UP ABOVE, BUT THEY NEVER NOTICE YOU.
EVERY BREATH YOU TAKE, THE MISERY OF IT ALL BURNS YOUR LUNGS.
THAT IS WHAT AWAITS YOU OUT THERE, KYOUKA.
YOUR *DEMON SNOW* IS AN AVATAR OF MASS-ACRE.
THAT IS YOUR SKILL.
...LIVING OUTSIDE THE MAFIA?
MAN-TIGER...
...GO AHEAD AND TELL HER.

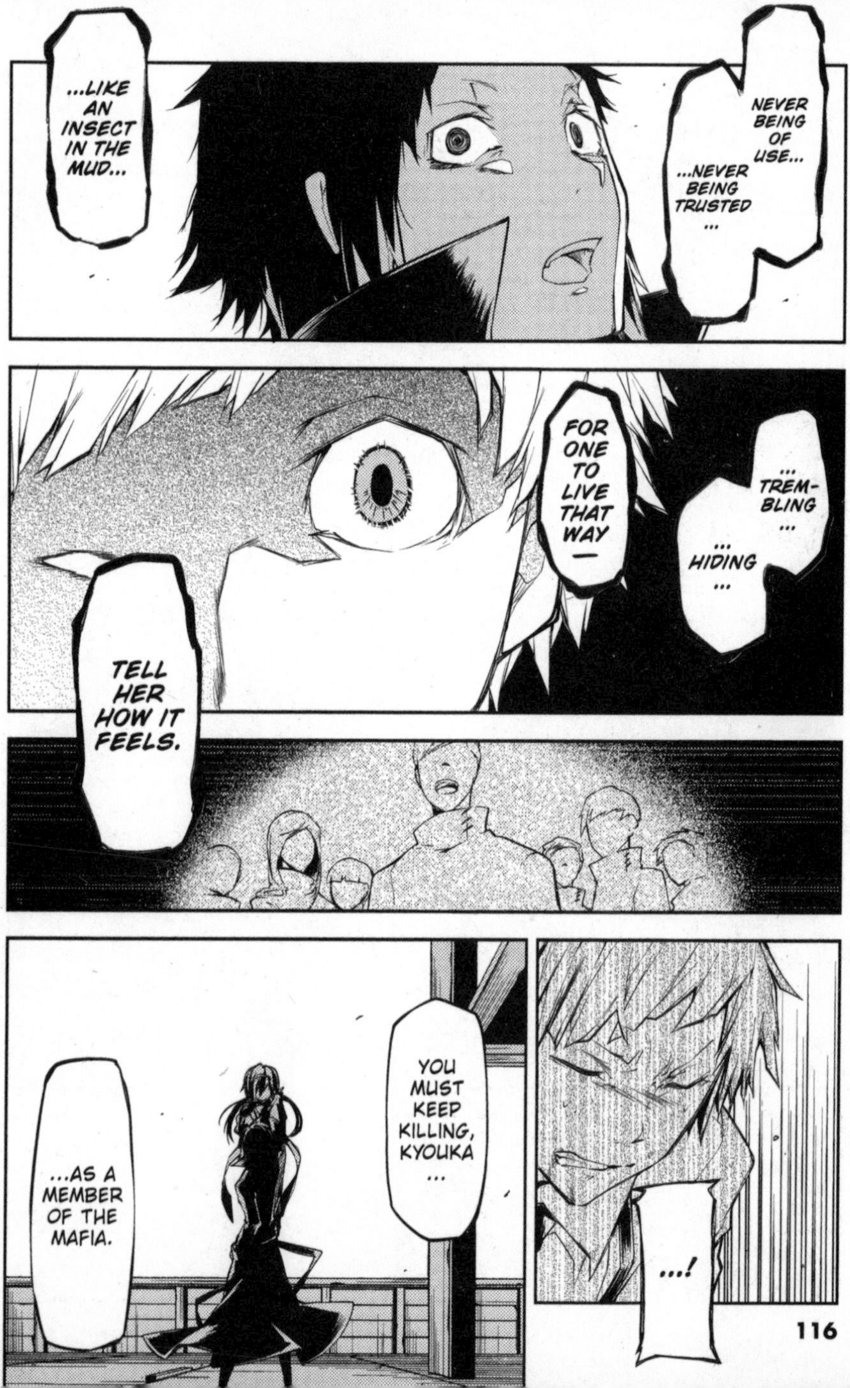
NEVER BEING OF USE...
...NEVER BEING TRUSTED ...
...LIKE AN INSECT IN THE MUD...
... TREM- BLING ... ... HIDING ...
FOR ONE TO LIVE THAT WAY —
TELL HER HOW IT FEELS.
...!
YOU MUST KEEP KILLING, KYOUKA ...
...AS A MEMBER OF THE MAFIA.

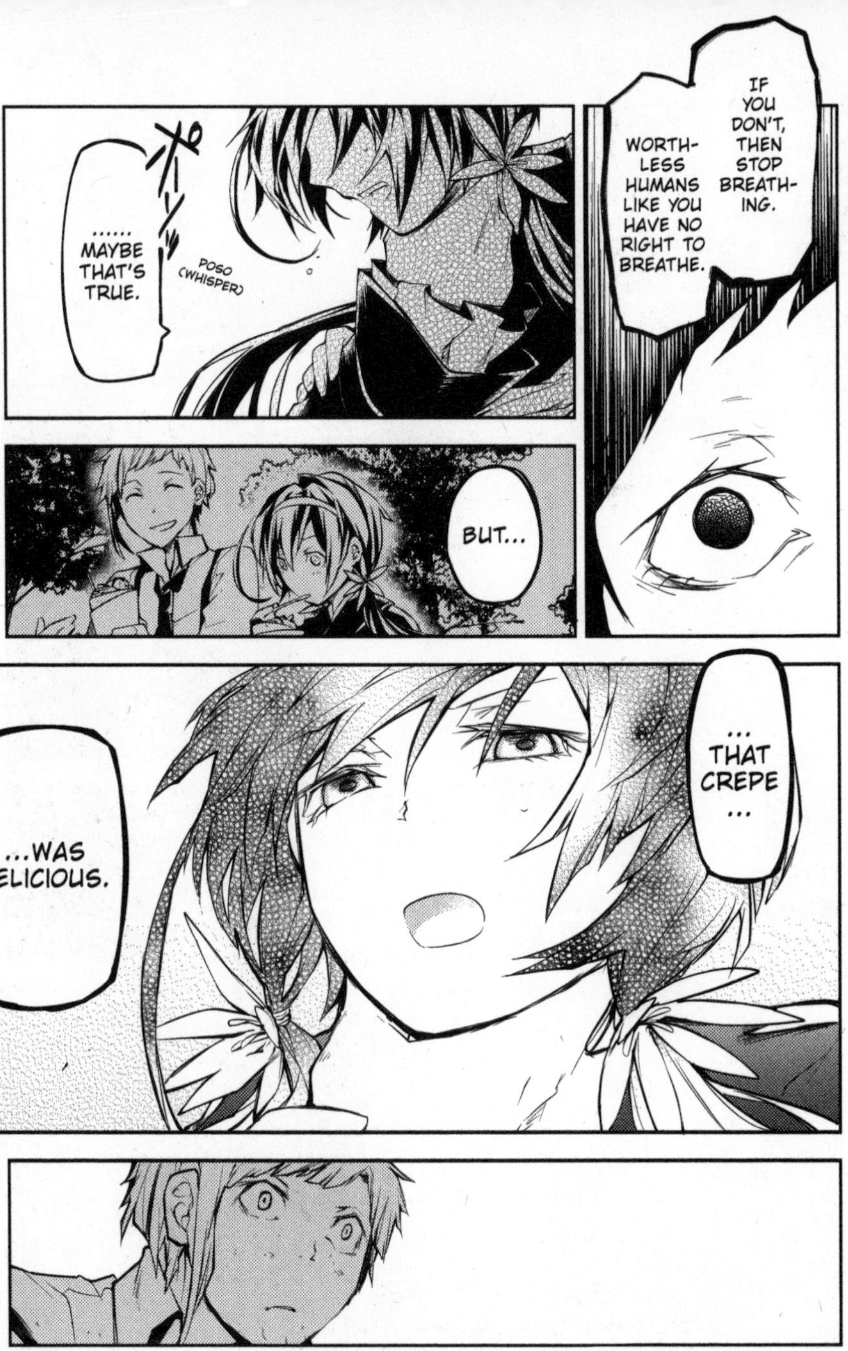
IF YOU DON'T, THEN STOP BREATHING.
WORTHLESS HUMANS LIKE YOU HAVE NO RIGHT TO BREATHE.
POSO (WHISPER)
......MAYBE THAT'S TRUE.
BUT...
...THAT CREPE...
...WAS DELICIOUS.

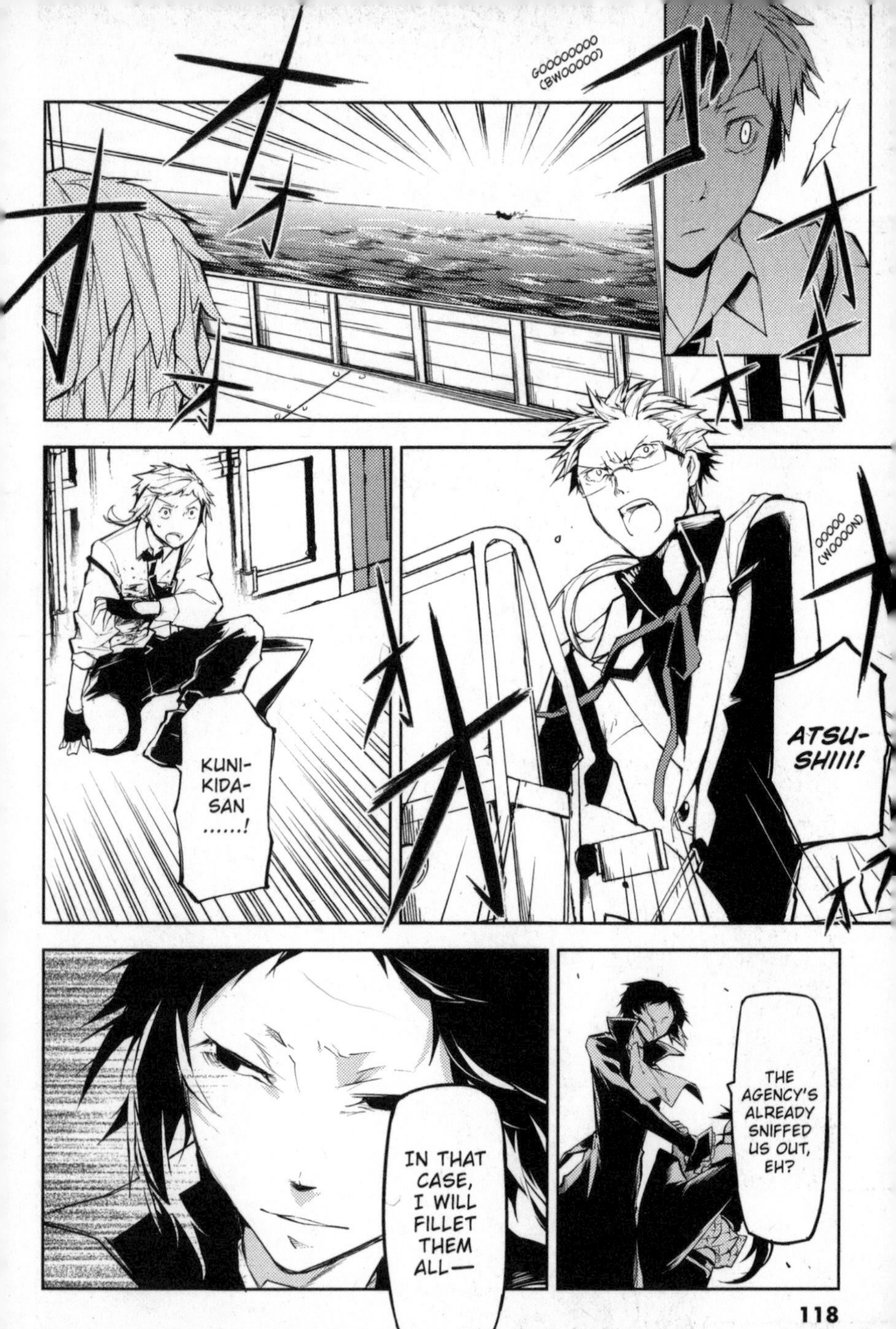
GOOOOOOOO (BWOOOOO)
ATSU-SHIII!
OOOOO (WOOOON)
KUNI-KIDA-SAN ......!
THE AGENCY'S ALREADY SNIFFED US OUT, EH?
IN THAT CASE, I WILL FILLET THEM ALL—

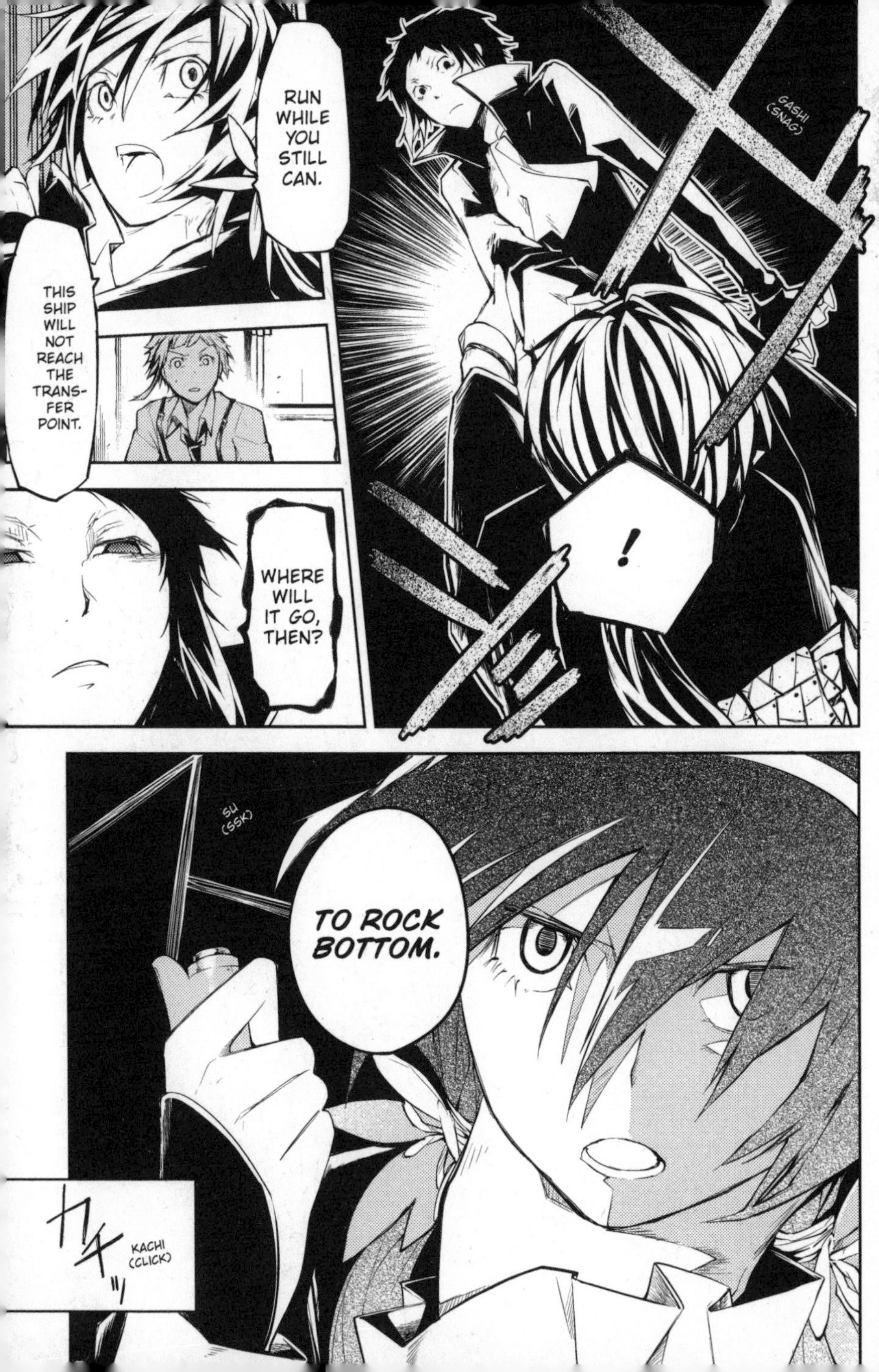
GASHI (SNAG)
!
RUN WHILE YOU STILL CAN.
THIS SHIP WILL NOT REACH THE TRANSFER POINT.
WHERE WILL IT GO, THEN?
SU (SSK)
TO ROCK BOTTOM.
カチッ
KACHI (CLICK)

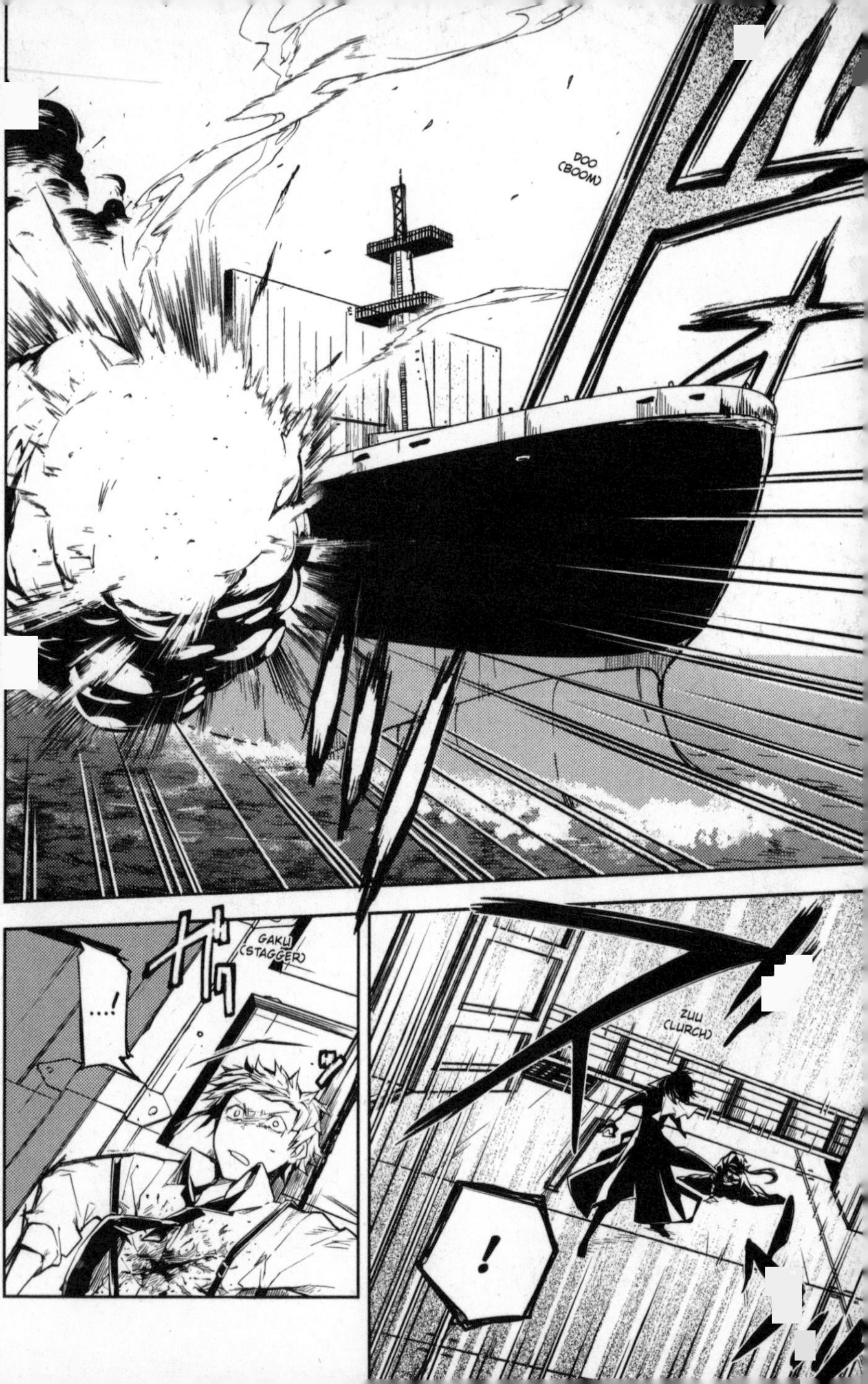
DOO
(BOOM)
ZUU
(LURCH)
!
GAKU
(STAGGER)
...!

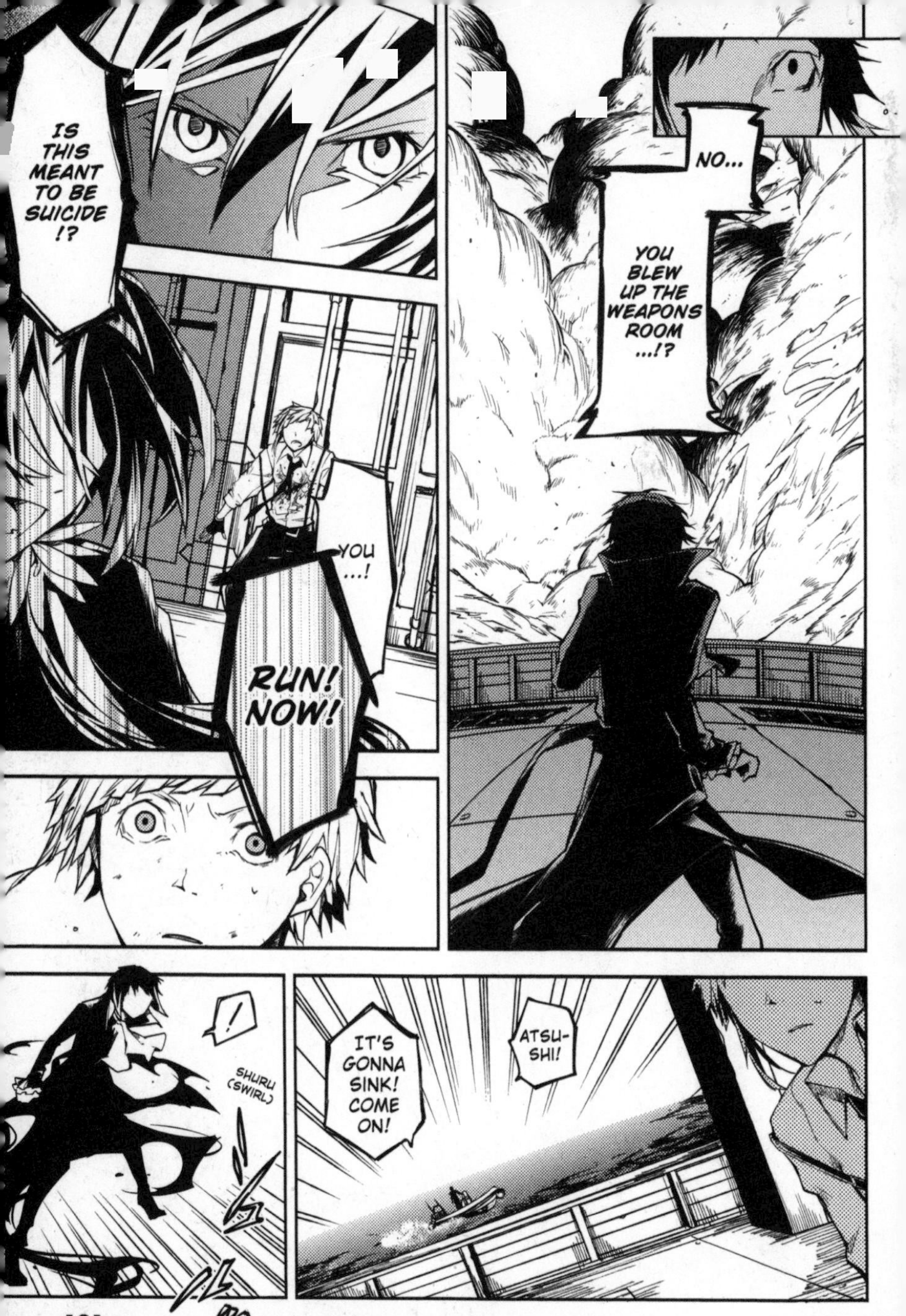
NO...
YOU BLEW UP THE WEAPONS ROOM ...!?
IS THIS MEANT TO BE SUICIDE !?
YOU ...!
RUN! NOW!
ATSU-SHI!
IT'S GONNA SINK! COME ON!
!
SHURU (SWIRL)

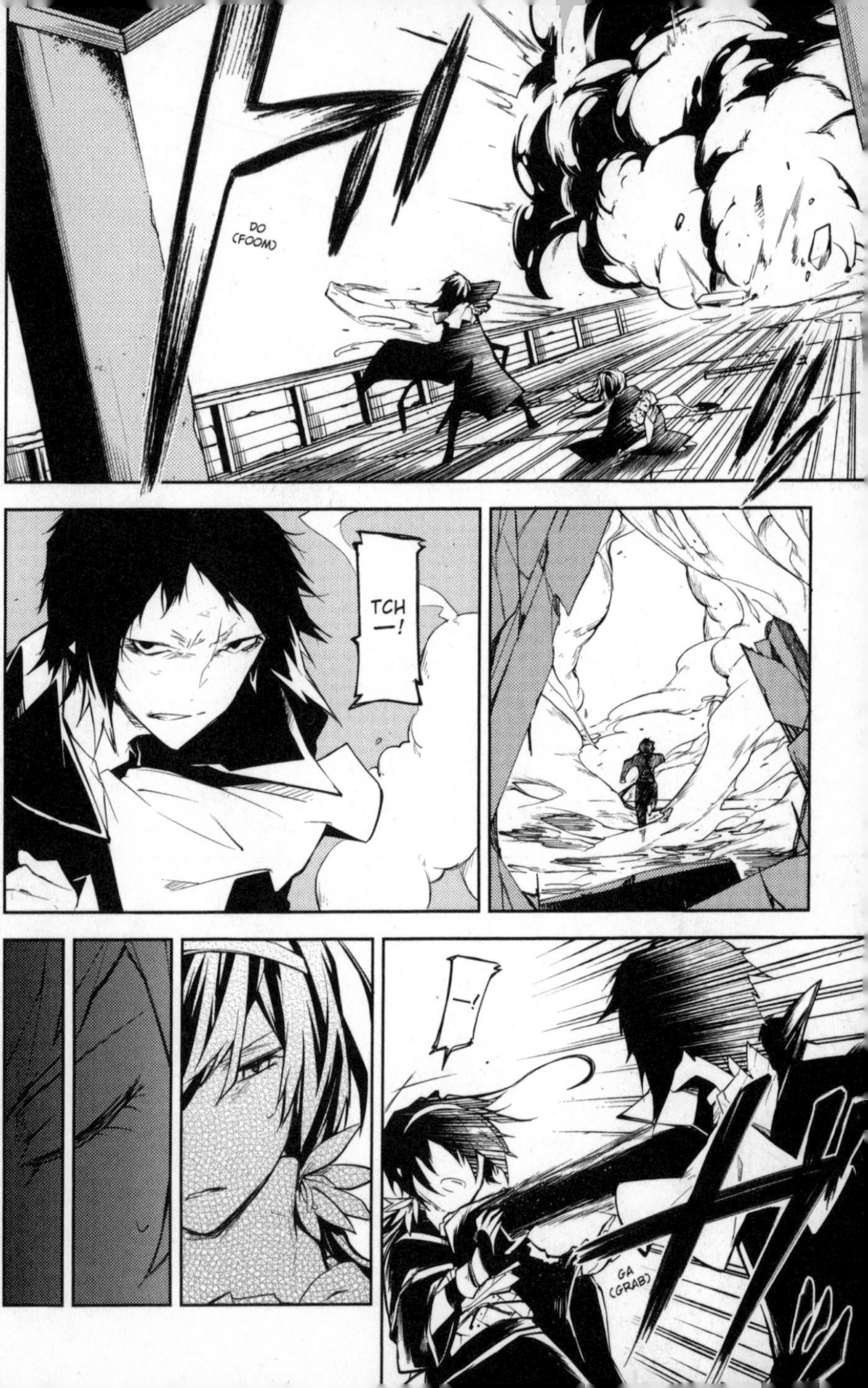
DO
(FOOM)
TCH
—!
—!
GA
(GRAB)

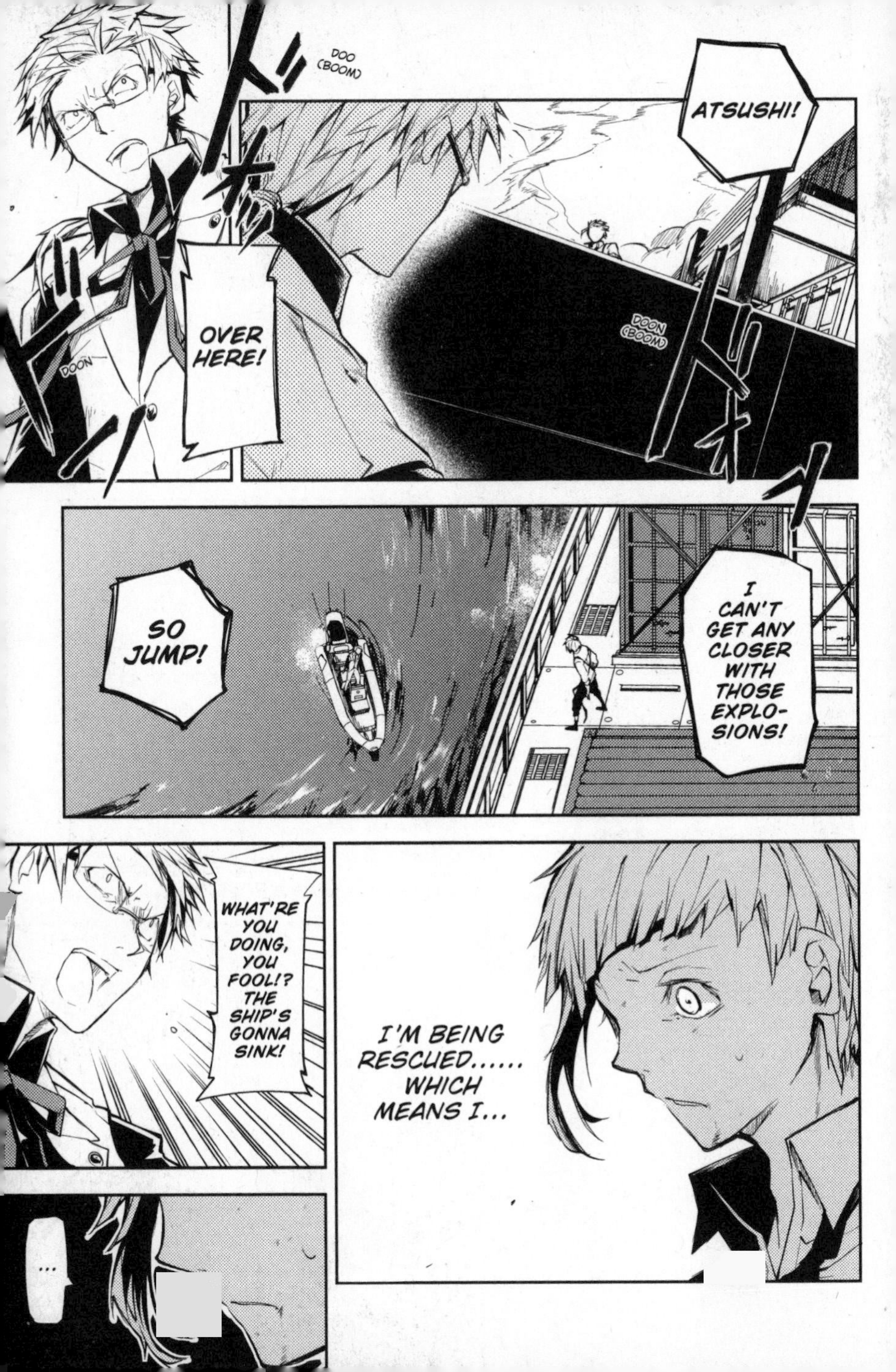
ATSUSHI!
DOON (BOOM)
DOO (BOOM)
OVER HERE!
DOON
I CAN'T GET ANY CLOSER WITH THOSE EXPLOSIONS!
SO JUMP!
I'M BEING RESCUED...... WHICH MEANS I...
WHAT'RE YOU DOING, YOU FOOL!? THE SHIP'S GONNA SINK!
...

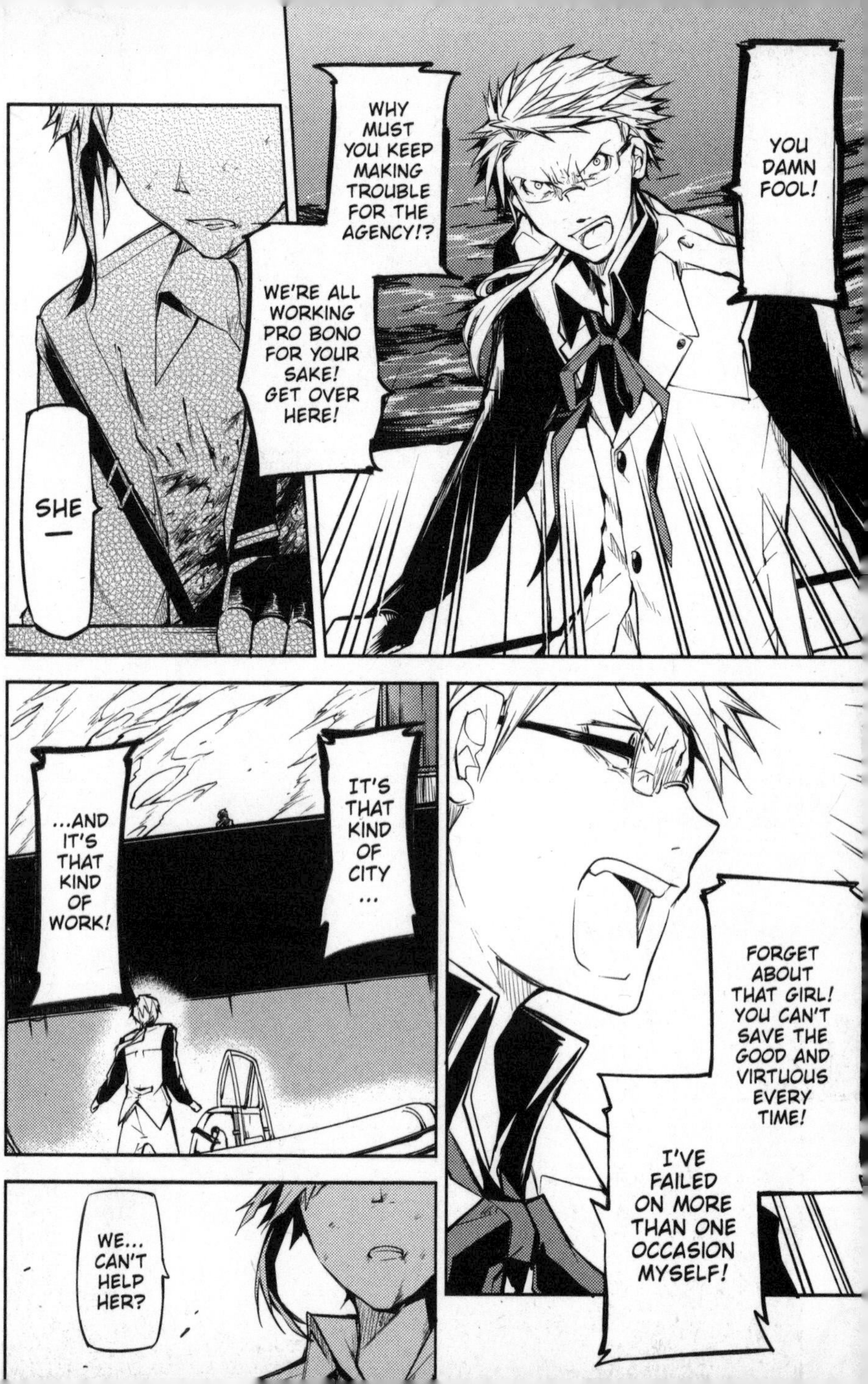
YOU DAMN FOOL!
WHY MUST YOU KEEP MAKING TROUBLE FOR THE AGENCY!?
WE'RE ALL WORKING PRO BONO FOR YOUR SAKE! GET OVER HERE!
SHE —
FORGET ABOUT THAT GIRL! YOU CAN'T SAVE THE GOOD AND VIRTUOUS EVERY TIME!
I'VE FAILED ON MORE THAN ONE OCCASION MYSELF!
IT'S THAT KIND OF CITY...
...AND IT'S THAT KIND OF WORK!
WE... CAN'T HELP HER?

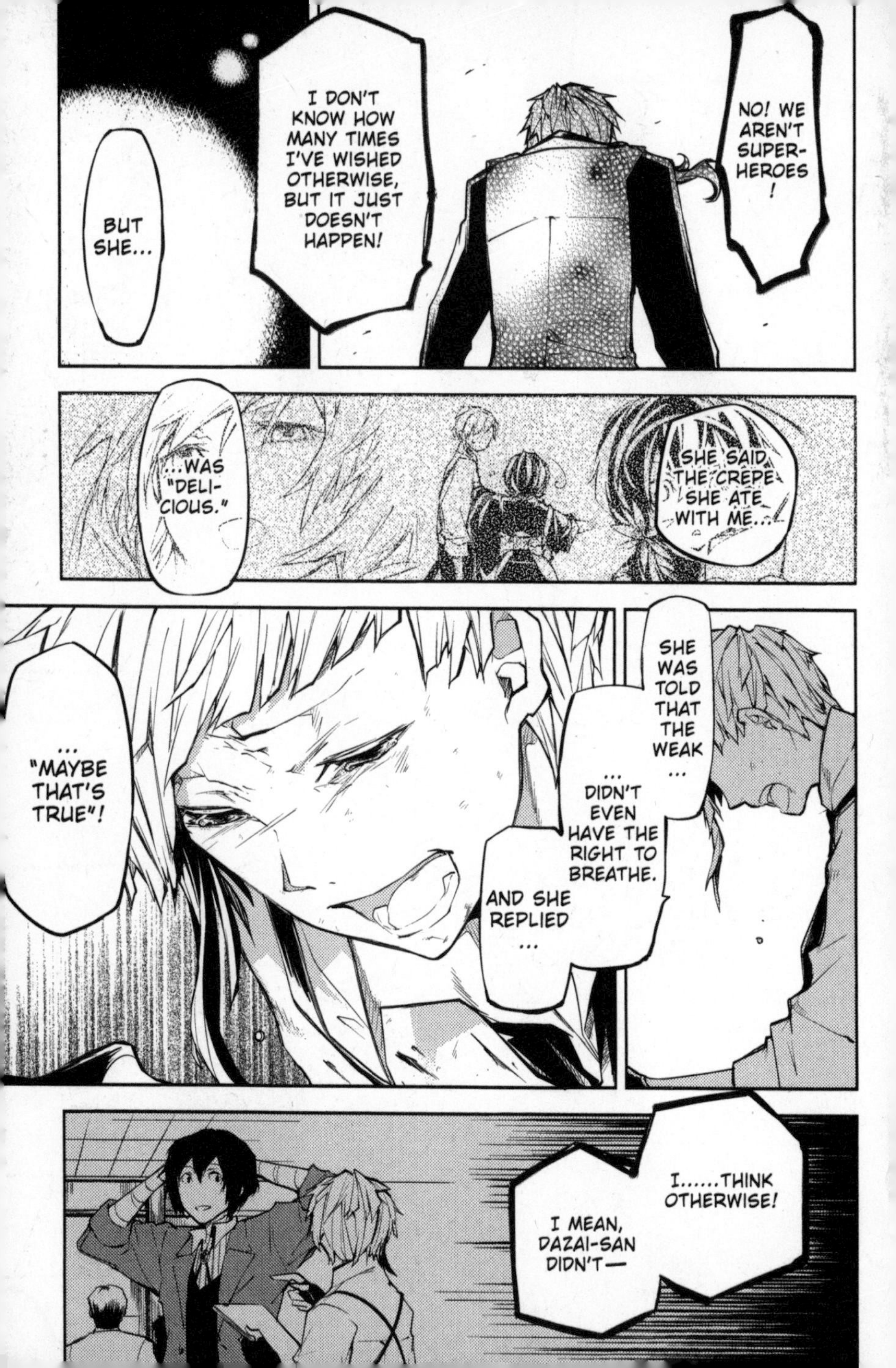
NO! WE AREN'T SUPER-HEROES!
I DON'T KNOW HOW MANY TIMES I'VE WISHED OTHERWISE, BUT IT JUST DOESN'T HAPPEN!
BUT SHE...
SHE SAID THE CREPE SHE ATE WITH ME...
...WAS "DELICIOUS."
SHE WAS TOLD THAT THE WEAK ...
... DIDN'T EVEN HAVE THE RIGHT TO BREATHE.
AND SHE REPLIED ...
... "MAYBE THAT'S TRUE"!
I......THINK OTHERWISE!
I MEAN, DAZAI-SAN DIDN'T—

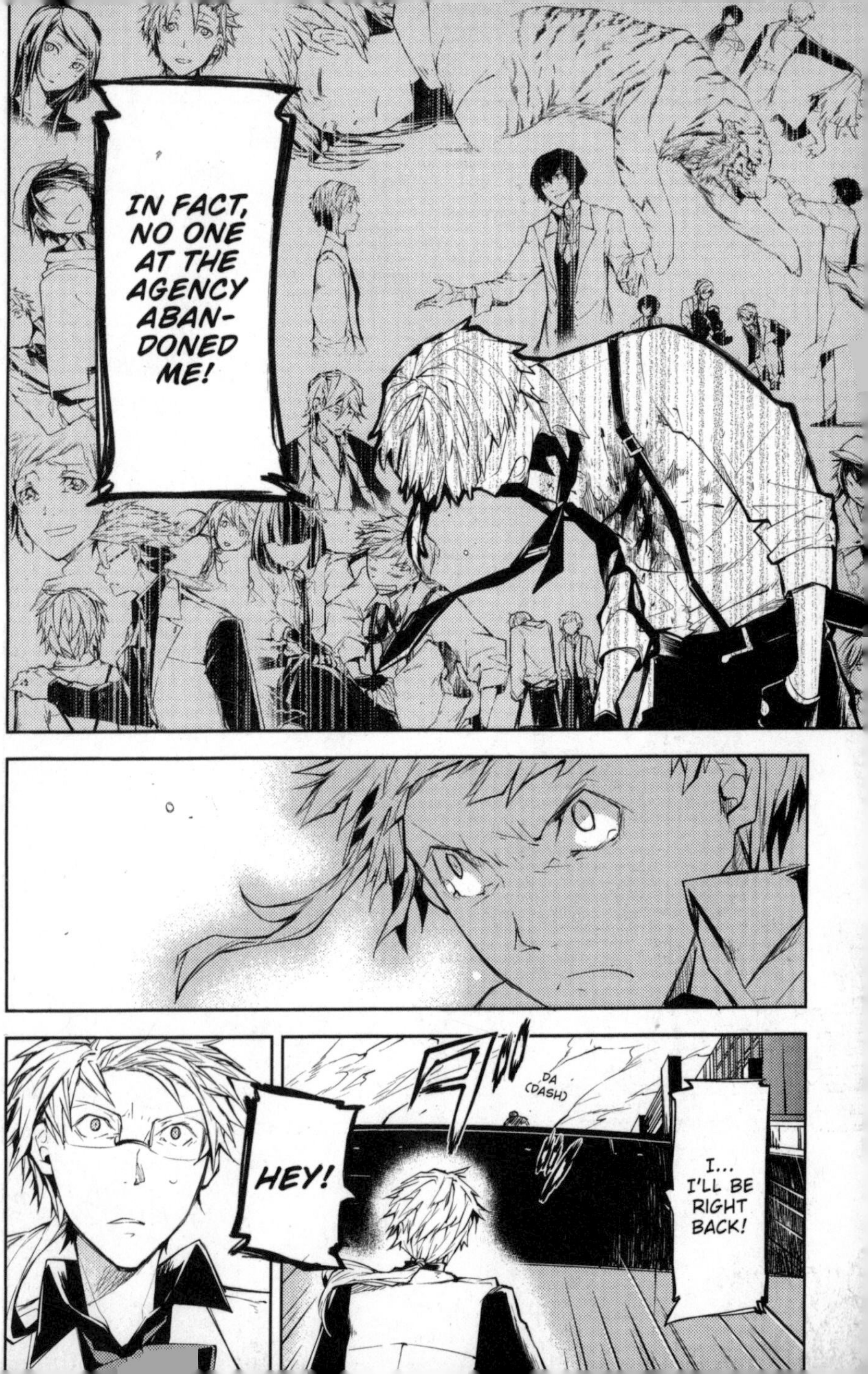
IN FACT, NO ONE AT THE AGENCY ABANDONED ME!
DA (DASH)
I... I'LL BE RIGHT BACK!
HEY!

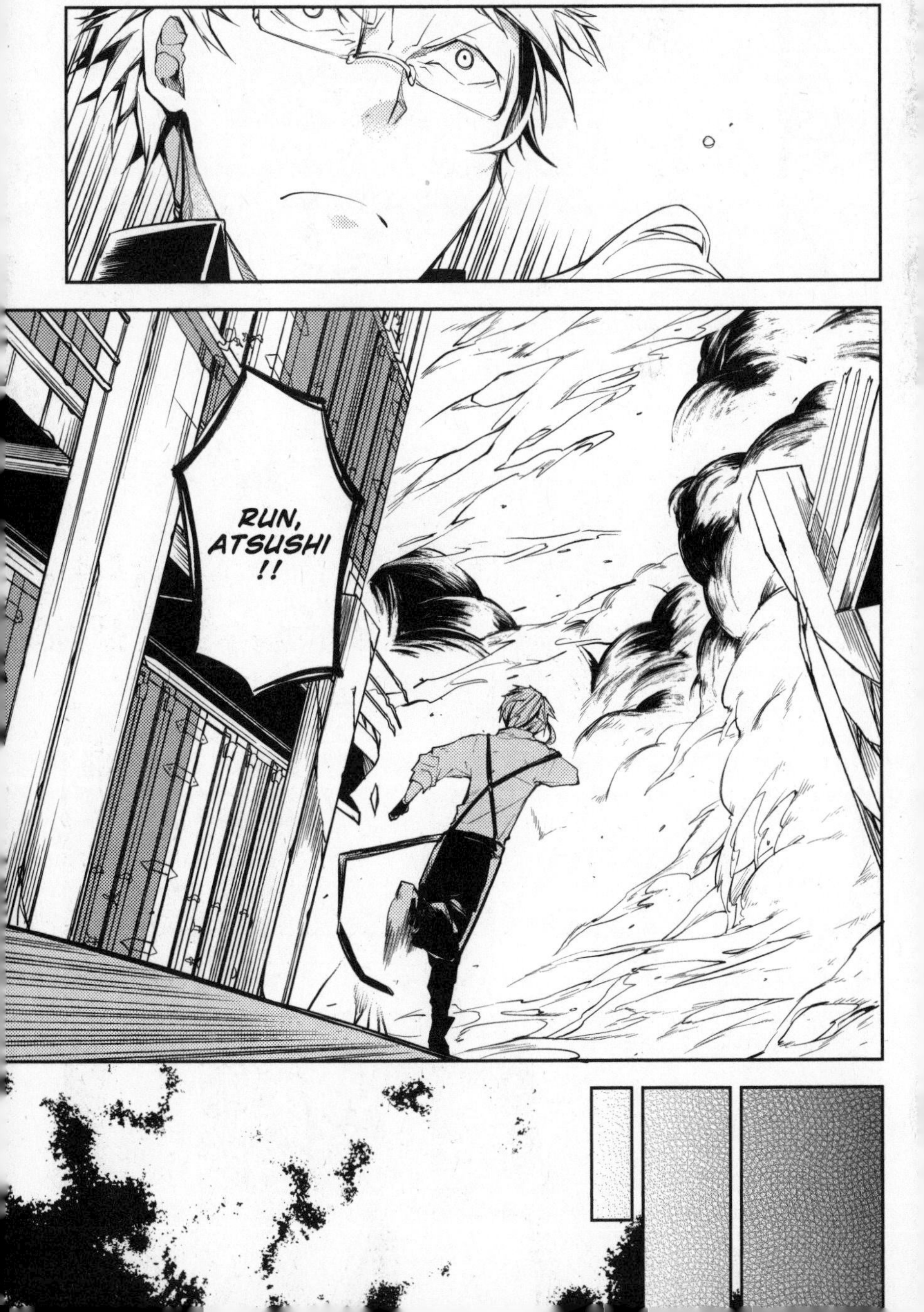
RUN, ATSUSHI !!

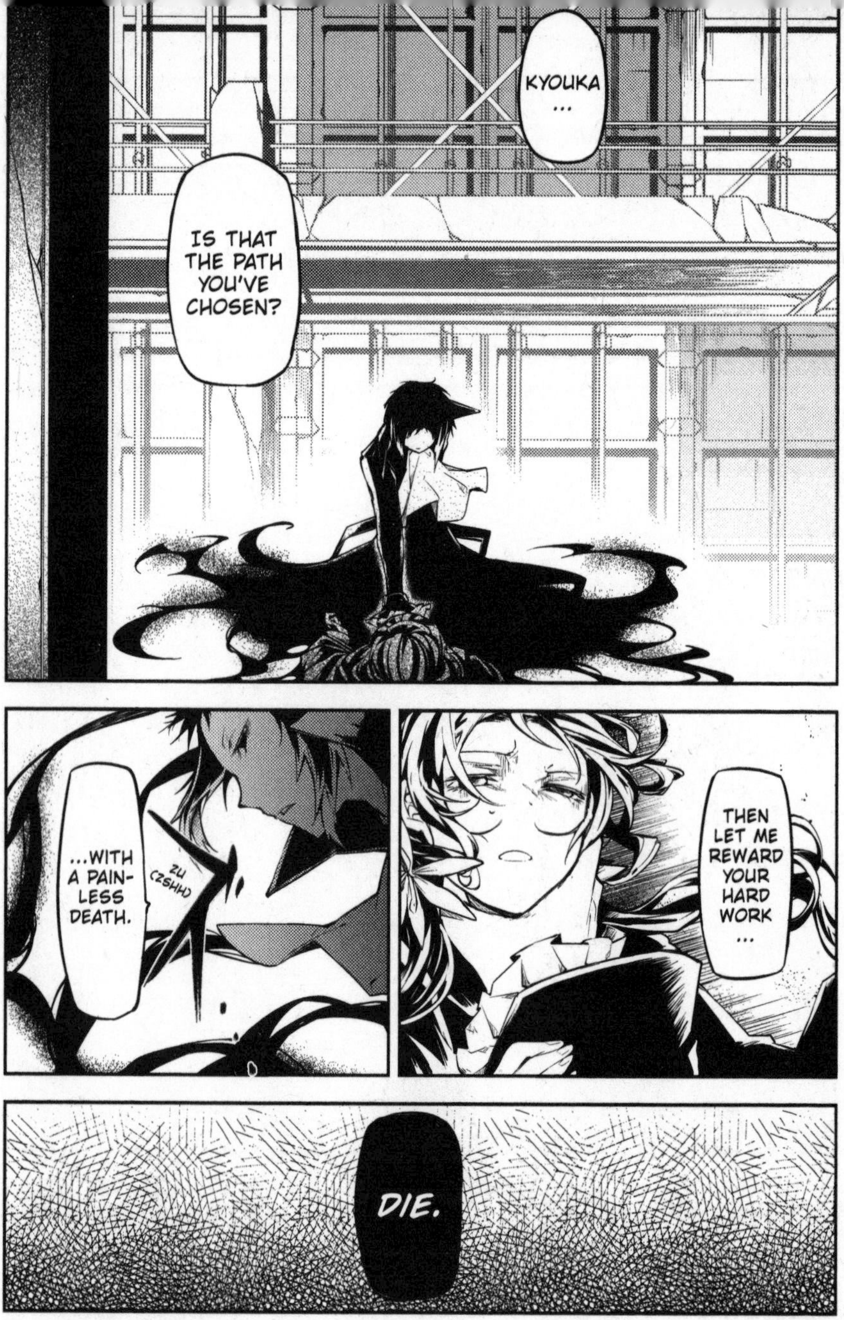
KYOUKA ...
IS THAT THE PATH YOU'VE CHOSEN?
THEN LET ME REWARD YOUR HARD WORK ...
...WITH A PAIN-LESS DEATH.
ZU (ZSHH)
DIE.

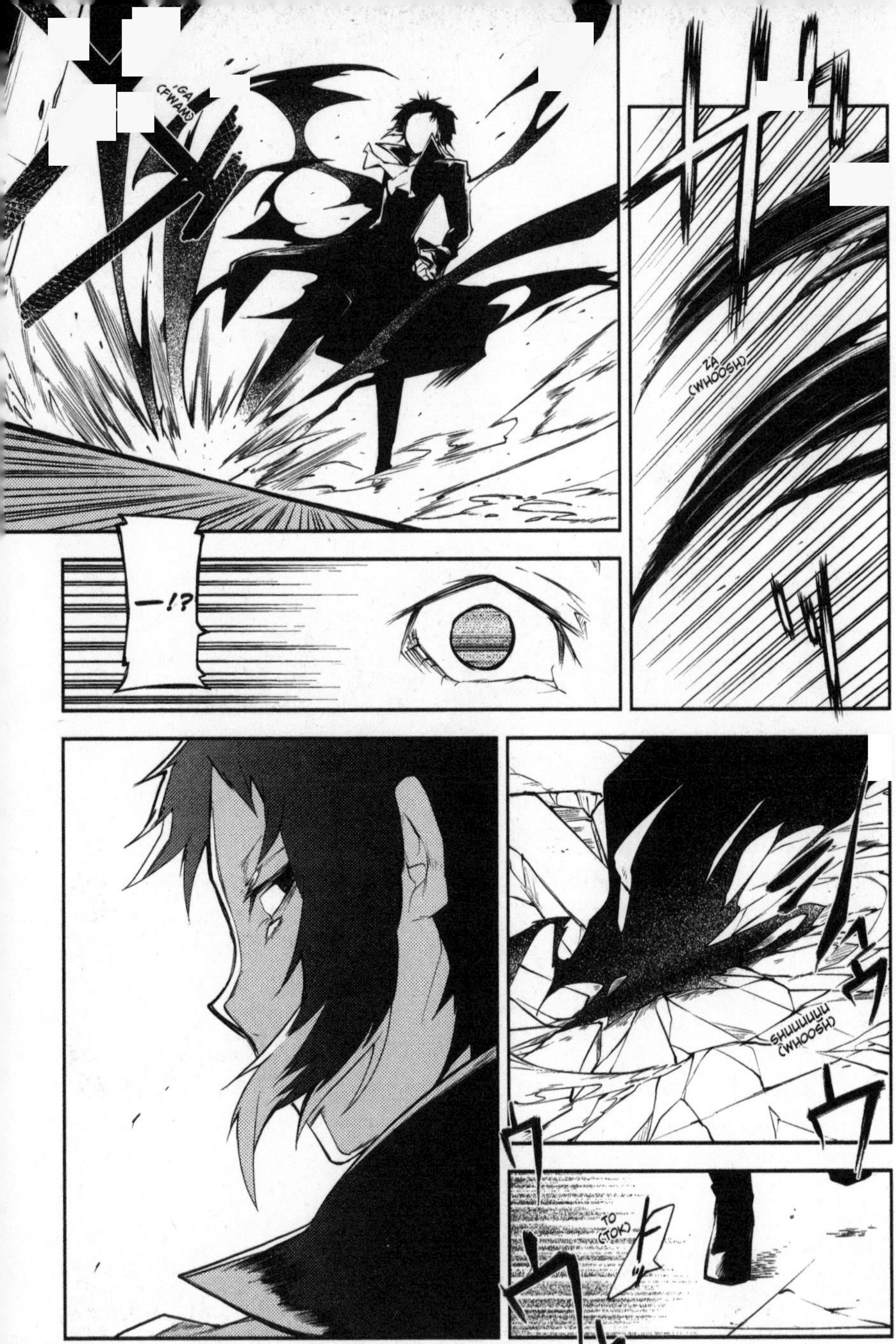
ZA
(WHOOSH)
GA
(FWAM)
—!?
SHUUUUUN
(WHOOSH)
TO
(TOK)

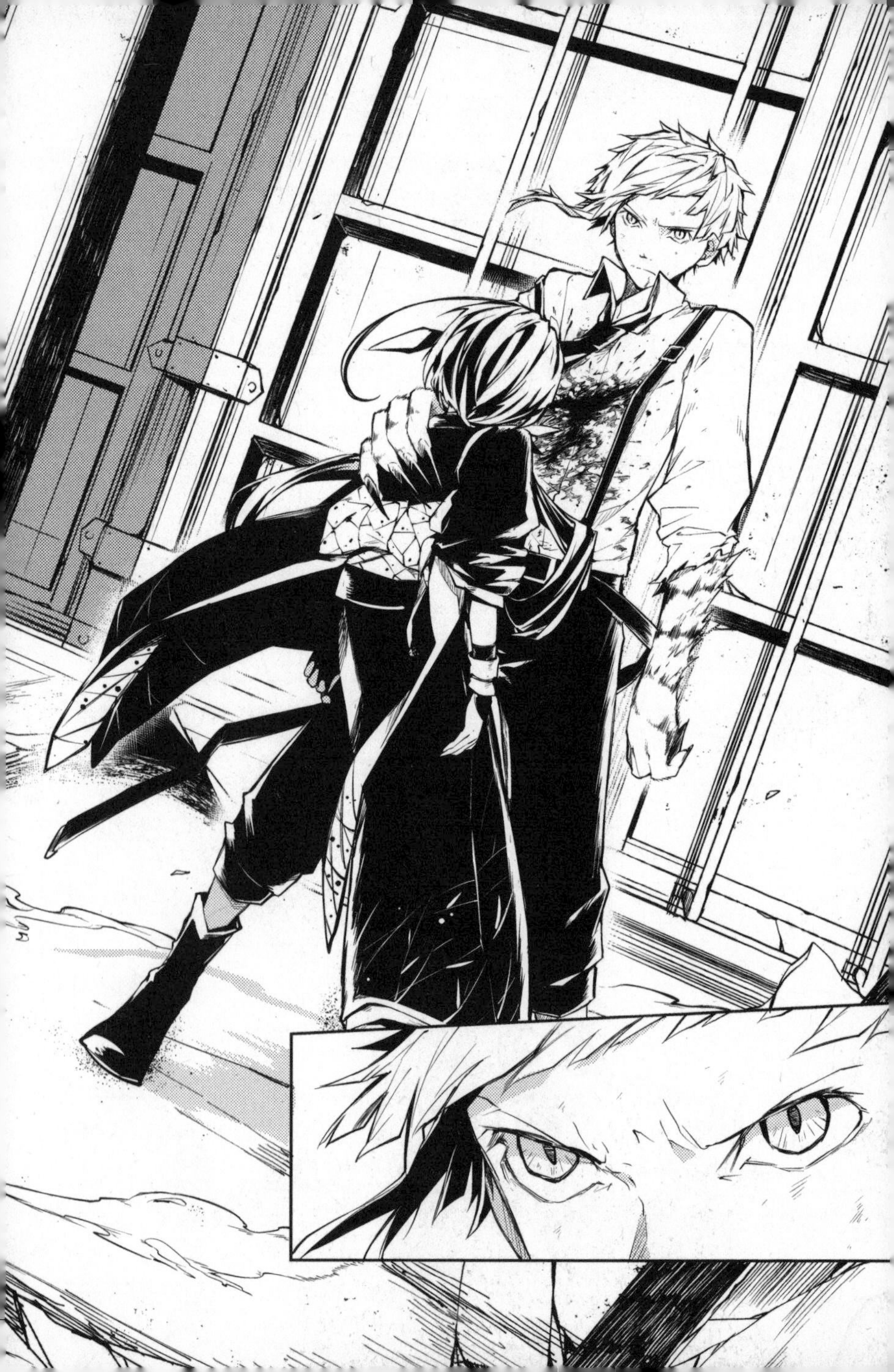

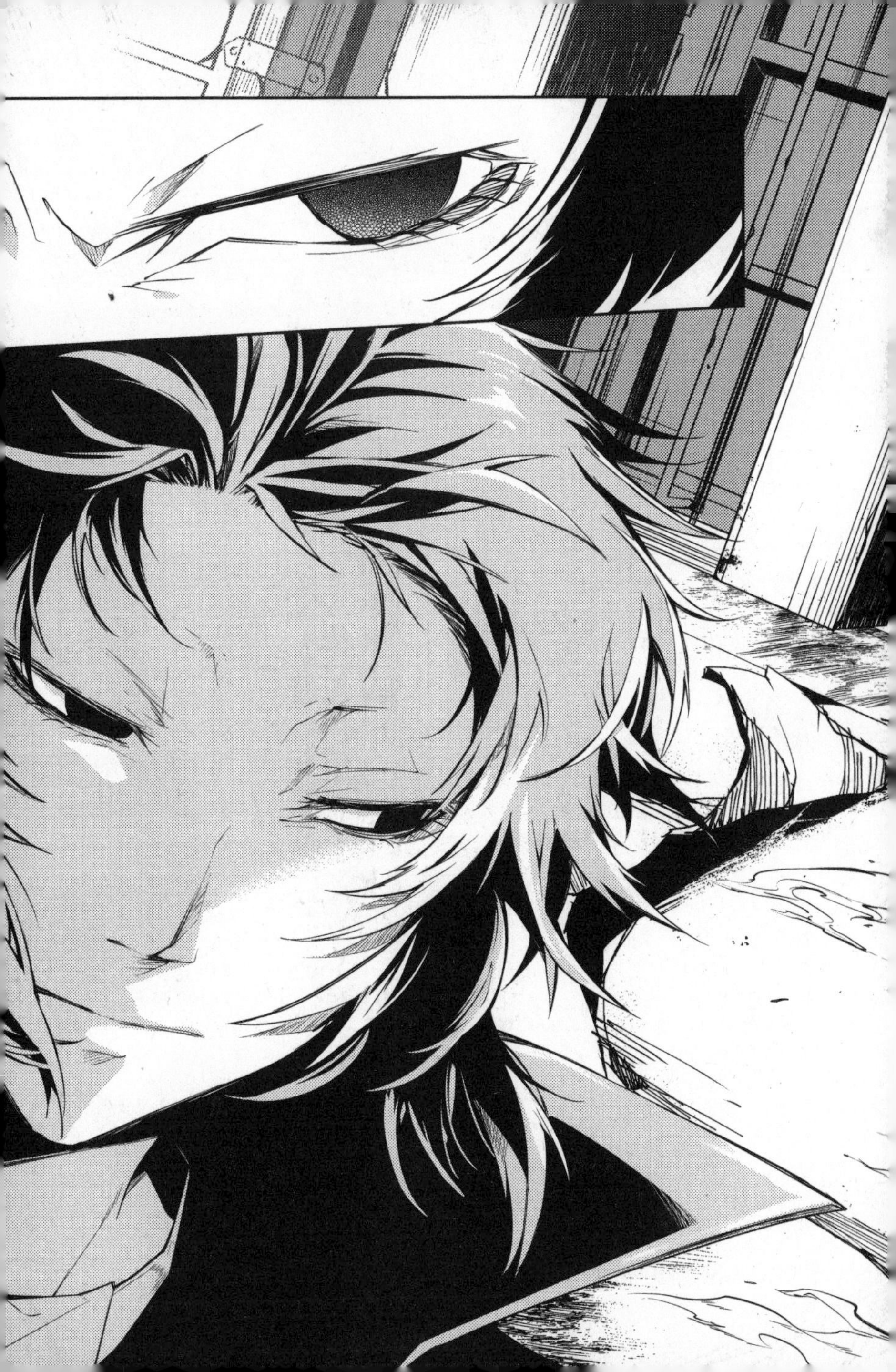

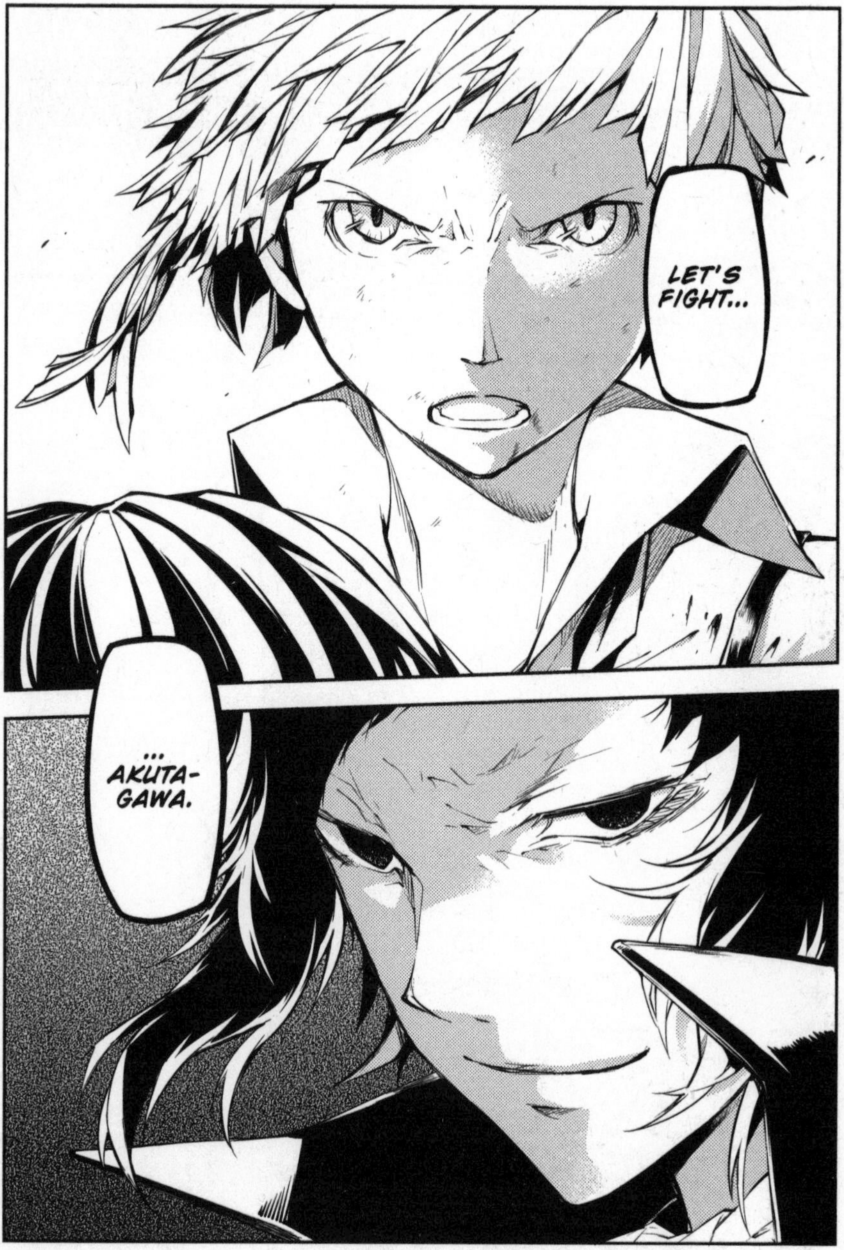
LET'S FIGHT...
... AKUTA-GAWA.

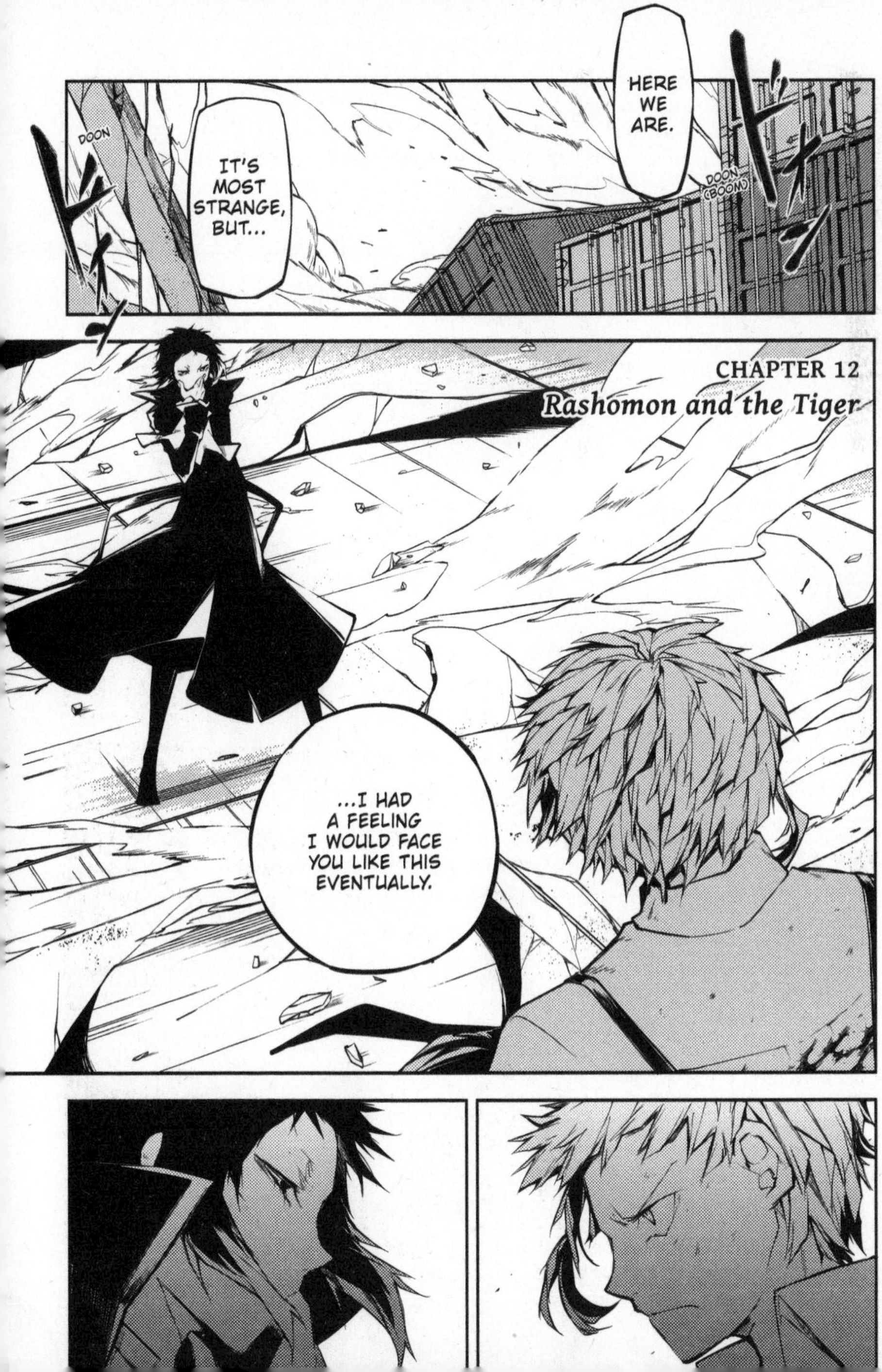
DOON (BOOM)
HERE WE ARE.
IT'S MOST STRANGE, BUT...
DOON
CHAPTER 12
Rashomon and the Tiger
...I HAD A FEELING I WOULD FACE YOU LIKE THIS EVENTUALLY.

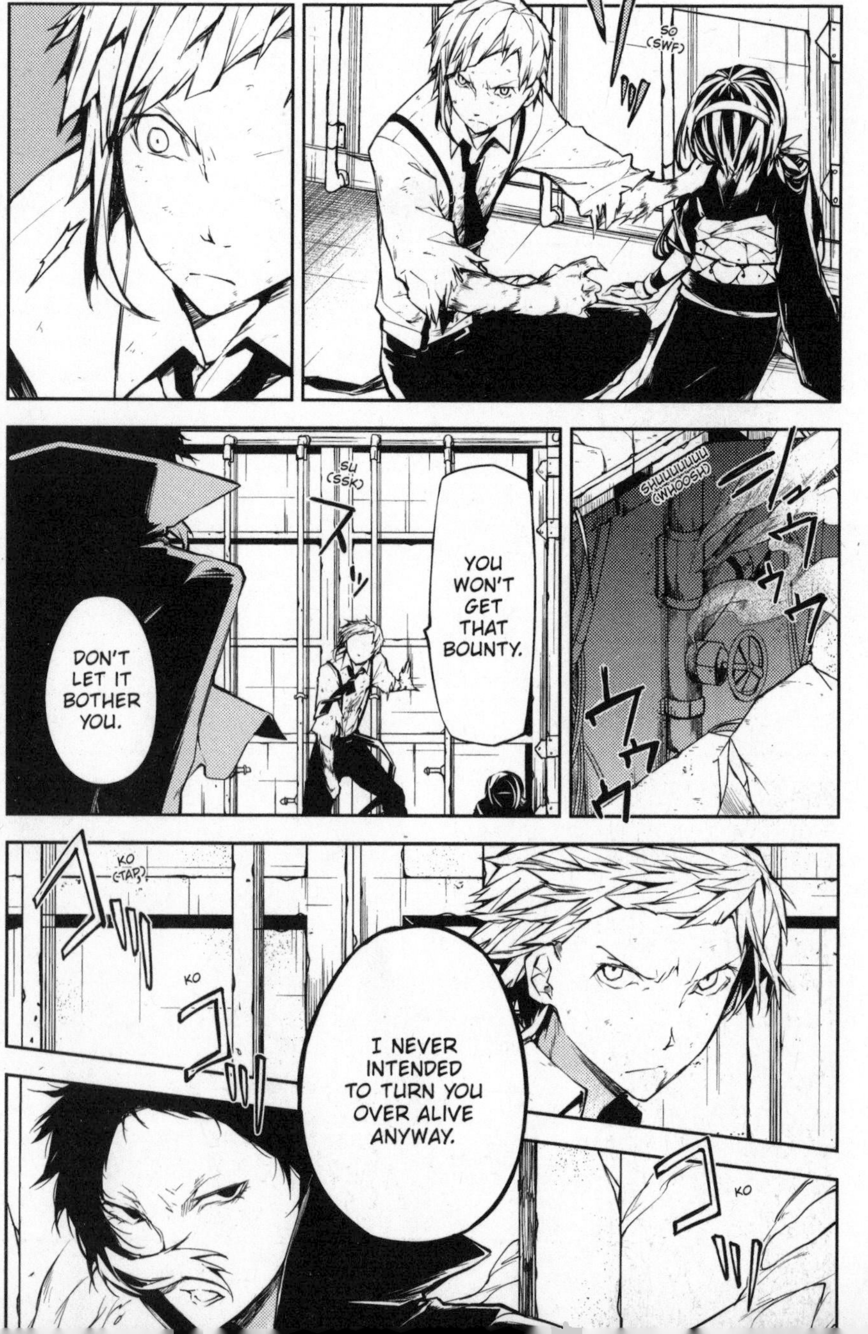

SO (SWF)
SHUUUUUUU (WHOOSH)
SU (SSK)
YOU WON'T GET THAT BOUNTY.
DON'T LET IT BOTHER YOU.
I NEVER INTENDED TO TURN YOU OVER ALIVE ANYWAY.
KO
KO (TAP)
KO

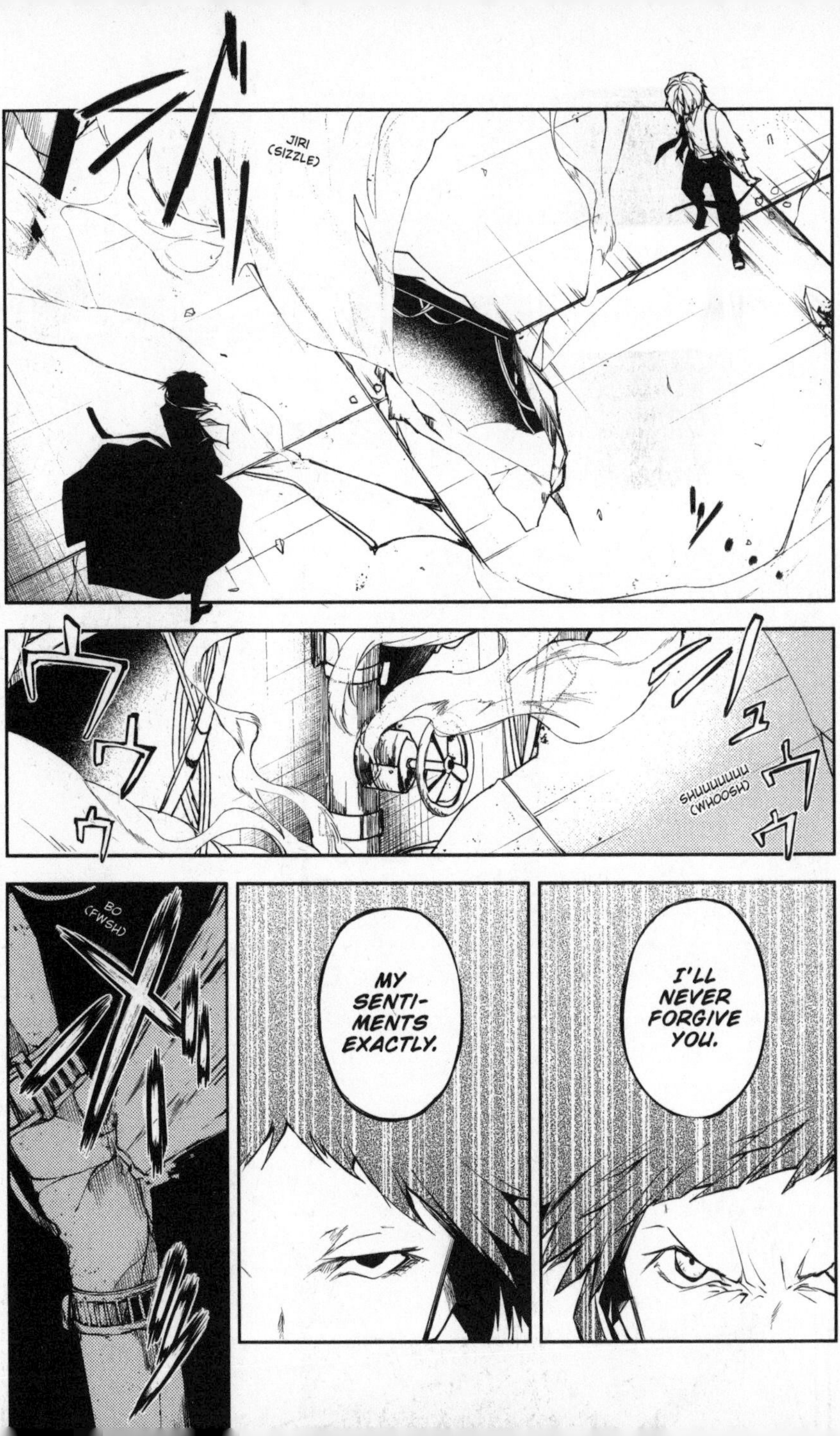
JIRI
(SIZZLE)
SHUNNNNNN
(WHOOSH)
I'LL NEVER FORGIVE YOU.
MY SENTI-MENTS EXACTLY.
BO
(FWSH)

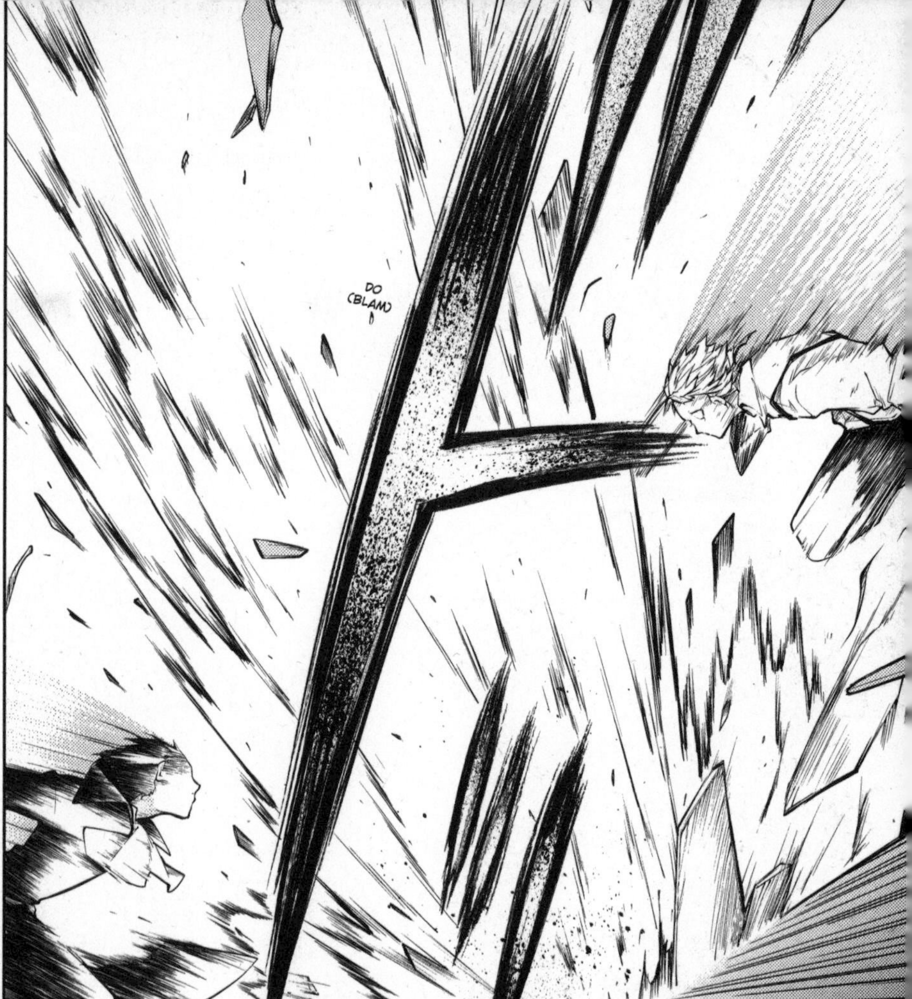
DO
(BLAM)
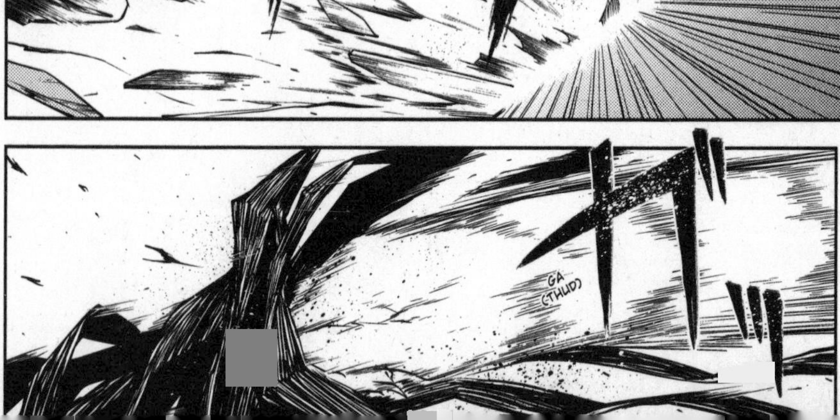
GA
(THUD)

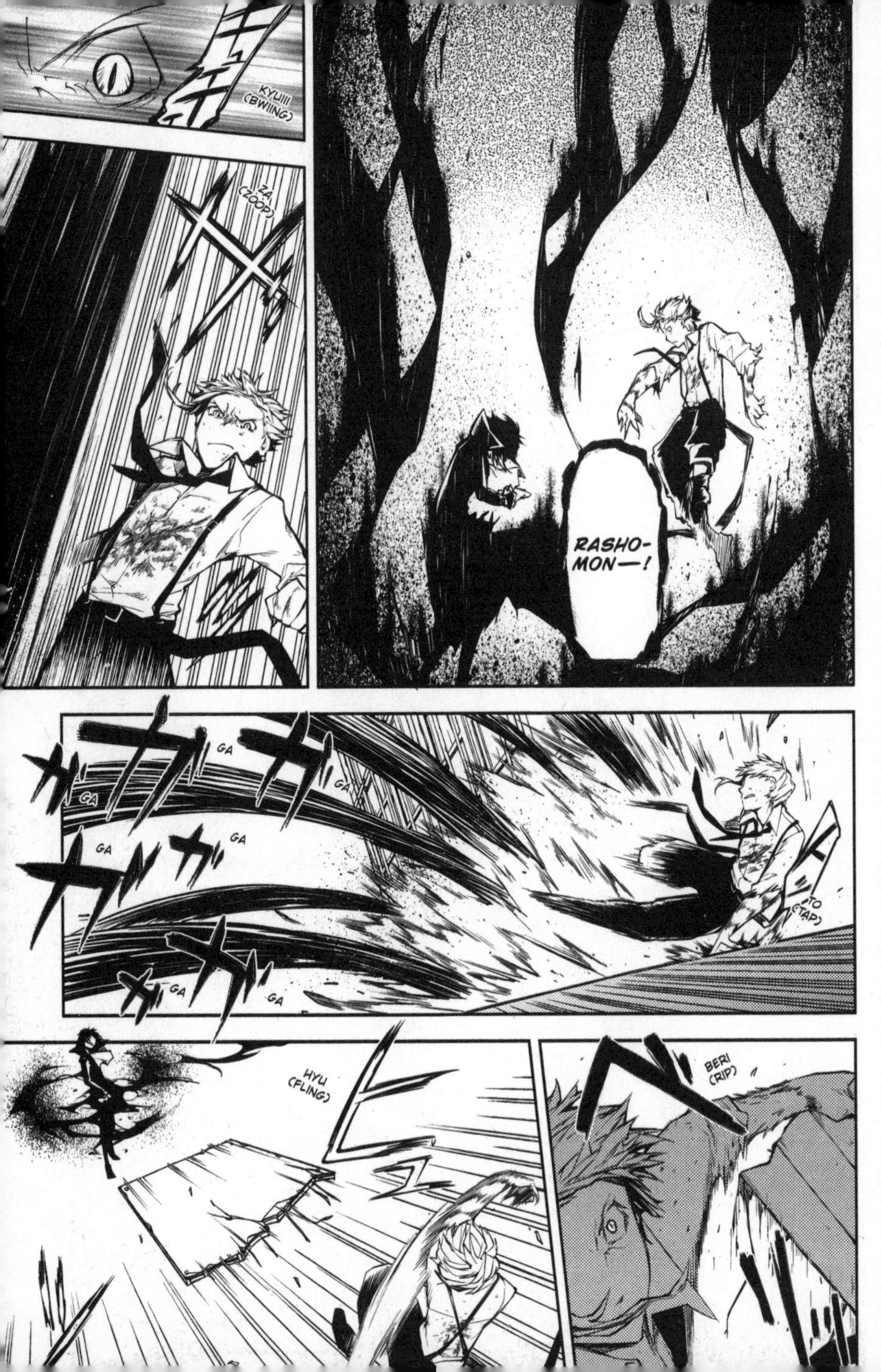
RASHO-
MON—!
KYUIII
(BWIING)
ZA
(ZOOP)
GA
GA
GA
GA
GA
GA
GA
TO
(TAP)
BERI
(RIP)
HYU
(FLING)

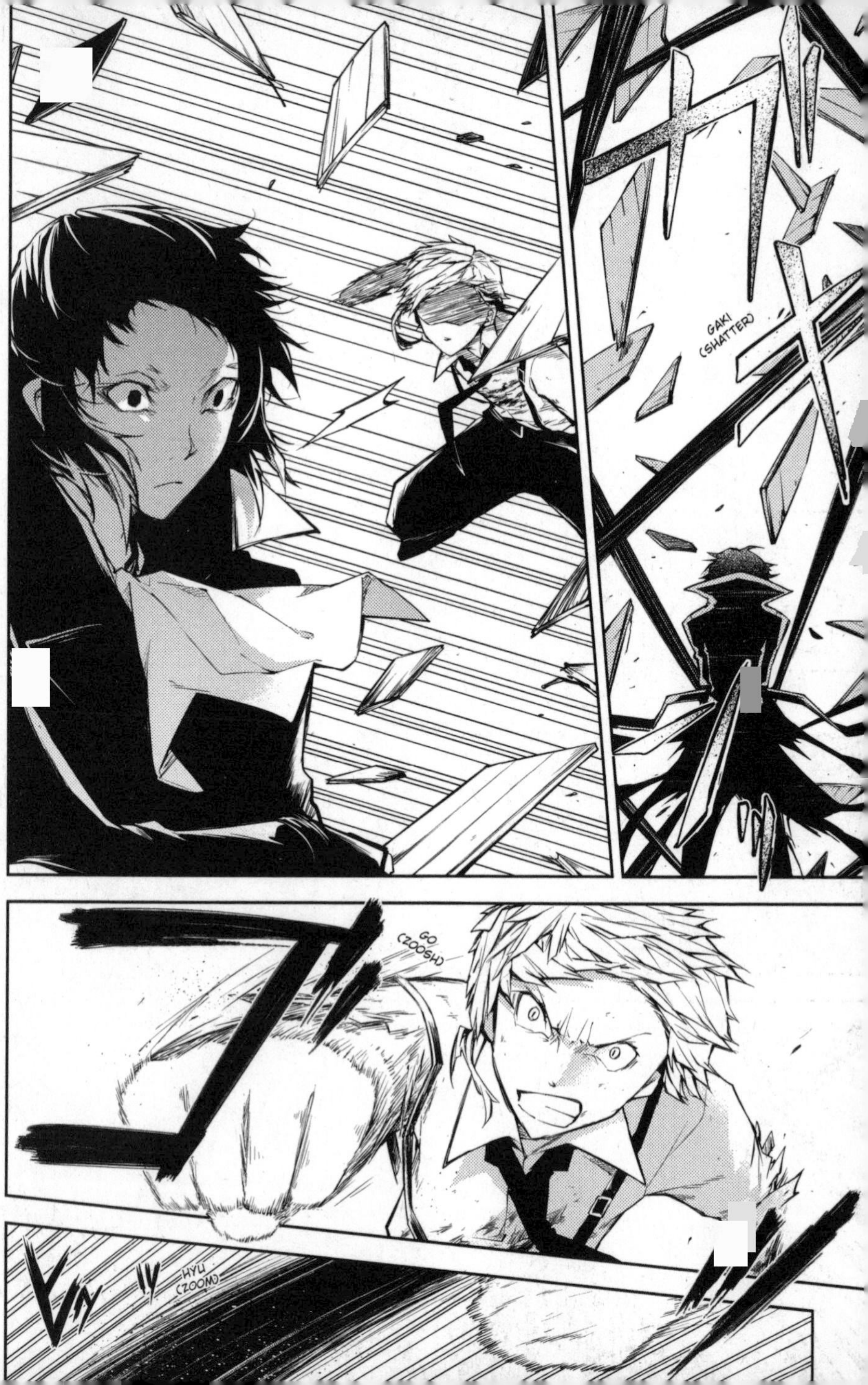
GAKI
(SHATTER)
GO
(ZOOSH)
HYU
(ZOOM)

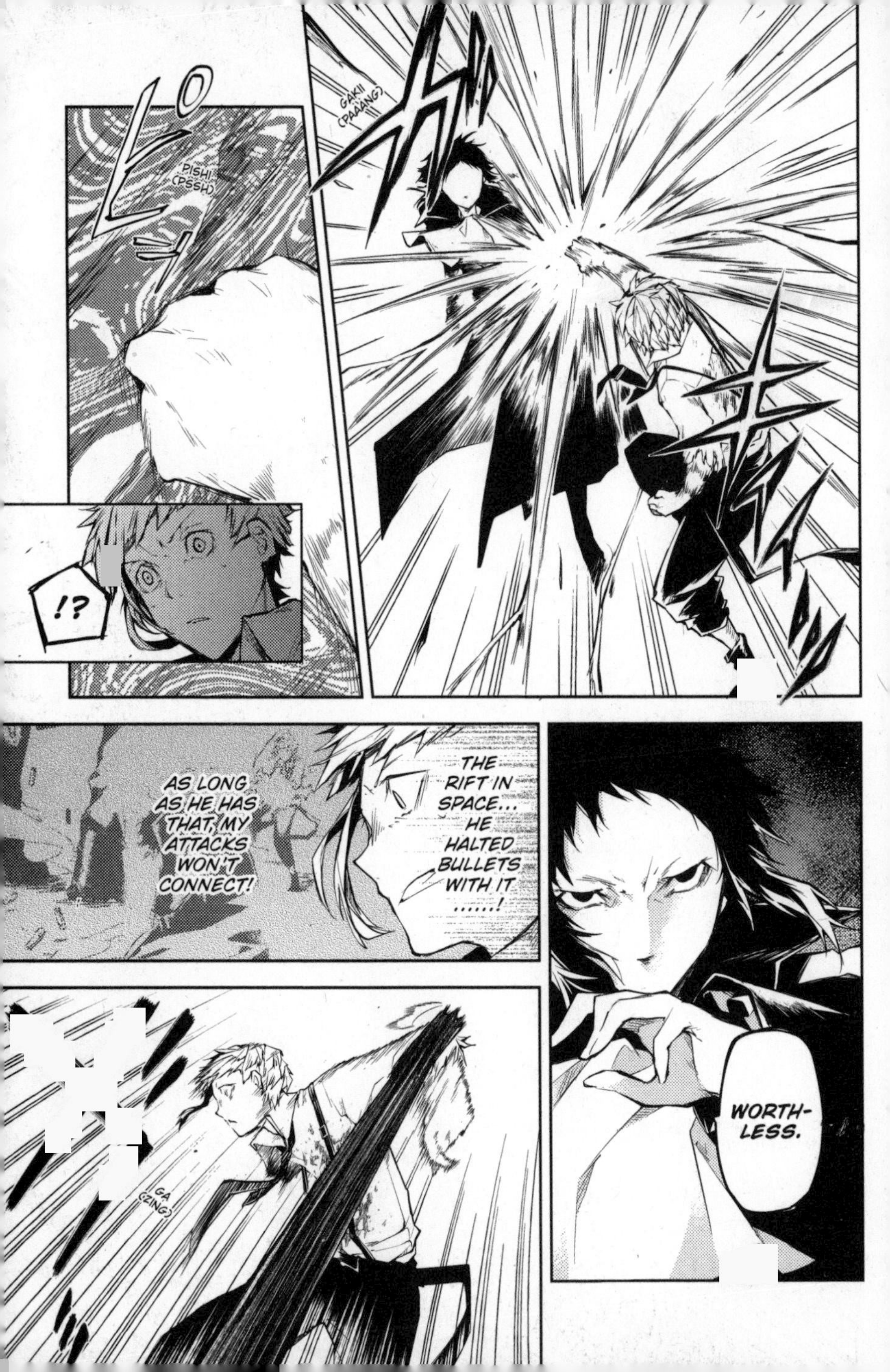
GAKII (PAAANG)
PISHI (PSSH)
!?
WORTH-LESS.
THE RIFT IN SPACE... HE HALTED BULLETS WITH IT ......!
AS LONG AS HE HAS THAT, MY ATTACKS WON'T CONNECT!
GA (ZING)

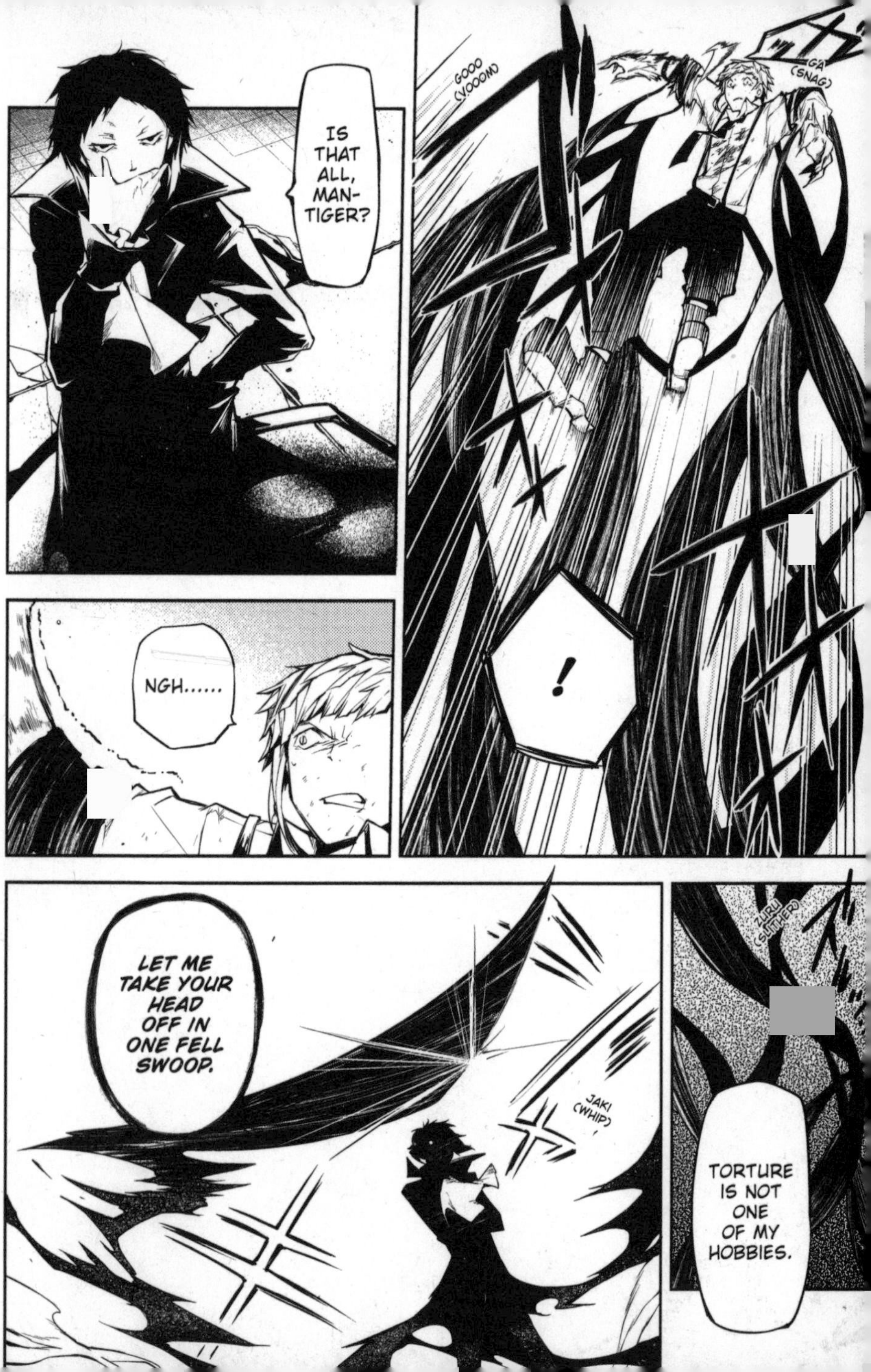
GOOO (VOOOM)
GA (SNAG)
!
IS THAT ALL, MAN-TIGER?
NGH......
ZURU (SLITHER)
TORTURE IS NOT ONE OF MY HOBBIES.
LET ME TAKE YOUR HEAD OFF IN ONE FELL SWOOP.
JAKI (WHIP)

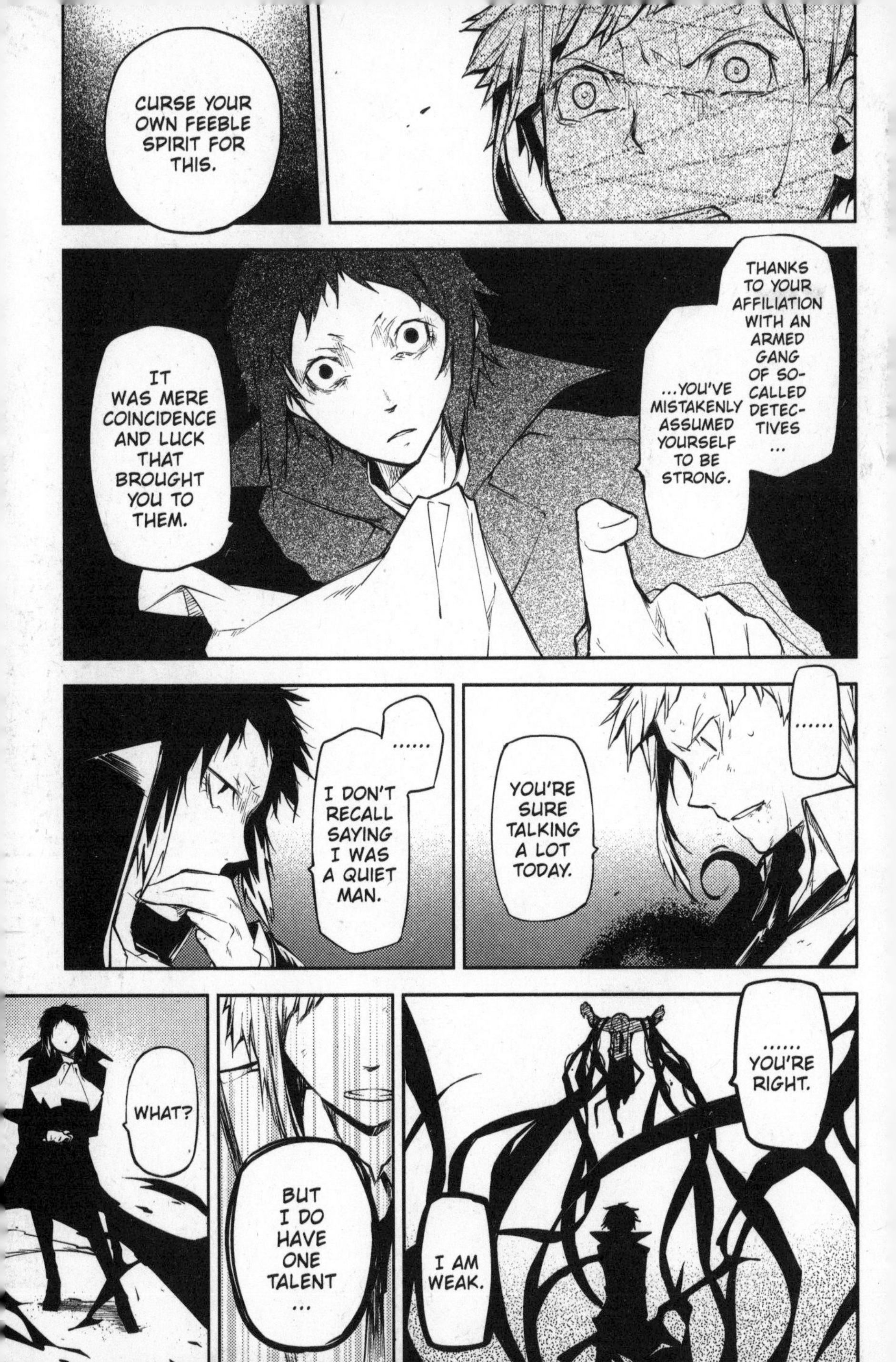
CURSE YOUR OWN FEEBLE SPIRIT FOR THIS.
THANKS TO YOUR AFFILIATION WITH AN ARMED GANG OF SO-CALLED DETECTIVES...
...YOU'VE MISTAKENLY ASSUMED YOURSELF TO BE STRONG.
IT WAS MERE COINCIDENCE AND LUCK THAT BROUGHT YOU TO THEM.
......
YOU'RE SURE TALKING A LOT TODAY.
......
I DON'T RECALL SAYING I WAS A QUIET MAN.
......YOU'RE RIGHT.
I AM WEAK.
BUT I DO HAVE ONE TALENT...
WHAT?

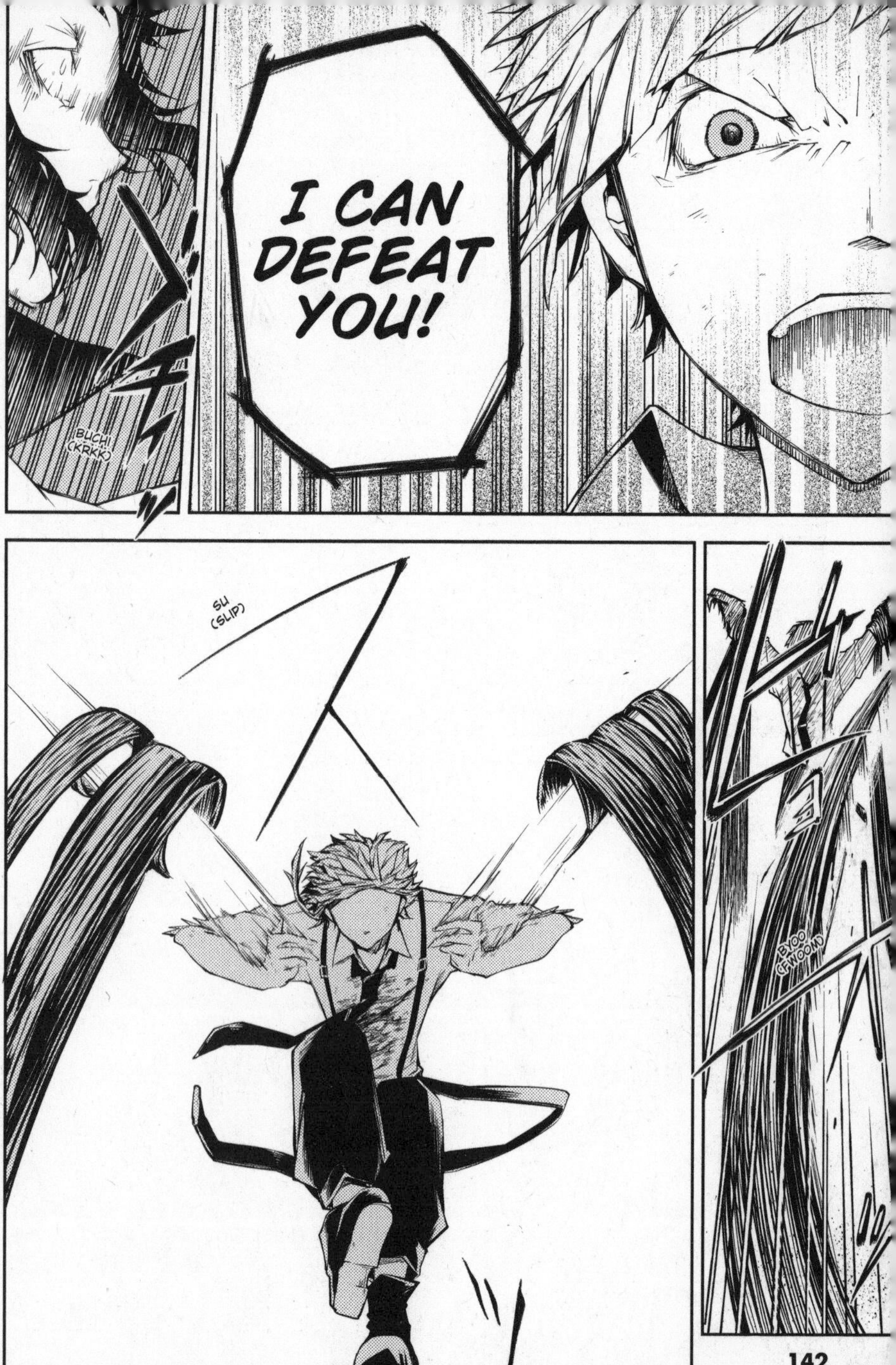
I CAN DEFEAT YOU!
BUCHI (KRKK)
BYOO (FWOOM)
SU (SLIP)

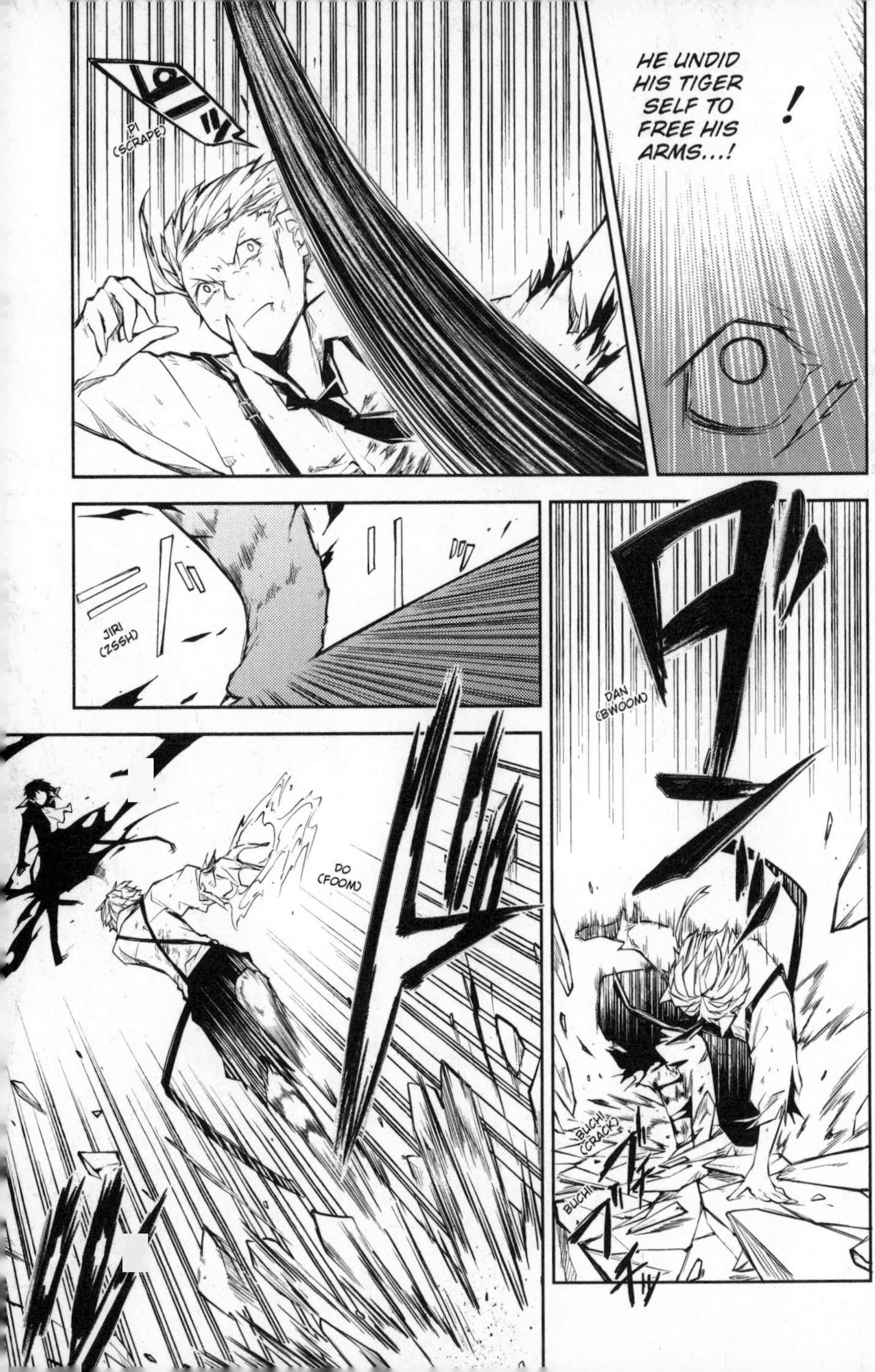
HE UNDID HIS TIGER SELF TO FREE HIS ARMS...!
!
PI (SCRAPE)
DAN (BWOOM)
BUCHI (CRACK)
BUCHI
JIRI (ZSSH)
DO (FOOM)

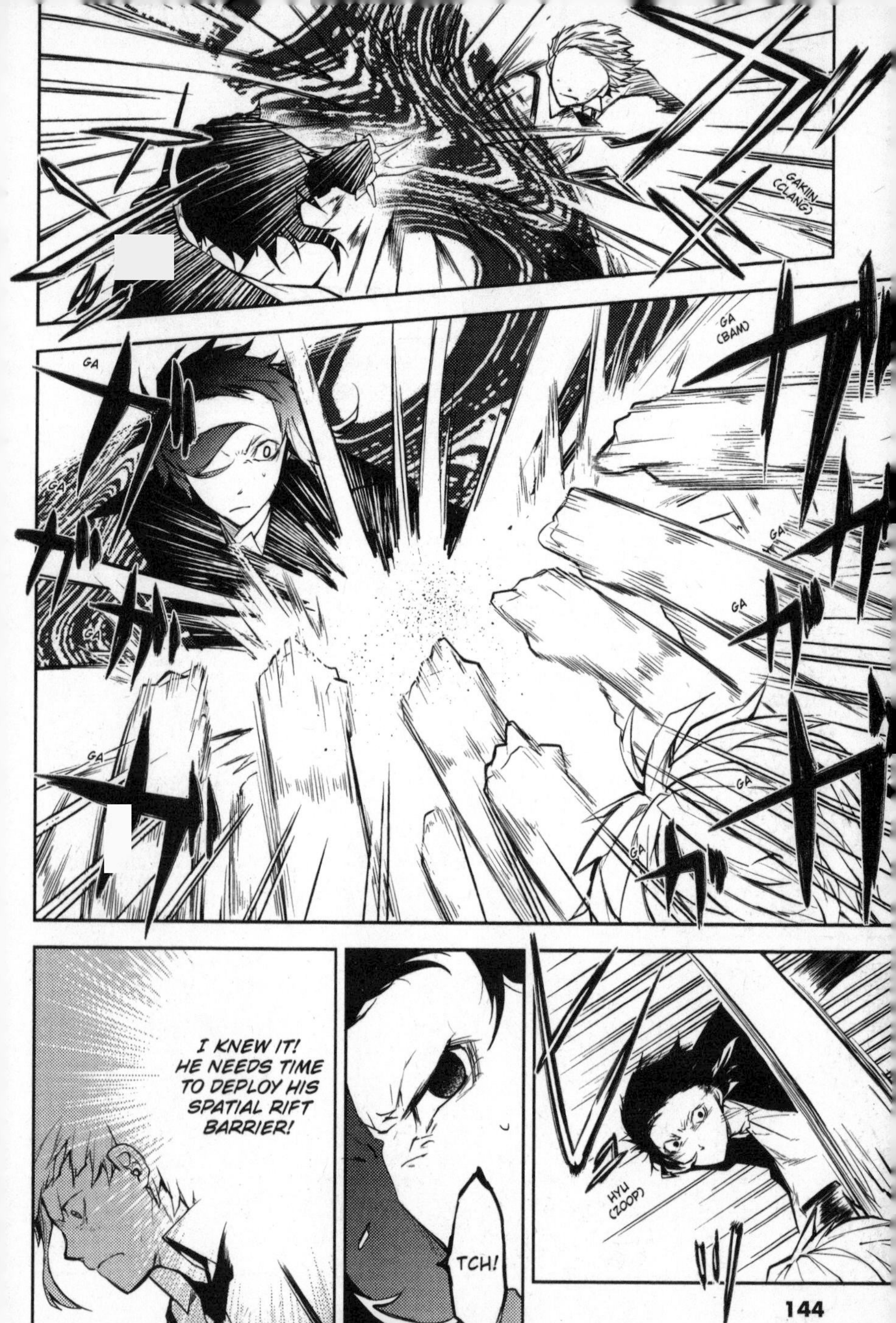
GAKIIN (CLANG)
GA (BAM)
GA
GA
GA
GA
GA
GA
GA
GA
HYU (ZOOP)
TCH!
I KNEW IT! HE NEEDS TIME TO DEPLOY HIS SPATIAL RIFT BARRIER!

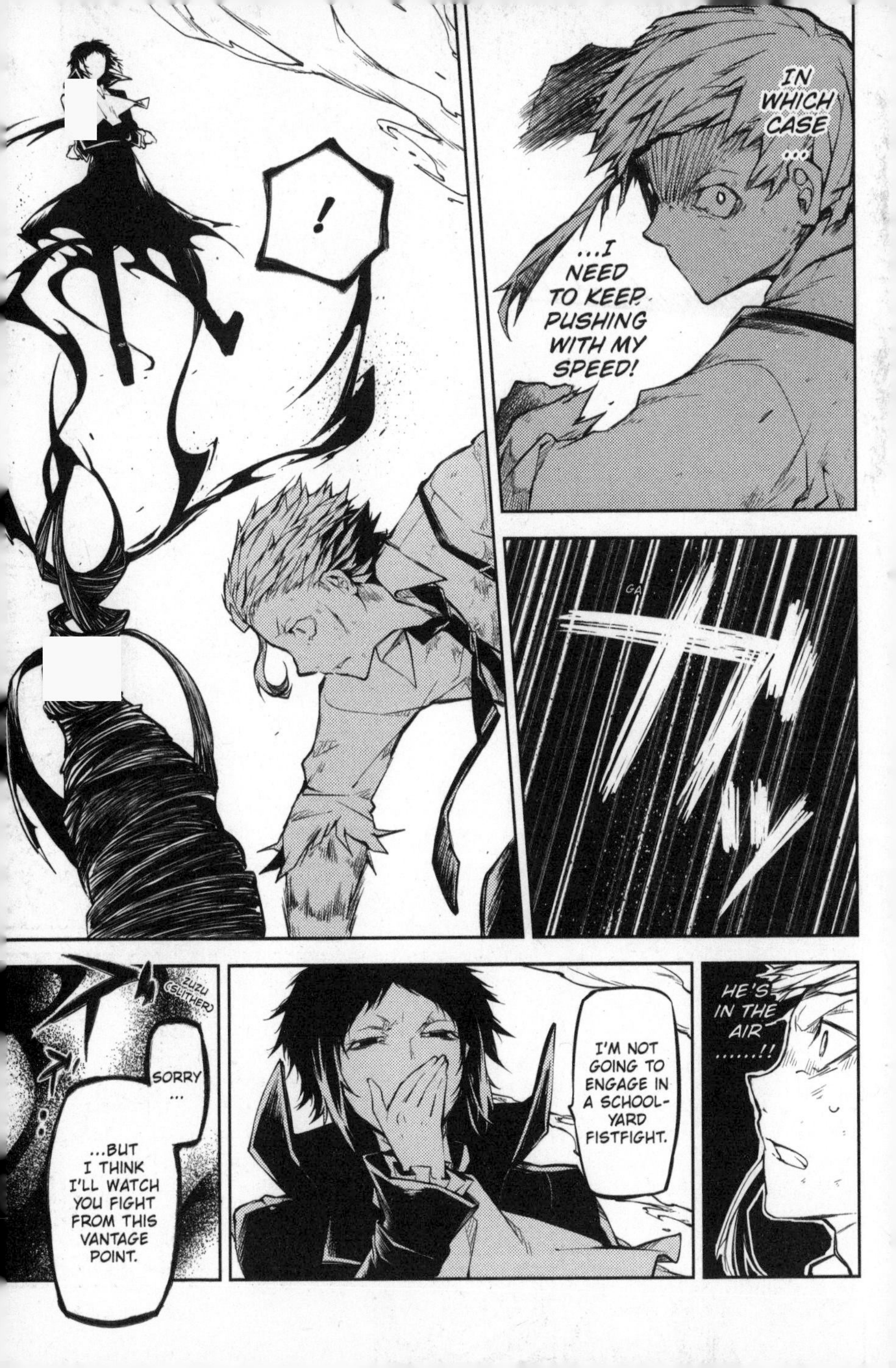
IN WHICH CASE ...
...I NEED TO KEEP PUSHING WITH MY SPEED!
GA
!
HE'S IN THE AIR ......!!
I'M NOT GOING TO ENGAGE IN A SCHOOL-YARD FISTFIGHT.
ZUZU (SLITHER)
SORRY ...
...BUT I THINK I'LL WATCH YOU FIGHT FROM THIS VANTAGE POINT.

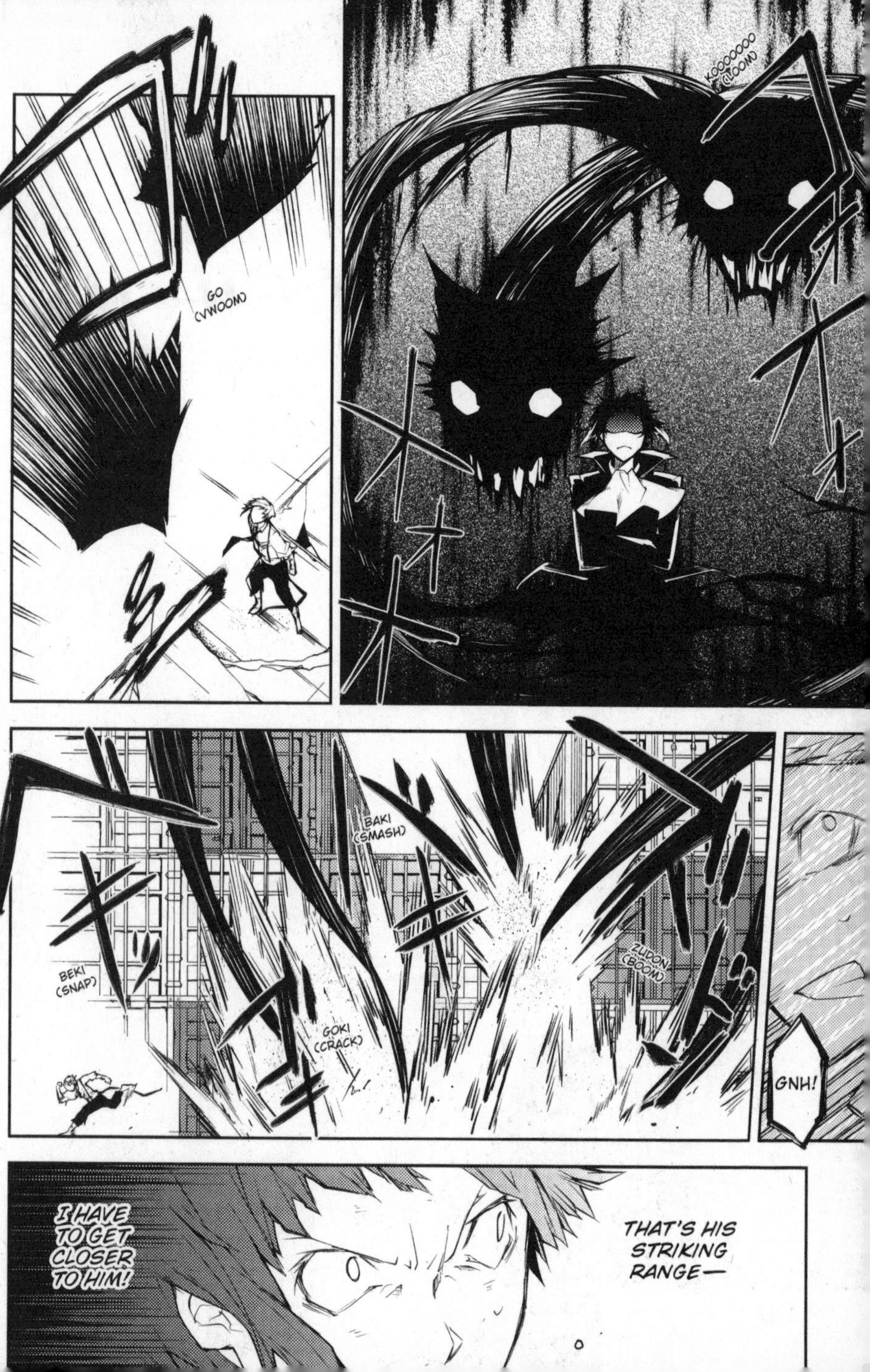
KOOOOOOO
(LOOM)
GO
(VWOOM)
GNH!
BAKI
(SMASH)
ZUDON
(BOOM)
GOKI
(CRACK)
BEKI
(SNAP)
THAT'S HIS STRIKING RANGE—
I HAVE TO GET CLOSER TO HIM!

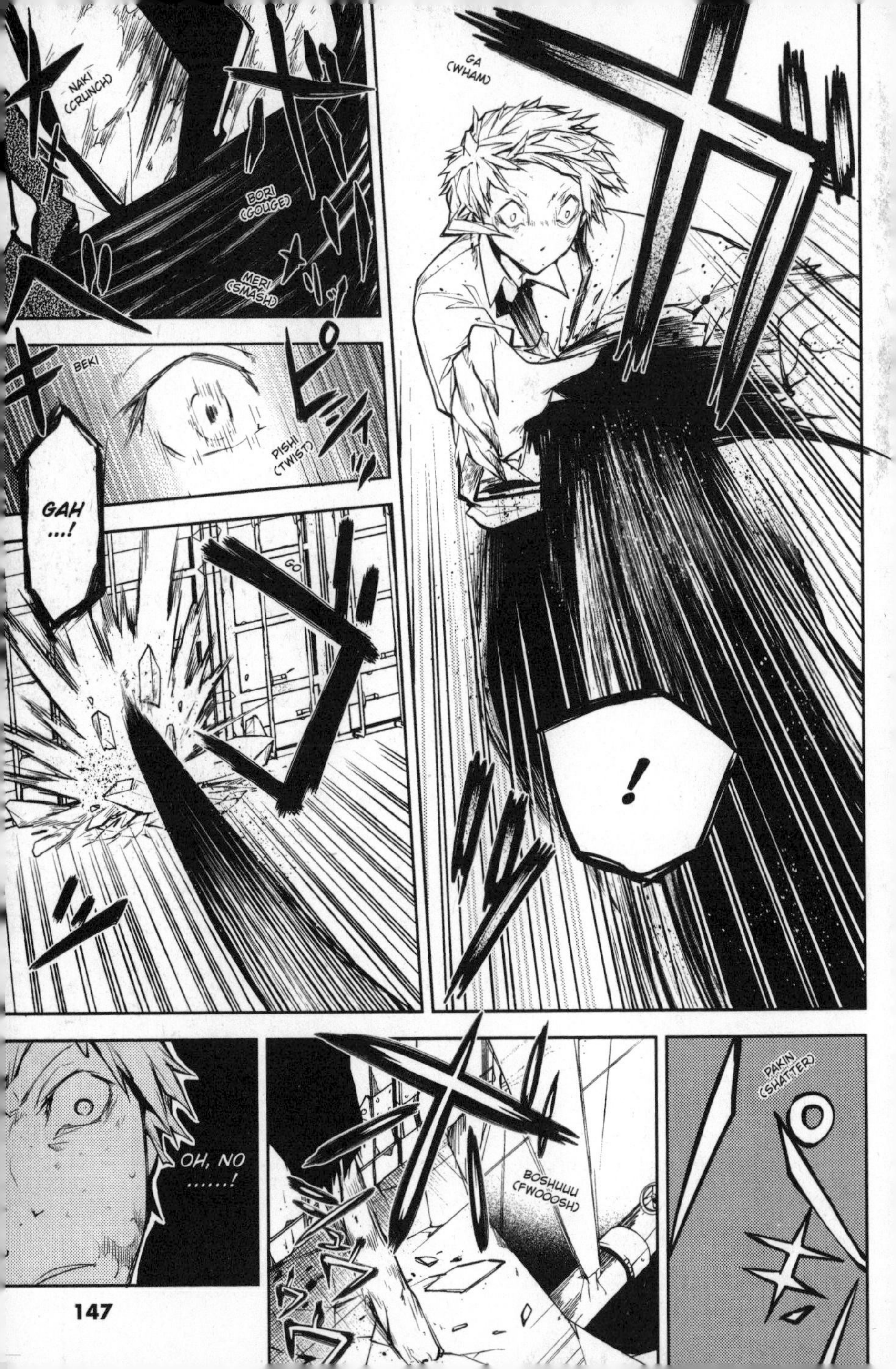
GA (WHAM)
!
NAKI (CRUNCH)
BORI (GOUGE)
MERI (SMASH)
BEKI
PISHI (TWIST)
GAH ...!
GO
PAKIN (SHATTER)
BOSHUUU (FWOOOSH)
OH, NO ......!

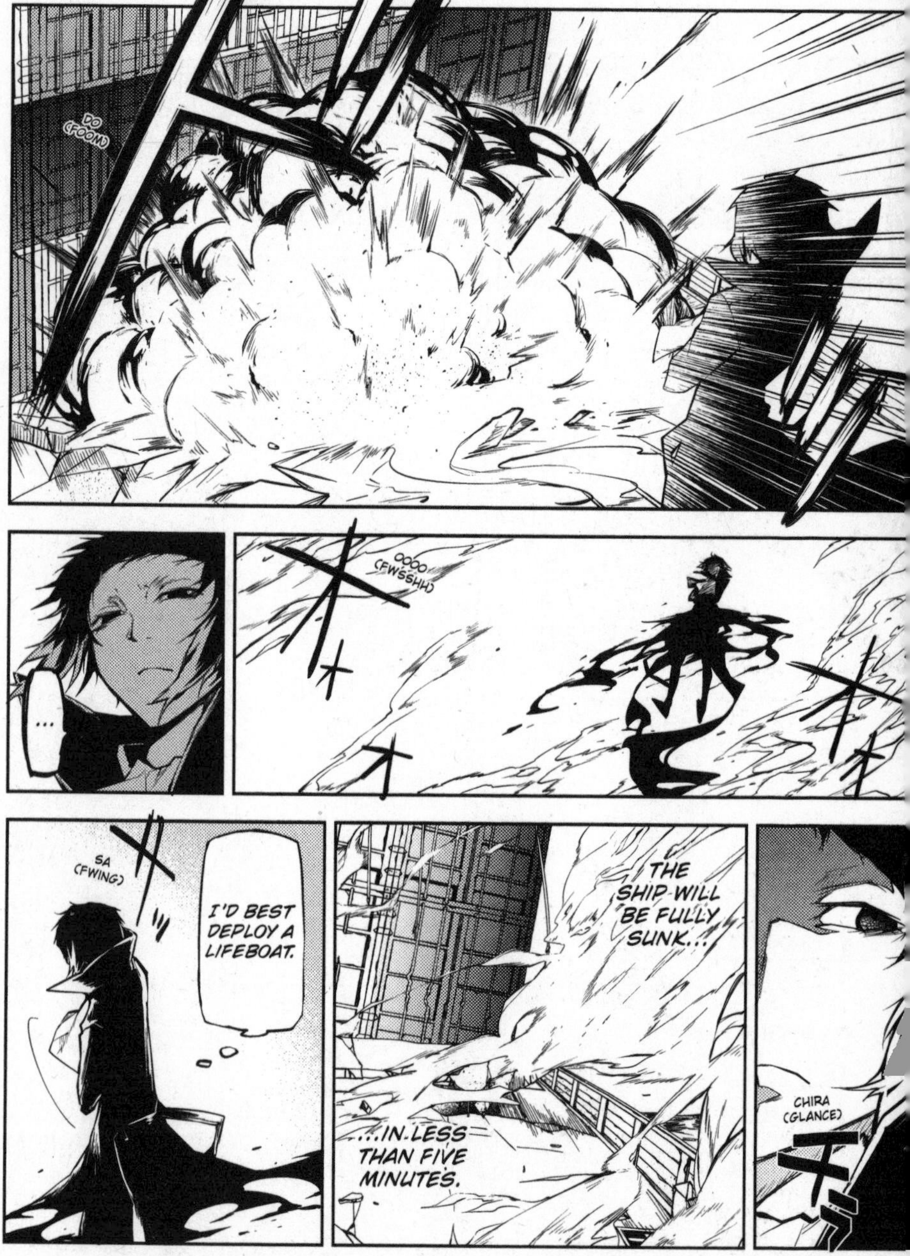
DO (FOOM)
OOOO (FWSSHH)
...
CHIRA (GLANCE)
THE SHIP WILL BE FULLY SUNK...
...IN LESS THAN FIVE MINUTES.
SA (FWING)
I'D BEST DEPLOY A LIFEBOAT.

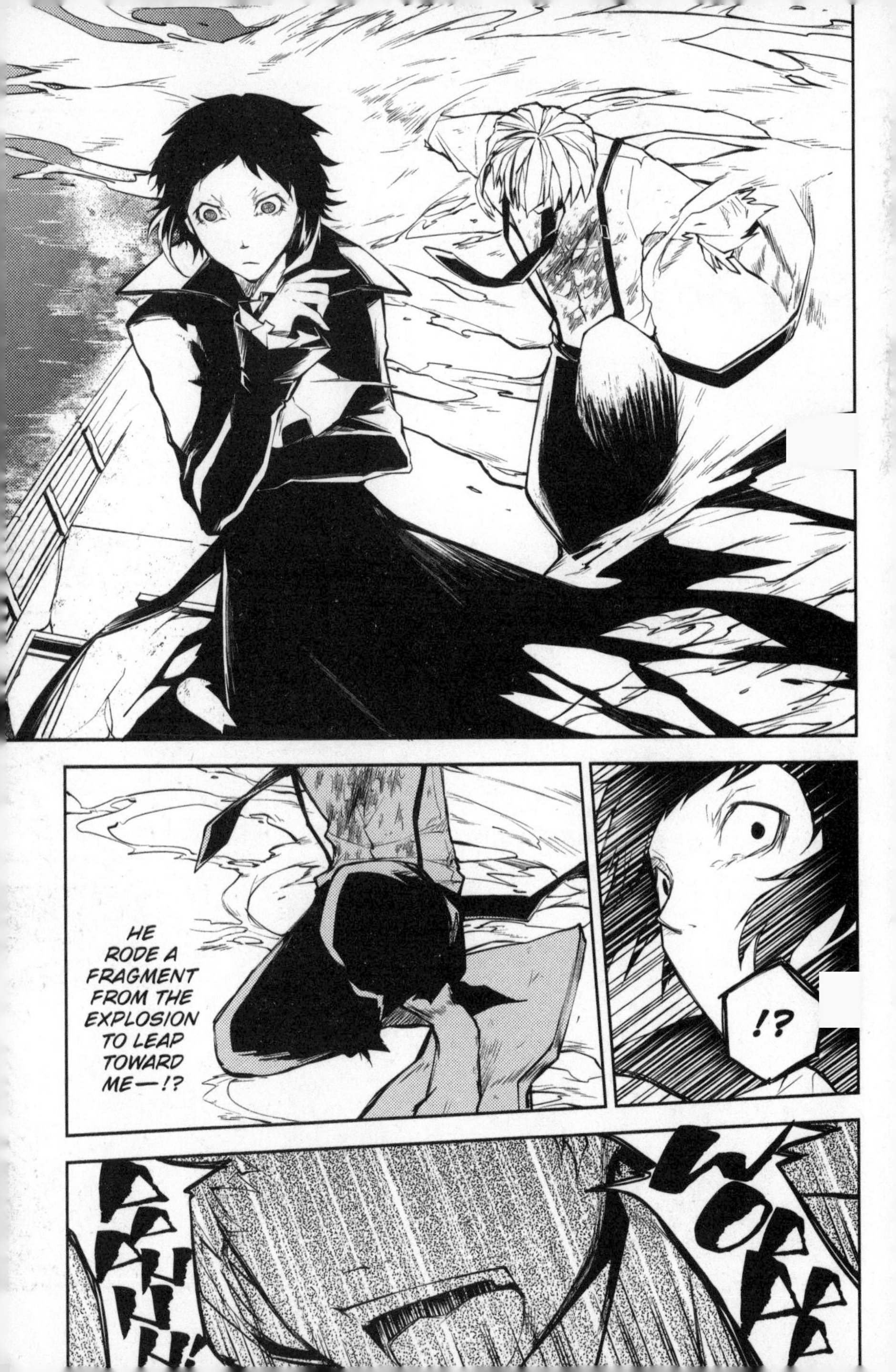
!?
HE RODE A FRAGMENT FROM THE EXPLOSION TO LEAP TOWARD ME—!?

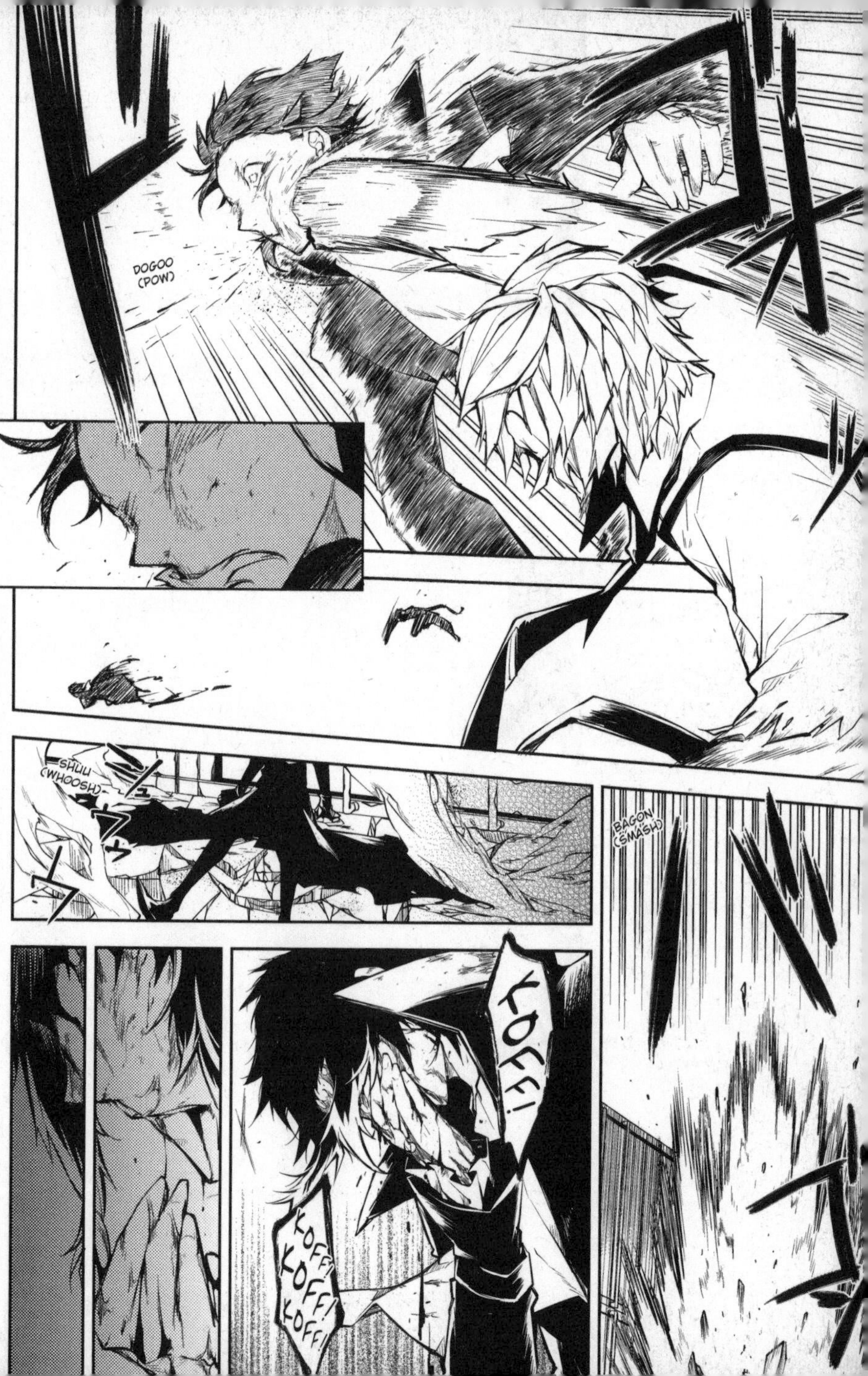
DOGOO (POW)
BAGON (SMASH)
SHUU (WHOOSH)
KOFF!
KOFF! KOFF! KOFF!

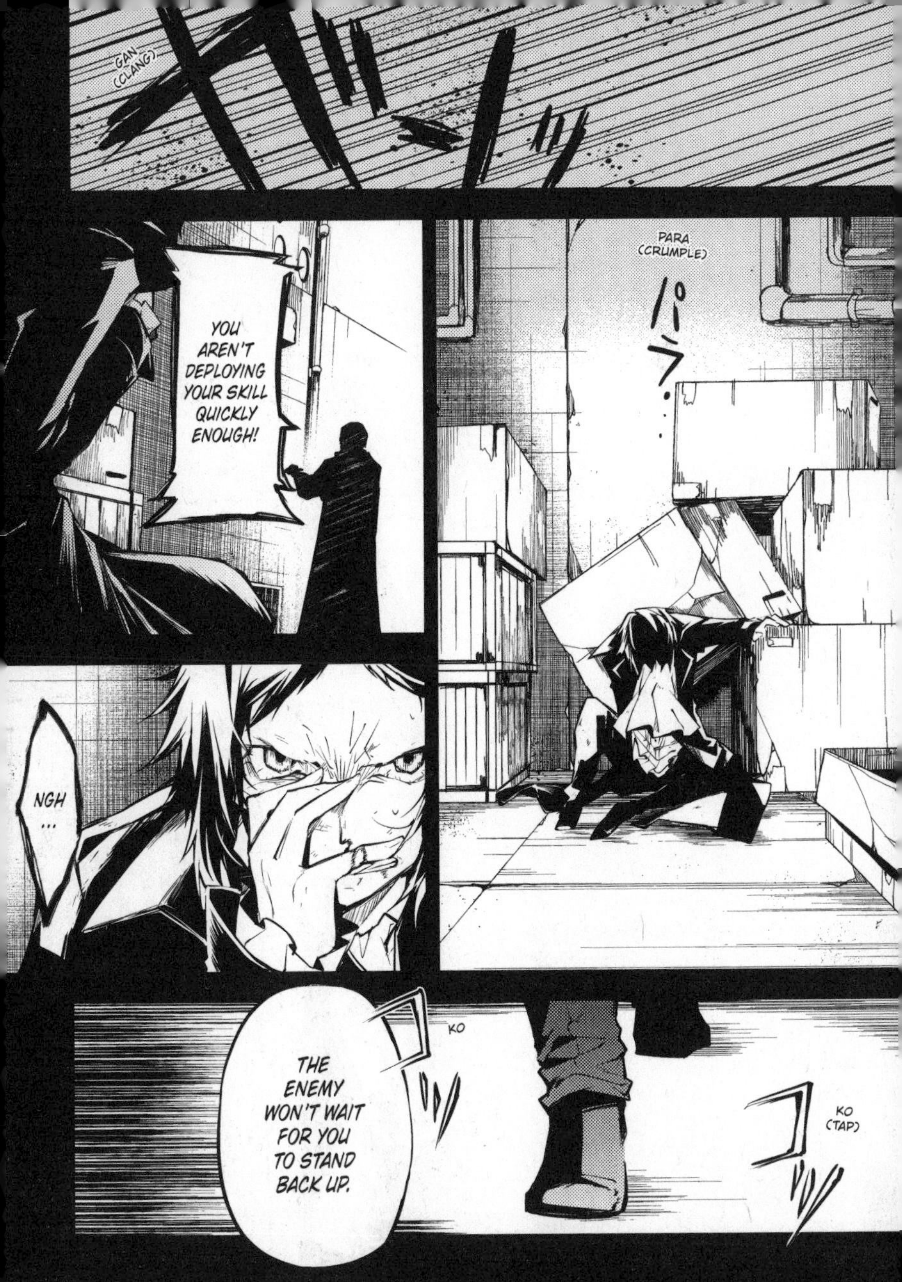
GAN (CLANG)
PARA (CRUMPLE)
YOU AREN'T DEPLOYING YOUR SKILL QUICKLY ENOUGH!
NGH ...
KO
KO (TAP)
THE ENEMY WON'T WAIT FOR YOU TO STAND BACK UP.

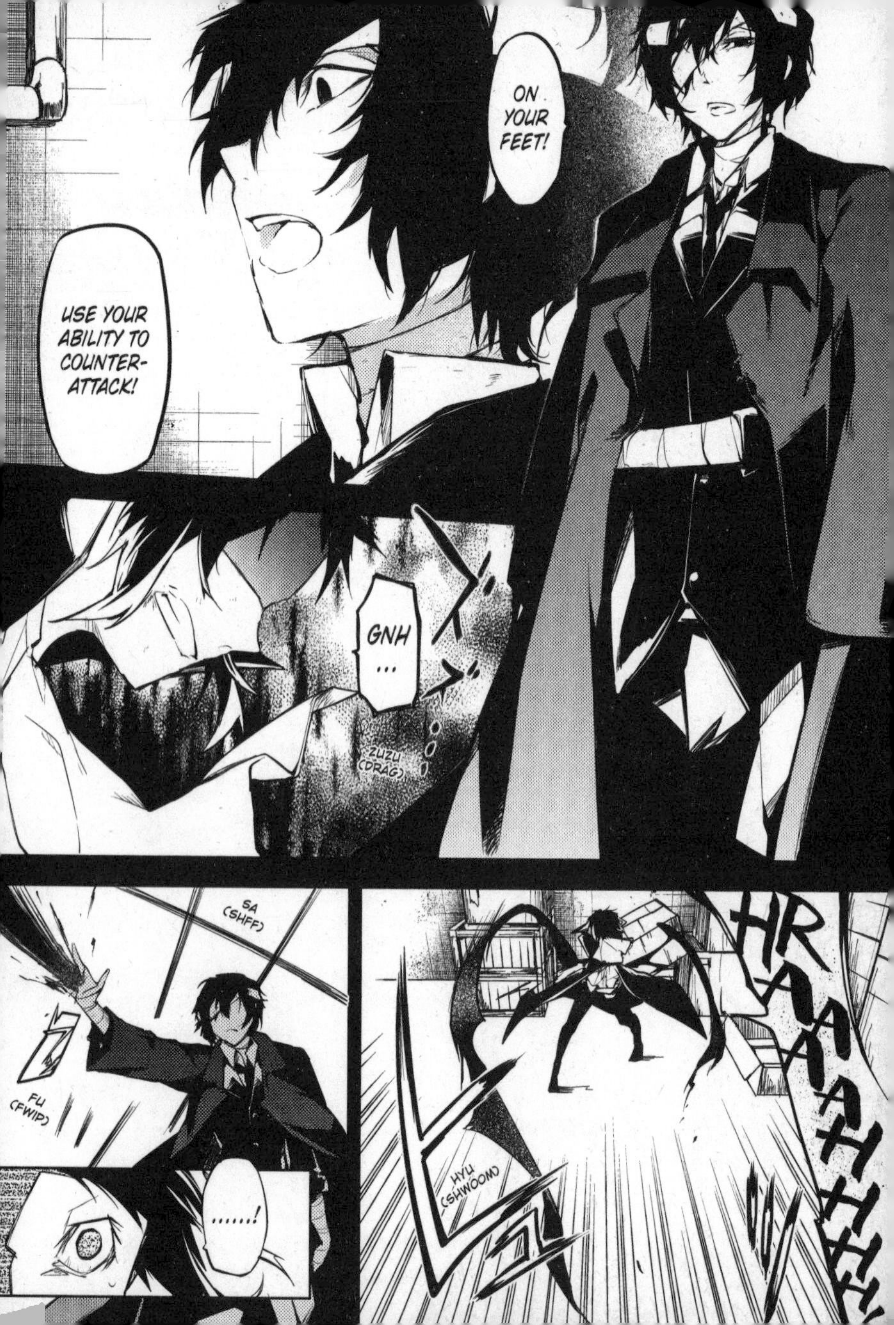
ON YOUR FEET!
USE YOUR ABILITY TO COUNTER-ATTACK!
GNH ...
ZUZU (DRAG)
HRAAAHHHHH!
HYU (SHWOOM)
SA (SHFF)
FU (FWIP)
......!

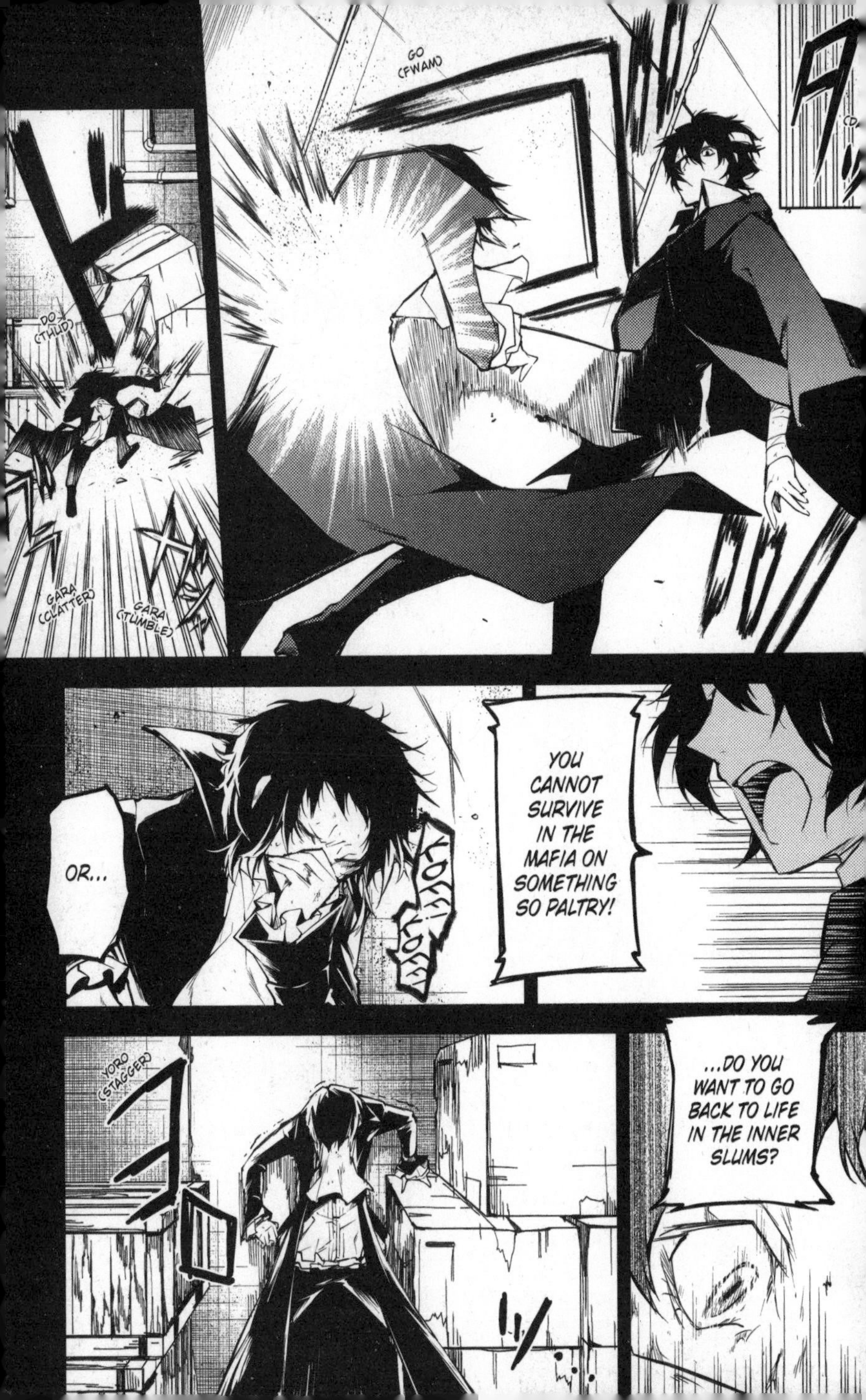
GO (FWAM)
DO (THUD)
GARA (CLATTER)
GARA (TUMBLE)
YOU CANNOT SURVIVE IN THE MAFIA ON SOMETHING SO PALTRY!
KOFF! KOFF
OR...
...DO YOU WANT TO GO BACK TO LIFE IN THE INNER SLUMS?
YORO (STAGGER)

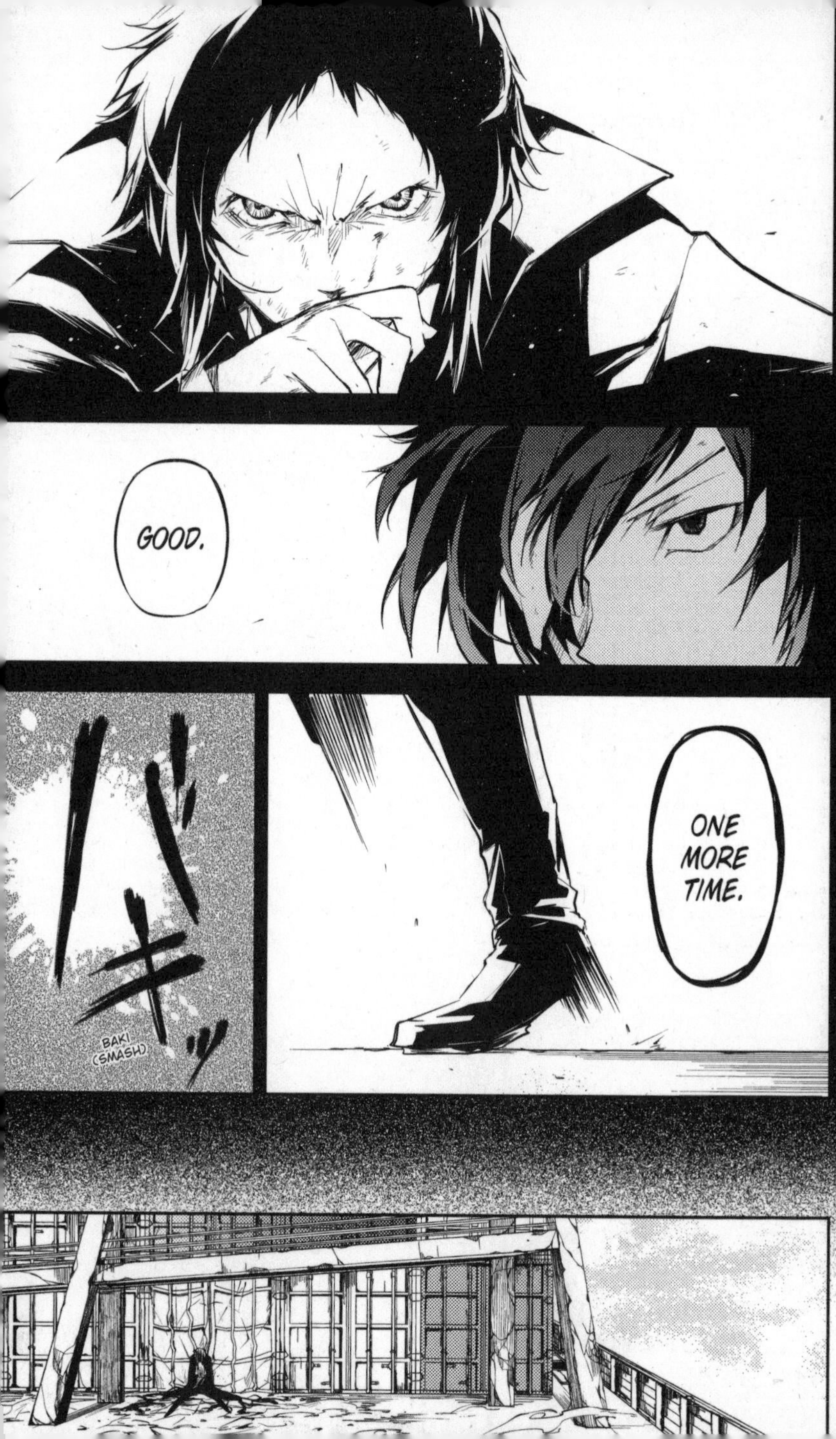
GOOD.
ONE MORE TIME.
BAKI (SMASH)

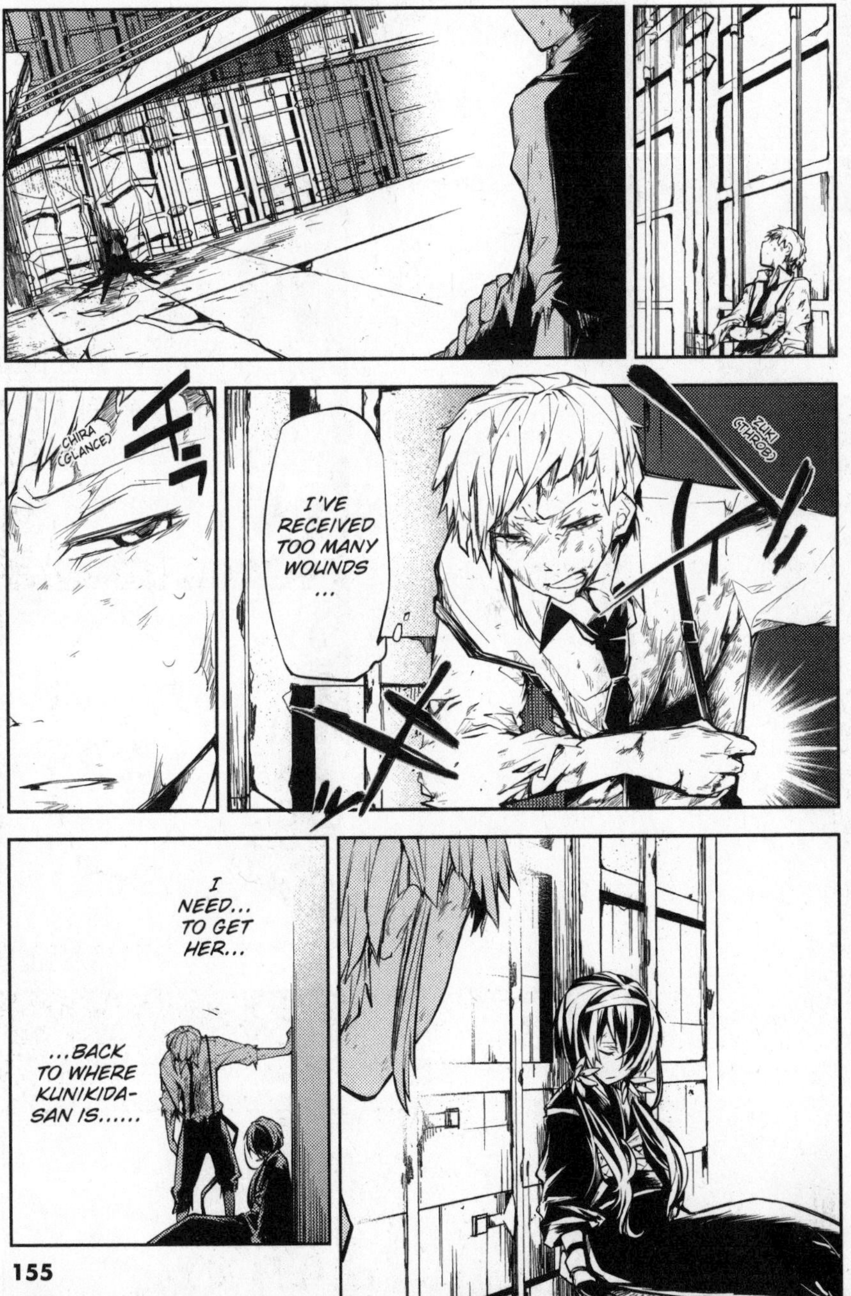
ZUKI (THROB)
I'VE RECEIVED TOO MANY WOUNDS...
CHIRA (GLANCE)
I NEED... TO GET HER...
...BACK TO WHERE KUNIKIDA-SAN IS......

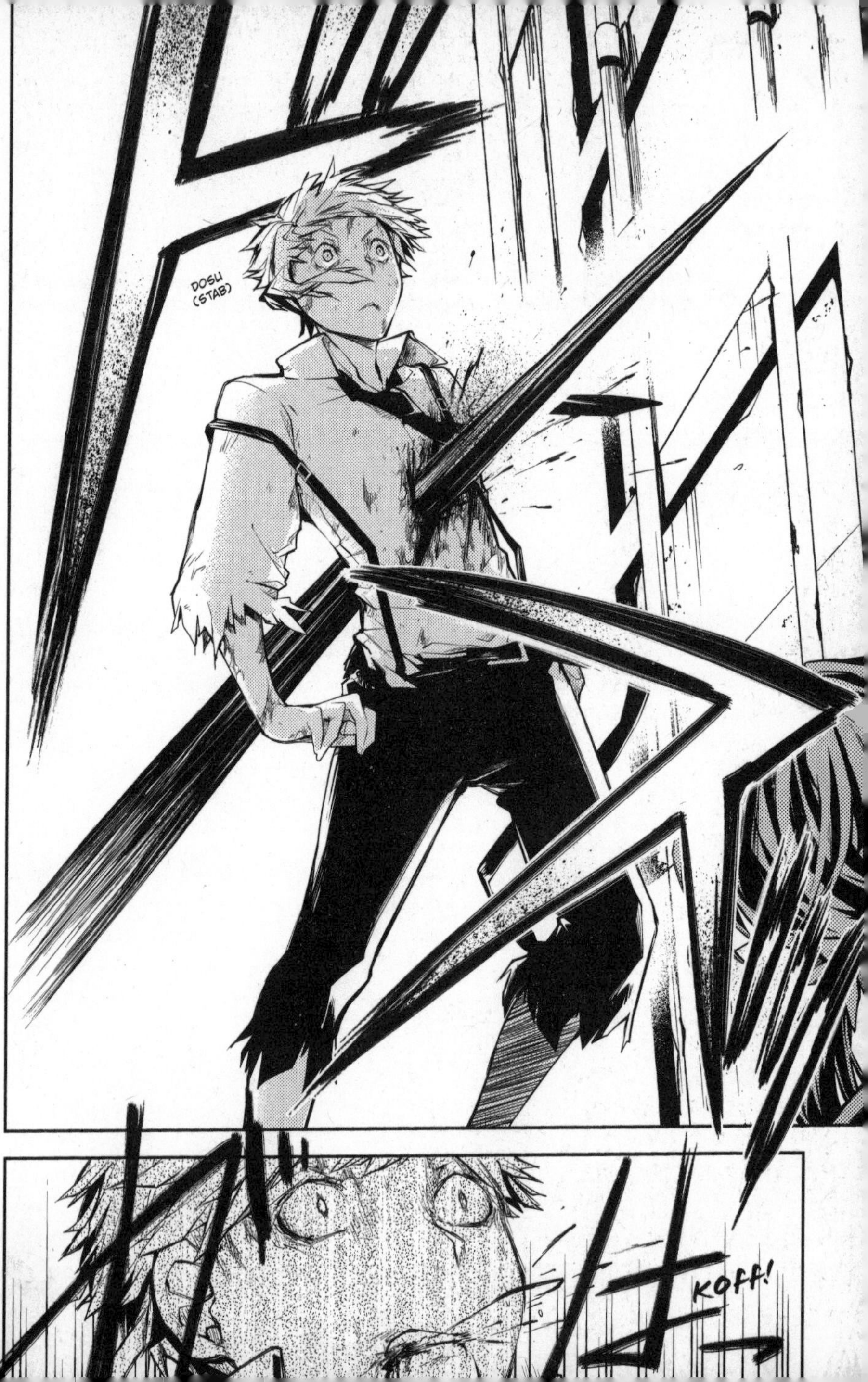
DOSU
(STAB)
KOFF!

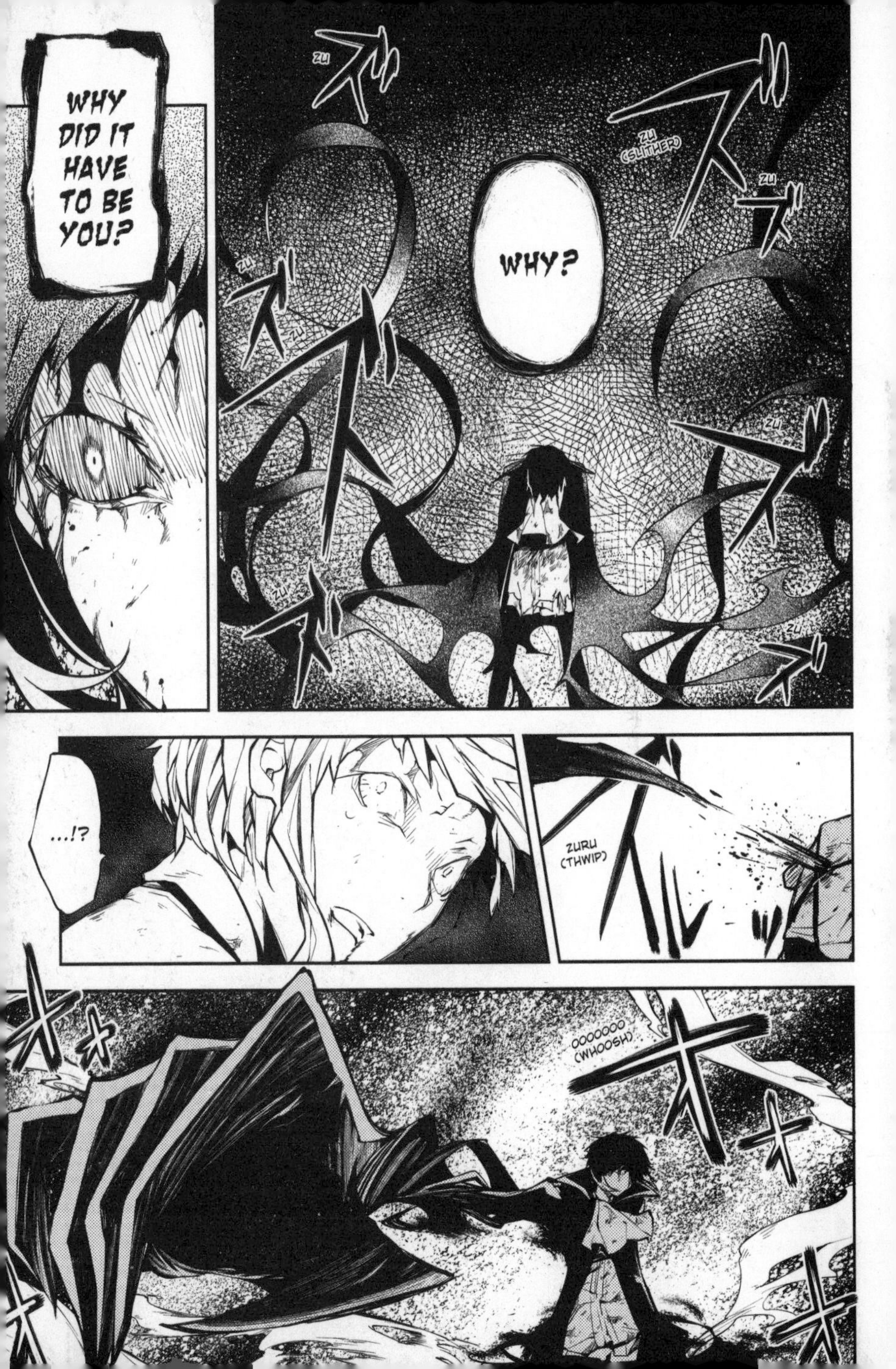

ZU (SLITHER)
ZU
ZU
WHY?
ZU
ZU
ZU
ZU
ZU
WHY DID IT HAVE TO BE YOU?
ZURU (THWIP)
...!?
OOOOOOO (WHOOSH)

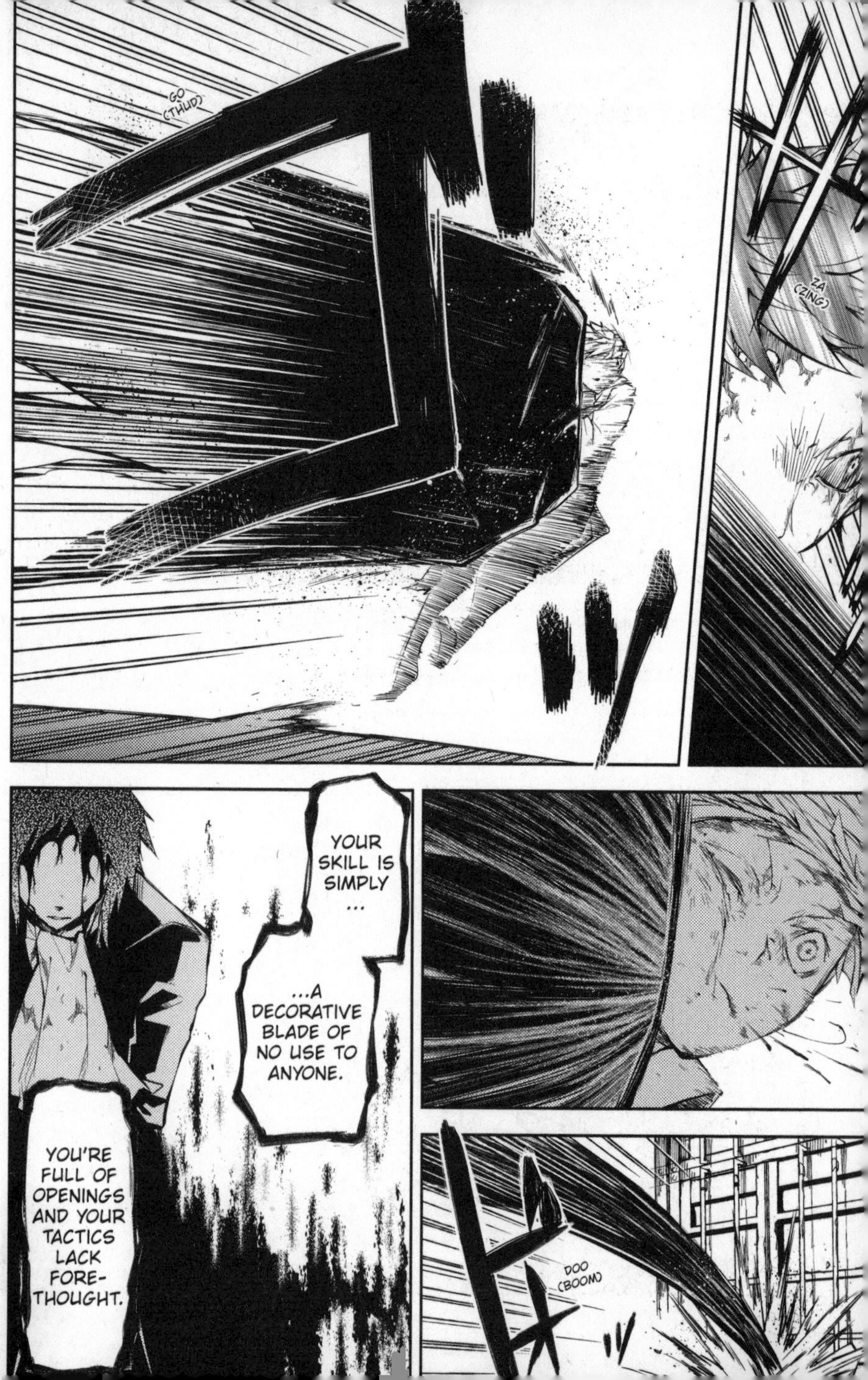
ZA (ZING)
GO (THUD)
DOO (BOOM)
YOUR SKILL IS SIMPLY ...
...A DECORATIVE BLADE OF NO USE TO ANYONE.
YOU'RE FULL OF OPENINGS AND YOUR TACTICS LACK FORE-THOUGHT.

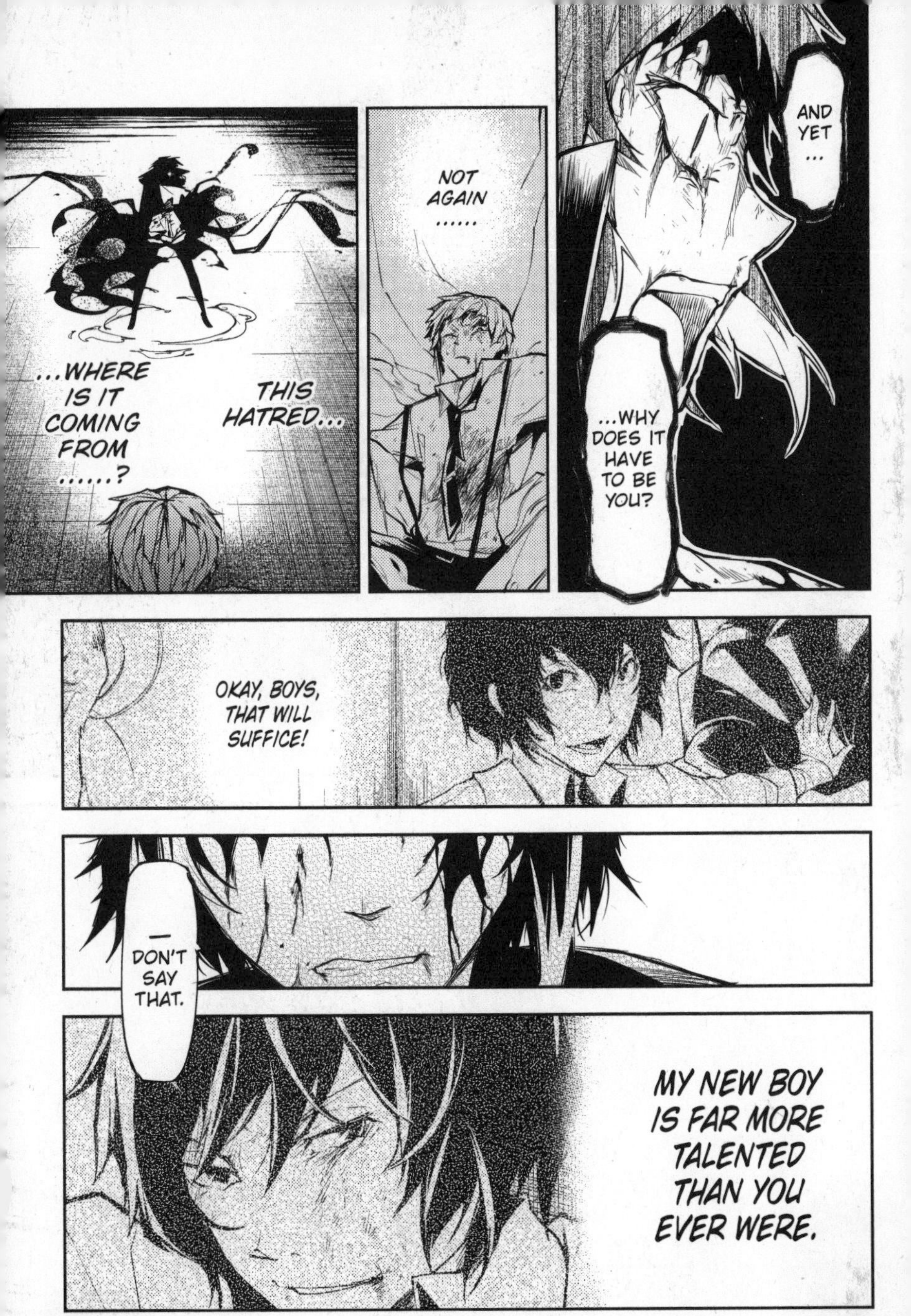
AND YET ...
...WHY DOES IT HAVE TO BE YOU?
NOT AGAIN ......
THIS HATRED...
...WHERE IS IT COMING FROM ......?
OKAY, BOYS, THAT WILL SUFFICE!
—DON'T SAY THAT.
MY NEW BOY IS FAR MORE TALENTED THAN YOU EVER WERE.

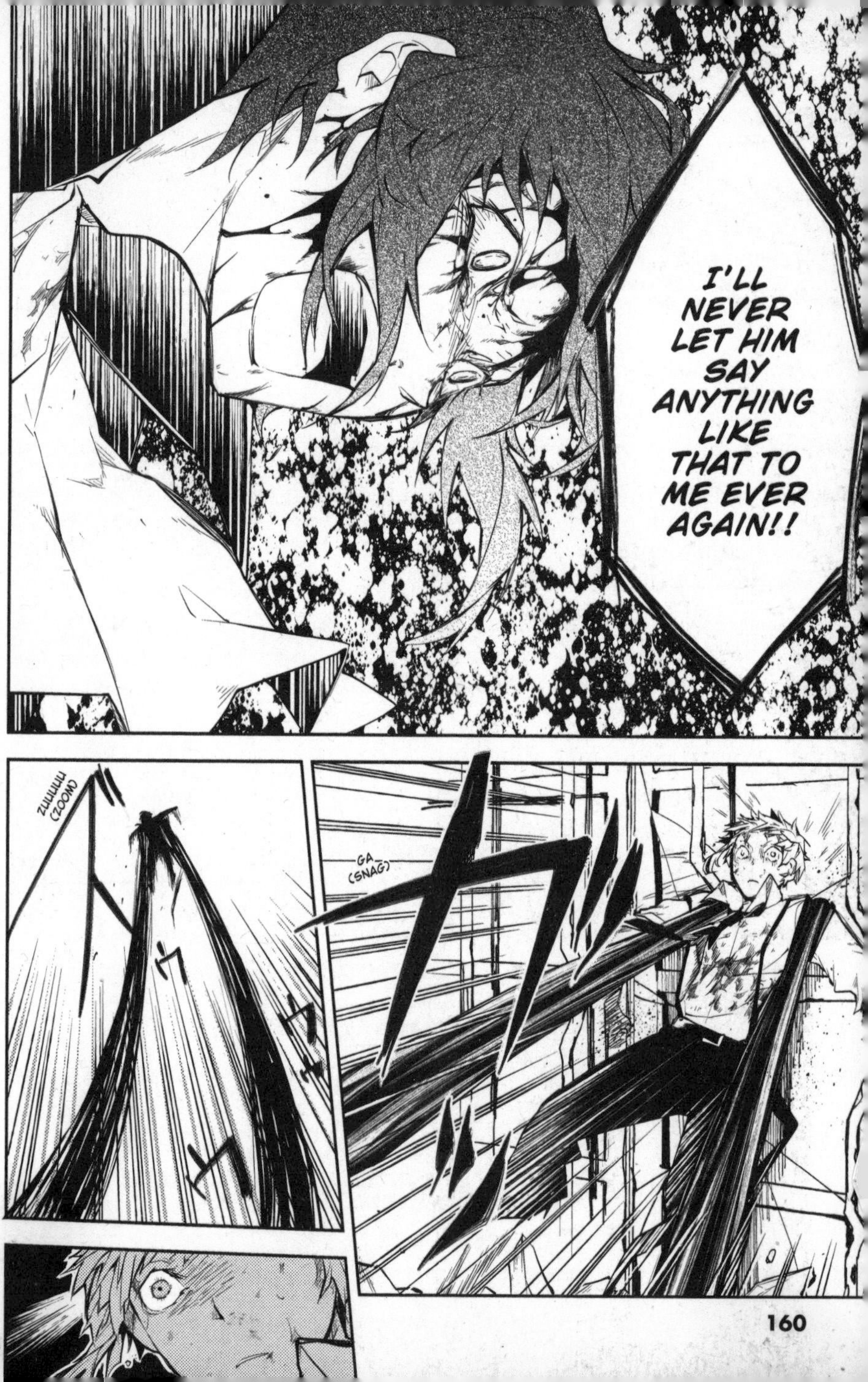
I'LL NEVER LET HIM SAY ANYTHING LIKE THAT TO ME EVER AGAIN!!
GA (SNAG)
ZUUUUUN (ZOOM)

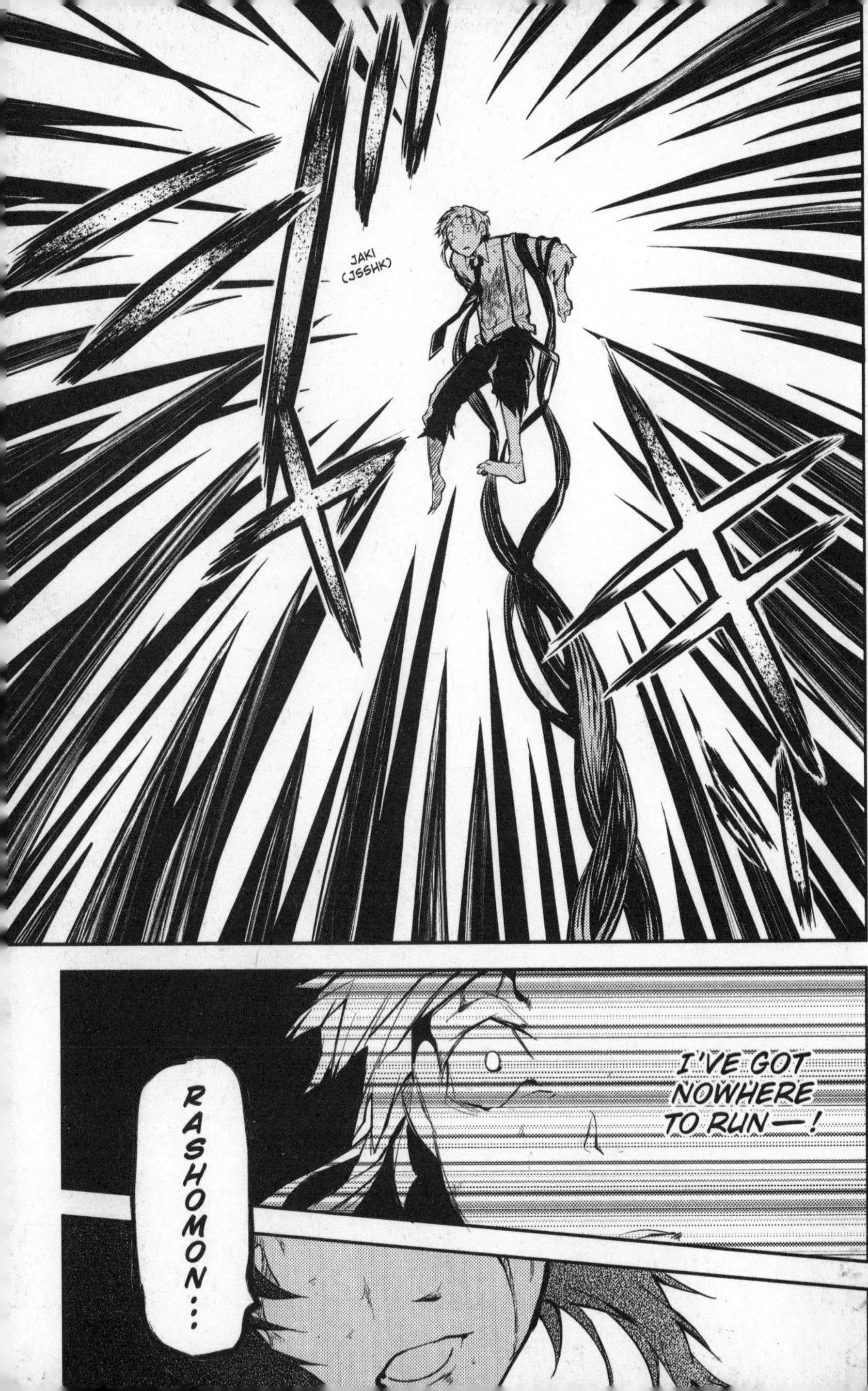
JAKI (JSSHK)
I'VE GOT NOWHERE TO RUN—!
RASHOMON...

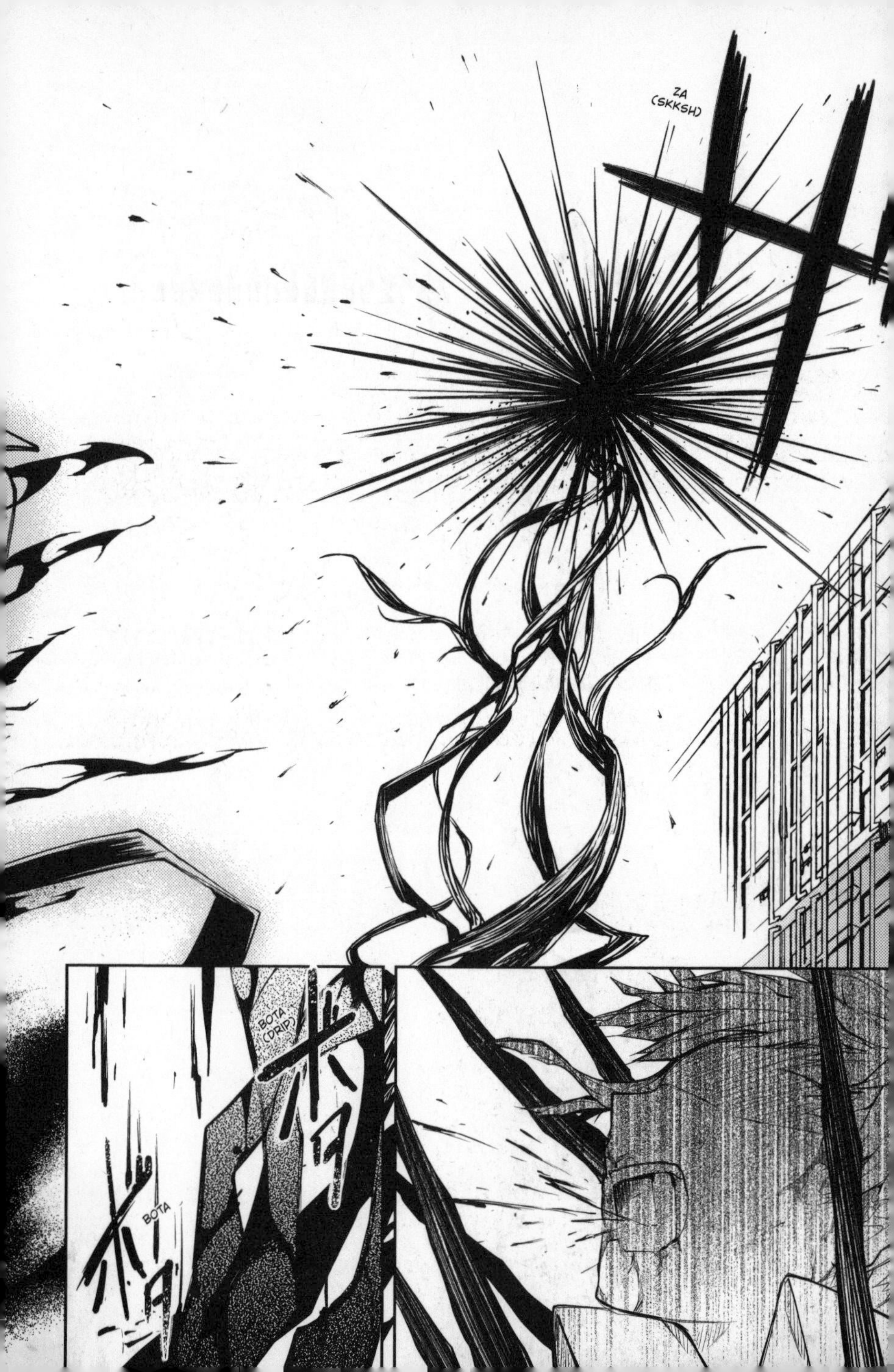
ZA
(SKKSH)
BOTA
(DRIP)
BOTA

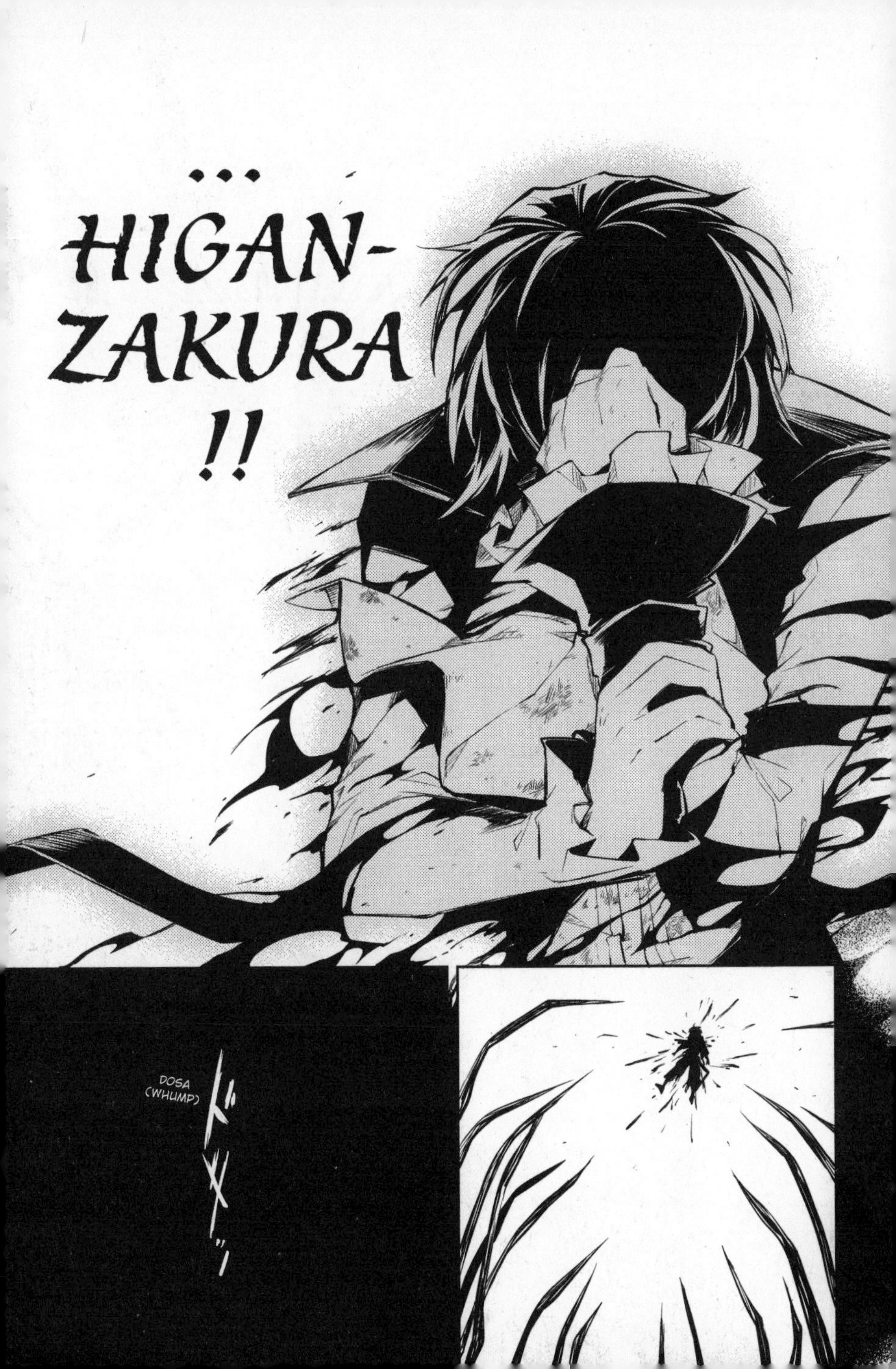
...HIGAN-ZAKURA!!
DOSA (WHUMP)

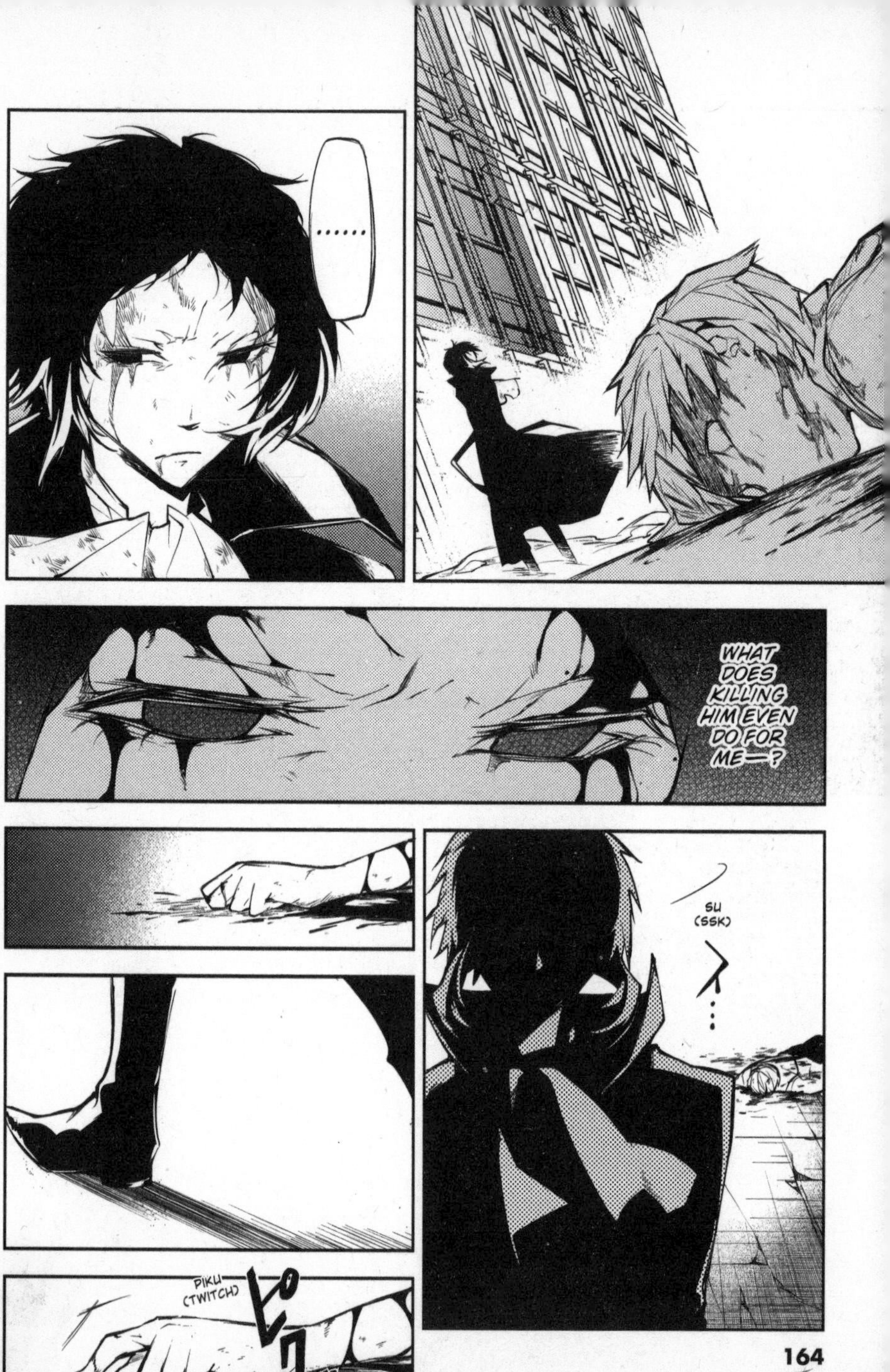
......
WHAT DOES KILLING HIM EVEN DO FOR ME—?
SU (SSK)
ス…
PIKU (TWITCH)
ピクッ

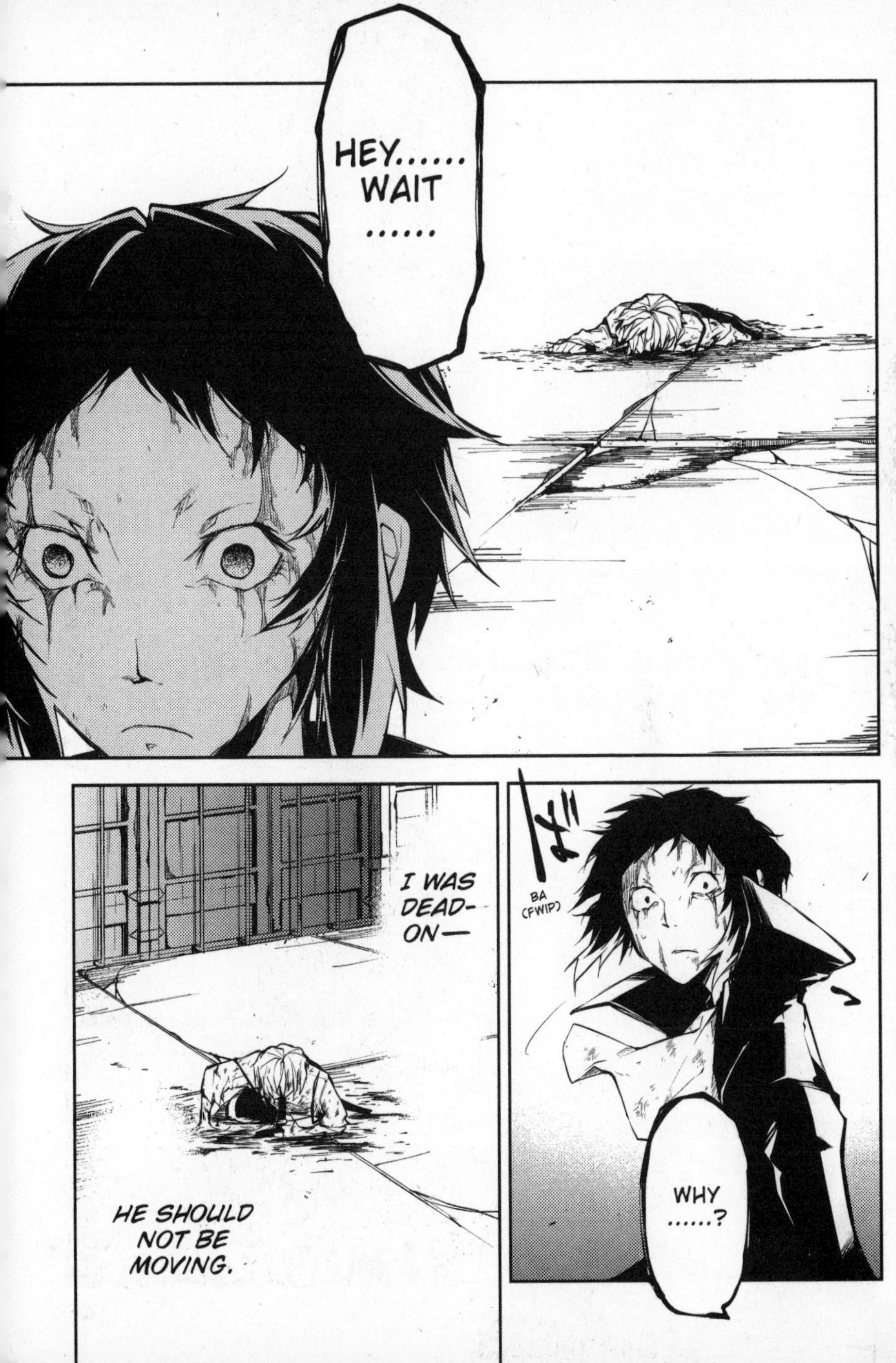
HEY...... WAIT ......
BA (FWIP)
WHY ......?
I WAS DEAD-ON—
HE SHOULD NOT BE MOVING.

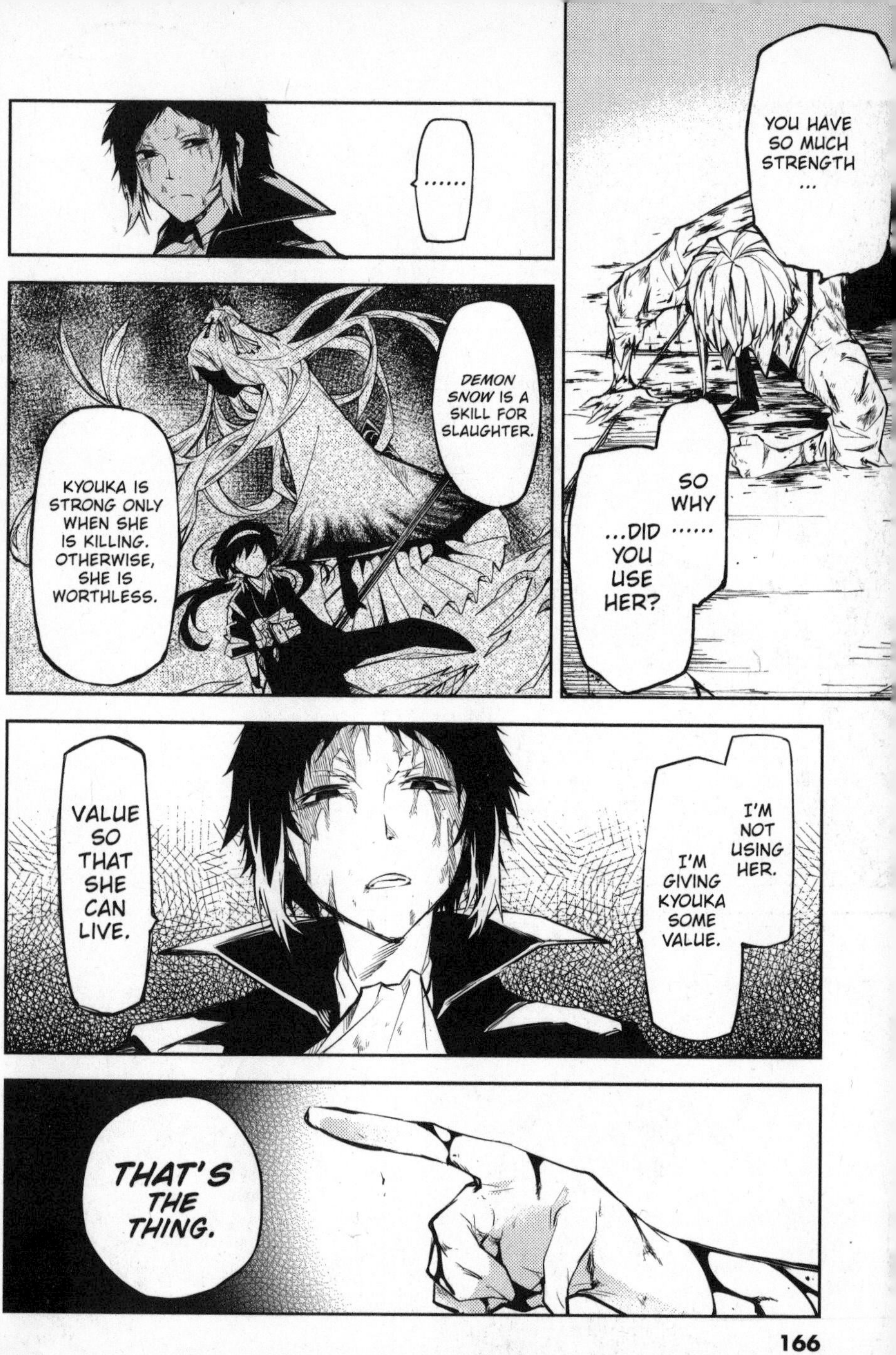
YOU HAVE SO MUCH STRENGTH ...
SO WHY ......
...DID YOU USE HER?
......
DEMON SNOW IS A SKILL FOR SLAUGHTER.
KYOUKA IS STRONG ONLY WHEN SHE IS KILLING. OTHERWISE, SHE IS WORTHLESS.
I'M NOT USING HER.
I'M GIVING KYOUKA SOME VALUE.
VALUE SO THAT SHE CAN LIVE.
THAT'S THE THING.

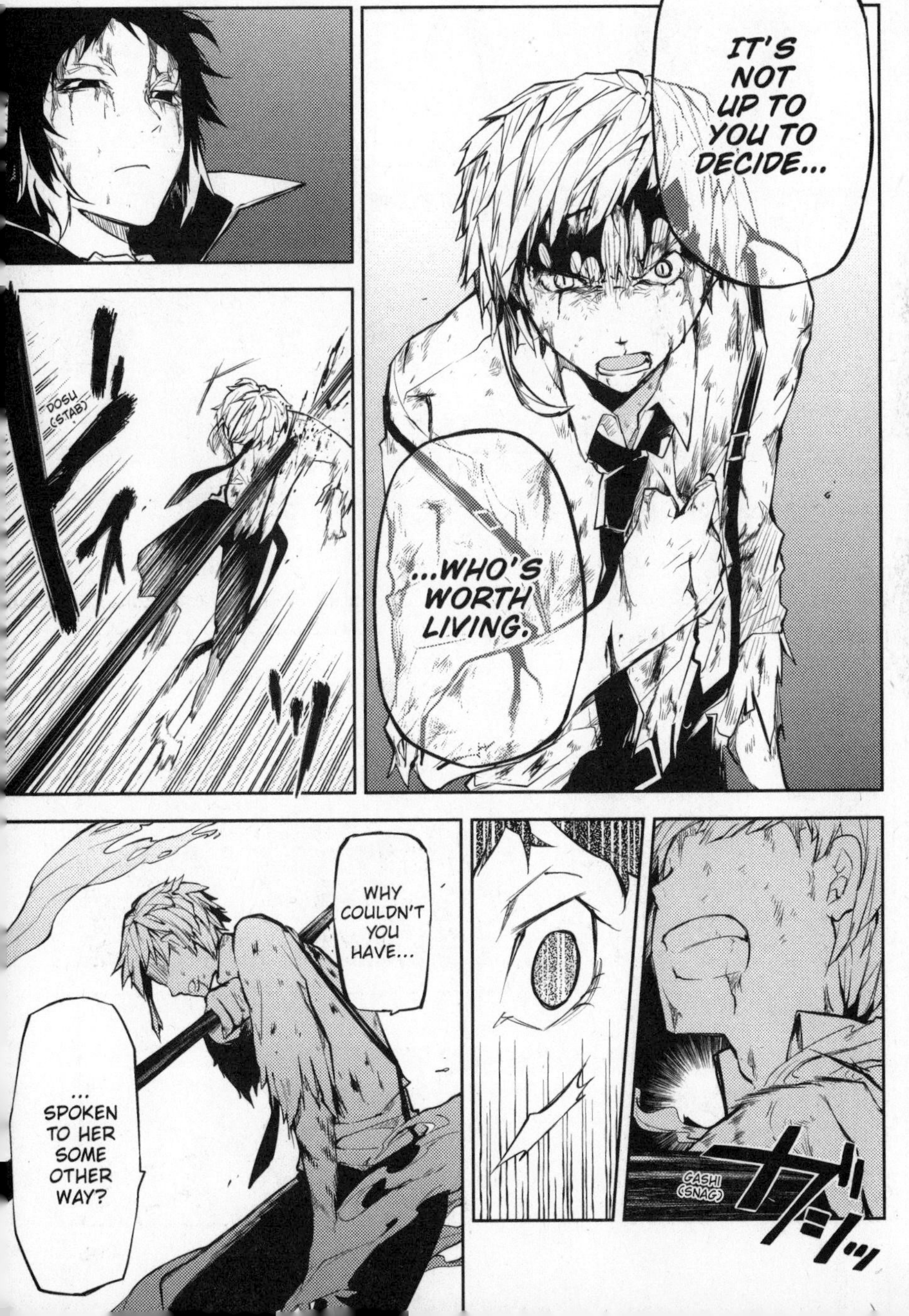
IT'S NOT UP TO YOU TO DECIDE...
...WHO'S WORTH LIVING.
DOSU (STAB)
GASHI (SNAG)
WHY COULDN'T YOU HAVE...
... SPOKEN TO HER SOME OTHER WAY?

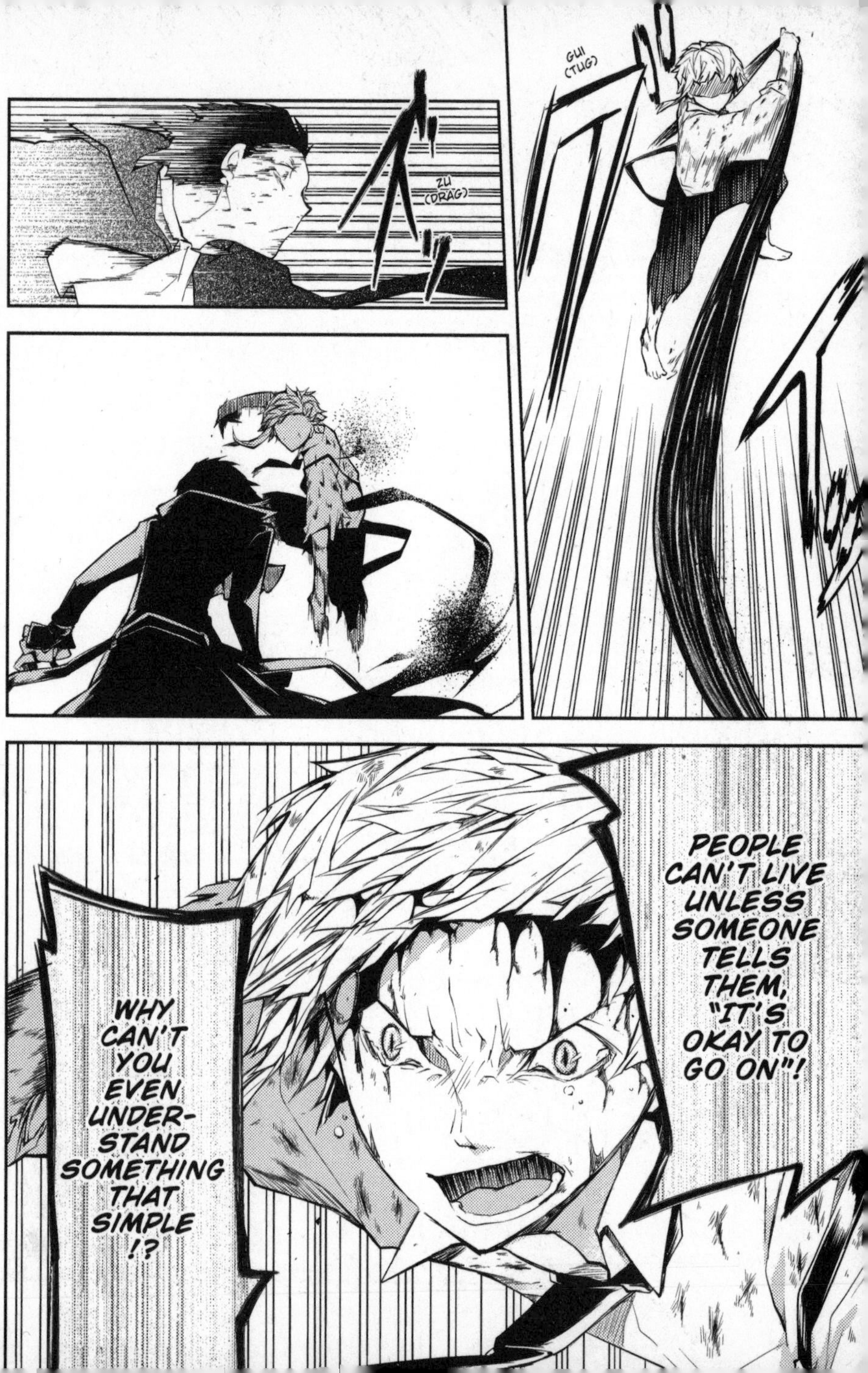
GUI
(TUG)
ZU
(DRAG)
PEOPLE CAN'T LIVE UNLESS SOMEONE TELLS THEM, "IT'S OKAY TO GO ON"!
WHY CAN'T YOU EVEN UNDER-STAND SOMETHING THAT SIMPLE !?

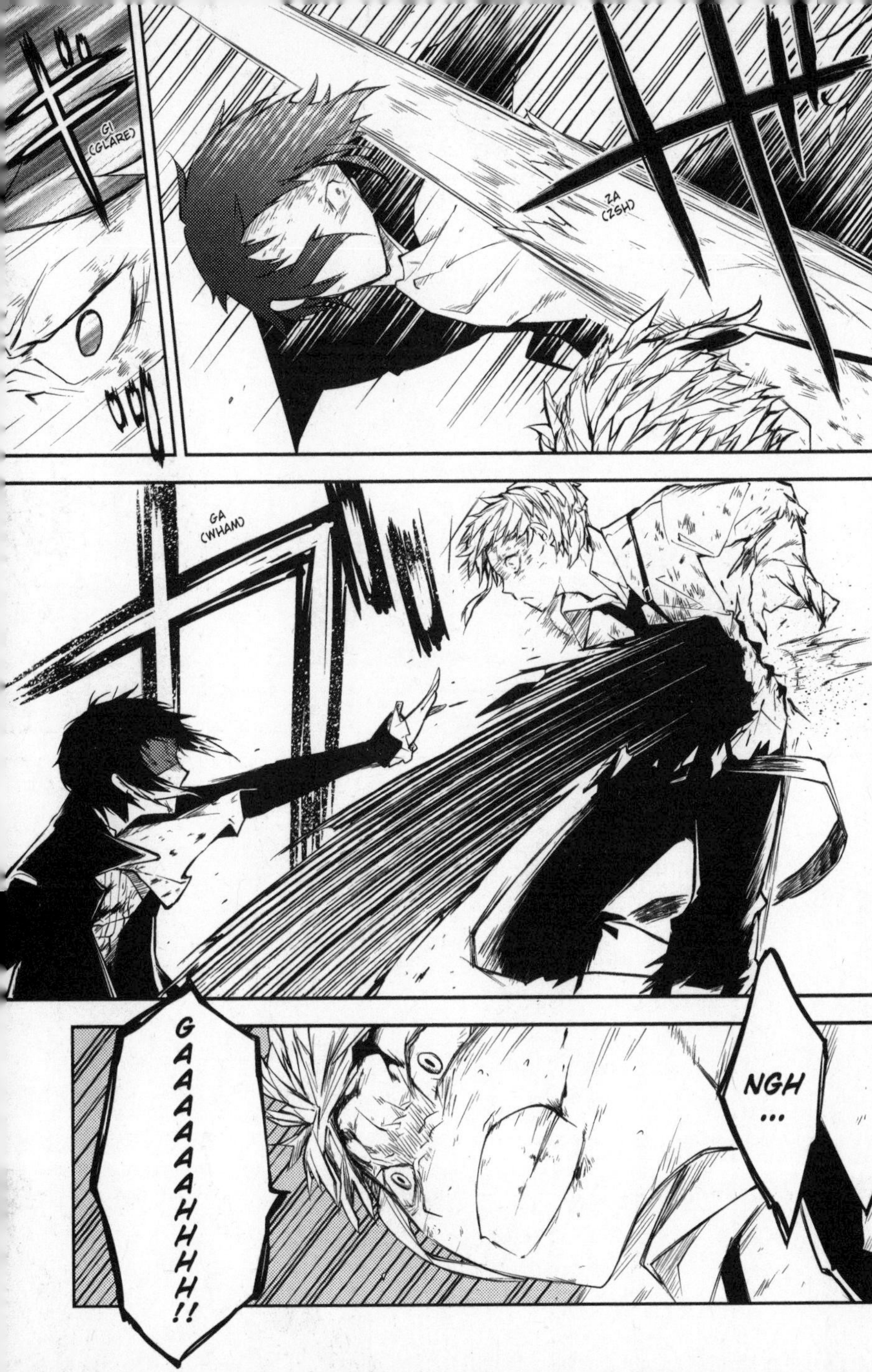
ZA (ZSH)
GI (GLARE)
GA (WHAM)
NGH ...
GAAAAAAHHHH!!

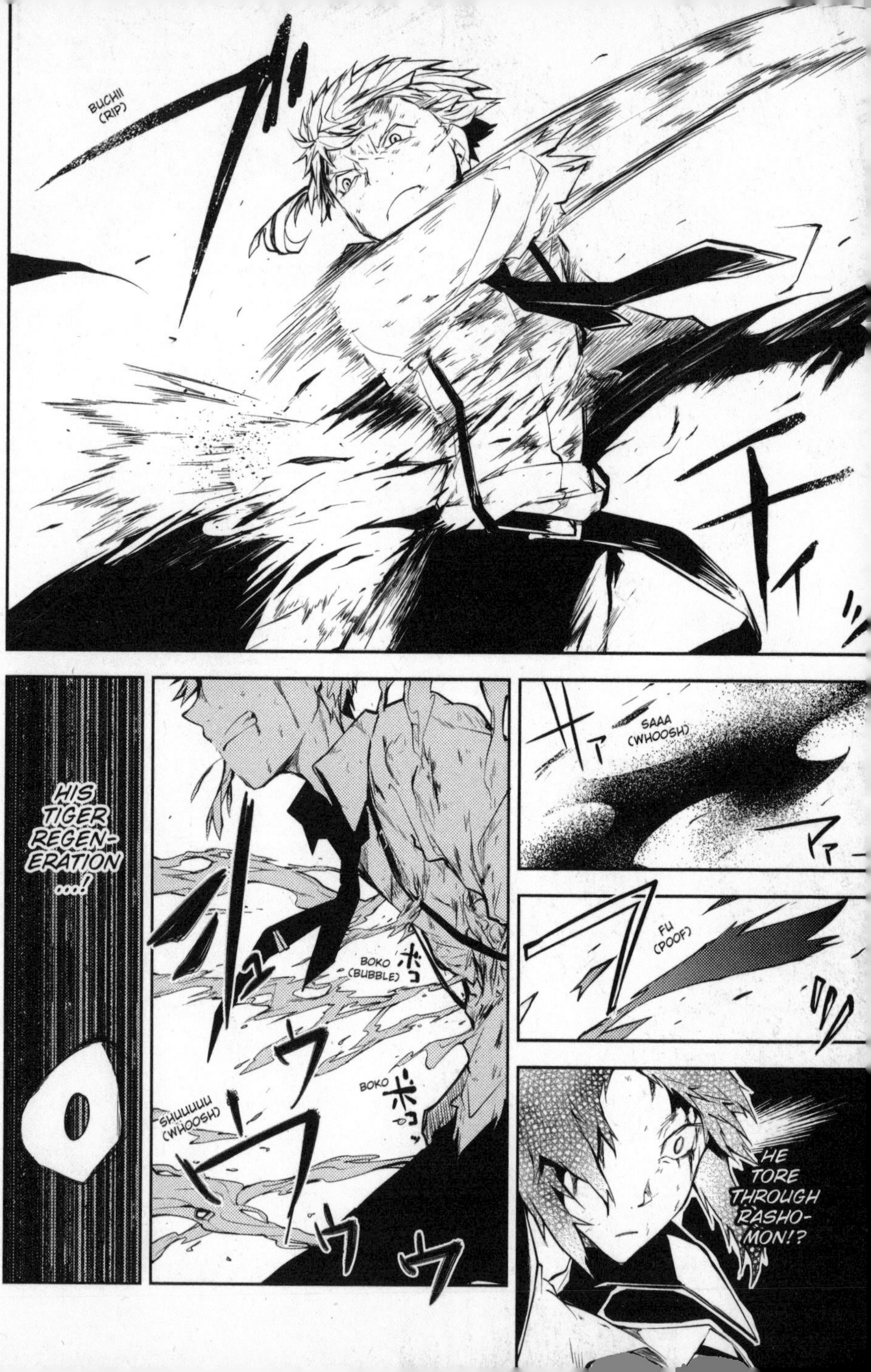
BUCHII (RIP)
SAAA (WHOOSH)
FU (POOF)
HE TORE THROUGH RASHO-MON!?
BOKO (BUBBLE)
BOKO
SHUUUUU (WHOOSH)
HIS TIGER REGEN-ERATION ...!

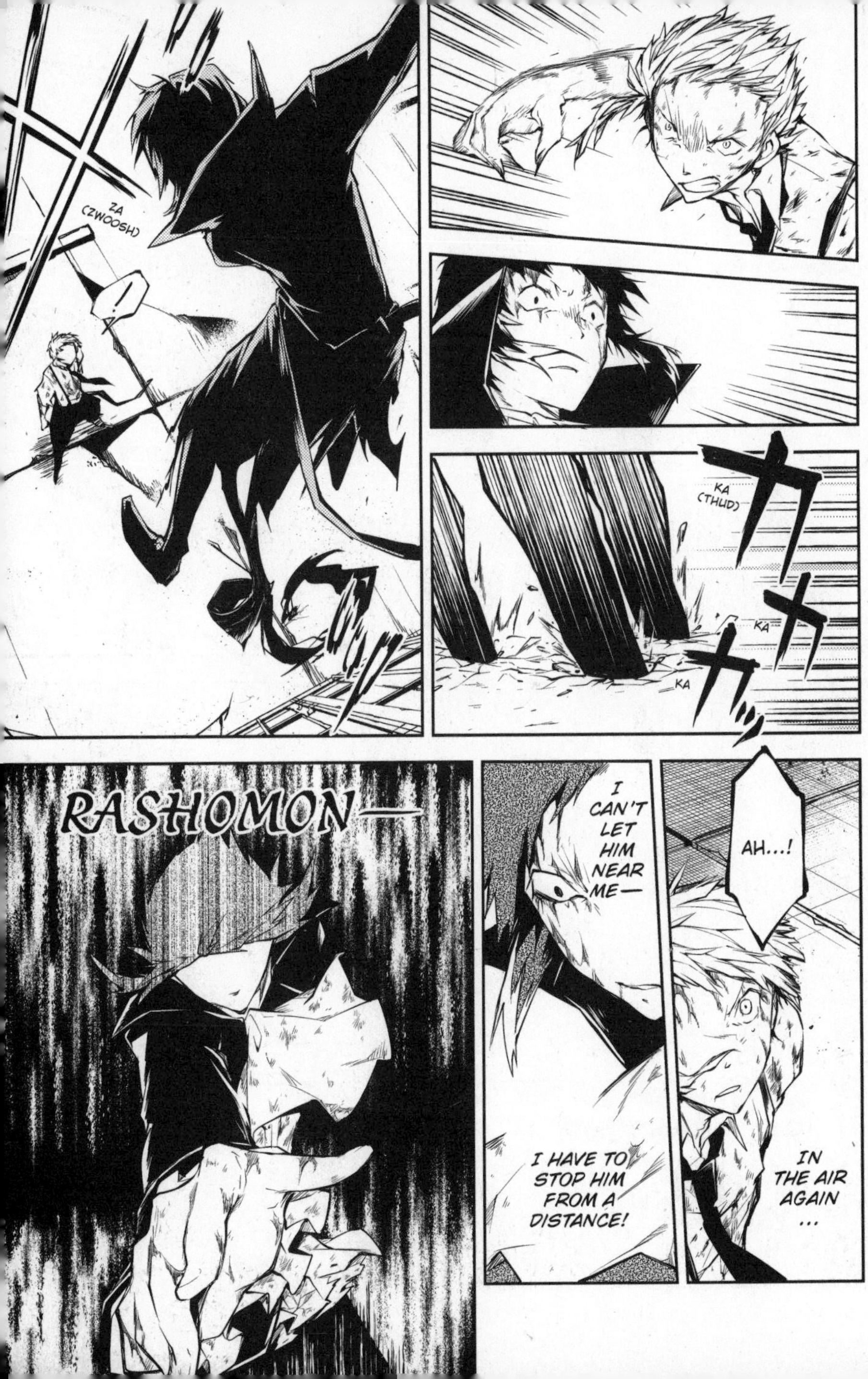
KA (THUD)
KA
KA
ZA (ZWOOSH)
!
AH...!
IN THE AIR AGAIN ...
I CAN'T LET HIM NEAR ME—
I HAVE TO STOP HIM FROM A DISTANCE!
RASHOMON—

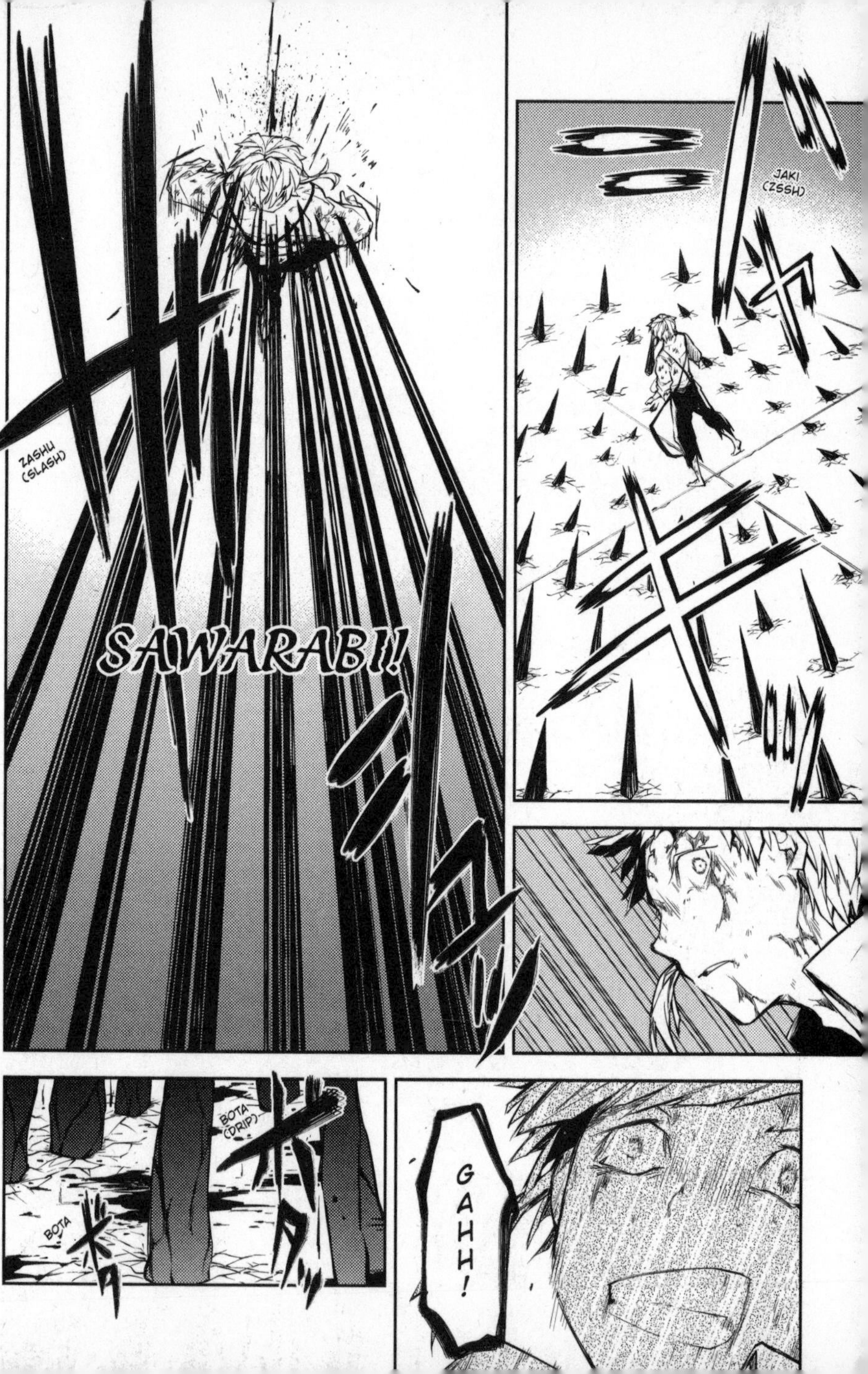
JAKI (ZSSH)
SAWARABI!
ZASHU (SLASH)
GAHH!
BOTA (DRIP)
BOTA

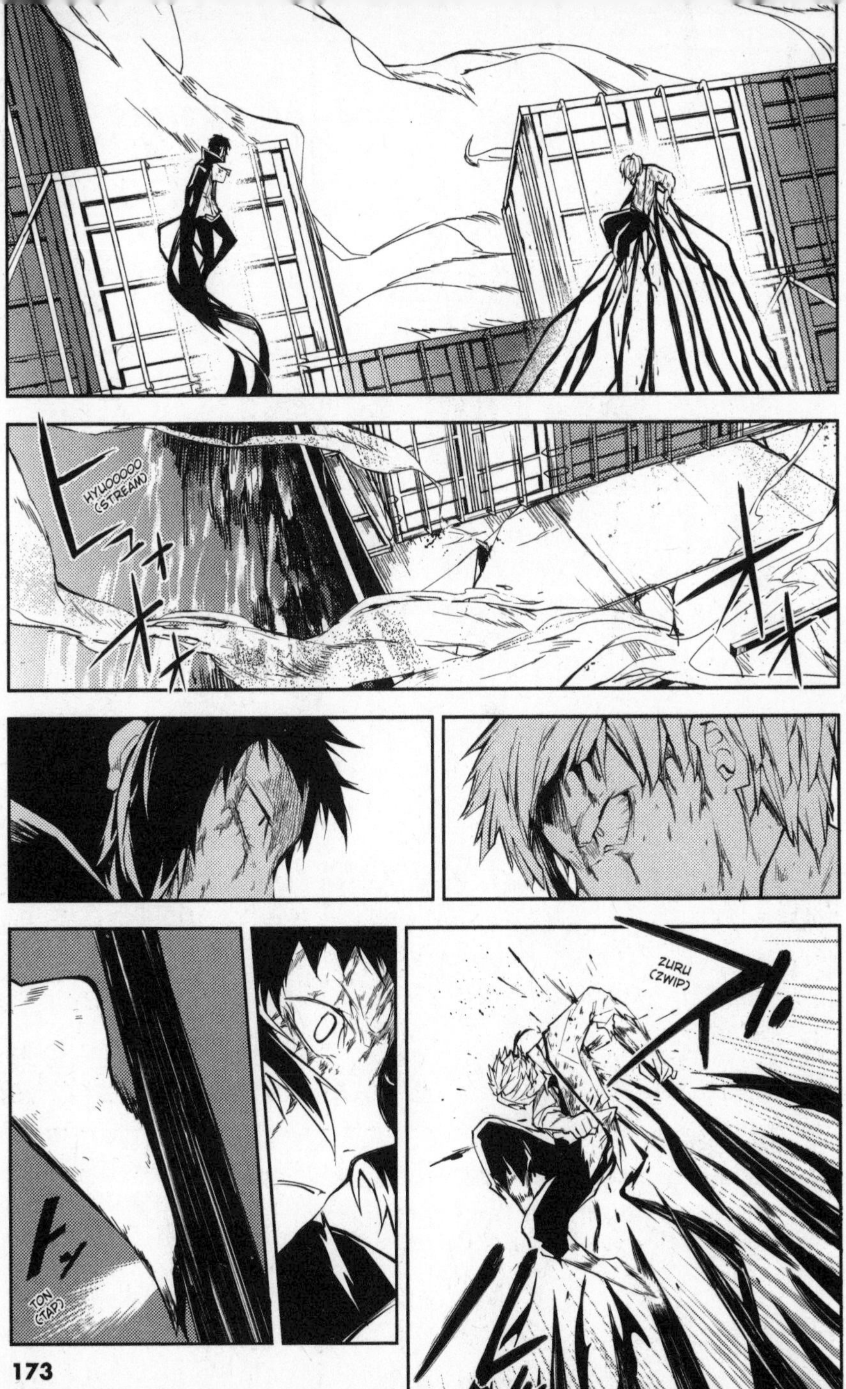
HYUOOOOO (STREAM)
ZURU (ZWIP)
TON (TAP)

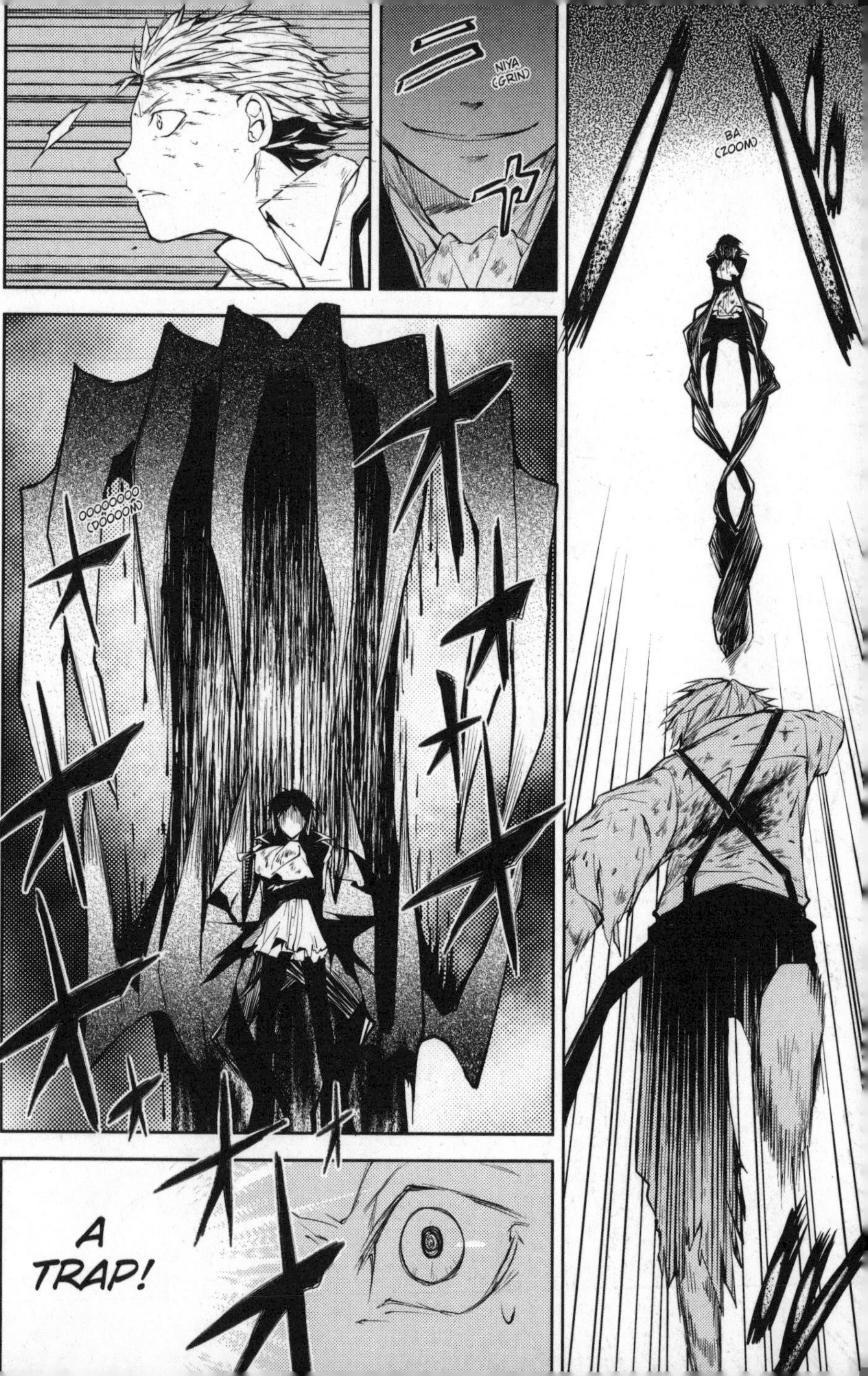
BA (ZOOM)
NIYA (GRIN)
OOOOOOOO (DOOOOM)
A TRAP!

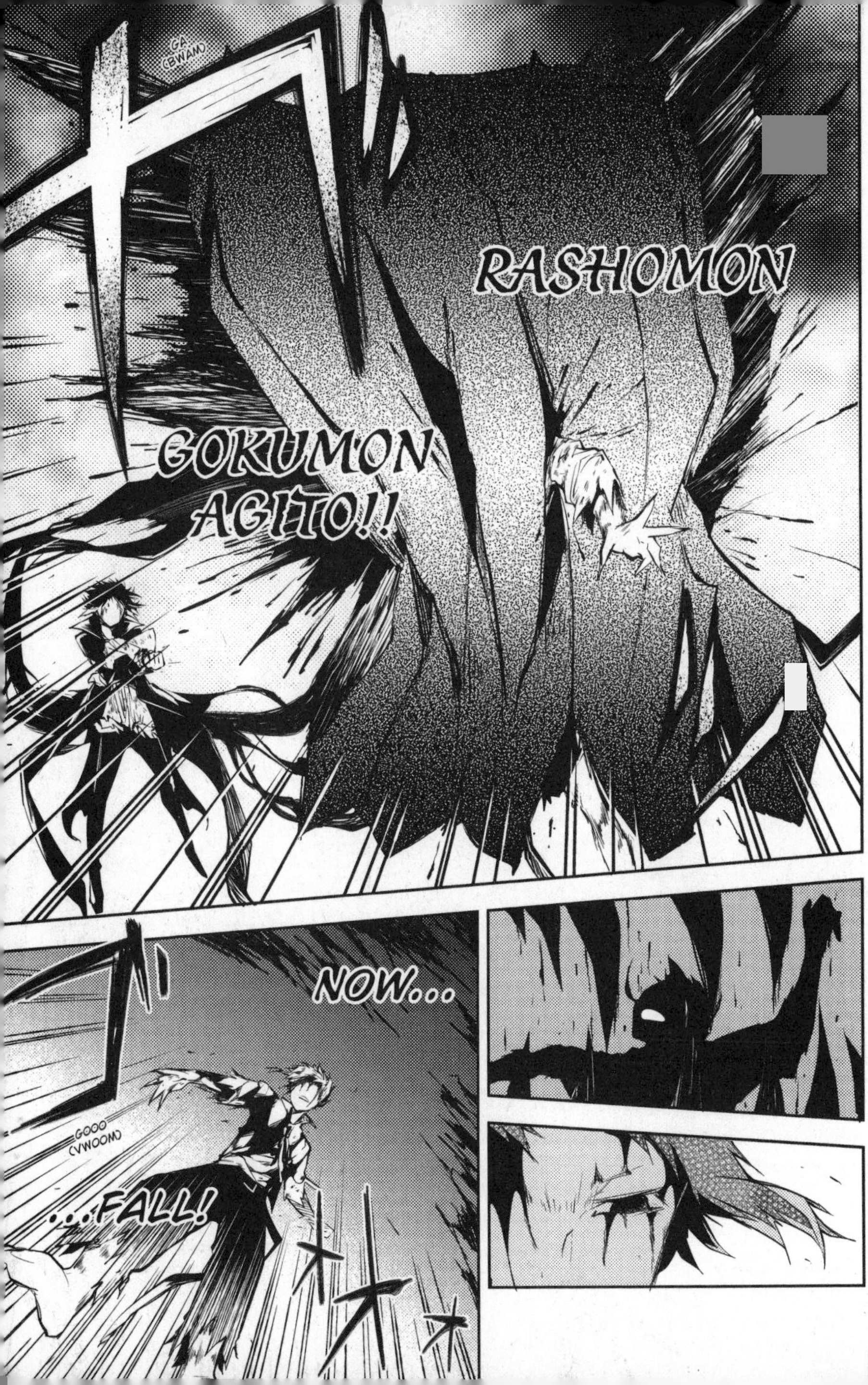
GA (BWAM)
RASHOMON
GOKUMON AGITO!!
NOW...
GOOO (VWOOM)
...FALL!

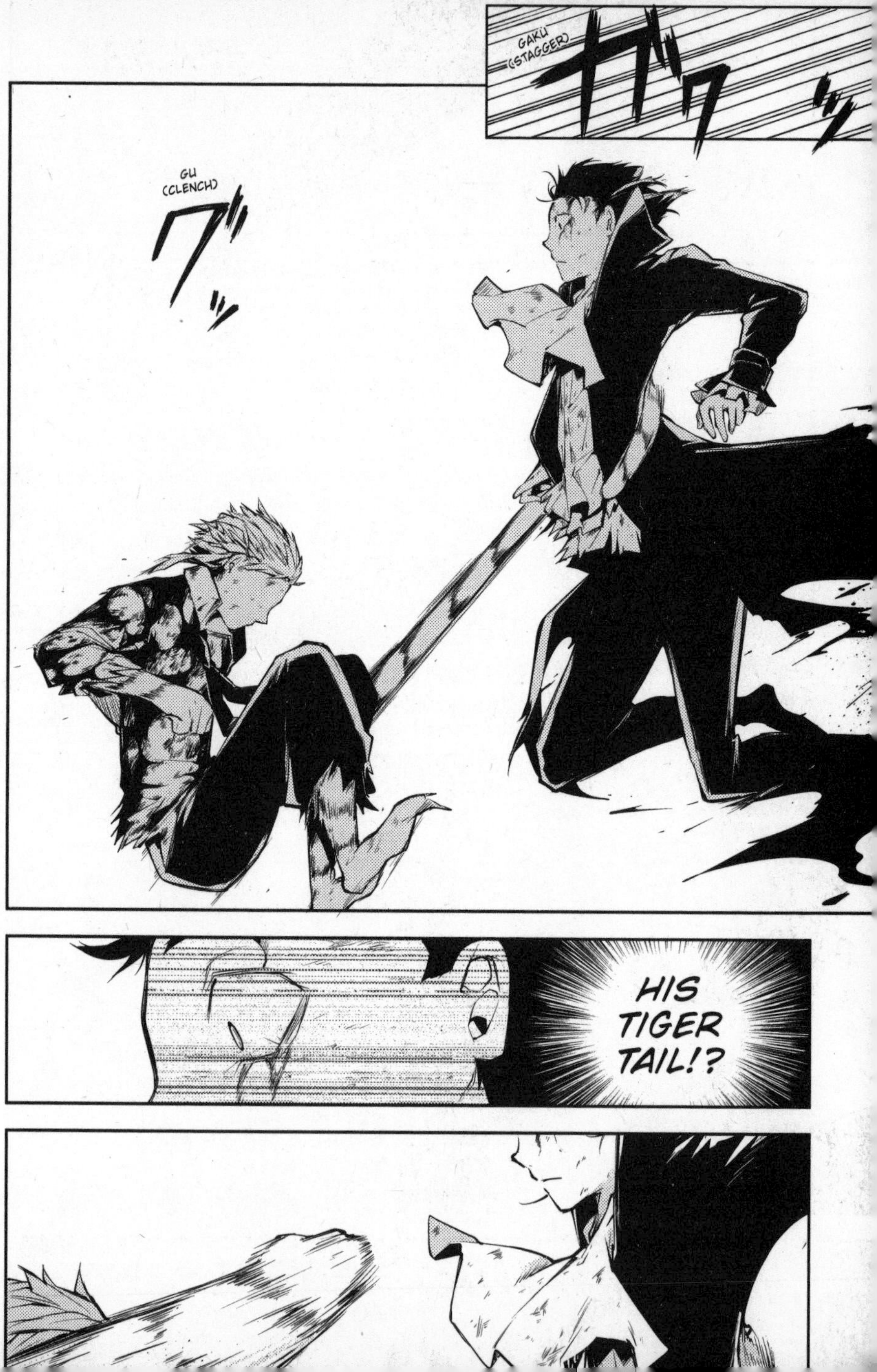
GAKU (STAGGER)
GU (CLENCH)
HIS TIGER TAIL!?

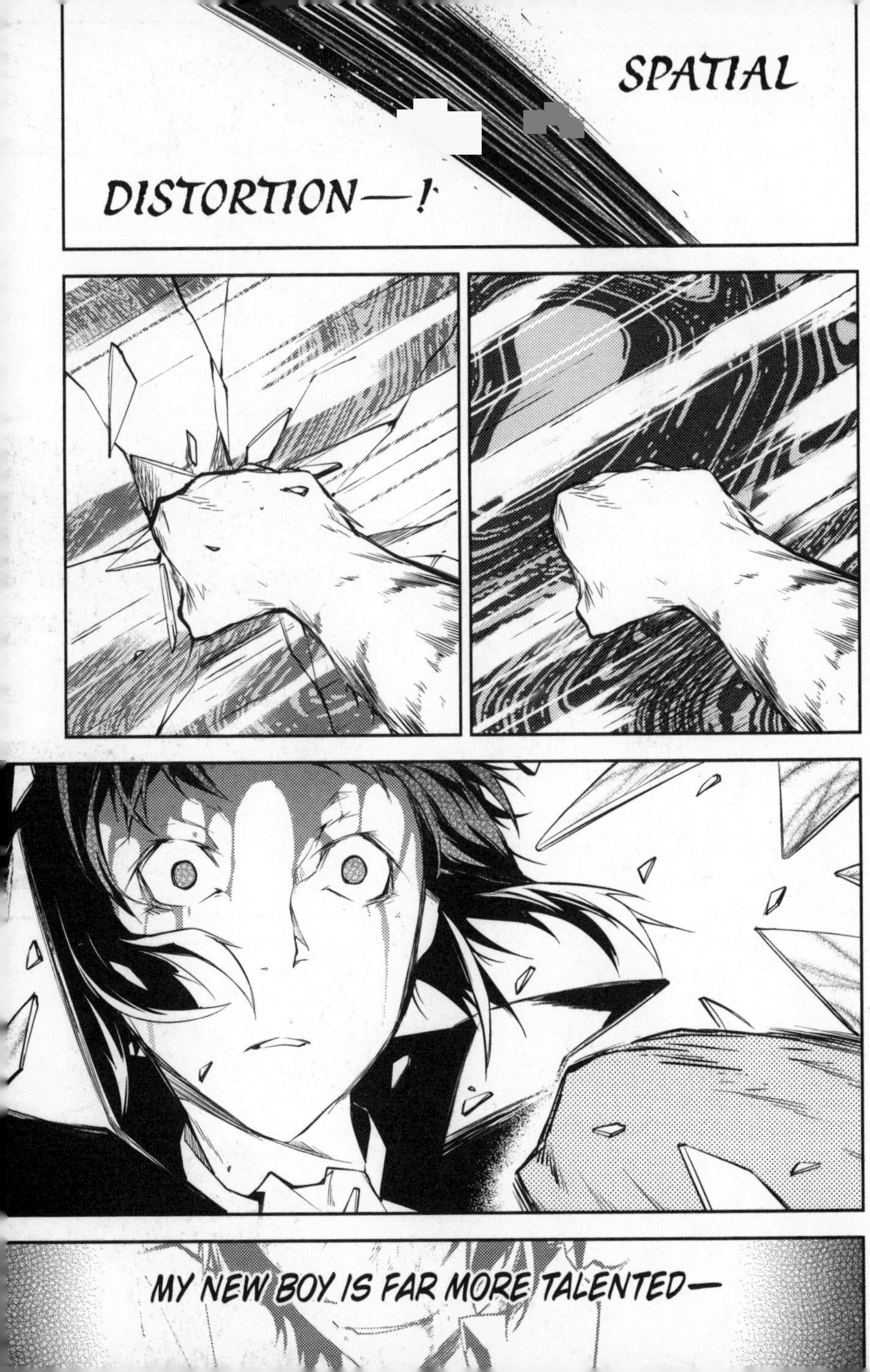
SPATIAL
DISTORTION—!
MY NEW BOY IS FAR MORE TALENTED—

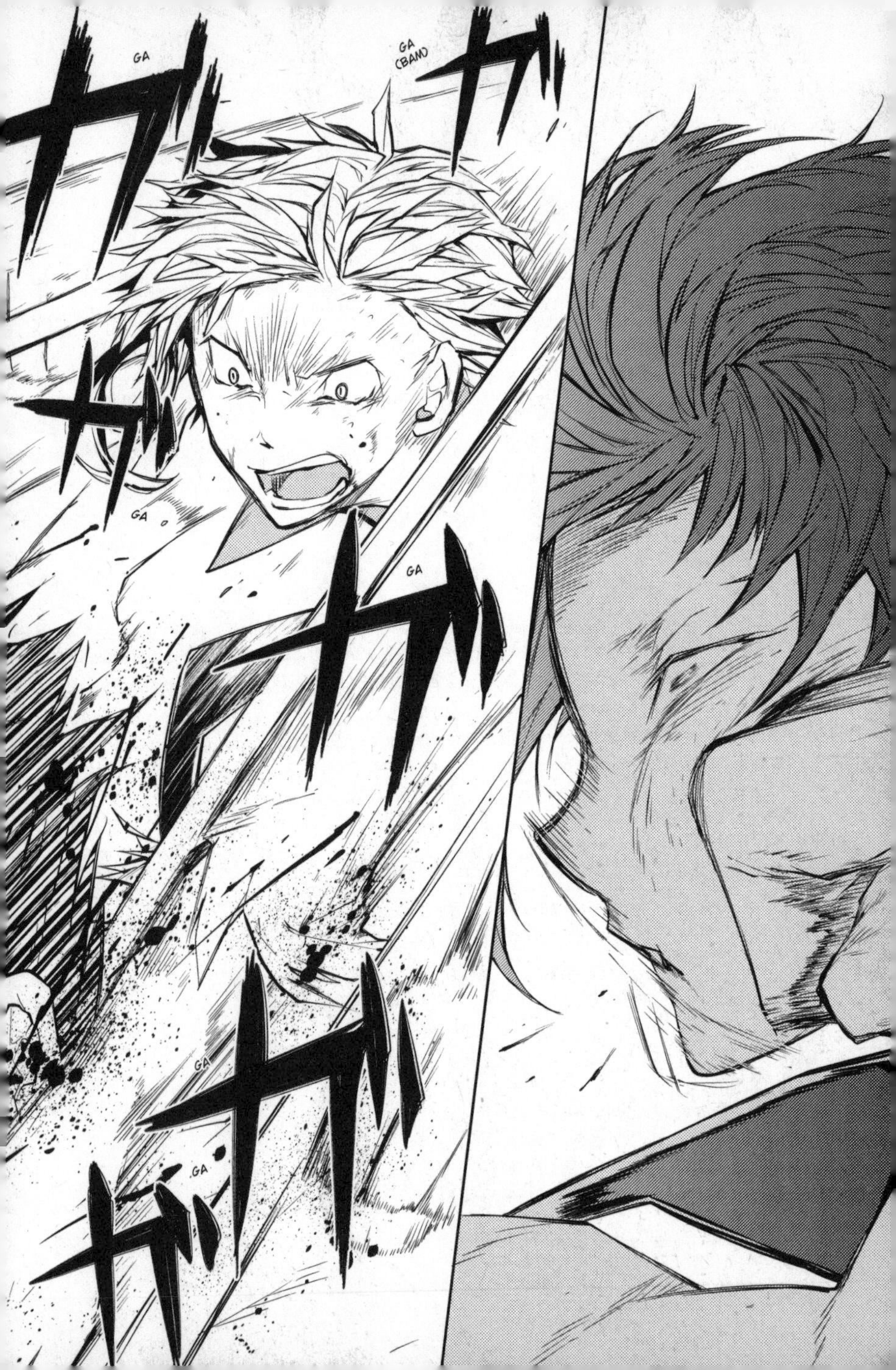
GA (BAM)
GA
GA
GA
GA
GA

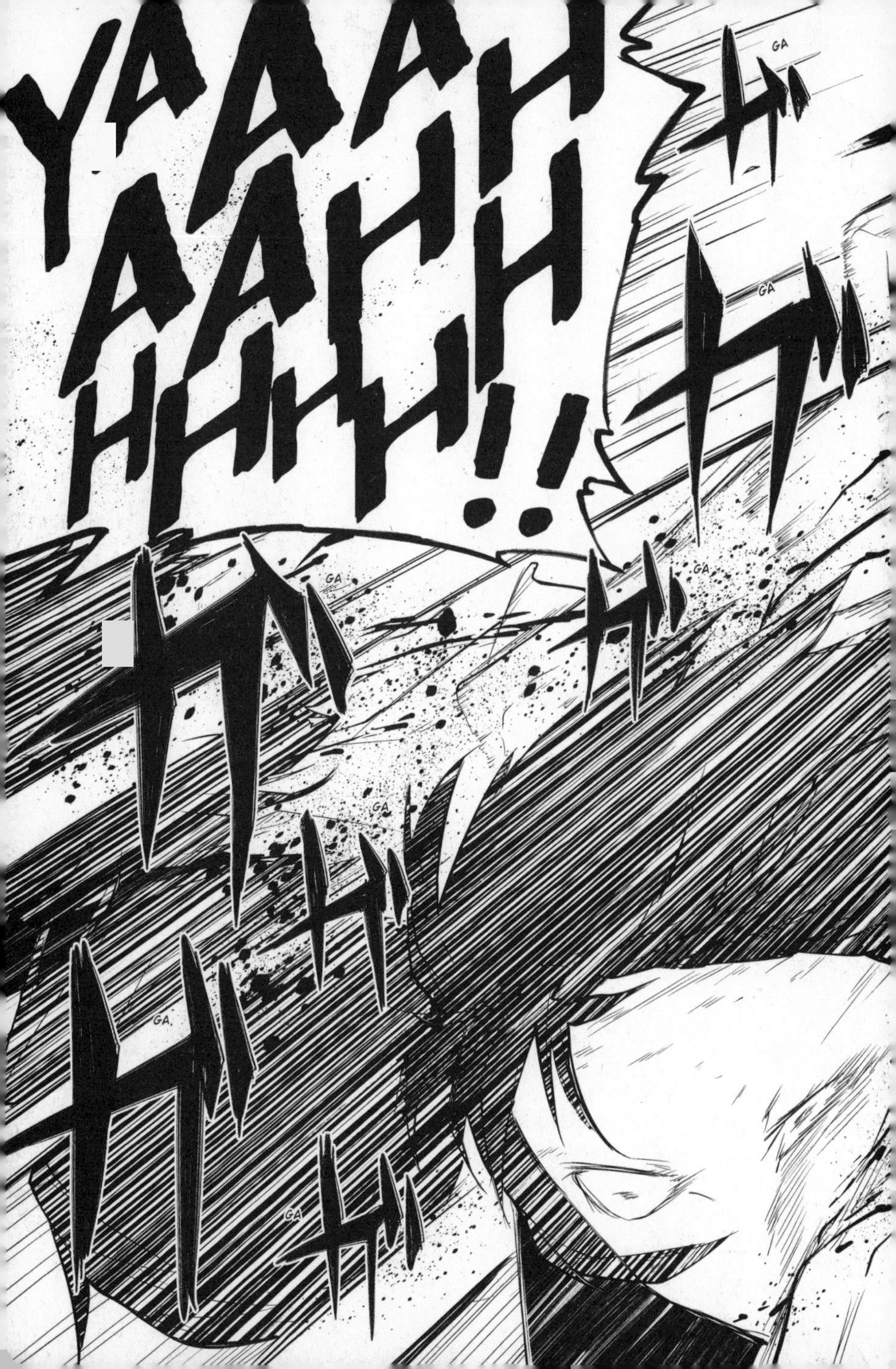
YAAHAAHHHHHH!!
GA
GA
GA
GA
GA
GA
GA

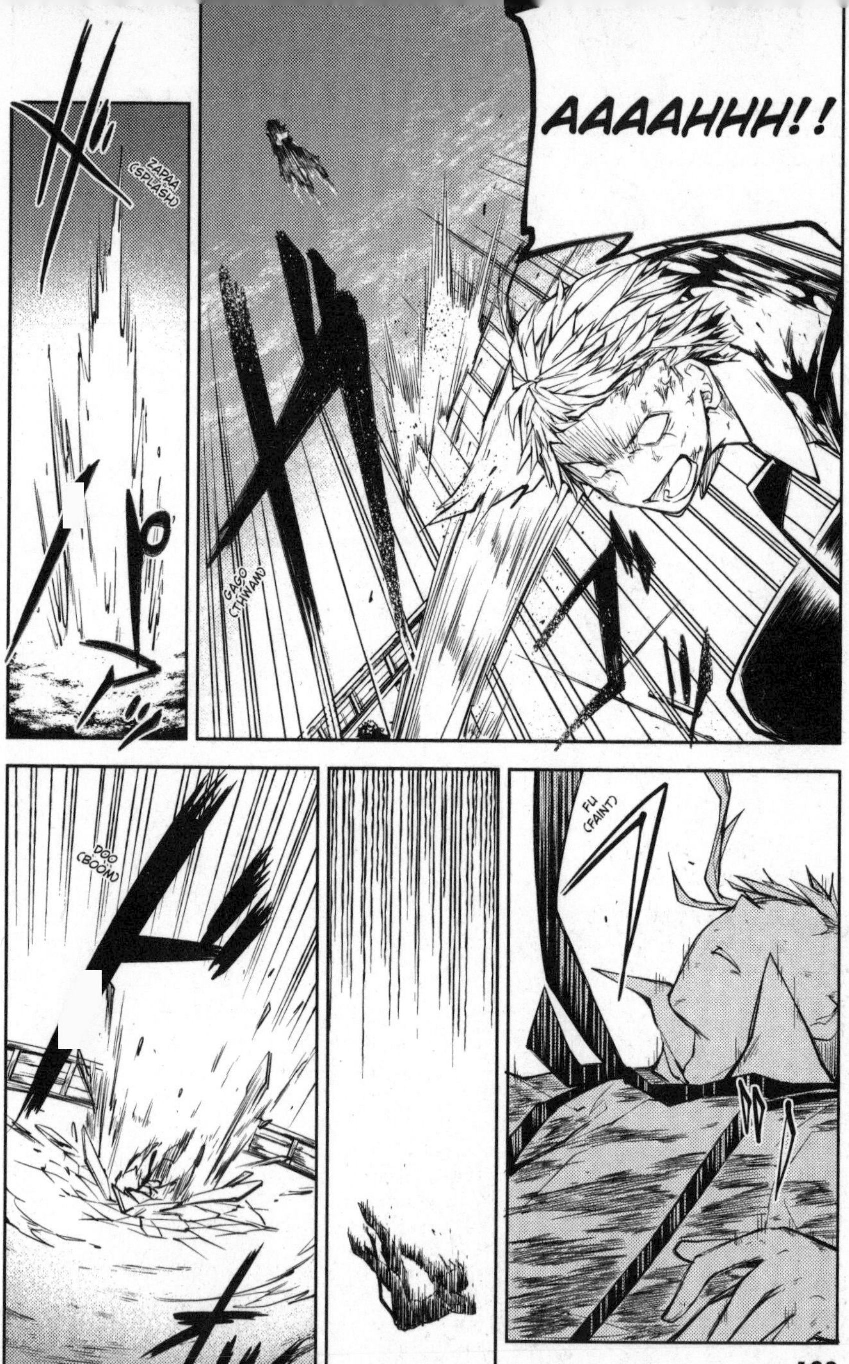
AAAAHHH!!
GAGO
(THWAM)
ZAPAA
(SPLASH)
FU
(FAINT)
DOO
(BOOM)

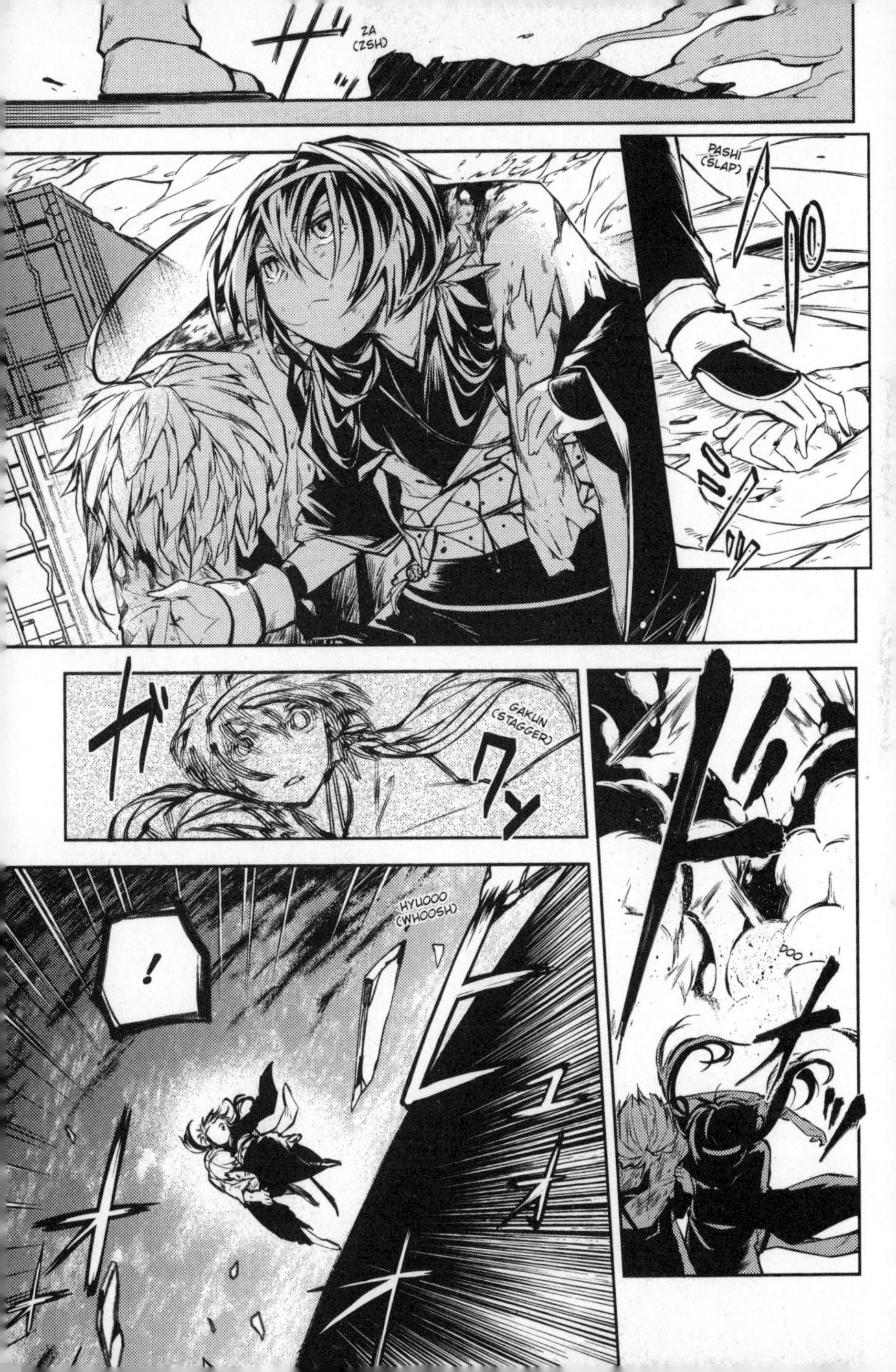
ZA
(ZSH)
PASHI
(SLAP)
DOO
GAKUN
(STAGGER)
HYUOOO
(WHOOSH)
!

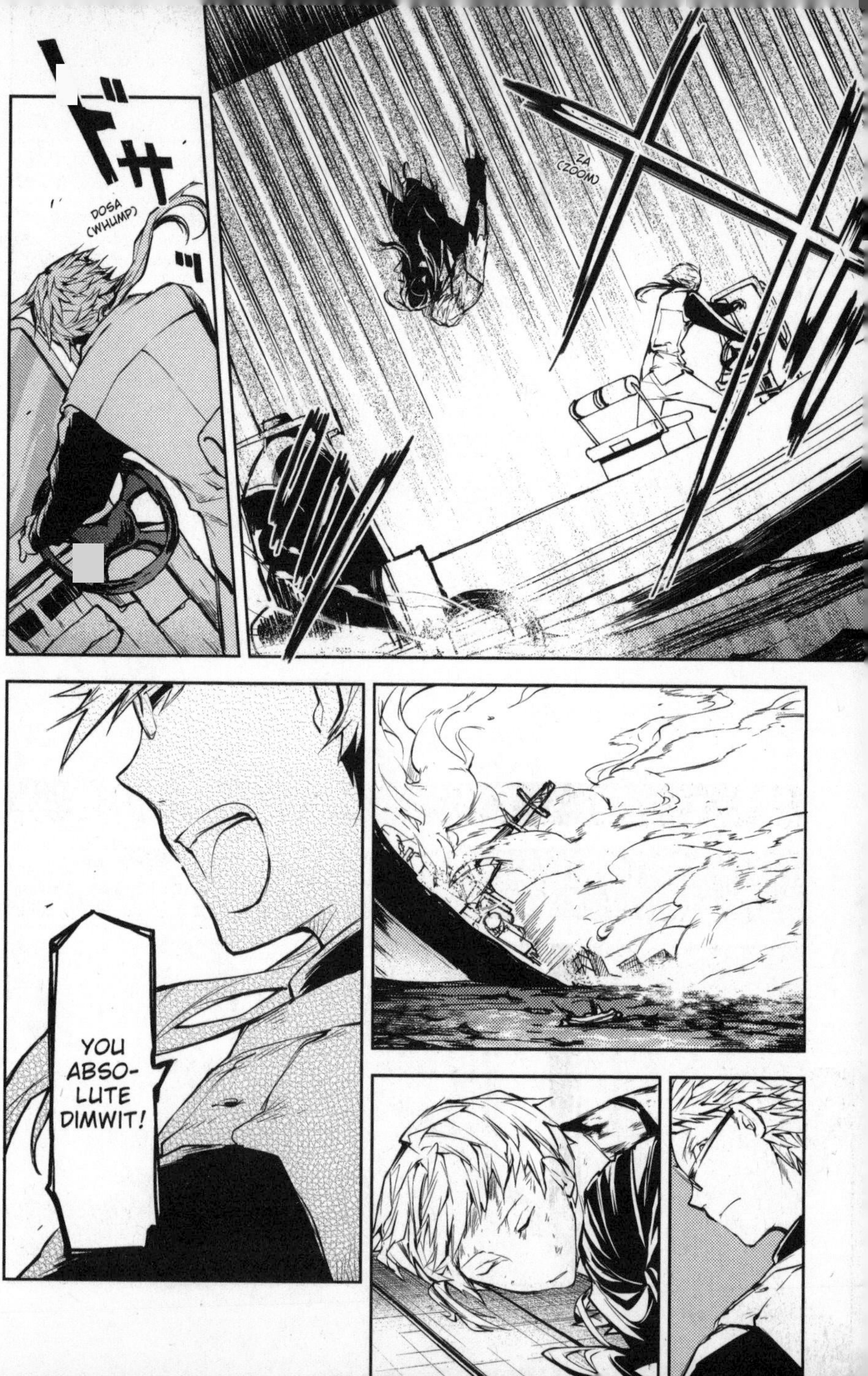
ZA (ZOOM)
DOSA (WHUMP)
YOU ABSOLUTE DIMWIT!

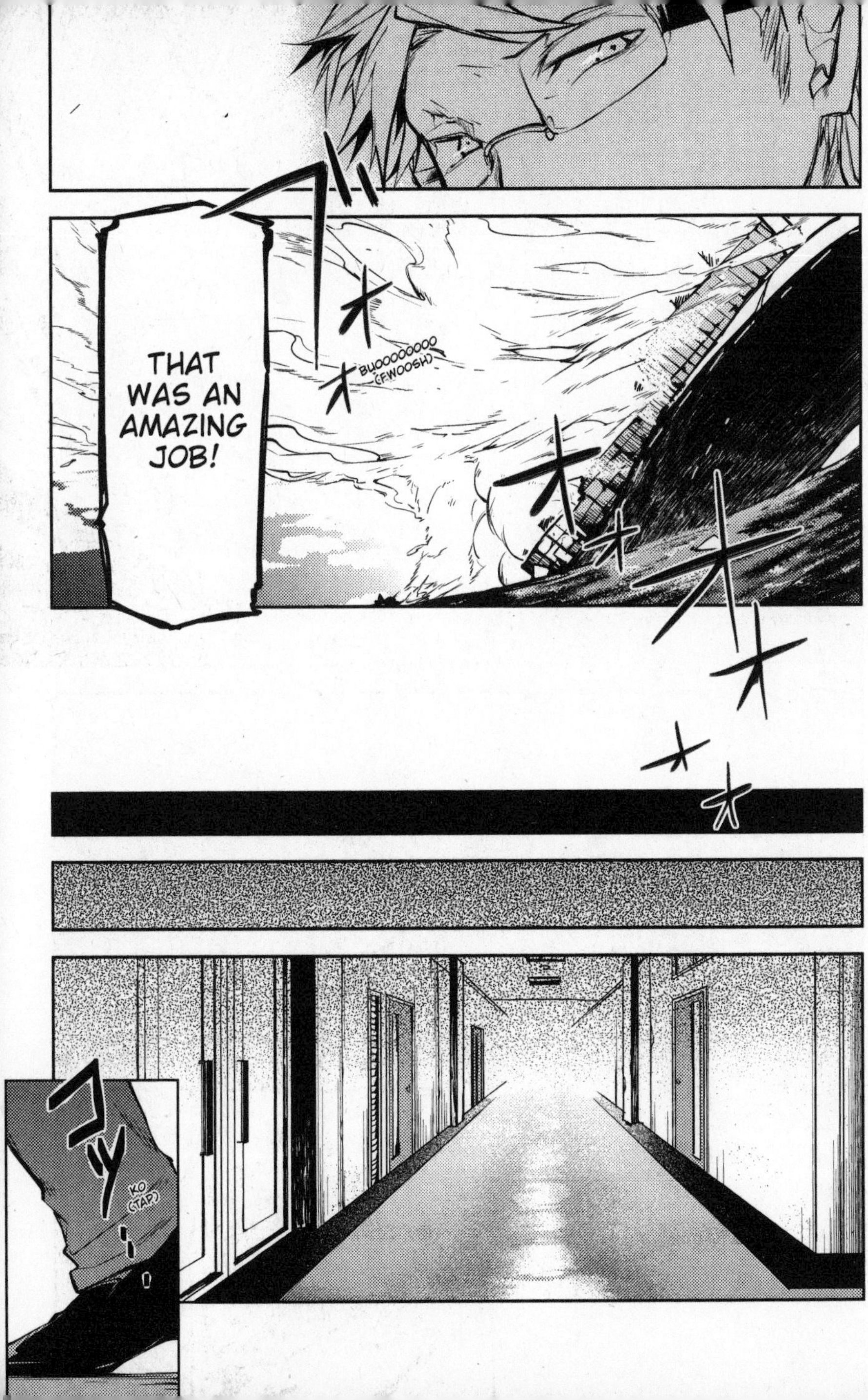
THAT WAS AN AMAZING JOB!
BUOOOOOOOO (FWOOSH)
KO (TAP)

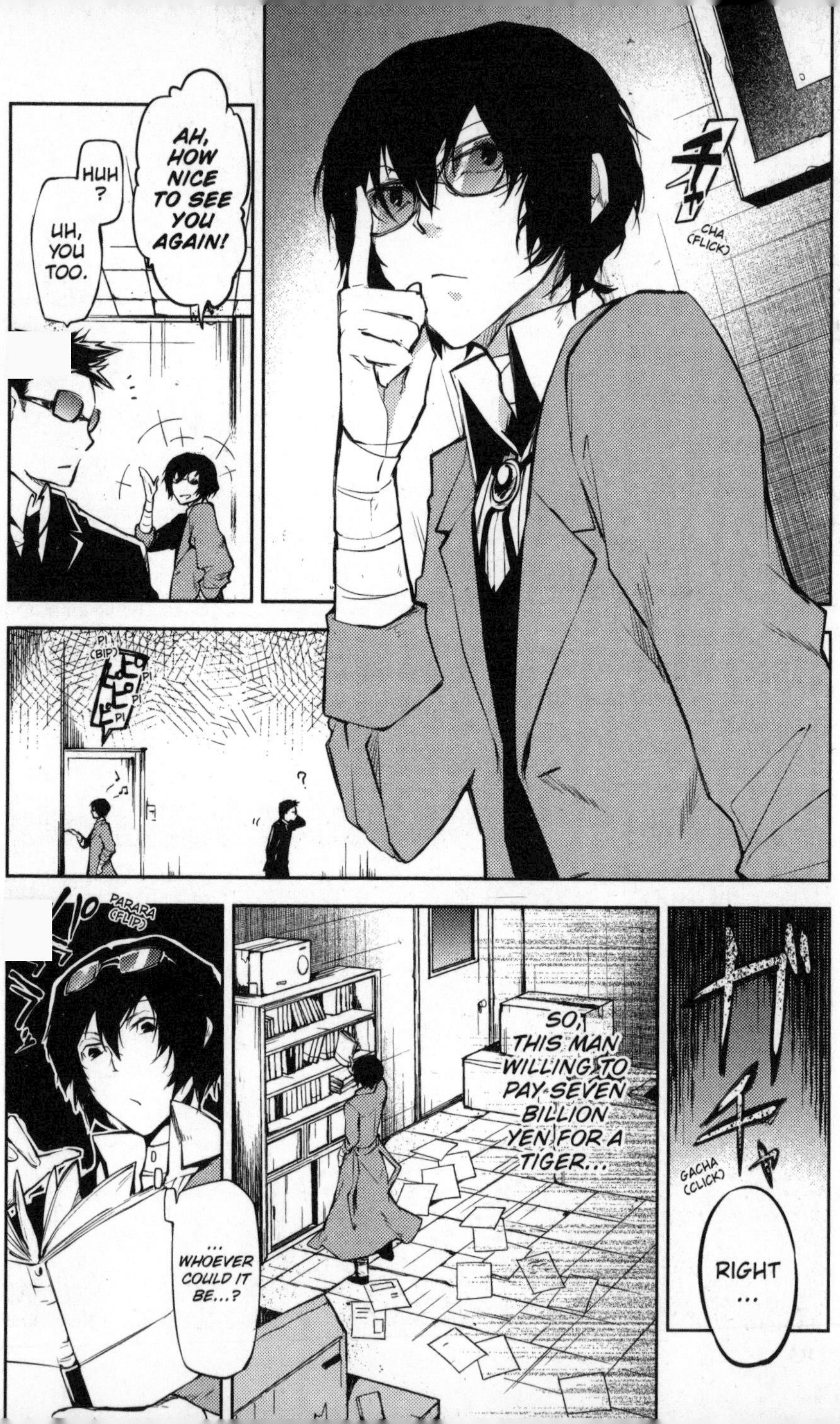
CHA (FLICK)
AH, HOW NICE TO SEE YOU AGAIN!
HUH ?
UH, YOU TOO.
PI (BIP) PI PI PI
GACHA (CLICK)
RIGHT ...
SO, THIS MAN WILLING TO PAY SEVEN BILLION YEN FOR A TIGER...
PARARA (FLIP)
... WHOEVER COULD IT BE...?

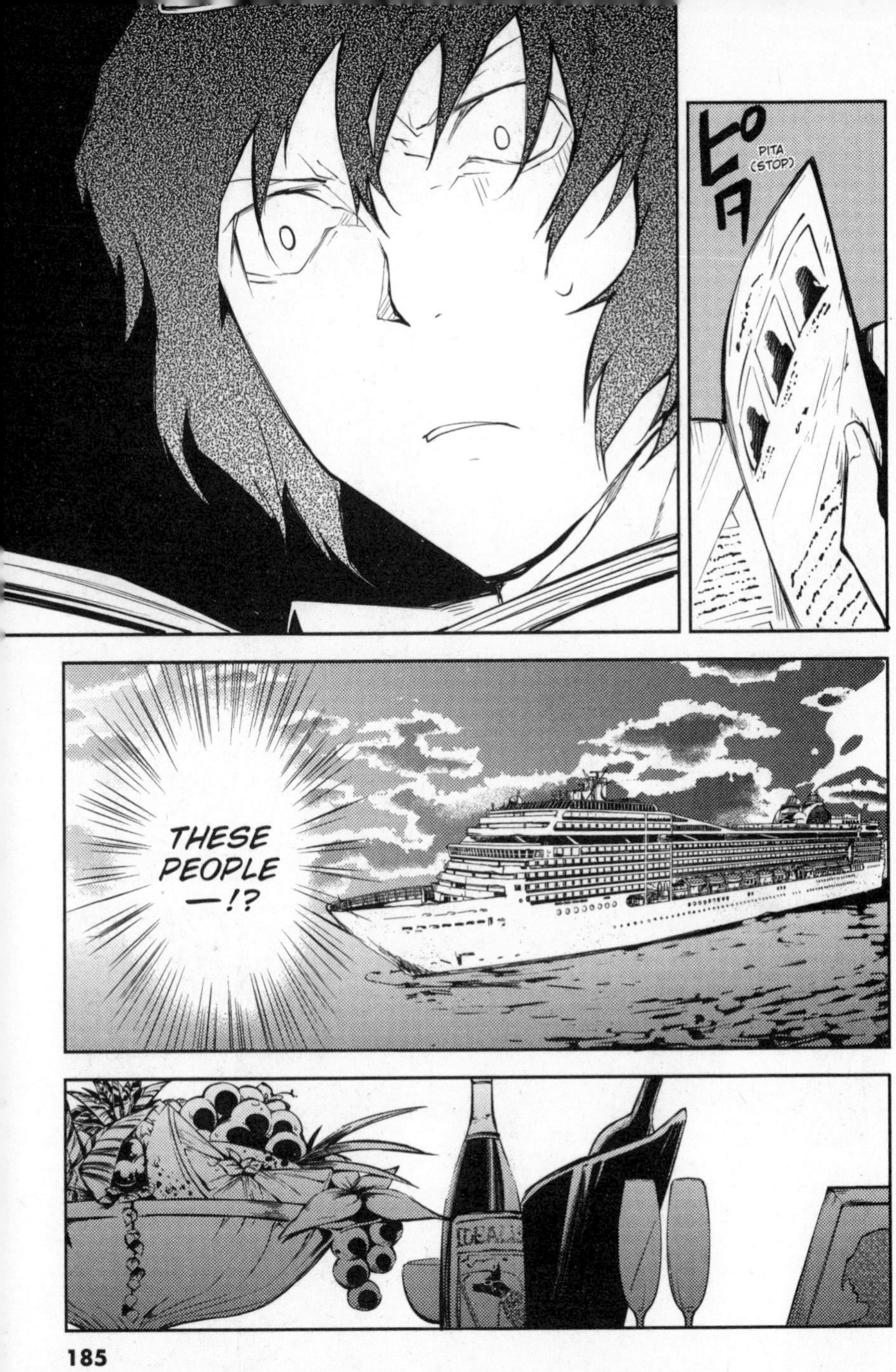
ピタ
PITA (STOP)
THESE PEOPLE —!?

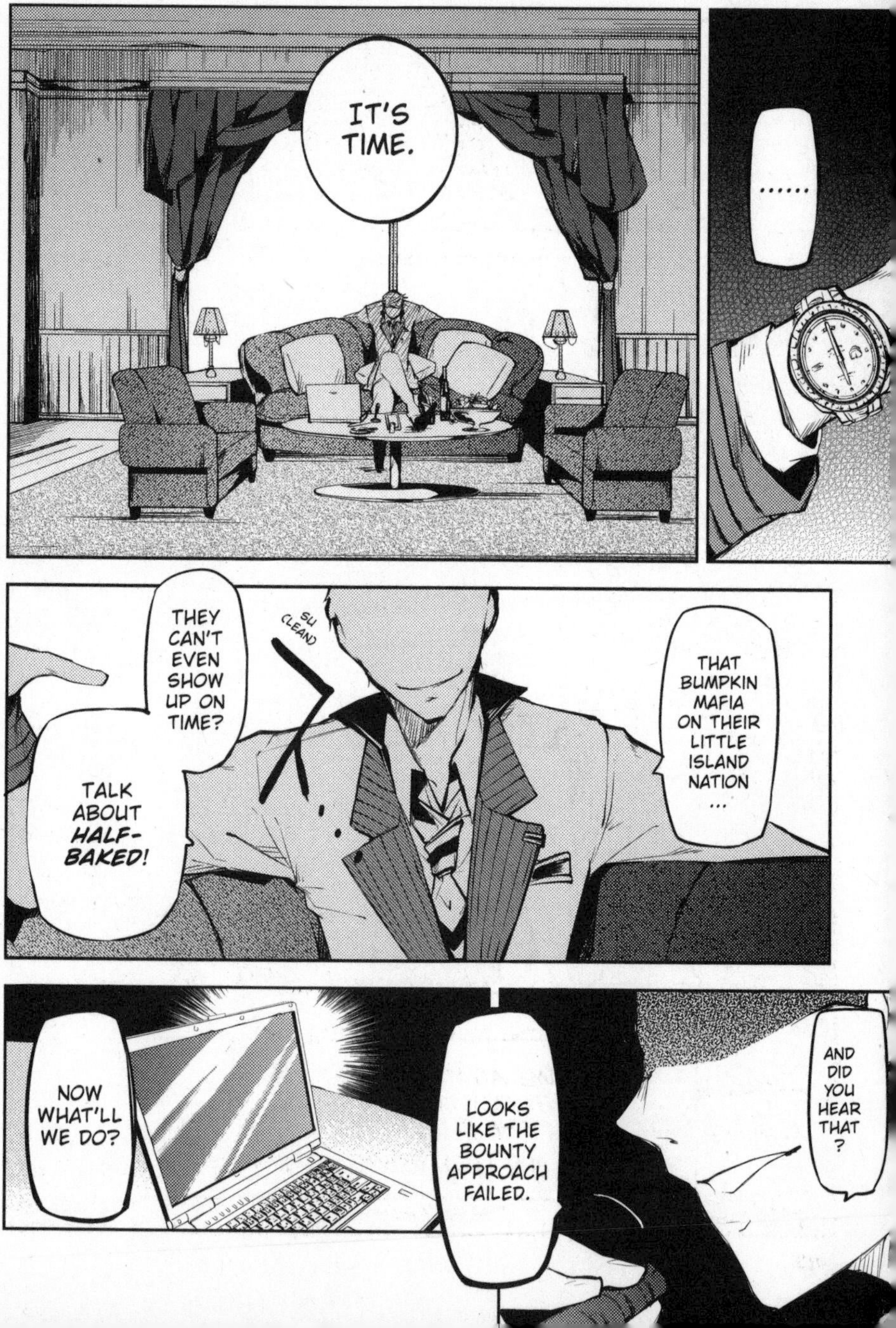
......
IT'S TIME.
THAT BUMPKIN MAFIA ON THEIR LITTLE ISLAND NATION...
SU (LEAN)
THEY CAN'T EVEN SHOW UP ON TIME?
TALK ABOUT ***HALF-BAKED!***
AND DID YOU HEAR THAT?
LOOKS LIKE THE BOUNTY APPROACH FAILED.
NOW WHAT'LL WE DO?

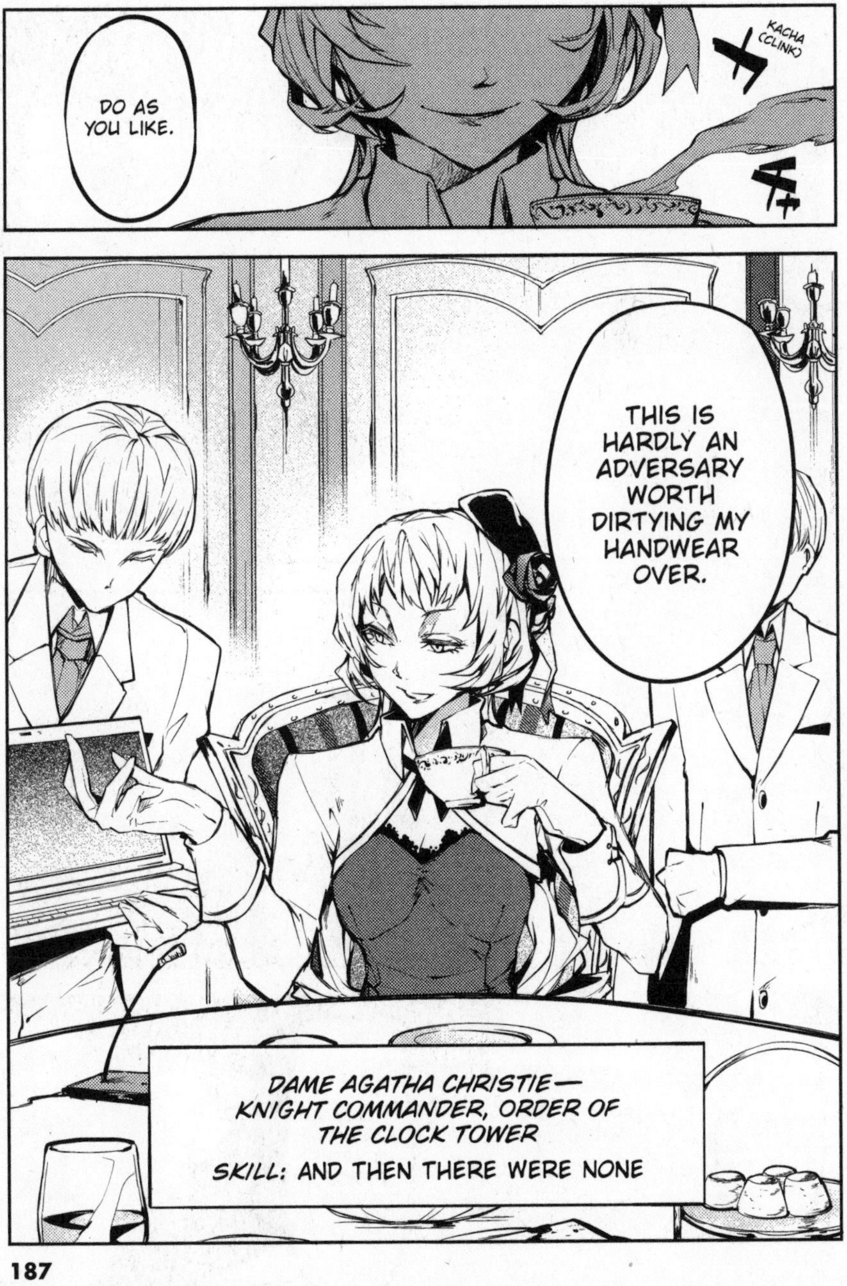
KACHA (CLINK)
DO AS YOU LIKE.
THIS IS HARDLY AN ADVERSARY WORTH DIRTYING MY HANDWEAR OVER.
DAME AGATHA CHRISTIE—KNIGHT COMMANDER, ORDER OF THE CLOCK TOWER
SKILL: AND THEN THERE WERE NONE

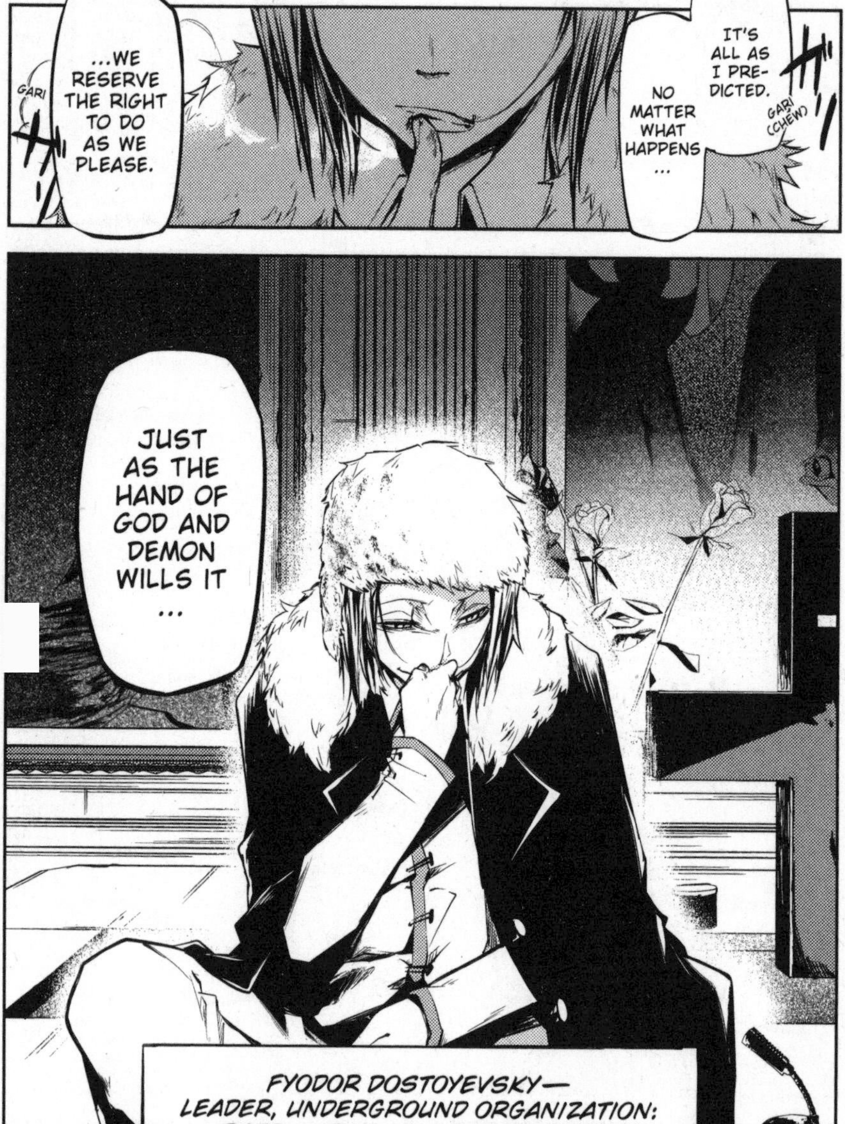

IT'S ALL AS I PRE-DICTED.
GARI (CHEW)
NO MATTER WHAT HAPPENS ...
...WE RESERVE THE RIGHT TO DO AS WE PLEASE.
GARI
JUST AS THE HAND OF GOD AND DEMON WILLS IT ...
FYODOR DOSTOYEVSKY— LEADER, UNDERGROUND ORGANIZATION: RATS IN THE HOUSE OF THE DEAD
SKILL: CRIME AND PUNISHMENT

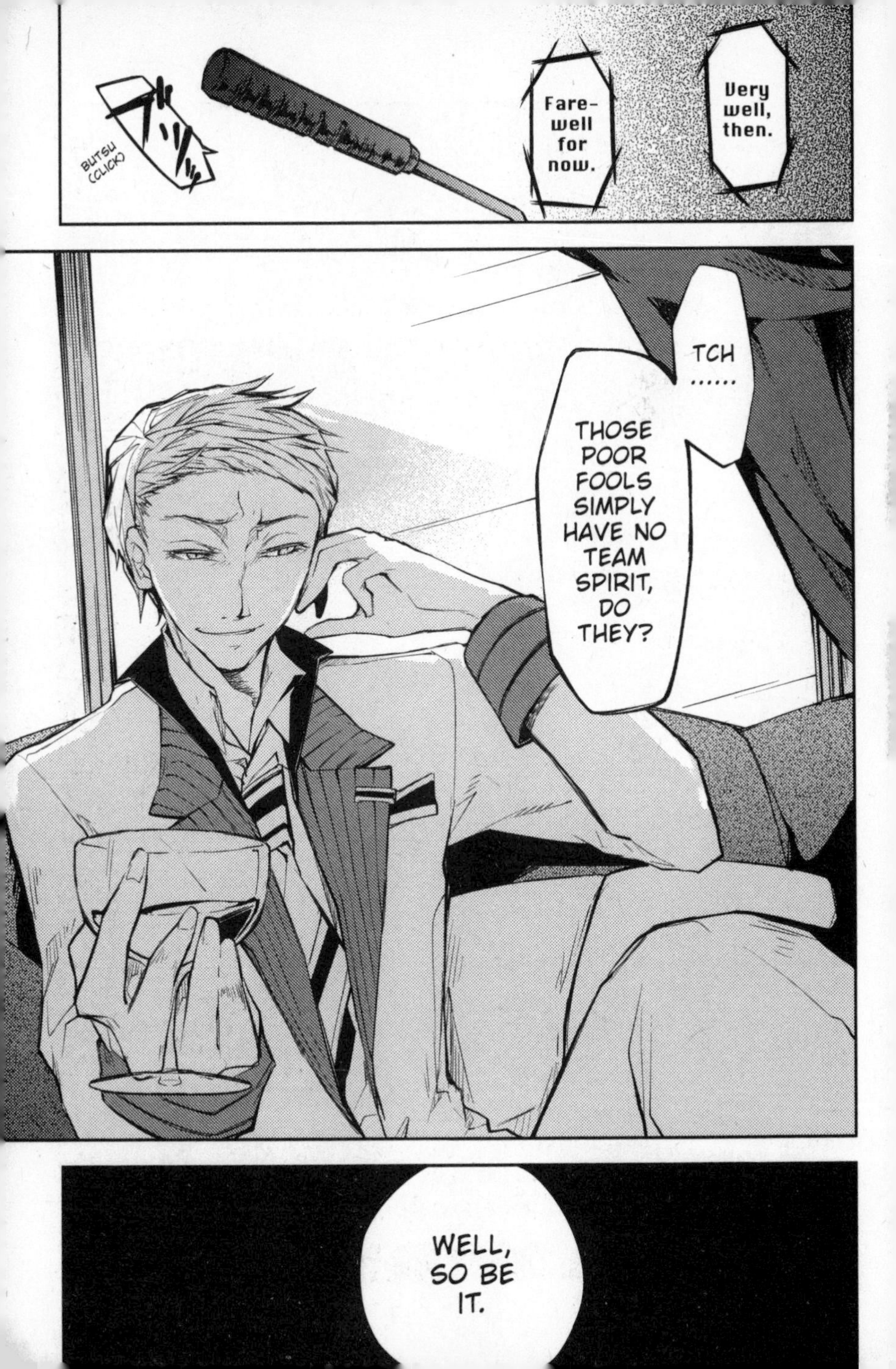
Very well, then.
Fare-well for now.
BUTSU (CLICK)
TCH ......
THOSE POOR FOOLS SIMPLY HAVE NO TEAM SPIRIT, DO THEY?
WELL, SO BE IT.

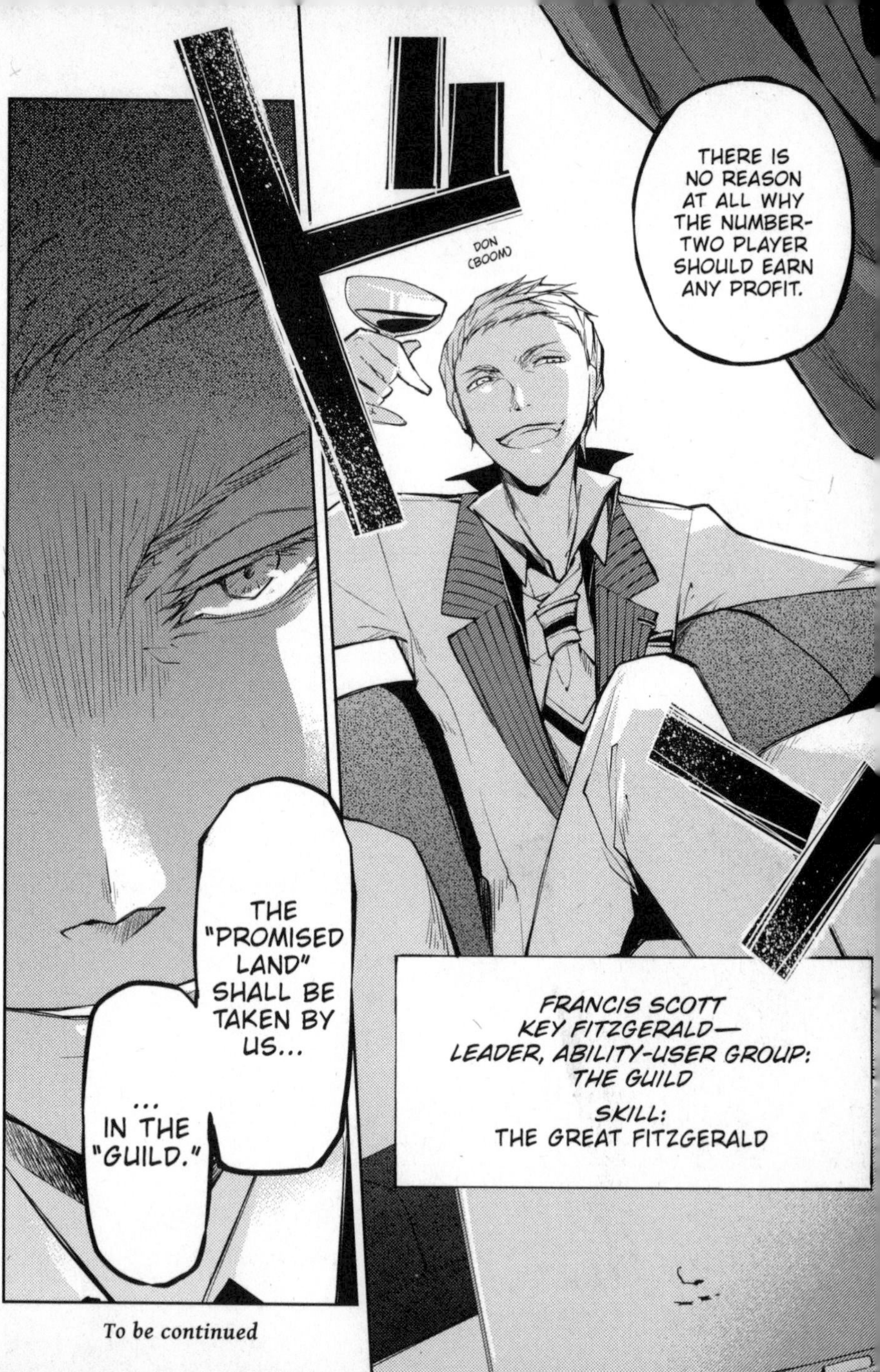
THERE IS NO REASON AT ALL WHY THE NUMBER-TWO PLAYER SHOULD EARN ANY PROFIT.
DON (BOOM)
FRANCIS SCOTT KEY FITZGERALD—LEADER, ABILITY-USER GROUP: THE GUILD
SKILL: THE GREAT FITZGERALD
THE "PROMISED LAND" SHALL BE TAKEN BY US...
... IN THE "GUILD."

To be continued

JUNICHIROU TANIZAKI

SKILL: **Light Snow**
Able to project illusions into physical space, like a smokescreen.

AGE: *18*

BIRTH DATE: *July 24*

HEIGHT: *174cm*

WEIGHT: *59kg*

BLOOD TYPE: *A*

LIKES: *Conger eel, Chinese food, cats*

DISLIKES: *Earthquakes*

Translation Notes

Page 163
Higanzakura is a type of cherry blossom, with *higan* meaning "spring equinox"—the time when *higanzakura* typically bloom. The higan cherry tree is one of the oldest species of cherry trees in Japan.

Page 172
Sawarabi means "freshly budding bracken," with bracken being a type of large fern.

Page 175
Gokumon Agito means "jaws of the prison gate."

BUNGO
STRAY DOGS

A *Dedication to* Bungo Stray Dogs

Yuu Okubo (translator, lecturer)

An adaptation is a sort of game of possibilities. It is something, especially so in the realm of modern and post-modern literature, that is commonly seen in any nation in the world. Japan is no exception, with names as lofty as Akutagawa, Dazai, and Atsushi Nakajima taking elements from the distant past and using then as material to weave their romances with.

Modern times, as well, have proven to be a personification of the growth process—the metamorphosis from youth to adulthood.

Boys and girls across the nation first learn by imitating others, then by creating work that differs from their ancestors, thus forging ahead. After all, the greatest names of modern literature are no different. Their mighty works are the result of their questioning of the world around them, taking the great tomes of domestic and international production and opening a path through their own awesome glories.

Bungo Stray Dogs is another example of adaptation taken to its extremes, depicting the great writers of our time as they engage in fantastic and mind-boggling adventures in their imaginary world. They have been resurrected from the dead in figurative fashion, given new appearances and dutifully apportioned with the tastes and customs of our modern era.

It allows us to explore what was and what could have been, with all these writers that came before us. What if the boy who ran roughshod all around the mountains behind his schoolyard found a companion to commiserate with? What if those swallowed by the darkness found a beam of light to turn to? Indeed, what if life, and all its wondrous possibilities, was given back to those who seek death for themselves?

Ah, what a joyous realm, this land of "adaptation" can provide to us!

Thus, the game continues, playing its sweet sound as it lurks around the morning mist. Let it take you as you close your eyes and behold the spring of youth renewed.

BUNGO STRAY DOGS

AUTHOR GUIDE (PART 1)

The characters of *Bungo Stray Dogs* are based on major literary figures from Japan and around the world! Here's a handy guide to help you learn about some of the writers who inspired the weird and wonderful cast of this series!

OSAMU DAZAI (1909-1948)

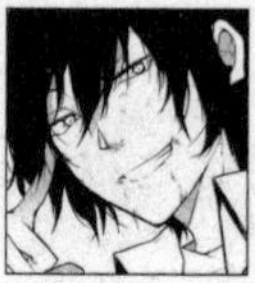

A brilliant writer who attempted suicide multiple times (before succeeding on his third try), Dazai is one of the most notable writers of "I-Novels"—first-person, semi-autobiographical works emphasizing darkness of the self. His most famous novel, *No Longer Human,* follows a man who goes through life feeling as if he is merely "acting" the part of a human.

ATSUSHI NAKAJIMA (1909-1942)

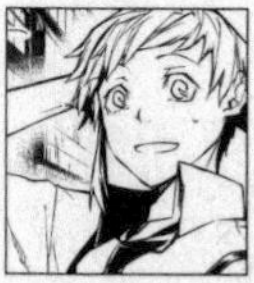

Although not politically active, Nakajima is known for his refusal to write propaganda stories for the Japanese government as so many of his peers did. The skill *Beast Beneath the Moonlight* references the short story "Tiger-Poet," about a man who transforms into a tiger because of his internal conflict between written and oral communication.

DOPPO KUNIKIDA (1871-1908)

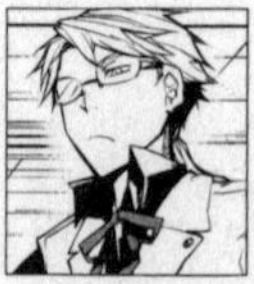

One of the fathers of Japanese naturalism as well as an author of romantic poetry, Kunikida fully embraced Western philosophy in his life and his writings. The skill *The Matchless Poet* does not refer to any specific work, but is based on his naturalist writing—a style that emphasizes accurate depiction of details.

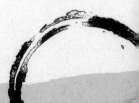

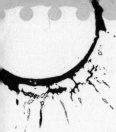

AKIKO YOSANO (1878-1942)

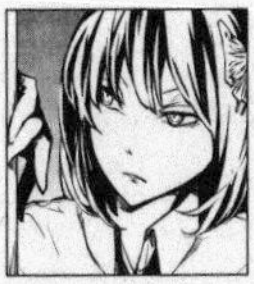

One of the most influential female poets in Japanese history, Yosano's is famous for her poems' expressions of feminine sensuality. Yosano was also staunchly anti-war—her poem "Thou Shalt Not Die" was written for her brother fighting in World War II. It tells him not to throw his life away for a country seemingly all too eager to sacrifice its people.

RYUUNOSUKE AKUTAGAWA (1892-1927)

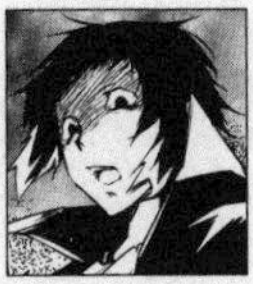

Akutagawa is the father of the Japanese short story. He took his own life at 35, inspiring Osamu Dazai's own fascination with suicide. Many of his stories are set in the 12th and 13th centuries, such as "Rashomon," a tale about a man struggling with the temptation to steal in order to avoid starvation. The Akutagawa Prize, named after the author, is Japan's most prestigious literary award.

KYOUKA IZUMI (1873-1939)

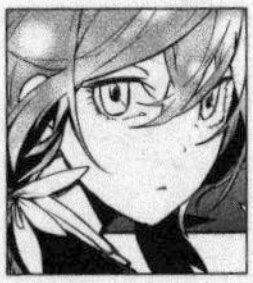

Unlike the *Bungo Stray Dogs* character, Izumi was a man. His works are known for creating worlds with a strong sense of the gothic and supernatural. The skill *Demon Snow*, as used by the character Kyouka, is named after Izumi's play *Demon Pond*, a story warning of the loss of generosity and respect for nature. It features a divine dragon named Shirayuki ("white snow").

CHUUYA NAKAHARA (1907-1937)

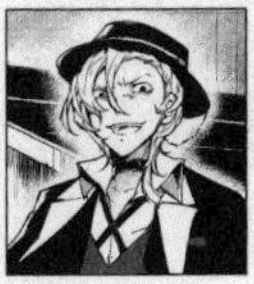

Famous for the lyrical qualities of his poems, Nakahara played with the rhythms of classic Japanese forms of poetry, such as waka, haiku, and tanka, while also taking influence from French styles. His poem "Upon the Tainted Sorrow" emphasizes hopelessness and the fleeting nature of life.

BUNGO
STRAY DOGS

Story: Kafka Asagiri   Art: Sango Harukawa

Translation: Kevin Gifford   †   Lettering: Bianca Pistillo

BUNGO STRAY DOGS Volume 3
©Kafka ASAGIRI 2013
©Sango HARUKAWA 2013
First published in Japan in 2013 by KADOKAWA CORPORATION, Tokyo.
English translation rights arranged with KADOKAWA CORPORATION, Tokyo through TUTTLE-MORI AGENCY, INC., Tokyo.

English translation © 2017 by Yen Press, LLC

Yen Press
1290 Avenue of the Americas
New York, NY 10104

Visit us at yenpress.com
facebook.com/yenpress
twitter.com/yenpress
yenpress.tumblr.com
instagram.com/yenpress

First Yen Press Edition: June 2017

Yen Press is an imprint of Yen Press, LLC.
The Yen Press name and logo are trademarks of Yen Press, LLC.

The publisher is not responsible for websites (or their content) that are not owned by the publisher.

Library of Congress Control Number: 2016956681

ISBNs: 978-0-316-46815-2 (paperback)
       978-0-316-46828-2 (ebook)

10 9 8 7 6 5 4

WOR

Printed in the United States of America